SECOND LANGUA
PROCESSING

Ask pts to reflect at end of test *2018*

Second Language Processing: An Introduction is the first textbook to offer a thorough introduction to the field of second language processing (SLP). The study of SLP seeks to illuminate the cognitive processes underlying the processing of a non-native language. While current literature tends to focus on one topic or area of research, this textbook aims to bring these different research strands together in a single volume, elucidating their particularities while also demonstrating the relationships between them. The book begins by outlining what is entailed in the study of SLP, how it relates to other fields of study, and some of the main issues shared across its subareas. It then moves into an exploration of the three major areas of current research in the field—phonological processing, lexical processing, and sentence processing. Each chapter provides a broad overview of the topic and covers the major research methods, models, and studies germane to that area of study. Ideal for students and researchers working in this growing field, *Second Language Processing* will serve as the go-to guide for a complete examination of the major topics of study in SLP.

Nan Jiang is Associate Professor of Second Language Acquisition at the University of Maryland, USA. He is the author of *Conducting Reaction Time Research in Second Language Studies* (2012) and numerous articles in leading journals of applied linguistics, second language acquisition, and psycholinguistics.

parsing into incorrect categ.

Reasons for difficulty c̄ phon. processing.
- *Lack of input/instruction*
- *Lack of experience c̄ sound in L1 (segment)*
- *⊖ transfer from L1*
- *Frequency of use of a sound (appears...)*
- *Amygdala blocking access due to overload*

Second Language Acquisition Research Series

Susan M. Gass and Alison Mackey, Series Editors

To view all of the books in this series, please visit:
www.routledge.com/Second-Language-Acquisition-Research-Series/book-series/LEASLARS

SECOND LANGUAGE PROCESSING

An Introduction

Influences:
AOA, Length of Residence, L1 Use,
L2 Learning experiences, L1 Typology.

Nan Jiang

→ Semantic & pragmatic language
can develop fully more
readily into native-like profic.
→ Phonological & Syntact. are generally more
difficult to develop native-
like proficiency

Routledge
Taylor & Francis Group

NEW YORK AND LONDON

First published 2018
by Routledge
711 Third Avenue, New York, NY 10017

and by Routledge
2 Park Square, Milton Park, Abingdon, Oxon, OX14 4RN

Routledge is an imprint of the Taylor & Francis Group, an informa business

© 2018 Taylor & Francis

Library of Congress Cataloging-in-Publication Data
Names: Jiang, Nan, 1959– author.
Title: Second language processing : an introduction / Nan Jiang.
Description: New York, NY : Routledge, [2018] | Series: Second language acquisition research series | Includes bibliographical references and index.
Identifiers: LCCN 2017051919 | ISBN 9780415708036 (hardback) | ISBN 9780415708043 (pbk.) | ISBN 9781134608324 (epub) | ISBN 9781134608393 (mobipocket/kindle)
Subjects: LCSH: Language and languages—Study and teaching—Psychological aspects. | Cognitive grammar—Psychological aspects. | Second language acquisition. | Education, Bilingual.
Classification: LCC P53.7 .J43 2018 | DDC 401/.93—dc23
LC record available at https://lccn.loc.gov/2017051919

ISBN: 978-0-415-70803-6 (hbk)
ISBN: 978-0-415-70804-3 (pbk)
ISBN: 978-1-315-88633-6 (ebk)

Typeset in Goudy
by Apex CoVantage, LLC

CONTENTS

ILLUSTRATIONS

Figures

Tables

PREFACE

Writing a book on second language processing (SLP) can be a challenging undertaking for anyone. It is more so for a non-native English speaker from a typologically different language background who did not have much exposure to English until age 21 (classroom) or 33 (naturalistic). The challenge lies in the sheer volume of research output in this area, the wide range of phenomena and topics examined, and the methodological diversity and technicality associated with it.

At the same time, there is a clear need for such a book. For a practical reason, many graduate programs in Second Language Acquisition, Second Language Studies, or Applied Linguistics offer a course on second language processing. A relatively comprehensive review of research in this area in a single volume, which has not been available, would be handy for such a course. More importantly, I see a great deal of overlap across subareas of SLP in both research questions and empirical findings, but there has been very limited interaction and communication across these areas. Four subareas of SLP can be identified: phonological processing, lexical processing, sentence processing, and bilingual processing, of which only the first three are included in this book due to space constraints. These subareas deal with the same participant population, i.e., second language (L2) or bilingual speakers; they attempt to examine the same phenomenon, i.e., language use by this population, and they approach this phenomenon from the same cognitive and psycholinguistic perspective, often with very similar methods and paradigms, and, more importantly, they share the same goal of understanding the mental processes involved in L2 or bilingual processing. Because of these similarities, research in these different areas overlap and has a great potential to inform each other. For example, the interaction of the two languages is a topic explored in all subareas of SLP. A person who reported findings of an L2 impact on L1 phonetic representation is likely to be interested in knowing similar L2 influence on L1 semantic representation. However, SLP researchers have traditionally focused themselves on one subarea. A person who does phonological processing research usually pays little attention to what is going on in lexical or sentence processing research, and vice versa. It is my hope that having an accessible overview of research in all these areas in a single volume will help bring these different lines of research into contact and encourage students and researchers to consider SLP issues from a broader perspective, which, I hope, will ultimately contribute to the establishment of SLP as a unified and coherent field of scientific inquiry.

This book is intended for graduate students and scholars who are interested in second language processing research for whatever reasons. It should be of particular interest to those in the fields of psycholinguistics, second language acquisition, applied linguistics. Research findings discussed in the book can also be informative to language teachers and administrators who hope to explore ideas for effective language teaching, and to those working in other applied field such as human–machine communication and clinical audiology who have to deal with non-native speakers.

The book consists of seven chapters. The first one provides a brief introduction to SLP research. It is followed by six chapters, two for each of the three subareas of SLP: phonological processing, lexical processing, and sentence processing. In writing these six chapters, I intended to provide sufficient background information about a topic before diving into the discussion of research questions and empirical findings. Due to space constraints, many topics had to be excluded or cut down from an earlier, more extensive version of the manuscript, such as the relationship between speech perception and production, the role of visual information on speech perception, the role of phonology in visual word recognition (independent of L1 transfer), the development of automaticity in lexical processing, early sentence processing research in L2, L2 speakers' sensitivity to semantic violations, L2 processing research done within the framework of language and thought (or linguistic relativity), and bilingual language processing. These topics are all an integral and important part of SLP research and have generated a great deal of research in recent years, so a lack of a detailed treatment of these topics in the book should not be taken as indicating otherwise. The review of research in each chapter is quite selective, as well. No attempt is made to provide an exhaustive review of all the published studies on a topic. Instead, I explain the issues and summarize findings by sampling a subset of these studies, with an effort not to miss seminal studies that have played a particularly important role in shaping the development of a topic.

In discussing SLP topics, I use some terms interchangeably. The use of one instead of the other usually reflects how these terms are used in the studies under discussion. For example, I make no distinction between *second language* and *foreign language*, unless a distinction is explicitly explained. The expression *second language* is used to refer to any non-native language, and thus it can be an individual's third or fourth language. *L2 speakers*, *L2 users*, *L2 learners*, and *non-native speakers* (NNS) usually refer to the same population. The same is true with *native speakers* (NS) and *L1 speakers*. Unless pointed out otherwise, semantic representation and conceptual representation are not differentiated. Additionally, in phonological processing research, researchers do not always stick strictly with the International Phonetic Alphabet. As a result, the use of phonetic or phonemic transcripts differ across studies. I use phonetic or phonemic symbols used in the original studies under discussion, which may result in some inconsistencies throughout the book. Readers are encouraged to refer to the original studies for clarification.

I am grateful to many who provided assistance in the process of this project. The editors at Routledge, Elysse Preposi, Leah Babb-Rosenfeld, Rebecca Novack, Kathrene Binag, and the series editors Susan Gass and Alison Mackey have been very helpful throughout the whole process. I would not have been able to complete this project without their hard work. I appreciate receiving a Research and Scholarship Award from the Graduate School of the University of Maryland which allowed me to concentrate on the writing of this book for a semester. Occasionally, I sent an inquiry or a section of a draft to researchers whose research was discussed and asked for feedback. I am most grateful to the following researchers who responded: Harald Clahsen, Robert DeKeyser, Tami Gollan, Alan Jeffs, Brian McWhinney, Xiaomei Qiao, Brent Wolter. I am also grateful to the students who participated in my Ph.D. seminar on SLP over the years for their thoughtful discussions. I also want to express my deepest appreciation to the five anonymous reviewers who reviewed drafts of the manuscript and provided very helpful comments and suggestions. I am particularly grateful to my wife Guiling Gloria Hu and my now six-year-old daughter Stephanie for allowing me to sit in front of my computer for as long as I did for the past four years when this project remained my primary focus. Without their support and understanding, I would never have been able to complete this project, no matter how imperfect it is.

ABBREVIATIONS

AJ	acceptability judgment
ANOVA	analysis of variance
AOA	age of acquisition or age of arrival
AR	accuracy rate
CBM	constraint-based model
CP	complementizer phrase
CPH	critical period hypothesis
CSL	Chinese as a second language
DO	direct object
DP	determiner phrases
EEG	electroencephalogram
ELAN	early left anterior negativity
ER	error rate(s)
ERP	event-related potentials
ERT	episodic recognition task
ESL	English as a second language
FCM	feature competition model
fMRI	functional magnetic resonance imaging
GJT	grammaticality judgment task
GP	garden path
GPE	garden-path effect
GPM	garden-path model
ISI	inter-stimulus intervals
L1	first language
L2	second language
LAN	left anterior negativity
LDT	lexical decision task
LOR	length of residence
MMN	mismatch negativity
MRI	magnetic resonance imaging
NL	native language

NLMM	native language magnet model
NNL	non-native language
NNS	non-native speaker(s)
NP	noun phrase
NS	native speaker(s)
PAM	perceptual assimilation model
PET	positron emission tomography
PLE	prime lexicality effect
PO	prepositional object
PP	prepositional phrase
RC	relative clause
RHM	revised hierarchical model
RRC	reduced relative clause
RST	reading span test
RT	reaction time(s)
SC	sentential complement
SJT	semantic judgment task
SLA	second language acquisition
SLM	speech learning model
SLP	second language processing
SOA	stimulus onset asynchrony
SOV	subject object verb
SPRT	self-paced reading task
SVO	subject verb object
UG	Universal Grammar
VOT	voice onset time
VP	verb phrase
WA	word association
WAT	word association task
WM	working memory
WST	word span test

Chapter 1

Introducing Second Language Processing

1.1 Introduction

The use of a language other than one's native language is common. This can be seen in the number of people who can use a language other than their native tongue. According to a survey by the European Commission published in February 2006, 56% of the 450 million people in the European Union "are able to hold a conversation in a language other than their mother tongue" (p. 8). In the USA, the number of people who speak a language other than English at home has increased significantly over the past four decades, from 23.1 million in 1980 to 60.6 million in 2011. The percentage of this population has also increased steadily from 11% in 1980 to 21% in 2011, according to the US census data. A majority of these people supposedly speak their native language at home and speak English as a second language (ESL) outside of home. These numbers do not include English native speakers in the USA who are able to speak another language such as Spanish, French, Japanese, and Chinese. Additionally, there is even a bigger number of ESL speakers in other parts of the world. In China alone, over 100 million school and university students are studying English, according to the Chinese Ministry of Education.

The use of a non-native language or a second language (L2) has become a phenomenon for scientific enquiry. Multiple approaches have been taken in this endeavor. One of them is to examine this phenomenon from a cognitive and psycholinguistic perspective. Second language processing (SLP) represents such an approach. In this approach, L2 use is viewed primarily as a cognitive event rather than, for example, a cultural, sociolinguistic, or pedagogical one. The primary goal of this research is to understand the mental processes and mechanisms involved in L2 use and what such knowledge can tell us about L2 acquisition. This focus on cognition is reflected in its reference to language use as language processing which represents an information processing approach to the study of human cognition, including language. In this approach, the human mind is considered as an information processor (or language processor) that has a limited processing capacity and storage and that relies on a set of algorithms or grammatical rules in handling linguistic input and output. In this context, the term *language processing* refers to both receptive and productive use of a language. Thus, SLP is concerned with the mental processes involved in the receptive and productive use of a second language.[1]

The study of the mental processes involved in language use by L2 or bilingual speakers can be traced back at least to James McKeen Cattell's (1887) research. As part of his effort to study the temporal issues related to mental processes, he examined the amount of time bilinguals needed to name pictures in their native language (NL) and non-native language (NNL) and to translate in both directions. He found that individuals needed 149–172 milliseconds (ms) more to name pictures in a NNL in comparison to naming them in their native or first language (L1), and that translation from L2 to L1 took less time than the reverse, both of which findings were replicated in more recent research.

The 1980s witnessed a significant increase in SLP studies. Some of the earliest SLP research included studies by Flege and Davidian (1984) and Flege and Hillenbrand (1984) on phonological processing, by Muchisky (1983), Koda (1988, 1989) on word recognition, and by Harrington (1987) and Kilborn and Cooreman (1987) on sentence processing. Substantial progress has been made in the past three decades in the development of theoretical frameworks (e.g., the proposal of L2 speech processing models), in the expansion of the scope of investigation (e.g., the wide range of structures involved in sentence processing research), in the number of discovered L2 processing phenomena (e.g., the interaction of L1 and L2 phonological representations, a larger frequency effect in L2 than in L1 in visual word recognition, a stronger presence of form-based lexical representation in the L2 lexicon), and in methodological advances (e.g., the application of the masked priming paradigm, the use of eye trackers, the electroencephalogram, and magnetic resonance imaging).

As it stands today, three SLP areas can be identified that have received the most attention: phonological processing, lexical processing, and sentence processing. The first area deals with speech perception and production among L2 speakers primarily at the segmental and suprasegmental levels, the second is about L2 word recognition and lexicosemantic representation and development, and the third focuses on syntactic structure building and the representation and processing of morphosyntactic and lexicosemantic knowledge in understanding sentences.

These three areas of SLP focus on three different aspects of language, and they sometimes deal with issues that are unique to that area. For example, the relationship between perception and production and the impact of degraded input on processing are topics unique to phonological processing research, the decomposition issue, i.e., whether certain linguistic units are represented and processed holistically or in an analytical manner, is primarily examined in lexical processing, and the relative importance of syntactic and semantic information in language processing concerns sentence processing only.

Suprasegmental = prosodic features
speech feature such as stress, ton

However, these three areas also share a great deal of similarities. They study the same population of L2 speakers and the same general phenomenon of language use by L2 speakers, and they share the same goal of understanding how L2 processing is similar to or different from L1 processing, they share the general methodological approach of comparing L2 speakers to L1 speakers, and they also share the same experimental approach and often draw from the same repertoire of experimental techniques and paradigms. Additionally, they also deal with very similar research questions. For example, the role of an individual's L1 linguistic knowledge in L2 processing is an important research topic across all three areas. Individuals' L2 learning profile, e.g., the age of onset, length of residence in the L2, and their proficiency, are factors frequently considered in the study of many topics across these areas. Consequently, research findings across these areas are likely to be related in one way or another.[2]

In the remainder of the chapter, I hope to highlight a few characteristics of SLP research shared by its subareas, and discuss some recurrent themes across these areas. In so doing, I hope to enhance the awareness of the similarities in research goals, research topics, research findings, and research methods across the different areas of SLP and promote SLP as a unified and coherent field of inquiry.

1.2 Characterizing SLP Research

SLP research enjoys several shared characteristics across its three areas. These characteristics help make SLP a coherent and unique field of inquiry. At the same time, these characteristics may help define the relationship between SLP and other fields, particularly psycholinguistics and second language acquisition (SLA). Four such characteristics can be identified.

1.2.1 A Cognitive Focus

First, the primary goal of SLP research is to understand the mental processes involved in L2 use, even though L2 use can be approached from a number of different perspectives. The study of foreign accent may serve as an example to illustrate this focus. Most adult L2 speakers speak with an accent. From a sociolinguistic perspective, one may ask whether the degree of accentedness has to do with their attitude toward the new language or culture, or whether it is affected by the person an individual is speaking to. These issues are legitimate and interesting issues to explore but they are of less interest to SLP researchers. Instead, their focus is more on the cognitive underpinnings of accented speech. They explore what acoustic features are similar or different in the mental representations of phonological categories between NNS and NS and the causes of any representational deviation that contributed to accented speech. Similarly, in studying lexical processing, SLP researchers are less concerned with how word recognition or literacy development is affected by individual differences in motivation, attitude, or socioeconomic background. Instead, they attempt to understand how lexical knowledge is represented and accessed in L2 word recognition in general and pay attention to linguistic and individual factors that may potentially affect lexical representation and access.

Given its focus on mental processes involved in L2 processing, SLP is deeply rooted in psycholinguistics and cognitive psychology. Indeed, many early L2 processing studies arose in the context of exploring general language processing issues such as the study of L2 sentence processing within the competition model (Gass, 1987; Harrington, 1987; Kilborn & Cooreman, 1987) and the study of the processing of non-native speech segments associated with the perceptual assimilation model (e.g., Best, McRoberts, & Goodell, 2001). Today's SLP research continues to rely heavily on psycholinguistics for conceptual frameworks, empirical findings, and research methods. Psycholinguistic findings obtained from L1 speakers often serve as a point of departure and baseline for comparison in many L2 processing research, such as the analysis of acoustic cues in speech perception (Section 3.2.1), morphological priming (Section 5.2.2), and relative clause attachment (Section 6.2.2). In light of this relationship, SLP may be considered as an extension of psycholinguistics from native language processing to L2 processing. It is not surprising in this sense that many leading scholars in SLP teach in a psychology department and many SLP empirical studies were published in psycholinguistics journals.

1.2.2 A Broader Scope Than L1 Psycholinguistics

Second, in extending language processing research from L1 to L2 speakers, SLP has to consider issues that are not usually considered in L1 psycholinguistic research, as L2 processing is more complicated and involves more factors. For example, for most L2 speakers, the L2 is learned after the establishment of an L1 and a related conceptual system. Thus, L1 influence and the nature of the L2-concept connections become unique issues to consider in studying L2 processing. Individuals also learn an L2 at variable ages, which raises the issue of how maturational factors may affect L2 acquisition and processing. The L1 and age factors combine to raise the acquirability issue, i.e., to what extent NNS are able to develop nativelike competence in a new language. For many individuals, an L2 is learned with less than optimal input. For example, classroom learners often do not have sufficient contextualized input or ample opportunities for meaningful interaction. This is likely to affect L2 learning and processing, too. Thus, L1, age, and input become three factors that are uniquely relevant to L2 processing research but less so in L1 processing research.

Other acquisition differences may also have processing ramifications. For example, unlike children learning their L1 where the development of speech and literacy is sequential, i.e., speech before literacy, L2 learners often learn to speak, listen, read, and write at the same time. This creates a unique situation with regard to the role of phonology and orthography in visual word recognition. Psycholinguists have found that phonology is actively involved in visual word recognition and attribute this finding to the development of speech before literacy (Bosman & De Groot, 1996; Davis, Castles, & Iakovidis, 1998). Now we have to wonder if phonology also plays a significant role in visual word recognition in an L2, as well. Additionally, the tendency for adults to rely on explicit knowledge or explicit learning may also result in two opposite patterns of behavior between L1 and L2 speakers, i.e., the presence of processing competence without explicit knowledge among L1 speakers and the presence of explicit knowledge without processing competence (i.e., automatic access of knowledge) among L2 speakers.

Thus, SLP research explores both issues that concern language processing in general and issues that are unique to L2 processing. The exploration of these L2-specific issues represents the unique contribution SLP makes to the broader field of cognitive science. It also provides important insights for understanding issues related to second language acquisition (SLA).

1.2.3 From Processing Data to Representation and Acquisition Issues

Representation, acquisition, and processing are closely related in SLP research. Mental representation refers to the information and knowledge that is stored in our mind in the form of symbols, images, or propositions. It reflects what we know. We behave in a certain way in language use because of the linguistic representation we have developed. I point to a tree and tell my daughter that it is a willow because I have a mental representation for this type of tree in my mind, i.e., a concept and/or an image, which includes probably its color and shape among other things, and a word that refers to this concept. A participant considers two acoustic signals, e.g., /i/ and /ɪ/ as in seat and sit, different sounds because there are two different phonetic categories represented in his or her mind, each corresponding to a different signal. From a cognitive perspective, the mental representation of our linguistic knowledge determines our linguistic behavior. The essence of language learning lies in the changes in an individual's mental representation of the language being learned. These changes may include the differentiation of two phonetic categories in phonological development, the creation of a new lexical entry in our lexicon in vocabulary acquisition, and the formation of a subject-verb agreement rule in learning syntax.

However, mental representations and their changes are often difficult to study directly, even with today's technology. Instead, we have to infer what linguistic knowledge is represented or how it has changed by examining a

[handwritten annotation: Orthography = everything to do w/ written text — spelling, hyphen, period]

language user's observable linguistic behavior. When this behavior is observed and measured in a controlled setting, it becomes processing data. They provide evidence, often through inferences, for understanding the mental representation and its changes, and thus for understanding acquisition. Thus, there is a close relationship between processing, representation, and acquisition.

In L1 processing research, processing data are often used to illuminate both the mental processes involved in language use and the representation of linguistic knowledge. For example, individuals' performance in the discrimination of speech sound segments may help reveal a) the acoustic cues used in auditory perception (i.e., processing strategies) and b) the acoustic space that phonetic categories occupy and their boundaries and relationships (i.e., mental representation of phonetic categories). The priming effect in word recognition, e.g., a faster recognition of the word *nurse* (the target) following the word *doctor* (the related prime) compared to following the word *teacher* (the control prime), may reflect how the lexicon is organized. In psycholinguistic research, at least where the participants are adults, individuals are treated as having reached a steady stage of language development. Thus, the goal of language processing research is to understand how language is processed and represented at this stage rather than language acquisition itself. In other words, psycholinguistic study of L1 processing involving adults is primarily concerned with processing and representation issues rather than acquisition issues.

SLP research is different from most psycholinguistic research in this respect. There are SLP topics that may be considered processing topics. For example, the use of orthographic vs. phonological information in L2 visual word recognition is a topic of processing strategies with less connection to L2 acquisition issues. However, a majority of SLP topics are related to L2 acquisition in one way or another. Either an SLP study was conceived and intended to understand L2 acquisition issues from the outset, or its findings shed light on some acquisition issues. For example, we study L2 phonological processing to study phonological development in L2 speakers, and we study semantic processing in order to explore whether adult NNS are able to develop a new and L2-specific semantic system.

This close connection between processing and acquisition can be seen in a shift of attention from processing to acquisition issues when a psycholinguistic finding is extended from L1 speakers to L2 speakers. Two examples suffice to illustrate this shift. The study of relative clause (RC) attachment examines whether a relative clause is interpreted as modifying the first or the second noun of a complex noun phrase. In Example 1.1, the underlined RC may be interpreted to modify the first noun phrases (NP) *the design* or the second NP *the furniture*. This research is done in psycholinguistics in the context of identifying universal processing principles (e.g., Cuetos & Mitchell, 1988), but when RC attachment is studied among L2 speakers, the purpose is often to understand whether L2 speakers are able to develop nativelike processing strategies (e.g., Dussias, 2003; Fernández, 2002) rather than the processing strategies themselves (see Section 6.2.2). The study of the broken agreement phenomenon provides another example. When presented with a sentence fragment (such as *the label on the bottles . . .*) and asked to complete the sentence, English NS were sometimes found to produce subject-verb agreement errors (by using *are* instead of *is* in this example). Psycholinguists have treated this phenomenon as a processing issue and studied it in both production and comprehension in order to determine what is the cause of such processing errors (e.g., Bock & Miller, 1991; Pearlmutter, Garnsey, & Bock, 1999). However, when the same phenomenon was examined among L2 speakers in reading comprehension, the purpose was to investigate whether they were able to develop a nativelike sensitivity to morphosyntactic errors (e.g., Jiang, 2004a, 2007a) (see Section 7.3.1).

1.1   *I like the design of the furniture that we discussed yesterday.*

These two examples illustrate that processing phenomena in psycholinguistics are often used in SLP to explore acquisition issues. If we consider processing, representation, and acquisition as a relationship of observable behavior (i.e., processing data) and their revelation about mental processes (representation and acquisition), then SLP and other psycholinguistic research differ in how far researchers go in interpreting processing data. Psycholinguists use processing data to understand processing strategies and processes and infer about the representation of linguistic knowledge. They usually do not go beyond that point (thus, processing → representation). SLP researchers take processing data as evidence for understanding L2 processing strategy and mental representations, as well. However, they often go one step further and interpret their processing data in relation to acquisition issues (thus, processing → representation → acquisition). Thus, SLP studies L2 processing in order to understand both L2 processing and L2 acquisition.

This characteristic of SLP makes it closely related to SLA research. Language acquisition is first and foremost a cognitive process. If the main goal of SLA research is to uncover the mental processes and mechanisms involved in the process of learning a non-native language, then this is exactly what SLP is about. The close relationship between processing and acquisition and the shared research goals make SLP an essential and integral part of SLA research. The importance of understanding processing for the sake of understanding acquisition is getting increasingly recognised. As rightly pointed out by Clahsen and Felser (2006), "theories of language acquisition are incomplete unless they also incorporate assumptions about processing" (p. 121). Thus, it is not surprising that SLP has become an integral part of the curriculum of many

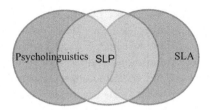

Figure 1.1 The Relationship Between SLP, Psycholinguistics, and SLA

graduate programs in SLA, Second Language Studies, and Applied Linguistics. Figure 1.1 illustrates the relationship between SLP, psycholinguistics (or cognitive science), and SLA.

1.2.4 An Experimental Approach That Emphasizes Vigorous Variable Manipulation and Control

Finally, SLP research is heavily, if not exclusively, quantitative and experimental in nature. L2 speakers' language behavior can be observed in multiple ways. The collection and analysis of language errors in L2 speakers' spontaneous L2 use, for example, played a significant role in the development of L2 theories in the early days of SLA research (e.g., Corder, 1967; Dulay & Burt, 1974). There are many classroom-based experimental SLA studies that examine the role of enhanced input, feedback, and task type in L2 acquisition. SLP research is different from these approaches for its lab-based experimental approach that emphasizes the observation and assessment of language behavior in a rigorously controlled setting. The control is often achieved by manipulating a variable under investigation while controlling other variables. Variable manipulation and control are often done by means of using a set of materials that are specifically developed for targeting a particular linguistic structure or phenomenon while holding other linguistic properties constant.

For example, in order to find out whether L1 translations are involved in L2 word recognition, one may construct two lists of English words that are matched in lexical properties such as frequency and length, but differ in the frequency of their Chinese translations. One list has high-frequency Chinese translations and the other has low-frequency translations. In this example, L1 translation frequency is the manipulated variable and lexical frequency and length are the controlled variables. Suppose that we ask a group of Chinese ESL speakers and a group of English native speakers (NS) to perform a lexical decision task on these items (mixed with a set of nonwords for the sake of the task). Their task is to decide as quickly as possible if a test item is an

English word or not. We would first expect English NS to show no difference in reaction time (RT) between the two conditions, as lexical properties are matched.[3] More importantly, if L1 translations are not involved in L2 word recognition, we would expect Chinese ESL participants to show no difference in RT, just as English NS do. However, if L1 translations are involved, we would expect Chinese ESL speakers to respond to the high-translation-frequency items faster than to the low-translation-frequency items. Thus, by isolating L1 translation frequency as a variable for investigation, we can reasonably link the processing data to our research question: a faster RT to the high-translation-frequency items among Chinese ESL speakers in the absence of such RT difference among English NS provides compelling evidence for the involvement of L1 translations in L2 word recognition.

For an example in sentence processing, even advanced Chinese ESL speakers like the present author have difficulty in producing nativelike accuracy in using plural forms in spontaneous communication, in spite of their explicit knowledge about plural marking. Thus, a question to explore is whether they are able to develop nativelike automatic access of this knowledge. To do so, we may construct sentences such as 1.2. Each sentence has a grammatical version and an ungrammatical version. As shown in the example, the two versions differ in plural marking but are identical otherwise. Again, such materials help isolate plural marking as a manipulated variable for investigation while controlling other factors that may affect an individual's reading time, such as vocabularies in the sentences, sentence length, structural complexity, and the familiarity of topics to the participants. We may use such materials in a self- paced word-by-word reading task in which Chinese ESL speakers and a group of English NS are asked to read for comprehension as quickly as possible and measure their comprehension rates and reading times. Based on previous research, we expect English NS to take longer in reading the underlined words in the ungrammatical version than those in the grammatical version. This delay suggests that even when they are asked to read for comprehension rather than for grammatical accuracy, they automatically notice the plural marking error, which results in a delay in reading. Chinese ESL speakers' performance under the same experimental condition can help determine if they have developed nativelike sensitivity to plural marking violations. If they also show a delay in reading the ungrammatical version, we can infer that they have also developed nativelike command of this feature. If they show no difference for the two conditions, we conclude that they have not developed nativelike competence about this structure.

1.2a. I like many of the books on the table.
1.2b. *I like many of the book on the table.

Both of these examples illustrate an important characteristic of the controlled experimental approach in SLP research: the isolation of a linguistic structure or phenomenon for investigation through the development of adequate test materials. Processing data obtained under such circumstances can be interpreted in relation to a processing or acquisition question with less ambiguity in that they allow fewer alternative explanations. While variable manipulation and control are achieved probably most frequently through test materials in SLP research, some variables have to be manipulated and controlled by identifying the right participant groups or tasks. For example, if the focus of a study is on the effect of onset age of L2 learning, one has to identify participants who differ in onset age but are comparable in other demographic and language learning background.

The experimental approach is also characterized by the use of a rich repertoire of experimental tasks and paradigms developed in psycholinguistics and cognitive science. These tasks allow one to target a specific cognitive process. For example, in order to name a picture such as a household object, one has to activate the concept related to the object before the name of the object is accessed and articulated. Thus, the picture-naming task can be used to examine the process of concept activation in language use. In a lexical decision task (LDT) in which individuals are asked to decide if a letter string is a word or not, they have to assess the mental representation of words or search the mental lexicon. Thus, this task can be used to examine lexical access or the organization of the lexicon. On the other hand, if individuals are first shown a list of words and then asked to decide if a subsequent stimulus word is among the words they saw earlier (i.e., the episodic recognition task, ERT), they have to search their episodic memory. Thus, even though the same set of words may be used, the two tasks (LDT and ERT) direct individuals' attention to different memory systems. We may also track individuals' eye movements or record individuals' blood flow or electrophysiological responses in the brain while they perform a linguistic task in order to determine what mental process or which part of the brain is involved.

These tasks and paradigms generate mostly three types of data: accuracy rates (AR) (or on the flip side error rates, ER), reaction time (RT), and brain responses. Phonological tasks such as identification and discrimination and sentence processing tasks such as grammaticality judgment typically produce AR data, even though RT data are sometimes gathered. AR data are often used as a relatively direct indication of how nativelike the participants' performance is. A high AR (in the form of a percentage or an A' score, for example) reflects a better command of linguistic knowledge or more nativelike representation. RT data are the dependent variable for many lexical and sentence processing tasks such as lexical decision, naming, self-paced reading, and eye tracking. However, the interpretation of RT data is much more complicated.

On the assumption that a more difficult task or a task involving more cognitive processes takes more time to perform, RT data may be interpreted as reflecting the level of difficulty or the number of cognitive processes involved. For example, native speakers (NS) are typically faster than non-native speakers (NNS) in performing the same task such as the LDT. This may be interpreted as reflecting a higher level of automaticity in recognizing L1 words than L2 words. More frequently, however, RT data are interpreted as a pattern in relation to the different conditions built in the design of a study. This pattern is often referred to as an effect. A faster RT in responding to concrete words than to abstract words is called a concreteness effect. A faster RT in responding to a target word (e.g., *nurse*) following a related word (e.g., *doctor*) than to the same target word following an unrelated word (e.g., *factor*) is referred to as a priming effect, or more specifically a semantic priming effect in this example. The presence or absence of an effect is then interpreted in relation to the research question under investigation. Brain responses that individuals produce while performing a linguistic task, as measured by electroencephalogram (EEG) or magnetic resonance imaging (MRI), also provide important information about what part of the brain is involved in relation to a specific linguistic task, which may reveal the processes and mechanisms involved in performing a linguistic task or provide evidence for language representation and processing in general.

Besides these three types of data, SLP studies may also use other data types. For example, in addition to eye fixation times which is a type of RT data, eye tracking studies also consider how often individuals look back (regression rates) and where they look in regression (regression sites). Proportion of fixations is the primary data where the visual world paradigm is used. Word association studies classify different types of responses and compute the percentage of each type of response. In studying speech production, it is common to ask native speakers to rate the accentedness or intelligibility of the speech produced by non-native speakers. The regression data, the fixation proportion data, the response type data, and the rating score data, along with the AR data, RT data, and brain response data, illustrate the use of a wide array of data types in SLP research.

The experimental approach is advantageous in several ways in comparison to the observation of linguistic behavior in naturalistic settings. The use of an appropriate task in combination with test materials specifically developed for the task and for a target phenomenon allows one to pinpoint a particular cognitive process or linguistic phenomenon for investigation and thus is more efficient than collecting data in naturalist settings. By controlling confounding variables, its results are generally less subject to multiple interpretations. By adopting online tasks to collect data while the cognitive process is ongoing, e.g., in a self-paced reading task, it offers a more sensitive measure for observing linguistic phenomena that are otherwise less observable. See Jiang (2012) for more about the advantages of this experimental approach and tasks that are frequently used in SLP research.

The experimental approach taken in SLP research may be criticized by some on the basis that the use of tasks such as lexical decision and word-by-word reading and materials such as isolated words and sentences do not represent real-life authentic language use. However, this criticism is off the mark if we consider the primary goal of SLP research, which is to understand the mental processes involved in language learning and use rather than how language use occurs in real-life situations. The experimental approach is adopted on the assumption that the basic mental processes involved in language use are the same regardless of the circumstances of language use. Visual word recognition involves the analysis of physical features of visual input, the recognition of letters, and the activation of a mental representation, regardless of whether the word appears in isolation or in a context, regardless of whether the word appears on a book page, on a computer monitor, or on a cell phone screen, and regardless of the socioeconomic background of the reader. Building a syntactical structure is a basic and essential part of sentence comprehension regardless of the listener–speaker relationship or the attitude of the speaker or listener. In short, a lab-based experimental approach in SLP research is based on the assumption that the basic mental processes involved in language use can be best studied in a controlled experimental setting.

To sum up, SLP studies language use by L2 speakers. In so doing, it aims to uncover the mental processes and mechanisms involved in L2 use and L2 acquisition. SLP is closely related to psycholinguistics in terms of the theoretical issues, conceptual frameworks, language phenomena, and methodological approaches. It distinguishes itself from other psycholinguistic research in focusing on L2 speakers and L2 use and in frequently relating processing data to acquisition issues. For the latter reason, it should be considered as an integral part of SLA. SLP research is usually lab-based and employs a variety of experimental tasks. Through vigorous variable manipulation and control, SLP studies produce results that permit more direct and unequivocal inferences about how L2 knowledge is acquired, represented, and accessed.

1.3 Recurrent Themes in SLP Research

SLP research examines both topics unique to a specific area and topics that are relevant to multiple areas. The latter topics often represent more basic issues facing SLP researchers and areas where researchers from different areas may benefit the most from knowing what is going on in other areas. Three such topics, or recurrent themes, are discussed in this section for illustrative purposes: the acquirability issue, L1–L2 interaction, and the nature of age effects.

1.3.1 The Acquirability of a Non-Native Language

One of the central issues in studying L2 learners from a cognitive perspective is whether they are able to attain nativelike command of a second language. This is referred to as the acquirability issue in this context. Sometimes this issue is brushed away on the argument that nativelike competence should not be the goal of L2 learning. This argument may make sense from a functional perspective, as less than nativelike command is often sufficient to allow the successful use of a non-native language for communication. However, from a cognitive perspective, this issue lies at the core of L2 acquisition and processing research, because identifying what is acquirable and what is not, and examining the circumstances and factors that affect acquirability are important means towards the goal of uncovering what is unique about L2 learning and processing and of understanding human cognition in general. Indeed, the issue has received a great deal of attention in SLP, particularly in L2 phonological and sentence processing research. In L2 phonological processing, the acquirability issue reveals itself as an issue of whether L2 speakers are able to develop nativelike and L2-specific phonetic categories so that they can perceive and produce L2 phonology with nativelike accuracy. In sentence processing research, the issue is whether L2 learners are able to develop nativelike morphosyntactic knowledge so that they can demonstrate a nativelike sensitivity to morphosyntactic errors in language use.

The acquirability issue is ultimately an empirical one. One may think that it can be resolved without much difficulty based on empirical evidence. The reality is much more complicated. In both phonological and sentence processing research, research findings are quite inconsistent and inconclusive.

In phonological processing research, some studies reported nativelike performance among L2 speakers in both speech perception and production. For example, Baker and Trofimovich (2006) showed that early Korean ESL learners were able to show an accuracy rate comparable to that of NS of English in the perception of English vowels, and the early ESL speakers in Archila-Suerte, Zevin, Bunta, and Hernandez (2012) also showed a nativelike pattern in a similarity judgment task involving the perception of four English vowels. In speech production, early Spanish and Korean ESL learners but not late learners in Flege (1991) and Kang and Guion (2006) produced a VOT (voice onset time) value similar to that of English NS in pronouncing English stops in spite of the difference between the languages. Adult L2 speakers were found to produce nativelike performance in some studies, as well. For example, three of the 22 adult French L2 speakers were found to produce French vowel durations that were similar to those of French NS in Birdsong (2007), two of the 30 adult Dutch L2 speakers were determined to be nativelike by a group of NS judges in Bongaerts, Mennen, and Slik (2000).

In contrast, many studies reported non-nativelike performance among both early and late L2 learners. What is particularly noteworthy is the findings from several studies about early L2 speakers' non-native performance. Among them are a series of studies published by a group of researchers based in Barcelona, Spain (Pallier, Bosch, & Sebastián-Gallés, 1997; Sebastián-Gallés & Soto-Faraco, 1999; Bosch, Costa, & Sebastián-Gallés, 2000; Sebastián-Gallés, Echeverría, & Bosch, 2005). They tested early Catalan L2 speakers with a Spanish background. The participants were all first exposed to Catalan at the age of 3 to 4, went through a bilingual education system, and were highly proficiency in their L2 Catalan. When the participants were asked to perform an AX discrimination task involving the Catalan /e/-/ɛ/ contrast, they produced an accuracy score significantly lower than that by Catalan NS. Similarly, only five out of the 31 early L2 Swedish speakers in Abrahamsson and Hyltenstam (2009) passed all four phonology tests showing nativelike performance, and early L2 German speakers in Rinker, Alku, Brosch, and Kiefer (2010) and Darcy and Krüger (2012) were found to be different from German NS in the perception of German-specific consonant and vowel contrasts in both behavioral and ERP (event-related potentials) measures. These findings present a sharp contrast with those demonstrations of nativelike performance by early and particularly late L2 speakers (Baker & Trofimovich, 2006; Flege, 1991; Kang & Guion, 2006).

Similar contradictory findings were obtained in sentence processing research where non-native speakers' sensitivity to morphosyntactic violations were examined (see Section 7.3 for more detail). In a series of studies (Jiang, 2004a, 2007a; Jiang, Novokshanova, Masuda, & Wang, 2011), we tested Chinese and Japanese ESL speakers in a self-paced word-by-word reading task with sentences such as 1.3. Their reading times were measured at the underlined positions of the sentences as an indication of their sensitivity to plural errors. English NS showed a reliable delay in reading the ungrammatical sentences, suggesting that they were sensitive to such errors. The Chinese and Japanese ESL speakers, however, showed no difference between the two versions, even though they were able to identify and correct such plural errors in an offline task. This lack of nativelike sensitivity to plural errors suggests that these ESL speakers had not developed a nativelike command of number marking knowledge. Several other studies replicated this lack of sensitivity among L2 speakers, e.g., involving the English third person singular -s for Japanese ESL speakers (Bannai, 2011; Shibuya & Wakabayashi, 2008), the Korean honorific marking for English learners of Korean (Mueller & Jiang, 2013), Spanish gender marking for English learners (Tokowicz & Warren, 2010).

1.3a. *They met some of the board members during their visit.*
1.3b. **They met some of the board member during their visit.*

At the same time, some other studies demonstrated nativelike sensitivity among NNS. Intermediate and advanced L2 Spanish speakers whose L1 was English were found to show a nativelike sensitivity to Spanish gender marking errors in Sagarra and Herschensohn (2010) and Foote (2011) where a self-paced reading task was adopted. Sensitivity to Spanish or French gender marking was also observed among advanced English-speaking learners in eye tracking data (Keating, 2009; Foucart & Frenck-Mestre, 2012).

There is also inconsistent electrophysiological evidence regarding this phenomenon. Some studies showed a nativelike sensitivity among NNS, as indicated by the presence of P600. This included English learners' processing of Spanish gender marking (Tokowicz & MacWhinney, 2005), German learners' processing of French person and number agreement (Frenck-Mestre, Osterhout, McLaughlin, & Foucart, 2008), English and Chinese learners' processing of Spanish number and gender agreement (Gillon Dowens, Vergara, Barber, & Carreiras, 2010; Gillon Dowens, Guo, Guo, Barber, & Carreiras, 2011). Other studies, however, showed a lack of such nativelike sensitivity (e.g., Chen, Shu, Liu, Zhao, & Li, 2007; Ojima, Nakata, & Kakigi, 2005). It is also quite common to see the demonstration of nativelike sensitivity in one ERP measure (usually P600) but not in another (usually LAN) (e.g., Frenck-Mestre et al., 2008; Gillon Dowens et al., 2011; Mueller, Hahne, Fujii, & Friederici, 2005).

Two factors are likely to have contributed to this inconclusive nature of findings in both phonological and morphosyntactic processing. One is the inconsistency in both the approaches and the criteria adopted to assess native-like performance across individual studies. To illustrate this variation, native-like pronunciation has been assessed in two different ways. One is to ask a group of NS judges to listen to the recordings made by the L2 speaking participants and decide if the speakers are NS of the language (e.g., Bongaerts et al., 2000; Schneiderman & Desmarais, 1988; Ioup, Boustagui, El Tigi, & Moselle, 1994). The other is to analyze the acoustic features such as the voice onset time (VOT) of voiced and voiceless stops (e.g., /t/, /d/) and compare the values with those produced by NS (e.g., Flege, 1991; Kang & Guion, 2006). As shown by Abrahamsson and Hyltenstam (2009), the NS judgment approach is much more lenient than the acoustic analysis approach. Only five out of the 31 Swedish L2 speakers who were judged by Swedish NS to be NS of Swedish passed all four acoustic analysis tests as NS in that study.

The specific criteria adopted in individual studies varied when the same approach was adopted, as well. For example, in studies where NS judges were asked to rate NNS pronunciation, the number of these judges varied a great deal, e.g., from three or four in Birdsong (2007) and Abu-Rabia and Kehat (2004) to 13 in Bongaerts et al. (1997) and Ioup et al. (1994) to 21 in Bongaerts et al. (2000). Assuming that an L2 speaker is more likely to be judged as an NS when fewer NS judges are involved, the number of judges will affect the results.

The same criterion issue applies to the assessment of nativelike sensitivity to morphosyntactic violations. Even though an effort is now made to use online data such as RT and ERP components which provide a better assessment than offline data such as grammaticality judgment accuracy, these online measures differ among themselves. For example, data collected with the eye tracking paradigm tended to show nativelike sensitivity than data collected with the self-paced reading paradigm, and L2 speakers have shown more nativelike ERP patterns when P600 was measured than when LAN was measured.

The second factor has to do with the effect of some intervening variables. Numerous such variables can affect the outcome of a study. In speech perception, the selection of the specific phonetic contrasts for investigation may represent the most important variable that can affect the results of a study. It is well documented that L2 speakers differ in their accuracy across L2 segments or phonetic contrasts. For example, Flege and MacKay (2004) tested Italian ESL speakers on nine English vowel contrasts in a discrimination task (Experiment 1). Their participants' accuracy rates, as assessed in A' scores, varied from a chance effect of 0.60 or lower for the /ɛ/-/æ/ and /ɒ/-/ʌ/ contrasts to a nativelike 0.95 for the /ə/-/ʌ/ contrast. Thus, which segments or contrasts to be used in a study will directly affect the results. Thus, it is not surprising that the non-nativelike performance of highly proficient Spanish-Catalan speakers was obtained with the most challenging Catalan vowel contrast of /e/ and /ɛ/ (e.g., Pallier et al., 1997; Sebastián-Gallés et al., 2005). Other variables such as the extent of the participants' continued use of L1 have also been shown to affect whether nativelike performance was to be observed (e.g., Flege, Schirru, & MacKay, 2003).

Many intervening variables can affect the outcome of individuals' performance in assessing morphosyntactic sensitivity, as well. One of them is the L1–L2 congruency. NNS are more likely to develop a nativelike command of a morphosyntactic structure if a similar structure is used in their L1, as shown in Tokowicz and Warren (2010) and Jiang et al. (2011). A second possible variable is the task. A nativelike P600 among NNS has been more frequently reported in ERP studies than a nativelike RT pattern in self-paced reading task. A plausible reason for this difference is that a grammaticality judgment task is often used in ERP studies on this topic (e.g., Gillon Dowens et al., 2011; Sabourin & Stowe, 2008) while the participants were usually asked to focus on reading for comprehension in a self-paced reading task. The participants' sensitivity may have been enhanced by being asked to concentrate on grammatical accuracy of the stimuli while performing the task in ERP studies. A third variable is the distance between the two ungrammatical elements of a sentence. NNS were found to be more likely to show a nativelike pattern in both RT and ERP studies when a morphosyntactic error involved two adjacent elements than an error involving two distant elements (e.g., Keating, 2009).

To sum up, the acquirability issue has surfaced in the study of L2 processing repeatedly. The essence of the issue is whether L2 learners are able to develop nativelike command of a non-native language. While the findings are not conclusive, there is compelling evidence to suggest that L2 learners have a considerable difficulty in attaining a nativelike competence in the area of phonology and morphosyntax. A review of the semantic processing literature suggests that nativelike semantic structures are difficult to develop at least where adult L2 learners are concerned. The acquirability issue is expected to continue to be on the center stage in L2 processing research. Progress on this topic, though, hinges on, among many other methodological considerations, the development of a set of widely shared criteria in assessing nativelikeness and the controlling of intervening variables that may affect participant performance.

1.3.2 L1–L2 Interaction

How an L2 speakers' L1 and L2 interact in language use represents another topic that have received a great deal of attention in all SLP areas. This interaction is first viewed primarily as a process of L1 influencing L2 use or L1 interfering with L2 acquisition. More recent research suggests that learning an additional language can also affect the representation and processing of a learner's L1. Thus, language interaction becomes truly bidirectional in nature.

The influence of an individual's L1 on L2 learning and use, or simply L1 effects, is probably the most prevalent finding in L2 processing research. In phonological processing, for example, research shows that it is difficult for an L2 speaker to perceive two L2 segments that are not distinguished in L1, such as the Catalan /e/-/ɛ/ contrast for Spanish speakers or the English /l/-/r/ contrast for Japanese speakers. L2 speakers whose L1s do not employ a suprasegmental property such as lexical tone or word stress as a distinctive feature often find it difficult to perceive and produce such features accurately (see Section 3.2.1 for more on the L1 effect in phonology). L1 effects occur in lexical processing, as well, as shown by the differential use of orthographic and phonological information in L2 word recognition by learners of different LT backgrounds (e.g., Koda, 1989, 1990), by a higher degree of decomposition in processing complex words by L2 speakers with a morphologically rich L1 (e.g., Portin et al., 2008), and by the difficulty L2 learners demonstrated in differentiating a semantic contrast that is not made in their L1 (e.g., Jiang, 2004b, 2007b). In sentence processing, L2 speakers were found to interpret ambiguous sentences on the basis of their L1 verb subcategorical specifications (e.g., Frenck-Mestre & Pynte, 1997) or on the basis of their L1 relative clause attachment preferences (e.g., Fernández, 2002), and they showed more difficulty in processing morphosyntactic structures that were not instantiated in their L1s (e.g., Jiang et al., 2011).

There is also evidence suggesting that learning an L2 can also affect L1 representations and processing. Probably the first piece of evidence for an L2 effect on L1 in phonology came from the finding reported by Flege (1987). English NS who spoke L2 French and lived in a French environment for an extended period of time were found to pronounce English stops with a voice onset time (VOT) value that lay between the typically longer English VOT and typically shorter French VOT. The same also happened to L1 French speakers who spoke L2 English and resided in the USA for an extended time period. An L2 effect in phonology has also been reported among L1 English speakers learning L2 Korean (Chang, 2012) and among Russian-English bilinguals (Dmitrieva, Jongman, & Sereno, 2010).

An L2 effect has also been found in semantic representation and processing. Pavlenko and Malt (2011) showed in an object naming task that speaking L2 English affected how Russian NS classified objects in their L1 Russian. Where monolingual Russian speakers named two objects with two different Russian names, *bokal* and *fuzher*, the Russian-English bilinguals in the study named the same two objects with a single Russian name *bokal*, (just as English NS would name them both as *glasses* in English). It seemed that these Russian ESL speakers had restructured two Russian concepts or meanings, {bokal} and {fuzher}, collapsing them into a single concept of {bokal}, as a result of learning English. Evidence of similar semantic restructuring is also present in studies reported by Pavlenko (2003), Pavlenko and Jarvis (2002), Athanasopoulos, Damjanovic, Krajciova, and Sasaki (2011), and Cook (2003).

The interaction between the two languages can be seen as occurring at two levels: mental representations and processing strategies. In the former case, L1 phonetic, lexical, and semantic categories are used in processing L2 input, which leads to L1 effects. In the reverse direction, the L1 mental representations change or are restructured as a result of being exposed to an L2, which leads to L2 effects on L1. All models of L2 phonological processing recognize that segmental and suprasegmental categories in an L2 are initially and may continue to be perceived on the basis of the existing L1 categories (see Section 2.5). These models provide a framework for understanding L1–L2 interaction in terms of mental representation. The psycholinguistic model of L2 lexical development outlined in Jiang (2000) also considers and explains L1–L2 interaction in terms of mental representation. For example, semantic transfer and lexical errors occur as a result of mapping L2 word form to L1 meanings in lexical representation.

Other L1–L2 interaction phenomena, such as the use of orthographic and phonological information in visual word recognition (Section 4.4.1), the degree of decomposition in processing complex words (Section 5.2.3), the preference of relative clause attachment (Section 6.2.2) are related more closely to the processing strategies L2 speakers adopt. Language interaction under these circumstances occur at the level of how language input is analyzed in language processing. It involves the type of computations an individual performs in processing language input rather than the mental representations involved. In comparison to the conceptualization of L1–L2 interaction in terms of mental representations, less attention has been given to specifying and theorizing about how L1–L2 interaction occurs at the level of processing strategies. It is possible that the encounter of a particular type of L2 linguistic input (e.g., a complex word) would automatically trigger the activation of a particular L1 processing strategy (e.g., decomposition) before L2-specific processing strategies are developed. It is also interesting to note that there is less evidence for an L2 effect on L1 at the level of processing strategy in the literature (except for relative clause attachment; see Section 6.2.2). For example, it is not clear whether adopting a more holistic processing strategy in L2 processing (Portin, Lehtonen, & Laine, 2007) would affect the processing the morphologically rich L1.

1.3.3 Documenting and Explaining Age Effects

Variable age of onset represents an important difference between L2 and L1 acquisition. The age factor has been considered in all areas of SLP either as a manipulated variable for investigation or as a controlled variable. The age issue and the acquirability issue are closely related. It is believed by many that a non-native language becomes less acquirable with an increasing age of onset. However, the debate on age effects is of a different nature from that on acquirability. Research related to L2 acquirability have generated inconsistent findings, which lead to different views on this issue. In contrast, age effects have been well documented. Early learners have usually demonstrated more nativelike performance than late learners. The controversy often lies in the explanation of the underlying causes of age effects. In the remainder of the section, I briefly summarize some findings of age effects across different areas, before discussing the different views regarding the causes of age effects (see DeKeyser, 2012 for an excellent review of the literature on this topic).

Age effects have surfaced in all SLP areas, even though it received more attention in phonological processing research than in the other areas. This research has compared children and adults, children of different onset ages, and individuals exposed to an L2 prior to, during, and after puberty. There is compelling evidence showing that younger learners outperform older learners in phonological processing across the board. This early-onset advantage has been shown in perception and production accuracy (e.g., Baker & Trofimovich, 2006; Flege, Munro, & MacKay, 1995; Flege, Yeni-Komshian, & Liu, 1999; Flege et al., 2006; Jia, Strange, Wu, Collado, & Guan, 2006), including in processing degraded input (e.g., Mayo, Florentine, & Buus, 1997; Meador, Flege, & MacKay, 2000). More nativelike performance among younger learners has also been found where phonological processing was assessed in terms of measures other than accuracy, such as assimilation (Baker, Trofimovich, Flege, Mack, & Halter, 2008) or categorization (Archila-Suerte et al., 2012) patterns, the size of the clear speech effect (Rogers, DeMasi, & Krause, 2010), and epenthesis patterns in perceiving consonant clusters (Parlato-Oliveira, Christophe, Hirose, & Dupoux, 2010).

There are multiple indications of age effects in other areas of L2 processing, as well. Guillelmon and Grosjean (2001) showed that only the early bilinguals showed a nativelike sensitivity to gender disagreement in an L2, Fernández (1999) demonstrated that early L2 learners were more nativelike than late L2 learners in the interpretation of ambiguous sentences involving relative clause attachment, Silverberg and Samuel (2004) found reliable L2–L1 semantic priming among early L2 learners, but not late L2 learners, Weber-Fox and Neville (1996) showed that the post-puberty L2 group behaved differently in both behavioral and ERP measures compared to both NS and younger L2 groups in both semantic and syntactic processing, and Kim, Relkin, Lee, and Hirsch (1997) found the involvement of the same cerebral regions in language production among L1 and early L2 speakers but different regions were involved between L1 and late L2 speakers.[4]

In the presence of this mounting evidence, multiple explanations of age effects have been proposed. This is where disagreements occur. We may classify these explanations into two categories. The neurophysiological approach asserts that as an individual gets older, the brain becomes more mature, which leads to the loss of flexibility. This adversely affects L2 learning among older learners. The cognitive approach attributes child–adult differences to the involvement of different cognitive processes and strategies in language learning among individuals of different ages. Such cognitive differences may or may not have their neurophysiological basis. Within each approach, different versions exist that differ in the specific mechanisms or processes used to explain age effects.

The neurophysiological approach attributes age-related differences to reduced brain plasticity as it matures. Two versions of this approach can be identified, one focusing on reduced plasticity at the cerebral level, and the other at the neuron level. In the case of the former, adults' reduced capability is viewed as an outcome of lateralization, the localization of the language function to the left hemisphere. According to this view, lateralization occurs around puberty, which leads to the specialization of the cortex for language learning. Any language learning that occurs after that point has to use whatever brain regions that remain available but are not specifically intended for language learning, which results in laborious language learning. This is the view adopted by Lenneberg (1967) and Penfield and Roberts (1959) in the proposal of the critical period hypothesis for language learning. Scovel (1969, 1988) adopted this view in explaining child–adult differences in L2 learning. At the neuronal level, the reduced brain plasticity is viewed as the increased difficulty for neurons to make new connections. This is the view adopted by Pulvermüller and Schumann (1994). Specifically, they attributed adults' reduced capability in language learning to myelination, a process whereby the axons of neurons become wrapped up by myelin, a substance in the glial cells. Myelination is a natural part of brain maturation and is necessary for rapid transmission of information across neurons, but it also reduces the neurons' capability of making new connections, which adversely affect the learning of a new language. According to these authors, "gradual maturation of the peri-sylvian region of the cortex leads to a loss of plasticity therein, making it hard to acquire phonological and syntactic knowledge" (p. 717).

A cognitive approach can be defined as one that explains age-related differences in terms of the cognitive processes or strategies involved in language learning among learners of different ages. Several specific versions can be put under this umbrella term. One version is Ullman's declarative/procedural model (Ullman, 2001, 2005). At the foundation of this model is the distinction between two separate memory systems, i.e., the declarative and procedural memories. They are believed to be involved in the learning of different aspects of language, with the declarative memory more involved in and better suited for the learning of the lexicon and the procedural memory more involved in learning grammatical rules. It is further believed that the two memory systems are associated with distinctive neural substrates and affected by body hormones and chemicals. The central claim of the model is that as individuals grow older, their body hormones and chemicals change. As a result, individuals tend to rely more on declarative memory than on procedural memory. In language learning, this means that while children learning their L1 use the right memory systems for learning different aspects of language, "young adult L2 learners should tend to rely heavily on declarative memory, even for functions that depend upon the procedural system in L1" (Ullman, 2005, p. 152). Thus, the age-related difference in language learning lies in the increasing involvement of the wrong memory system (i.e., the declarative memory) for learning what is best handled by the procedural memory (i.e., the grammatical rules) in older learners.

A second version of the cognitive approach explains age effects in terms of the different learning processes or strategies involved in language learning among learners of different ages. Several specific proposals have been made depending on how they define or classify these learning processes. Krashen (1981) believed that children subconsciously acquire a language while adults tend to learn it consciously. In Felix's (1985) competition model, it is argued that children's success in learning L1 lies in the use of a language-specific learning module, but as individuals grow older, they develop better general cognitive skills which lead them to use "a general problem-solving module" which is not best suited for language learning. Bley-Vroman (1990) expressed a similar idea in his fundamental difference hypothesis. He asserted that children rely on "a domain-specific language acquisition device" in L1 acquisition but adults have to adopt "a general problem-solving cognitive system" because the former "no longer operates in adults" (p. 23). Another cognitive explanation of age effects is suggested by DeKeyser (2000; DeKeyser & Larson-Hall, 2005) on the basis of a distinction between implicit and explicit learning. According to this view,

> children necessarily learn implicitly; adults necessarily learn largely explicitly. As a result, adults . . . falter in those areas in which explicit learning is ineffective, that is, where rules are too complex or probabilistic in nature to be apprehended fully with explicit rules. Children, on the other hand, cannot use shortcuts to the representation of structure, but eventually reach full native speaker competence through long-term implicit learning from massive input.
>
> (DeKeyser & Larson-Hall, 2005, p. 103)

A similar proposal has been put forward by Archila-Suerte et al. (2012) in the context of explaining age effects in phonological processing. These authors also suggested that, unlike children learning both L1 and L2 implicitly, adult learners have to rely on explicit or higher-cognitive processes in L2 learning.

The proposal that adults seem to rely on cognitive processes different from those used by children is often made on the basis of a more developed cognitive capacity among adults. In Krashen's proposal, the child–adult difference was attributed to the onset of the formal operations stage. In his words, "Formal Operations causes an increase in our ability to learn but damages our ability to acquire" (1981, p. 8) and is "at least partly responsible for a fossilization of progress in subconscious language acquisition". Another explanation is offered in the form of the "less-is-more" hypothesis by Newport (1990). She suggested that due to limited perceptual and memorial abilities, children tend to represent and store smaller pieces of linguistic input which makes componential analysis of language easier. In contrast, "the adult's greater capabilities, and the resulting more complete storage of complex words and sentences, may make the crucial internal components and their organization more difficult to locate and may thereby be a counterproductive skill" (1990, p. 26).

A third version of the cognitive approach is the L1 entrenchment view: younger and older learners differ in how well established their L1 system is and thus in how much interference the L1 produces in L2 learning. Older learners are likely to have a better consolidated L1 which is likely to produce more interference in L2 learning. For example, auditory input is more likely to be perceived with the established L1 phonetic categories among older learners. The same point can be made in semantic processing, as well. L1 entrenchment has been taken as a cause of age-related differences in L2 learning particularly in the L2 phonological processing literature (Flege, 2003; Kuhl, 2000). Flege, for example, linked age effects to L1 influence by arguing that

> as L1 phonetic categories develop slowly through childhood and into early adolescence, they become more likely to perceptually assimilate L2 vowels and consonants. If instances of an L2 speech sound category persist in being identified as instances of an L1 speech sound, category formation for the L2 speech sound will be blocked.
>
> (2003, p. 328)

This approach is able to explain the role of other factors such as continued L1 use in L2 acquisition in that older L2 learners are more likely to continue to use their L1 which will lead to more L1 interference in L2 learning. The L1 entrenchment explanation is viewed as a cognitive approach here as it explains age effects in terms of what mental representations have been established and involved at the time of L2 learning.

These cognitive explanations differ among themselves in whether the cognitive differences are linked to neurophysiological changes. For example, Ullman's (2001, 2005) model links the two memory systems to distinctive neural substrates. Kuhl's (2000) native language magnet model attributes age effects to neural commitment as a result of learning an L1. No claim is made in other cognitive explanations about any neurophysiological basis underlying the change in cognitive processes across the life span.

The cognitive explanations differ from the neurophysiological explanations and differ among themselves with regard to whether adults still retain the ability to attain a nativelike command of the new language. A neurophysiological explanation implies that an adult's brain is no longer flexible enough for the development of nativelike competence. Thus, its answer is generally negative. A weak version of this view is to limit this inability to the development of phonology, as suggested by Scovel (1969). The cognitive explanations, however, do not always imply the permanent loss of the ability to attain nativelike proficiency. Some proponents of a cognitive explanation contend that adult learners can still develop nativelike competence in an L2. Krashen (1981, 1982) explicitly stated that adults can acquire when they are provided with sufficient comprehensible input. Flege has repeatedly asserted that adults maintain the same ability as children do in developing nativelike phonology (e.g., 1981, 1995, 2003). A similar view has been expressed by Ullman (2005), Birdsong (2007), Best and Tyler (2007), and Wayland and Li (2008) with various qualifications. However, Bley-Vroman (1990) seemed to be more skeptical about this prospect.

In short, age effects have been well documented in multiple L2 processing areas. Learners of younger onset ages are usually more likely to produce nativelike performance than older learners are. Multiple explanations of the cause of this age effect have been proposed, some focusing on the loss of brain plasticity, and others on the involvement of different learning processes or strategies. It should be pointed out that these explanations are largely speculative in nature at this stage. Empirical evidence that can link age-related differences to the changes in brain plasticity or cognitive processes has yet to be obtained.

1.4 Conclusion

Three distinct but related areas of SLP can be identified: phonological processing, lexical processing, sentence processing. Each of these areas has its unique and specific focuses. Nevertheless, they share the same primary goal of improving our understanding of the cognitive processes involved in L2 processing, there is a great deal of overlap in the research questions they explore, the research findings from the three areas are often related, and they all adopt an experimental approach. Because of these similarities and of the fact that they have generated the most amount of research in SLP, they can be characterized as the core areas of a coherent and unified field of SLP.

While they are expected to continue to be where most SLP research will be generated, SLP research is also likely to expand to less explored areas such as L2 production, L2 discourse processing, and the relationship between second language and thought.

Given its primary goal of understanding L2 cognition, SLP can be best characterized as basic research. At the same time, research findings in this field may offer many practical applications or insights for dealing with practical issues. For example, research on the intelligibility of non-native speech is highly relevant to human–machine communication, clinical audiology, and wherever a "non-native factor" is important (see Van Wijngaarden, Steeneken, & Houtgast, 2002). Many topics are also directly related to language teaching. For example, research on L2 phonological processing has led Kuhl to suggest that phonological instruction should aim at providing "exaggerated acoustic cues, multiple instances by many talkers, and mass listening experience" (Kuhl, 2000, p. 11855). The research on the integration of new words in the lexicon (Section 4.4.3) and semantic development in L2 (Section 5.4.1) offers insights on the causes of L2 learners' difficulty in vocabulary use and strategies for effective vocabulary teaching. The finding of the larger frequency effect in L2 word recognition (Section 4.4.2) may provide new insights for the development of tools for measuring vocabulary knowledge or lexical development. Findings from such basic research has not been given much attention in pedagogy-related research, as pointed out by Derwing and Munro (2005). It certainly takes a collaborative effort between SLP researchers and researchers of applied fields to help realize the full potentials SLP has to offer in dealing with practical problems.

Notes

1   The term *second language* or *L2* refers to any non-native language learned after the onset of the first or native language and is used interchangeably with *non-native language* in this book. It can be an individual's third or fourth language.

2   An area of research closely related to SLP is bilingual language processing. They are related in the sense that L2 speakers are usually also bilingual speakers, and thus researchers in these two areas study essentially the same population and the same general phenomenon of language use by this population. Additionally, the two areas are both concerned with the cognitive processes involved in language processing. However, bilingual language processing has a focus different from that of SLP. While SLP research is primarily concerned with the comparison of L2 speakers to L1 speakers, the latter is more concerned with the comparison between bilingual speakers and monolingual speakers. This difference leads to differences in perspectives and the type of questions raised. For a quick example, the structure of the mental lexicon is of a great deal of interest to both lexical processing and bilingual processing researchers. But they ask different questions. Bilingual processing researchers want to know if bilinguals have a single integrated lexicon or two separate lexicons, one for each language. L2 lexical processing researchers, on the other hand, often assume that there are two lexicons and they want to know whether the L1 and L2 lexicons are structured in a similar or different way. Bilingual language processing is not covered in this book. For those who are interested in this research, several handbooks and reviews are available that provide detailed but accessible coverages of the diverse research topics in the area (Bhatia & Ritchie, 2004; De Groot & Kroll, 1997; Jiang, 2015; Kroll & De Groot, 2005; Schweitzer, 2015).

3   A reliable difference between the two conditions among English NS means that the two sets of materials are not matched in lexical properties that affect RT, and thus have to be revised before testing L2 speakers.

4   There are studies that have reported no difference between late and early L2 learners (e.g., in brain activities in Chee, Tan, & Thiel, 1999 and Illes et al., 1999, in the size of the cross-language priming effects in Perea, Duñabeitia, & Carreiras, 2008, in sensitivity to morphosyntactic violation in Foote, 2011, and in L2 object naming and rating patterns in Malt & Sloman, 2003). However, these studies constituted a minority, and there is always the possibility that the age of onset did not differ sufficiently to show an age effect, or the particular task or materials used did not tap a process that responded to the age manipulation in these studies. Some studies even showed an older-age advantage (e.g., Aoyama, Flege, Guion, Akahane-Yamada, & Yamada, 2004; Aoyama, Guion, Flege, & Yamada 2008; Oh et al., 2011; Wang & Kuhl, 2003). This usually occurs at the very initial stage of language development (e.g., Aoyama et al.) or with individuals with little exposure to the target language (Wang & Kuhl). Children tended to catch up and surpass older learners with continued exposure to the target language.

5   Not considered in this discussion are the affective explanations that consider child–adult differences in L2 learning in terms of motivation, ego boundary, and attitude (e.g., Moyer, 2007).

References

Abrahamsson, N. & Hyltenstam, K. (2009). Age of onset and nativelikeness in a second language: Listener perception versus linguistic scrutiny. *Language Learning*, 59, 249–306.

Abu-Rabia, S. & Kehat, S. (2004). The critical period for second language pronunciation: Is there such a thing? *Educational Psychology, 24*, 77–97.

Aoyama, K., Flege, J. E., Guion, S. G., Akahane-Yamada, R., & Yamada, T. (2004). Perceived phonetic dissimilarity and L2 speech learning: The case of Japanese /r/ and English /l/ and /r/. *Journal of Phonetics, 32*, 233–250.

Aoyama, K., Guion, S. G., Flege, J. E., & Yamada, T. (2008). The first years in an L2-speaking environment: A comparison of Japanese children and adults learning American English. *International Review of Applied Linguistics in Language Teaching, 46*, 61–90.

Archila-Suerte, P., Zevin, J., Bunta, F., & Hernandez, A. E. (2012). Age of acquisition and proficiency in a second language independently influence the perception of non-native speech. *Bilingualism: Language and Cognition, 15*, 190–201.

Athanasopoulos, P., Damjanovic, L., Krajciova, A., & Sasaki, M. (2011). Representation of colour concepts in bilingual cognition: The case of Japanese blues. *Bilingualism: Language and Cognition, 14*, 9–17.

Baker, W. & Trofimovich, P. (2006). Perceptual paths to accurate production of L2 vowels: The role of individual differences. *IRAL, 44*, 231–250.

Baker, W., Trofimovich, P., Flege, J. E., Mack, M., & Halter, R. (2008). Child-adult differences in second-language phonological learning: The role of cross-language similarity. *Language and Speech, 51*, 317–342.

Bannai, M. (2011). The nature of variable sensitivity to agreement violations in L2 English. *EUROSLA Yearbook, 11*, 115–137.

Best, C. T., McRoberts, G., & Goodell, E. (2001). Discrimination of non-native consonant contrasts varying in perceptual assimilation to the listeners native phonological system. *Journal of the Acoustical Society of America, 109*, 775–794.

Best, C. T. & Tyler, M. D. (2007). Nonnative and second language speech perception: Commonalities and complementaries. In O.-S. Bohn & M. J. Munro (Eds.), *Language experience in second language speech learning* (pp. 13–34). Amsterdam: John Benjamins.

Bhatia, T. K. & Ritchie, W. C. (Eds.). (2004). *The handbook of bilingualism*. Malden, MA: Blackwell Publishing.

Birdsong, D. (2007). Nativelike pronunciation among late learners of French as a second language. In M. J. Munro & O.-S. Bohn (Eds.), *Second language speech learning: The role of language experience in speech perception and production* (pp. 99–116). Amsterdam: John Benjamins.

Bley-Vroman, R. (1990). The logical problem in foreign language learning. *Linguistic Analysis, 20* (1–2), 3–47.

Bock, K. & Miller, C. A. (1991). Broken agreement. *Cognitive Psychology, 23*, 45–93.

Bongaerts, T., Mennen, S., & Slik, F. V. D. (2000). Authenticity of pronunciation in naturalistic second language acquisition: The case of very advanced late learners of Dutch as a second language. *Studia Linguistica, 54*, 298–308.

Bongaerts, T., Van Summeren, C., Planken, B., & Schils, E. (1997). Age and ultimate attainment in the pronunciation of a foreign language. *Studies in Second Language Acquisition, 19*(4), 447–465.

Bosch, L., Costa, A., & Sebastián-Gallés, N. (2000). First and second language vowel perception in early bilinguals. *European Journal of Cognitive Psychology, 12*, 189–221.

Bosman, A. M. T. & De Groot, A. M. B. (1996). Phonologic mediation is fundamental to reading: Evidence from beginning readers. *The Quarterly Journal of Experimental Psychology, Section A: Human Experimental Psychology, 49A*, 715–744.

Cattell, J. M. (1887). Experiments on the association of ideas. *Mind, 12*, 68–74.

Chang, C. B. (2012). Rapid and multifaceted effects of second-language learning on first-language speech production. *Journal of Phonetics, 40*, 249–268.

Chee, M. W., Tan, E. W., & Thiel, T. (1999). Mandarin and English single word processing studied with functional magnetic resonance imaging. *The Journal of Neuroscience, 19*, 3050–3056.

Chen, L., Shu, H., Liu, Y., Zhao, J., & Li, P. (2007). ERP signatures of subject and verb agreement in L2 learning. *Bilingualism: Language and Cognition, 10*, 161–174.

Clahsen, H. & Felser, C. (2006). Continuity and shallow structures in language processing. *Applied Psycholinguistics, 27*, 107–126.

Cook, V. (Ed.). (2003). *Effects of the second language on the first.* Clevedon: Multilingual Matters.

Corder, S. P. (1967). The significance of learner's errors. *IRAL, 5*, 161–170.

Cuetos, F. & Mitchell, D. C. (1988). Cross-linguistic differences in parsing: Restrictions on the late-closure strategy in Spanish. *Cognition, 30*, 73–105.

Darcy, I. & Krüger, F. (2012). Vowel perception and production in Turkish children acquiring L2 German. *Journal of Phonetics, 40*, 568–581.

Davis, C., Castles, A., & Iakovidis, E. (1998). Masked homophone and pseudohomophone priming in children and adults. *Language and Cognitive Processes, 13*, 625–651.

De Groot, A. M. B. & Kroll, J. F. (Eds.). (1997). *Tutorials in bilingualism: Psycholinguistic perspectives.* Mahwah, NJ: Lawrence Erlbaum Associates.

DeKeyser, R. M. (2000). The robustness of critical period effects in second language acquisition. *Studies in Second Language Acquisition, 22*, 499–534.

DeKeyser, R. M. (2012). Age effects in second language learning. In S. Gass & A. Mackey (Eds.), *Routledge handbook of second language acquisition* (pp. 442–460). London: Routledge.

DeKeyser, R. M. & Larson-Hall, J. (2005). What does the critical period really mean? In J. Kroll & A. M. B De Groot (Eds.), *Handbook of bilingualism: Psycholinguistic approaches* (pp. 88–108). New York: Oxford University Press.

Derwing, T. M. & Munro, M. J. (2005). Second language accent and pronunciation teaching: A research-based approach. *TESOL Quarterly, 39*(3), 379–397.

Dmitrieva, O., Jongman, A., & Sereno, J. (2010). Phonological neutralization by native and non-native speakers: The case of Russian final devoicing. *Journal of Phonetics, 38*, 483–492.

Dulay, H. C. & Burt, M. K. (1974). Natural sequences in child second language acquisition. *Language Learning, 24*, 37–53.

Dussias, P. E. (2003). Syntactic ambiguity resolution in L2 learners: Some effects of bilinguality on L1 and L2 processing strategies. *Studies in Second Language Acquisition, 25*, 529–557.

Felix, S. W. (1985). More evidence on competing cognitive systems. *Second Language Research, 1*, 47–72.

Fernández, E. M. (1999). Processing strategies in second language acquisition: Some preliminary results. In E. C. Klein & G. Martohardjono (Eds.), *The development of second language grammars: A generative approach* (pp. 217–239). Amsterdam: John Benjamins.

Fernández, E. M. (2002). Relative clause attachment in bilinguals and monolinguals. In R. R. Heredia & J. Altarriba (Eds.), *Bilingual sentence processing* (pp. 187–215). Amsterdam: Elsevier.

Flege, J. E. (1981). The phonological basis of foreign accent: A hypothesis. *TESOL Quarterly, 15*, 443–455.

Flege, J. E. (1987). The production of 'new' and 'similar' phones in a foreign language: Evidence for the effect of equivalence classification. *Journal of Phonetics, 15*, 47–65.

Flege, J. E. (1991). Age of learning affects the authenticity of voice-onset time (VOT) in stop consonants produced in a second language. *The Journal of the Acoustical Society of America, 89*, 395–411.

Flege, J. E. (1995). Second-language speech learning: Theory, findings, and problems. In W. Strange (Ed.), *Speech perception and linguistic experience: Issues in cross-language research* (pp. 233–272). Baltimore, MD: York Press.

Flege, J. E. (2003). Assessing constraints on second-language segmental production and perception. In A. Meyer & N. Schiller (Eds.), *Phonetics and phonology in language comprehension and production, differences and similarities* (pp. 319–355). Berlin: Mouton de Gruyter.

Flege, J. E., Birdsong, D., Bialystok, E., Mack, M., Sung, H., & Tsukada, K. (2006). Degree of foreign accent in English sentences produced by Korean children and adults. *Journal of Phonetics, 34*, 153–175.

Flege, J. E. & Davidian, R. D. (1984). Transfer and developmental processes in adult foreign language speech production. *Applied Psycholinguistics, 5*, 323–347.

Flege, J. E. & Hillenbrand, J. (1984). Limits on phonetic accuracy in foreign language speech production. *The Journal of the Acoustical Society of America, 76*, 708–721.

Flege, J. E. & MacKay, I. R. (2004). Perceiving vowels in a second language. *Studies in Second Language Acquisition, 26*, 1–34.

Flege, J. E., Munro, M. J., & MacKay, I. R. (1995). Effects of age of second-language learning on the production of English consonants. *Speech Communication, 16*, 1–26.

Flege, J. E., Schirru, C., & MacKay, I. R. (2003). Interaction between the native and second language phonetic subsystems. *Speech Communication, 40*, 467–491.

Flege, J. E., Yeni-Komshian, G. H., & Liu, S. (1999). Age constraints on second-language acquisition. *Journal of Memory and Language, 41*, 78–104.

Foote, R. (2011). Integrated knowledge of agreement in early and late English-Spanish bilinguals. *Applied Psycholinguistics, 32*, 187–220.

Foucart, A. & Frenck-Mestre, C. (2012). Can late L2 learners acquire new grammatical features? Evidence from ERPs and eye-tracking. *Journal of Memory and Language, 66*, 226–248.

Frenck-Mestre, C., Osterhout, L., McLaughlin, J., & Foucart, A. (2008). The effect of phonological realization of inflectional morphology on verbal agreement in French: Evidence from ERPs. *Acta Psychologica, 128*, 528–536.

Frenck-Mestre, C. & Pynte, J. (1997). Syntactic ambiguity resolution while reading in second and native languages. *The Quarterly Journal of Experimental Psychology A, 50*(1), 119–148.

Gass, S. M. (1987). The resolution of conflicts among competing systems: A bidirectional perspective. *Applied Psycholinguistics, 8*, 329–350.

Gillon Dowens, M. G., Guo, T., Guo, J., Barber, H., & Carreiras, M. (2011). Gender and number processing in Chinese learners of Spanish—Evidence from event related potentials. *Neuropsychologia, 49*, 1651–1659.

Gillon Dowens, M. G., Vergara, M., Barber, H. A., & Carreiras, M. (2010). Morphosyntactic processing in late second-language learners. *Journal of Cognitive Neuroscience*, 22, 1870–1887.

Guillelmon, D. & Grosjean, F. (2001). The gender marking effect in spoken word recognition: The case of bilinguals. *Memory and Cognition*, 29, 503–511.

Harrington, M. (1987). Processing transfer: Language-specific processing strategies as a source of interlanguage variation. *Applied Psycholinguistics*, 8, 351–377.

Illes, J., Francis, W. S., Desmond, J. E., Gabrieli, J. D., Glover, G. H., Poldrack, R., Lee, C. J., & Wagner, A. D. (1999). Convergent cortical representation of semantic processing in bilinguals. *Brain and Language*, 70, 347–363.

Ioup, G., Boustagui, E., El Tigi, M., & Moselle, M. (1994). Reexamining the critical period hypothesis. *Studies in Second Language Acquisition*, 16, 73–98.

Jia, G., Strange, W., Wu, Y., Collado, J., & Guan, Q. (2006). Perception and production of English vowels by Mandarin speakers: Age-related differences vary with amount of L2 exposure. *The Journal of the Acoustical Society of America*, 119, 1118–1130.

Jiang, N. (2000). Lexical representation and development in a second language. *Applied Linguistics*, 21, 47–77.

Jiang, N. (2004a). Morphological insensitivity in second language processing. *Applied Psycholinguistics*, 25, 603–634.

Jiang, N. (2004b). Semantic transfer and its implications for vocabulary teaching in a second language. *The Modern Language Journal*, 88, 416–432.

Jiang, N. (2007a). Selective integration of linguistic knowledge in adult second language learning. *Language Learning*, 57, 1–33.

Jiang, N. (2007b). Semantic representation and development in steady-state second language speakers. *Review of Applied Linguistics in China*, 3, 60–91.

Jiang, N. (2012). *Conducting reaction time research in second language studies*. London: Routledge.

Jiang, N. (2015). Six decades of research on lexical representation and processing in bilinguals. In J. Schweitzer (Ed.), *Cambridge handbook of bilingual processing* (pp. 29–84). Cambridge, MA: Cambridge University Press.

Jiang, N., Novokshanova, E., Masuda, K., & Wang, X. (2011). Morphological congruency and the acquisition of L2 morphemes. *Language Learning*, 61, 940–967.

Kang, K. H. & Guion, S. G. (2006). Phonological systems in bilinguals: Age of learning effects on the stop consonant systems of Korean-English bilinguals. *The Journal of the Acoustical Society of America*, 119, 1672–1683.

Keating, G. D. (2009). Sensitivity to violations of gender agreement in native and nonnative Spanish: An eye-movement investigation. *Language Learning*, 59, 503–535.

Kilborn, K. & Cooreman, A. (1987). Sentence interpretation strategies in adult Dutch-English bilinguals. *Applied Psycholinguistics*, 8, 415–431.

Kim, K. H., Relkin, N. R., Lee, K. M., & Hirsch, J. (1997). Distinct cortical areas associated with native and second languages. *Nature*, 388, 171–174.

Koda, K. (1988). Cognitive process in second language reading: Transfer of L1 reading skills and strategies. *Second Language Research*, 4(2), 133–155.

Koda, K. (1989). Effects of L1 orthographic representation on L2 phonological coding strategies. *Journal of Psycholinguistic Research*, 18, 201–222.

Koda, K. (1990). The use of Ll reading strategies in l.2 reading. *Studies in Second Language Acquisition, 12,* 393–410.

Krashen, S. D. (1981). *Second language acquisition and second language learning.* Oxford: Pergamon Press.

Krashen, S. D. (1982). *Principles and practice in second language acquisition.* Oxford: Pergamon Press.

Kroll, J. F. & De Groot, A. M. B. (Eds.). (2005). *Handbook of bilingualism: Psycholinguistic approaches.* Oxford: Oxford University Press.

Kuhl, P. K. (2000). A new view of language acquisition. *Proceedings of the National Academy of Sciences of the United States of America, 97,* 11850–11857.

Lenneberg, E. (1967). *Biological foundations of language.* New York: Wiley.

Malt, B. C. & Sloman, S. A. (2003). Linguistic diversity and object naming by nonnative speakers of English. *Bilingualism: Language and Cognition, 6,* 47–67.

Mayo, L. H., Florentine, M., & Buus, S. (1997). Age of second-language acquisition and perception of speech in noise. *Journal of Speech, Language, and Hearing Research, 40,* 686–693.

Meador, D., Flege, J. E., & MacKay, I. R. (2000). Factors affecting the recognition of words in a second language. *Bilingualism: Language and Cognition, 3,* 55–67.

Moyer, A. (2007). Do language attitudes determine accent? A study of bilinguals in the USA. *Journal of Multilingual and Multicultural Development, 28,* 502–518.

Muchisky, D. M. (1983). Relationships between speech and reading among second language learners. *Language Learning, 33,* 77–102.

Mueller, J. L., Hahne, A., Fujii, Y., & Friederici, A. D. (2005). Native and nonnative speakers' processing of a miniature version of Japanese as revealed by ERPs. *Journal of Cognitive Neuroscience, 17,* 1229–1244.

Mueller, J. L. & Jiang, N. (2013). The acquisition of the Korean honorific affix (u)si by advanced L2 learners. *Modern Language Journal, 97,* 318–339.

Newport, E. L. (1990). Maturational constraints on language learning. *Cognitive Science, 14,* 11–28.

Oh, G. E., Guion-Anderson, S., Aoyama, K., Flege, J. E., Akahane-Yamada, R., & Yamada, T. (2011). A one-year longitudinal study of English and Japanese vowel production by Japanese adults and children in an English-speaking setting. *Journal of Phonetics, 39,* 156–167.

Ojima, S., Nakata, H., & Kakigi, R. (2005). An ERP study of second language learning after childhood: Effects of proficiency. *Journal of Cognitive Neuroscience, 17,* 1212–1228.

Pallier, C., Bosch, L., & Sebastián-Gallés, N. (1997). A limit on behavioral plasticity in speech perception. *Cognition, 64,* B9–B17.

Parlato-Oliveira, E., Christophe, A., Hirose, Y., & Dupoux, E. (2010). Plasticity of illusory vowel perception in Brazilian-Japanese bilinguals. *The Journal of the Acoustical Society of America, 127,* 3738–3748.

Pavlenko, A. (2003). Eyewitness memory in late bilinguals: Evidence for discursive relativity. *International Journal of Bilingualism, 7,* 257–281.

Pavlenko, A. & Jarvis, S. (2002). Bidirectional transfer. *Applied Linguistics, 23,* 190–214.

Pavlenko, A. & Malt, B. C. (2011). Kitchen Russian: Cross-linguistic differences and first-language object naming by Russian-English bilinguals. *Bilingualism: Language and Cognition, 14,* 19–45.

Pearlmutter, N. J., Garnsey, S. M., & Bock, K. (1999). Agreement processes in sentence comprehension. *Journal of Memory and Language, 41*, 427–456.

Penfield, W. & Roberts, L. (1959). *Speech and brain-mechanisms*. Princeton: Princeton University Press.

Perea, M., Duñabeitia, J. A., & Carreiras, M. (2008). Masked associative/semantic priming effects across languages with highly proficient bilinguals. *Journal of Memory and Language, 58*, 916–930.

Portin, M., Lehtonen, M., Harrer, G., Wande, E., Niemi, J., & Laine, M. (2008). L1 effects on the processing of inflected nouns in L2. *Acta Psychologica, 128*, 452–465.

Portin, M., Lehtonen, M., & Laine, M. (2007). Processing of inflected nouns in late bilinguals. *Applied Psycholinguistics, 28*, 135–156.

Pulvermüller, F. & Schumann, J. H. (1994). Neurobiological mechanisms of language acquisition. *Language Learning, 44*, 681–734.

Rinker, T., Alku, P., Brosch, S., & Kiefer, M. (2010). Discrimination of native and non-native vowel contrasts in bilingual Turkish–German and monolingual German children: Insight from the Mismatch Negativity ERP component. *Brain and Language, 113*, 90–95.

Rogers, C. L., DeMasi, T. M., & Krause, J. C. (2010). Conversational and clear speech intelligibility of/bVd/syllables produced by native and non-native English speakers. *The Journal of the Acoustical Society of America, 128*, 410–423.

Sabourin, L. & Stowe, L. A. (2008). Second language processing: When are first and second languages processed similarly? *Second Language Research, 24*, 397–430.

Sagarra, N. & Herschensohn, J. (2010). The role of proficiency and working memory in gender and number agreement processing in L1 and L2 Spanish. *Lingua, 120*, 2022–2039.

Schneiderman, E. I. & Desmarais, C. (1988). The talented language learner: Some preliminary findings. *Second Language Research, 4*, 91–109.

Schweitzer, J. (Ed.). (2015). *Cambridge handbook of bilingual processing*. Cambridge, MA: Cambridge University Press.

Scovel, T. (1969). Foreign accents, language acquisition, and cerebral dominance. *Language Learning, 19*(3–4), 245–253.

Scovel, T. (1988). *A time to speak: A psycholinguistic inquiry into the critical period for human speech*. Rowley, MA: Newbury House.

Sebastián-Gallés, N., Echeverría, S., & Bosch, L. (2005). The influence of initial exposure on lexical representation: Comparing early and simultaneous bilinguals. *Journal of Memory and Language, 52*, 240–255.

Sebastián-Gallés, N. & Soto-Faraco, S. (1999). Online processing of native and non-native phonemic contrasts in early bilinguals. *Cognition, 72*, 111–123.

Shibuya, M. & Wakabayashi, S. (2008). Why are L2 learners not always sensitive to subject-verb agreement? *EUROSLA Yearbook, 8*, 235–258.

Silverberg, S. & Samuel, A. G. (2004). The effect of age of second language acquisition on the representation and processing of second language words. *Journal of Memory and Language, 51*, 381–398.

Special Eurobarometer 243 (February 2006). Europeans and Their Languages. European Commission: Directorate-General for Communication.

Tokowicz, N. & MacWhinney, B. (2005). Implicit vs. explicit measures of sensitivity to violations in L2 grammar: An event-related potential investigation. *Studies in Second Language Acquisition, 27*, 173–204.

Tokowicz, N. & Warren, T. (2010). Beginning adult L2 learners' sensitivity to morphosyntactic violations: A self-paced reading study. *European Journal of Cognitive Psychology, 22*(7), 1092–1106.

Ullman, M. T. (2001). The neural basis of lexicon and grammar in first and second language: The declarative/procedural model. *Bilingualism: Language and Cognition, 4*, 105–122.

Ullman, M. T. (2005). A cognitive neuroscience perspective on second language acquisition: The declarative/procedural model. In C. Sanz (Ed.), *Mind and context in adult second language acquisition: Methods, theory, and practice* (pp. 141–178). Washington, DC: Georgetown University.

Van Wijngaarden, S. J., Steeneken, H. J., & Houtgast, T. (2002). Quantifying the intelligibility of speech in noise for non-native talkers. *The Journal of the Acoustical Society of America, 112*, 3004–3013.

Wang, Y. & Kuhl, P. K. (2003). Evaluating the 'critical period' hypothesis: Perceptual learning of Mandarin tones in American adults and American children at 6, 10 and 14 years of age. In *Poster presented at the 15th International Congress of Phonetic Sciences* (pp. 1537–1540). Retrieved from http://128.95.148.60/kuhl/pdf/wang_kuhl_2003.pdf (Accessed on January 1, 2016).

Wayland, R. P. & Li, B. (2008). Effects of two training procedures in cross-language perception of tones. *Journal of Phonetics, 36*, 250–267.

Weber-Fox, C. M. & Neville, H. J. (1996). Maturational constraints on functional specializations for language processing: ERP and behavioral evidence in bilingual speakers. *Journal of Cognitive Neuroscience, 8*, 231–256.

Chapter 2

Phonological Processing in L2
Concepts, Methods, and Models

2.1 Introduction

Understanding speech as intended and producing it in an intelligible way are the most basic skills involved in language use, but they are also the most challenging aspects of language learning for many L2 speakers. Many individuals find it extremely difficult to rid themselves of an L2 accent. They also find it hard to understand L2 speech in less than optimal conditions, such as over the phone or in a noisy environment.[1] A great deal of research has been done to understand the perception and production of speech sounds and other phonological units by L2 speakers. This research attempts to understand how the processes involved in L2 perception and production are similar to or different from L1 perception and production, what makes speech perception and production in a non-native language difficult, and what factors may affect the development of nativelike phonology in an L2. Research on L2 phonological processing is unique in comparison to other processing areas in that it is closely tied to phonological development. Processing data are obtained and interpreted with close attention to what they can tell us about phonological development in an L2. Thus, this research best illustrates the close relationship between processing and acquisition.

This chapter provides an introduction to concepts, methods, and theoretical models related to L2 phonological processing. It begins with a description of the speech production process and the acoustic cues that are used in speech perception. It then provides examples to illustrate how languages differ in many aspects of phonology. Many of these differences have been used as the target phenomena for studying L2 phonological processing. It is then followed by a description of the frequently used research methods in this area and a summary of models of L2 phonological processing.

2.2 Speech Production and Acoustic Cues

Most speech sounds are produced when airflow originated from the lungs passes through the larynx and the vocal tract. This airflow can be modified in this process to produce different speech sounds. One way to modify the airflow is to adjust the opening between the vocal folds (also known as vocal cords), the two pieces of mucous membrane positioned horizontally in the larynx. When the opening is narrow, the airflow would cause the vocal folds to vibrate resulting in voiced sounds (i.e., vowels and voiced consonants). Otherwise, voiceless sounds are produced. We may raise the soft palate (or velum) to block the airway leading to the nasal cavity to produce oral sounds, or lower it to produce nasal sounds. Finally, we may position the tongue and lips differently to affect the shape of the vocal tract (i.e., the airway), the amount of constriction the airflow encounters, and where the constriction occurs, all of which will affect the sounds we eventually produce.

When we regulate the airflow and manipulate the shape of the vocal tract, we change the acoustic properties associated with the speech sounds. One of the most important acoustic properties is the frequency of sound waves. A speech sound we hear is made of periodically repeating waves of air molecules. Frequency in this context refers to the number of periodic repetitions of sound waves, or cycles, in a second. It is measured in hertz (Hz) after German physicist Heinrich Rudolf Hertz. The frequencies of sound waves are initially created as a result of the vibration of the vocal folds, and then modified when the airflow hits the surfaces of the vocal tract. When we position our speech organs such as the tongue and lips differently, we create different shapes of the vocal tract through which the airflow passes. This, in turn, leads to the creation of different frequencies of the sound waves, and thus different sounds.

More specifically, a speech sound consists of sound waves of different frequencies, all of which form the frequency spectrum of a sound. At the lowest end of the spectrum is the frequency of the vibration of the vocal folds. It is referred to as the *fundamental frequency*, or F_0 (pronounced as F zero). Males, females, and children differ in the structure of the vocal folds (in terms of thickness and length). This difference leads to the difference in the rate of vocal fold vibration (e.g., the thicker vocal folds of males result in a slower rate of vibration), which in turn results in difference in fundamental frequency. That is how we are able to tell the voice of a male, a female, or a child. The sound waves of other frequencies form the harmonics of a sound. These sound waves have the frequencies that are the whole-number multiples of the fundamental frequency. They resonate with the fundamental frequency and thus are acoustically prominent. Sound waves of such resonant frequencies are known as *formants*. They are usually numbered as Formant 1 (or F_1), Formant 2 (or F_2), and so on, beginning from the lowest frequency of the spectrum following F_0. These formants reflect the articulatory changes made in speech production. For example, F_1 is inversely correlated with tongue height. A high tongue position leads to greater pharyngeal space which produces lower F_1. Thus, high vowels have lower F_1s. F_2 is correlated with tongue retraction (or frontness). A front tongue position leads to a higher F_2.

In a *spectrogram*, which is a visual representation of a speech signal, a formant can be identified as a darker and denser band of frequencies (Figure 2.1a).

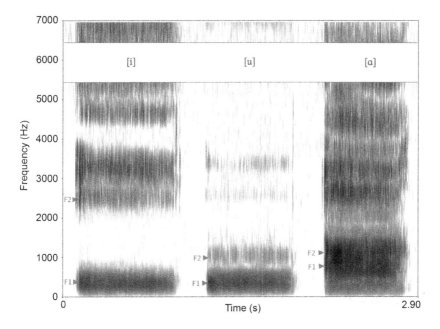

Figure 2.1a Graphic Illustration of Acoustic Cues

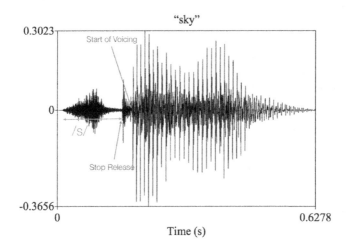

Figure 2.1b

In phonological processing research, these frequencies are referred to as or said to provide *spectral cues* for speech perception.

When speech sounds are produced in syllables, their pronunciation is often influenced by the neighboring sounds, a phenomenon referred to as

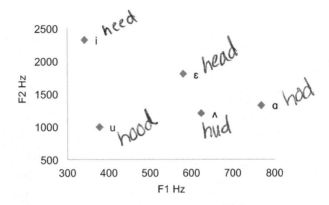

Figure 2.2 FI and F2 Frequencies (in Hz) of Five English Vowels, /i/, /ɛ/, /ɑ/, /ʌ/, and /u/, as Pronounced in *Heed, Head, Hod, Hud, Hood*, Based on the Male Data in Table V in Hillenbrand, Getty, Clark, and Wheeler (1995)

coarticulation. In the cases of vowels, this influence may be seen in the change of the formants during the transition from a consonant to a vowel or from a vowel to a consonant. The formant frequency may rise, drop, or remain flat. This is often referred to as formant direction, transition, movement, or contour. Formant directions also provide spectral cues in speech perception.

In addition to manipulating the shape of the vocal tract, we can control how long airflow is blocked or constricted, or how long or how soon the vocal folds vibrate, thus affecting the duration of a sound segment. The amount of time a segment or the transition from one sound to another takes is often referred to as the duration, length, or quantity property of a sound and is said to provide *temporal cues* in speech perception. A good example of how *temporal cues* may help differentiate speech sounds is the role of *voice onset time* (*VOT*) in the differentiation of word-initial voiced and voiceless stops. *VOT* refers to the duration between the release of air pressure and the vibration of the focal folds in producing words such as *tie* and *die* (see Figure 2.1b).[2] In English, for example, voiced stops are usually produced with a short *VOT* (usually 30 ms or shorter) than voiceless stops (usually 40 ms or longer).

These spectral and temporal cues, which can take a variety of forms in the context of an actual syllable or word, provide the primary information for the discrimination of most speech sounds. For example, research shows that vowels, when produced in isolation, can be best differentiated based on the frequencies of the first two formants (Fant, 1973; Klein, Plomp, & Pols, 1970). This allow us to show the acoustic differences among vowels in a two-dimensional space with each dimension representing one of the two formants, as shown in Figure 2.2. For another example, the frequency and direction of

Table 2.1 Example of Phonetic Contrasts and Their Primary Acoustic Cues

Phonetic Contrasts and Examples	Primary Acoustic Cues
Vowels in isolation, /i e u/	F1 and F2 frequencies
Vowels in syllables, *pet, peat; bet, beat*	F1 and F2 frequency and transition
Voicing in initial stops, *pea, bee*	voice onset time (VOT)
Voicing in final stops, *tap, tab*	duration of the preceding vowel
Voicing in final fricatives, *bus, buzz*	duration of the preceding vowel
Place of articulation in oral stops and nasals, *deed, bead; need, mead*	F2 starting frequency and transition
Initial liquids, *lead, read*	F3 starting frequency and transition
Chinese tone	F0 pitch contour

the third formant are the primary cues for differentiating the English liquids /l/ and /r/.

More examples of the primary acoustic cues used to differentiate English phonetic contrasts can be found in Table 2.1.

The fact that a primary cue often provides sufficient information for discriminating a phonetic contrast does not mean that there is only a single cue involved in perception. On the contrary, a phonetic contrast can be perceived on the basis of multiple cues. For example, both spectral and temporal cues help to distinguish English tense (e.g., /i/, /u/, /ɑ/) from lax (e.g., /ɛ/, /æ/, /ə/) vowels (Fox, Flege, & Munro, 1995). While F_0 contour is the primary acoustic cue for differentiating Mandarin lexical tones, vowel duration, and amplitude envelope (i.e., the variation of amplitude over time) may also help differentiate tones (Blicher, Diehl, & Cohen, 1990; Whalen & Xu, 1992). Word stress can be differentiated on the basis of three cues: F_0, duration, and intensity (e.g., Fry, 1955; Lieberman, 1960; Sluijter & van Heuven, 1996; Zhang & Francis, 2010).

The process of segmental perception is one in which a listener perceives and analyzes the acoustic input and matches the input to the phonetic category represented in his or her mind. Accurate perception of a speech sound is dependent on the presence of a mental representation of a phonetic category for the sound. When such a category is available and when the incoming input is perceived to sufficiently match the represented category, the sound is recognized. For example, accurate perception of the English vowel /æ/ can only be achieved when a phonetic category for this vowel is represented in the listener's mind. For a monolingual Chinese speaker whose native language does not have this vowel, the same stimulus is likely to be perceived as something else, e.g., the closest sound recognized in Chinese. Thus, the essence of phonological development and accurate phonological processing lies in the formation of new phonetic categories specific to the target language. However, this can be a complex and challenging process, due to numerous and often very subtle phonetic and phonological differences between languages. Some of such differences are discussed in the following section.

2.3 Cross-Linguistic Differences in Sound Systems

There are numerous differences in phonology between any two languages. These differences often become target phenomena for studying L2 phonological processing, so a good understanding of these differences will help better appreciate the research issues under investigation, the methodology adopted, and the findings reported in a published study. This section explains many of the differences that one often encounters in reading the L2 phonological processing literature. It is organized around the three levels of phonological representations: the sound inventory and acoustic details, distinctive features, and phonotactics.

2.3.1 The Sound Inventory and Acoustic Details

Human beings employ a large number of sounds in speech communication. According to Ladefoged (2004), the world's languages contain approximately 200 vowels and 600 consonants. However, any individual language only uses a subset of these sounds, and languages differ in how many sounds they use. Take the number of vowels, for example. Spanish and Japanese have five vowels or monophthongs, but German has 18. Most languages seem to have a number between the two, for example, 6 in Mandarin Chinese, 8 in Catalan, 9 in Korean, 12 in Dutch and English, 14 in French. Similarly, languages vary in the number of consonants they employ. Hawaiian has 8 consonants, French 18, and Nepali 27 (Clements, 2003). A survey of 317 human languages indicated that the number of segments can vary between 11 in one language and 141 in another, with the inventory size of 20 to 37 being typical (Maddieson, 1984).

Languages also differ in the specific subset of sounds they employ, regardless of the size of the inventory. A sound may be used in one language, but not in another. This results in a different inventory of sounds for each language. For example, Chinese does not have interdental consonants /θ/ and /ð/ that are in English, as in the words *three* and *that*. English does not have retroflex consonants such as /ʂ/ and /ʐ/ that are available in Chinese. Many languages have diphthongs, but French does not (except for Quebec French). Mandarin Chinese and French share a similar vowel /y/, as in the French word *début* (beginning) and in the Mandarin word *yu* (rain), but it is not used in English.

Even when similar sounds are shared between two languages, subtle differences may exist in the acoustic details of the sounds. For example, both English and Spanish share the vowels /i/ and /e/, but they are produced with significantly higher F_2 in English than in Spanish (Bradlow, 1995). English and Korean both have stops, and they can be classified as voiced and voiceless stops based on VOT in both languages. However, different from English, Korean stops can also be differentiated in terms of the onset F_0 of the following vowel. Thus, two stops may both have a long VOT but differ in the onset F_0 of the following vowel, resulting in two different phonemes. Consequently, instead of having a two-way voiced/voiceless distinction in English, Korean has a three-way classification for stops: fortis stops that have short VOT and high F_0, lenis stops that have medium to long VOT and low F_0, and aspirated stops that have long VOT and high F_0 (Chang, 2012). Thomson, Nearey, and Derwing (2009) also showed that even though both Mandarin and English have the vowel /u/, the English /u/ is much higher in F_1 and F_2 frequencies than the Chinese /u/.

The subtle differences in similar sounds across languages were empirically demonstrated by Chung et al. (2012) who compared the pronunciation of three vowels, /i/, /a/, and /u/, that are shared in five languages: Cantonese, English, Greek, Japanese, and Korean. Two primary acoustic cues, F_1 and F_2, were measured and compared of these vowels as they were produced by native speakers of each of these languages. A number of differences were found. For example, the F_1 of /a/ was higher in English and Japanese than in the other three languages, and /u/ and /a/ showed more cross-language differences than /i/. Furthermore, the three vowels occupied a larger acoustic space in Cantonese than in the other four languages (you can visualize the Cantonese vowels being more spread out than those of the other languages if they are all shown in Figure 2.2).

2.3.2 Distinctive Features

A distinctive feature is a phonetic property that helps define natural classes of speech sounds and distinguish a phonetic category or a set of phonetic categories from another. Some of these features are more related to the distinction of vowels, some to that of consonants, and still some being suprasegmental. Some features frequently occurring in phonological processing literature are described below, each followed by illustrations of how languages differ in them.

2.3.2.1 Voicing

A speech sound can be voiced or voiceless. The former is produced with the vibration of the vocal folds and the latter without. All vowels are voiced sounds, but consonants can be voiced or voiceless. Voicing is a contrastive feature employed in many languages. In English, for example, a voiceless consonant has a voiced counterpart. Thus, /t/, /p/, /k/, /f/, /s/, /θ/, and /ʃ/ are voiceless consonants, and their voiced counterparts are /d/, /b/, /g/, /v/, /z/, /ð/, and /ʒ/. However, not all languages use voicing as a distinctive feature. In Chinese, for example, some voiceless stops do not have their voiced counterparts. Furthermore, in languages that do employ the voicing distinction, there are often subtle differences in where the boundary is set between voiced and voiceless sounds. As discussed earlier, the acoustic cue for word-initial voicing is the VOT, which is longer for voiceless sounds than for voiced sounds. The phonetic boundary is around 30 ms to 40 ms in English. Thus, a stop+vowel syllable that is produced with a VOT of 20 ms is perceived as having a voiced stop, but a VOT of 50 ms would result in the perception of a voiceless stop. In French, however, the voicing boundary is located at the VOT of 0 ms, as demonstrated by Caramazza and Yeni-Komshian (1974). Such voicing boundary difference across languages has direct perceptual consequences. For example, the same stop+/a/ syllable with a VOT of 20 ms were perceived as having a voiced stop by English NS, but as having a voiceless stop by French speakers, as shown in Caramazza & Yeni-Komshian.

2.3.2.2 Aspiration

A consonant can be produced with or without a strong burst of air, thus resulting in an aspirated or non-aspirated sound. Languages also differ in whether aspiration serves as a distinctive feature. For example, aspiration is a distinctive feature in Chinese, but not in English. A Chinese stop, such as /t/, has an aspirated (/tʰ/) and non-aspirated (/t/) counterpart and they are two different phonemes, e.g., /tʰi/ meaning *substitute*, and /ti/ meaning *ground* when pronounced in the fourth tone. The aspirated and non-aspirated versions of an English stop are allophones of the same phoneme. When the word *speak* is pronounced as /spʰik/ rather than /spik/, it sounds strange, but it is still understood as *speak* by English NS.

2.3.2.3 Length

The duration of a sound segment can be manipulated so that it is short or long. This is often referred to as the length, duration, quantity, or temporal feature or cue. Length serves as a distinctive feature in some languages such as German, Japanese, Korean, Estonian, Finnish, Swedish, to name just a few. Length can be a distinctive feature for both vowels and consonants, as well. In Japanese, for example, a consonant may be a shorter *singleton* or a longer *geminate*. Thus, *oto* and *otto* (meaning *sound* and *husband*, respectively) are a minimal pair whose two members only differ in the length of the consonant /t/. It is the same with vowels. /kado/ means *corner*, and /kaado/ means *card* (see more examples in

Hayes-Harb, 2005 and Tajima, Kato, Rothwell, Akahane-Yamada, & Munhall, 2008). While the length contrast is usually binary, classifying sounds into short and long ones, it is possible to have a three-way classification. For example, a vowel in Estonian can be short, long, or overlong (Meister & Meister, 2011). *oh.* Other languages do not employ length as an independent distinctive feature, such as English and Spanish. Temporal cues may help distinguish sounds in such languages, but they usually co-vary with a primary cue rather than function as a primary cue. For example, English vowels and Mandarin tones differ in length, but F_1/F_2 frequency and pitch contour are considered primary cues in these cases, respectively.

2.3.2.4 Word Stress

In some languages, a word with multiple syllables is pronounced such that one syllable is produced with more force and thus perceived as more prominent than other syllables. Such words are said to have a word stress. Compared with unstressed syllables, a stressed syllable is usually pronounced with a higher F_0, a longer duration, and a greater intensity. Thus, F_0, duration, and intensity are the three acoustic correlates associated with word stress (Cutler, 2005; Fry, 1955; Lieberman, 1960). Languages differ in whether word stress (or word accent) is employed as a distinctive feature. In languages such as Chinese and Japanese, word stress does not play a significant role. In some other languages, e.g., French and Bengali, stress falls consistently on the syllable of the same position of a word, e.g., the last syllable, and are thus said to have a fixed stress. A third class of languages, such as English and Spanish, have variable stress patterns in that stress falls on different syllables in different words. In these latter languages, stress can be a distinctive feature in that it affects the meaning of words. For example, the word *record* is a noun when the stress is on the first syllable, but is a verb when the second syllable is stressed. Languages also differ in the acoustic cues used in the perception of word stress. English word stress is associated with four cues of varying reliability: vowel quality, F_0, duration, and intensity (or amplitude) (Fry, 1955; Lieberman, 1960), but vowel quality is not associated with the perception of stress in Spanish (Zhang & Francis, 2010). In some languages such as English and Dutch, but not in others such as Spanish, a reduced vowel is often used in an unstressed syllable (Cooper, Cutler, & Wales, 2002).

2.3.2.5 Lexical Tone

When a word is pronounced with a unique pitch pattern that helps differentiate meaning, the word is said to have a lexical tone. Languages also differ in whether tone is used as a distinctive feature. Tone is employed in Mandarin, Cantonese, Vietnamese, Thai, Norwegian, for example, but not in English,

Spanish, and French. Tonal languages also differ in how many tones they recognize. Mandarin has four tones, Thai has five, and Vietnamese and Cantonese have six. Research (e.g., Coster & Kratochvil, 1984; Gandour, 1983; Whalen & Xu, 1992) indicated that tones differ primarily in pitch contour which includes F_0 frequency at the onset of a syllable that carries the tone, and the movement or direction of F_0 throughout the syllable. Additionally, they can be differentiated on the basis of amplitude contour, length, and voice quality. Tonal languages may differ in what cues other than pitch contour also provide reliable information for tone perception. For example, length can help distinguish Mandarin tones in non-continuous speech, particularly between the third and the rest of the tones, and voice quality was found to be associated with tone perception in Vietnamese (Vu, 1981).

A speech perception phenomenon that is associated with these features is categorical perception. It refers to the perception of auditory tokens varying along an acoustic continuum as members of often two contrasting categories rather than separate and graded categories. Take the voicing feature for English stops for example. A syllable-initial alveolar stop in the syllable /_ɪp/ is perceived either as a voiceless stop /t/ or a voiced stop /d/ depending on the length of their VOT. Given the voicing boundary at 30 ms in English, all tokens with a VOT shorter than 30 ms are perceived to have a voiced stop, i.e., *dip*. All tokens with a VOT value on the other side of the boundary, e.g., 40 ms, 50 ms, and 60 ms, are perceived to be *tip*.

2.3.3 Phonotactics

Phonotactics deals with how sound segments are sequenced in a language. In any given language, some sounds are allowed to go together but not others. For example, a consonant sequence of /spr/ is allowed in English, but not a sequence of /zpr/. Similarly, /blim/ is a legal combination in English even if it is not a word, but /zlim/ is not. The existence of words such as *grizzly* suggests that the combination of /zl/ is allowed in English. Thus, the illegality of /zlim/ has to do with the fact that /zl/ appears at the word-initial position, which is not allowed in English (except for loanwords such as *zloty*, which is a Polish monetary unit). These two examples illustrate two phonotactic restrictions: sequencing restrictions and distributional restrictions. The former determines what phonemes are allowed to appear together and in what order, and the latter determines where a phoneme or a sequence of phonemes can appear in a syllable or word.

Languages differ in phonotactic restrictions. Many sound sequences are allowed in one language, but not in another. For example, consonant clusters are common in English, French, German, but they are rare in Japanese, Korean, and Chinese. In addition to such general differences, a language may also have very specific and often idiosyncratic phonotactic restrictions which make cross-language comparison very complicated. For example, /sp/ is legal at the word-initial position in English, but not /sb/. The release of the stop consonant at the word-final position, such as *stop*, is optional in English, but unreleasing such stops is obligatory in Korean (Chang & Mishler, 2012). A /s/+consonant cluster such as /sp/ can occur in word-initial, word-medium, and word-final positions in English, but it is illegal at the word-initial and word-final positions in Spanish (Altenberg, 2005). Numerous consonants and consonant clusters can appear at the word-final position in English, but no consonant or consonant clusters can appear at the word-final position in Spanish except for /s, n, r, l, d/ and for loanwords (Dalbor, 1969; Goldstein, 2001). A common consonant cluster in English /sn/ is not allowed in Catalan, and /st/ cannot appear word-initially in that language, either (Davidson, 2010). Sequences such as /kt/, /tf/, /dv/ can occur at the onset position in Polish but not in English (Davidson, 2006). Obstruent voicing contrasts (e.g., /p/-/d/, /s/-/z/) occur word-initially in both English and Dutch, but they occur word-finally only in English, as voiced obstruents are not allowed at this position in Dutch (Broersma, 2010). Languages also differ in how often a segment or a combination of segments is used, even when the combination is allowed in these languages. For example, a labial+alveolar cluster such as /pt/ can be found in English, Spanish, and Japanese, but the frequency of such sequences varied a great deal across these languages, from 1.567% in English to 0.647% in Spanish to 0.003% in Japanese (Massaro, Cohen, Gesi, & Heredia, 1993).

In sum, languages differ in the size of the sound inventory, in the specific phonetic categories in the inventory, in the acoustic details of these categories, in the phonetic features that are used to distinguish meaning, and in phonotactic constraints. Cross-linguistic differences in phonology may differ between pairs of languages, e.g., with Language A being phonologically more similar to Language B than to Language C. However, numerous and subtle differences exist between any two languages, including two languages that are believed to be similar or are historically or typologically related. Thus, developing a native-like phonology in an L2 involves substantial learning and often proves to be a challenging task for L2 learners, regardless of their L1 and L2 pairing.

2.4 Research Methods

Phonological processing research is empirical in nature. Once a research question is identified, a plan needs to be in place for data collection, which typically involves the observation of individuals' performance while they are engaged in a phonological activity. A variety of such activities, or experimental tasks, have been adopted for this purpose. They help produce three types of data: accuracy scores or measures, reaction times, and neurophysiological observations.

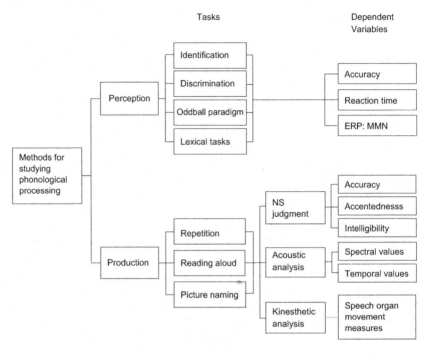

Figure 2.3　Overview of Research Methods for Studying Speech Perception and Production by NNS

These data then have to be analyzed, evaluated, and interpreted. Some frequently used methods are summarized in Figure 2.3 and described below.

2.4.1 Assessing Perception

In a perceptual task, a stimulus or a set of stimuli are presented to a participant who is asked to make a decision about them. The decision, or the task, is usually of two types: stimulus identification (e.g., what sound is the stimulus?) and stimulus discrimination (e.g., are the two segments the same?). However, the specific form of the task may vary across studies to suit the need of the study and the stimuli used. There is also much inconsistency in the literature regarding how the tasks are labelled. Frequently used labels are identification, discrimination, classification, categorization tasks. They are often used to refer to the same task in different studies, or two different tasks are labelled with the same name across studies. It is not rare to find the use of different names for the same task by the same author(s). It is desirable to use a single label for a task, and use different labels for different tasks. With this in mind, four different tasks are described below, each with its own label.

2.4.1.1 The Identification Task

In this paradigm, a single stimulus is presented to a participant who has to identify which sound segment (or word) it is. There are two versions of the task: the free-choice identification task and the forced-choice identification task. In the former case, no choice is provided and a participant is asked to write down whatever they believe they heard (e.g., Bohn & Best, 2012, Exp. 2). In the forced-choice identification task which is more frequently used, choices are provided to a participant who has to identify the stimulus based on the choices provided. A two-choice identification task is most common where two alternatives are given, for example, two segments such as /w/ or /v/, /l/ or /r/, or two words such as *ray* or *lay* (e.g., Bohn & Best, 2012; Bradlow, Pisoni, Akahane-Yamada, & Tohkura, 1997; Bürki-Cohen, Grosjean, & Miller, 1989; Cooper et al., 2002). A participant has to decide whether they heard *ray* or *lay*. More choices can be provided depending on the need of the study, such as three in Rallo Fabra and Romero (2012); four in Kong and Zeng (2006) and Cebrian (2006); six in Parlato-Oliveira, Christophe, Hirose, and Dupoux (2010); nine in Escudero and Williams (2011); ten in Bent, Kewley-Port, and Ferguson (2010); and 15 in De Jong, Silbert, and Park (2009). An "open-ended" variant of the task is to provide a few choices but also include a choice for "other" which makes the task less forced than a typical forced-choice task (e.g., Massaro et al., 1993). In the identification task, the participants typically respond by pressing a designated key or writing down the number correspondent to the alternative, or mark the alternative they believed they heard in other ways.

2.4.1.2 The Discrimination Task

In this task, two or more stimuli are presented to a participant who has to decide whether they are the same or different. It has three versions. In the two-stimulus version, two stimuli are presented and a participant has to decide whether they are the same or different. When a participant is specifically asked to decide whether the second stimulus is the same as the first, it is referred to as the AX discrimination task. The second and more widely used version is the ABX task in which three stimuli are presented (labelled as A, B, and X). Two of them are phonetically or phonemically identical, and the other is different from the other two. A participant has to decide whether the X stimulus is the same as the A or B stimulus. The X stimulus can be placed at any of the three positions, thus resulting in three different variants of the task, ABX, AXB, XAB. Most three-stimulus discrimination studies employed the first two, but occasionally one can find the third one (e.g., Escudero, Benders, & Lipski,

2009). A third version of the task, sometimes referred to as the "oddity task" or "oddity paradigm" (Strange & Shafer, 2008), is similar to the second version in presenting three stimuli in a trial but it is different from the second version in that no target stimulus (i.e., the X stimulus in the second version) was specified. Instead, a participant is asked to identify the stimulus among the three stimuli that is different from the other two. This "odd" stimulus can be at any of the three positions (e.g., Aoyama, Flege, Guion, Akahane-Yamada, & Yamada, 2004; Darcy & Krüger, 2012; Flege & MacKay, 2004; Rallo Fabra & Romero, 2012; Tsukada et al., 2005).

Note that the three-stimulus versions of the discrimination task (the second and third versions) differ in how many sequences of the stimuli are possible. The AXB task (or its other two variants) allow a maximum of four different sequences: AAB, ABB, BBA, BAA where the underline middle stimulus is the X (the same being true of ABX, i.e., ABA, BAA, BAB, ABB). The oddity task allows six: AAB, ABB, BAA, BBA, ABA, BAB. It is common to have all possible sequences allowed by a task in the stimulus set so as to minimize response bias and guessing. It is also common to use three stimuli of each triad that are different in physical properties, e.g., by using recordings from different speakers. For example, in a sequence of AAB where the middle A is the X, it can be a stimulus that is phonologically identical to the first A but both A and B are pronounced by another person. This allows the assessment of speech perception independently of physical similarities. Also note that these different versions of the discrimination task differ in memory load and stimulus predictability, as pointed out by Strange and Shafer (2008), with the oddity task being most demanding in this regard. These are important issues to keep in mind, as factors such as memory load and stimulus predictability may affect individuals' performance. For example, different memory load required by the AX and ABX tasks has been used to explain different results in perceptual outcomes (Dupoux, Sebastián-Gallés, Navarrete, & Peperkamp, 2008). The AXB discrimination task is often favored for its advantages of less memory load as the target stimulus X is right next to the other two members of the triad.

The identification and discrimination tasks are used in combination of both nonsense syllables and real words. In the former case, the segments under investigation (often vowels) are embedded in a syllable. For example, the vowels were placed in a /s_t/ syllable in Rallo Fabra and Romero (2012). In the latter case, real words containing the target segments are used. For example, Ingvalson, McClelland, and Holt (2011) used minimum pairs such as *lock–rock* to test the perception of /l/-/r/ contrast. These tasks can also be used together with both naturally produced tokens (digitally modified or unmodified) and synthesized tokens. As pointed out by Hallé, Best, and Levitt (1999), the use of synthesized tokens allows the assessment of participants' sensitivity to fine-grained differences along a specific acoustic dimension, e.g., by creating stimuli that differ in F_3 in six steps of equal intervals. While these two methods are used as untimed tasks in a majority of studies, timed versions are used as well (e.g., Chang & Mishler, 2012) which generate response latency as well as accuracy data.

2.4.1.3 The Oddball Paradigm

This is a paradigm used mostly in research in which mismatch negativity (MMN), an auditory event-related potential component, is recorded as data. MMN is a negative waveform that is usually recorded at frontal central sites approximately 100 ms to 250 ms after the onset of a stimulus that is different from the preceding stimuli. It is believed to be a result of automatic notice of a mismatch of memory traces registered in the left auditory cortex when language-specific stimuli are used (Näätänen, 2001, 2002). Thus, it is taken as an indication of an individual's sensitivity to a phonetic contrast. In L2 research, the observation of an MMN in response to an L2 phonetic contrast is considered as evidence for the development of nativelike phonetic representation.

Where the oddball paradigm is used, the stimuli typically consist of a standard stimulus (or simply standard), and one or more deviant stimuli (or deviants). The standard and deviant stimuli differ phonetically in a way that is related to the purpose of the investigation. For example, to determine if an individual has developed the English /i/-/ɪ/ contrast, /i/ may serve as a standard, and /ɪ/ as a deviant, or vice versa. To assess where the voicing boundary is located among French-English bilingual speakers, a stimulus with a VOT of 30 ms may serve as a standard, and stimuli with a VOT of −10 ms, 0 ms, 20 ms, and 50 ms may serve as deviants. A deviant is usually presented after several exposures of the standard. Thus, a test item may consist of a sequence of /i/, /i/, /i/, /ɪ/, where the repeated presentations of the standard serve to establish a memory trace for a phonetic category and the presentation of the deviant helps determine if individuals are sensitive to the /i/-/ɪ/ contrast. The MMN is measured by subtracting the amplitude elicited by a standard from that by a deviant during a predetermined time window (i.e., 100 ms to 250 ms after the onset of the deviant). If the participants have developed a nativelike sensitivity to the phonetic contrast under investigation, an MMN is expected. The absence of an MMN is interpreted as indicating a lack of such development. A unique aspect of this method is that participants are not asked to perform any task on the stimuli (and thus the term "passive oddball paradigm" is sometimes used, e.g., Nenonen, Shestakova, Huotilainen, & Näätänen, 2003; Shestakova, Huotilainen, Čeponien, & Cheour, 2003). Instead, they are often asked to ignore them or to be engaged in a task that directs their attention away from the stimuli, thus strengthening the claim that any observed MMN reflects a preattentive cognitive process.

2.4.1.4 Lexical Tasks

Some lexical tasks are also used to study phonological processing issues, albeit less commonly. In Pallier, Colomé, and Sebastián-Gallés (2001), for example, an auditory LDT task was used to determine whether L2 speakers would treat an L2 minimal pair as two different words or the same word, and this was done by assessing whether a repetition priming effect could be observed of minimal pairs in a LDT. An auditory LDT was also used by Sebastián-Gallés, Echeverría, and Bosch (2005) who used response accuracy to determine if Spanish-Catalan speakers were able to differentiate two Catalan vowels /e/ and /ɛ/ in word recognition. A different version of the lexical decision task was adopted in McAllister, Flege, and Piske (2002). Instead of being asked to decide whether a stimulus was a word or not, the participants were presented with a phrase defining a word, which was then followed by a stimulus. Their task was to decide whether or not an auditorily presented stimulus was a phonologically correct word based on the definition. The stimuli used in such lexical decision tasks were usually manipulated around the phonetic contrasts under investigation, for example, vowel contrasts in Pallier, Colomé, and Sebastián-Gallés and vowel duration contrasts in McAllister, Flege, and Piske. The participants' accuracy and reaction time in performing the lexical task provide means for assessing whether they have developed L2-specific phonetic contrasts.

2.4.2 Assessing Production

The study of speech production usually adopts a method that consists of two components: the elicitation of speech samples and the evaluation of the speech samples.

2.4.2.1 Speech Sample Elicitation

The most frequently used tasks for speech elicitation are repetition (or mimicking, mimicry), reading aloud, and picture naming. Where the first task is adopted, an auditory input is provided as a prompt, and the participant is asked to repeat what they hear. A participant may be asked to repeat what they hear immediately following the prompt, as in De Jong, Hao, and Park (2009), or after a delay as in Flege, Yeni-Komshian, and Liu (1999). The latter option, which is usually adopted to avoid direct imitation by the participants, is achieved by asking the participant to repeat only after they hear a signal. The repetition or mimicking task can be used with words or sentences and with or without visual input (e.g., Davidson, 2006; Ingvalson et al., 2011; Hao, 2012; MacKay, Flege, Piske, & Schirru, 2001; MacKay, Meador, & Flege, 2001).

In a reading-aloud task, a participant is asked to read aloud words, sentences, or paragraphs that are presented to them visually. Where words serve as stimuli, it is common to embed them in carrier phrases such as "take a ___" (Flege, 1991), "I said ___ this time" (Lee, Guion, & Harada, 2006) or "___ is the word" (Kang & Guion, 2006) to maintain a constant phonetic environment for different types of words. The picture-naming task is similar to the reading-aloud task except that the visual stimuli are pictures. It may be used with or without other visual stimuli such as words and with or without auditory prompts (e.g., Altenberg, 2005; Baker, Trofimovich, Flege, Mack, & Halter, 2008; Baker & Trofimovich, 2006; Oh et al., 2011). Some circumstances may call for the use of other visual stimuli in a production task. For example, in the study of the production of Swedish vowel duration by NNS, McAllister et al. (2002) decided not to use words as visual stimuli for the reason that vowel duration is orthographically coded and thus may provide a cue for the NNS participants, leading to overperformance. Instead, they used a combination of pictures and definitions to avoid the problem.

As far as the visual stimuli are developed according to the phonetic phenomenon under investigation, it usually does not take a long list of words or sentences to obtain the necessary speech samples for evaluation. For example, to compare the production of English vowels by children and adult learners, Baker et al. (2008) used only 12 words, three for each of the four English vowels under investigation. Similarly, Lee, Guion, and Harada used 19 words to represent stressed and unstressed syllables, Kang and Guion used three words for each of the five conditions, thus a total of 15 words, and Flege, Munro, and MacKay (1995a) used five sentences to elicit speech samples for the study of the production of English consonants by Italian speakers. It is also common to ask the participants to record multiple tokens of the same stimuli, and either use all the tokens or use the last tokens as samples for analysis. The latter practice is based on the assumption that the last tokens are better representations of an individual's speech samples (e.g., Baker et al., 2008; Oh et al., 2011).

2.4.2.2 Speech Sample Evaluation

The second phase of data collection in studying production is the evaluation of the speech samples collected from NNS. Two methods are used frequently for this purpose: acoustic analysis and NS judgment. In the former case, acoustic values of a predetermined phonetic feature such as vowel duration, F_0, F_1, or F_2 values are measured with the help of a software program such as Praat (Boersma & Weenink, 2016). These values are compared to those obtained from NS speakers to determine, for example, whether speech produced by the participants is nativelike, whether independent variables such as age, length of residence, type of phonetic contrasts, L1–L2 similarity affect production accuracy, or whether significant progress has been made over the course of L2 learning (e.g., Cebrian, 2006; Rallo Fabra & Romero, 2012; Flege, 1991; Flege, Munro, & MacKay, 1995b; Oh et al., 2011; Zhang, Nissen, & Francis, 2008).

In the second method, speech samples produced by NNS are given to a group of NS listeners for evaluation. Two evaluation methods are the most common: NS identification and NS rating. Where the identification method is adopted, speech samples are presented to NS listeners who are asked to identify the stimuli. For example, in order to determine whether a NNS can produce the two English vowels /i/ and /ɪ/ accurately, he or she may be asked to read English words such as *beat, bit, heat, hit*. The recordings are then presented to NS listeners for the identification of the words, e.g., in a forced-choice identification task. Where sentences are used, NS listeners are often asked to transcribe them word for word. The identification or transcription accuracy by NS listeners is then used as an indication of the production accuracy or intelligibility of the NNS speaker (e.g., Behrman & Akhund, 2013; Burda, Scherz, Hageman, & Edwards, 2003; Munro & Derwing, 1995a, 1995b; Rogers & Dalby, 2005; Wilson and Spaulding, 2010; Winters & O'Brien, 2013).

Where the NS rating method is adopted, NS listeners serve as judges to rate the performance of NNS in terms of either accentedness or intelligibility. They may be asked to provide a rating score for each test item elicited from NNS, or to provide a global assessment of the accentedness of the speaker. Even though this rating method has been used widely in the study of L2 production, a great deal of variability exists in its application across studies, which may affect the interpretation of the results. Four aspects of this method deserve special attention. The first one is the rating scale. Two rating scales are most common, a five-point scale (e.g., Abu-Rabia & Kehat, 2004; Birdsong, 2007; Bongaerts, Planken, & Schils, 1995; Bongaerts, Van Summeren, Planken, & Schils, 1997) and a nine-point scale (e.g., Flege et al., 2006; Guion, Flege, & Loftin, 2000; Ingvalson et al., 2011; Munro, Derwing, & Flege, 1999), usually with 1 indicating very strong accent and 5 or 9 indicating nativelike pronunciation. Scales of other resolution have also been used, such as binary rating of native and non-native in Abrahamsson and Hyltenstam (2009); four points in Flege, Frieda, and Nozawa (1997); six points in Moyer (1999); and seven points in Levi, Winters, and Pisoni (2007). According to Southwood and Flege (1999), a nine-point scale offers better validity in being able to reduce the ceiling effect, which explains why a nine-point scale has been used in studies reported by Flege and associates.

The second is the number of NS judges. Some judges are more lenient than others. The rating results from Abrahamsson and Hyltenstam (2009) illustrate this inter-rater inconsistency very well. There was a great deal of disparity among the ten NS judges in the evaluation of the participants in most age groups in that study. For example, five participants in the adolescence group were rated as nativelike by five judges and non-nativelike by the other five judges. These results illustrate the risk of using a small number of NS judges. However, the number of NS judges used varied considerably across studies, e.g., three in Birdsong (2007); four in Abu-Rabia and Kehat (2004); five in Guion, Flege, and Loftin (2000); nine in Piske, MacKay, and Flege (2001); ten in Flege et al. (1999), Baker et al. (2008), and Abrahamsson and Hyltenstam (2009); 12 in Ingvalson et al. (2011); 13 in Ioup, Boustagui, El Tigi, and Moselle (1994); 18 in Flege et al. (2006); 21 in Bongaerts, Mennen, and Slik (2000).

The third one is the NS–NNS ratio in the speech samples to be rated. It is common to include speech samples produced by NS controls so that the NS judges will be presented with a mixture of speech samples from both NS and NNS for the rating task. Flege and Fletcher (1992) found that the inclusion of a higher proportion of NS samples would lead to a lower rating score for NNS speech. The effect of the NS–NNS ratio on rating results has not received much attention, as can be seen in the wide range of NS–NNS ratios across studies. Here are some numbers in published studies (the first being the number of NS controls and the second being the number of NNS participants): 3 and 4 in Ioup et al. (1994), 17 and 22 in Birdsong (2007), 10 and 31 in Bongaerts et al. (1997), 18 and 90 in Piske et al. (2001), 20 and 195 in Abrahamsson and Hyltenstam (2009), 24 and 240 in Flege et al. (1999).

Finally, different criteria have been used to determine nativelike performance. It is common to compare the mean rating scores on NS and NNS speech samples to determine nativelikeness of NNS as a group. However, it becomes more complicated when individual non-native speakers' performance is evaluated. One strategy is to define nativelikeness based on the lowest rating scores assigned to NS. In Birdsong (2007), NS received rating scores varying between 4.5 to 5 on a five-point scale. Thus, any NNS that received a score of 4.5 or higher by all three judges was considered to have reached nativelike level. A similar approach was adopted in Abrahamsson and Hyltenstam (2009). All NS in the study were considered nativelike by at least nine out of the ten judges, so nativelike rating by nine judges was adopted as a criterion for evaluating NNS performance. A different approach was taken in Flege et al. (1995b), Bongaerts et al. (1997), and Bongaerts et al. (2000). They adopted a two-standard-deviation criterion. Thus, any NNS who received a mean rating score that was within the range of two standard deviations from the NS mean was considered nativelike.

The rating scale, the number of NS raters, the proportion of speech samples from NS, and the criterion for determining nativelikeness all potentially affect the rating results and the conclusion to be drawn. However, no protocol or guidelines have been developed to enhance the validity and reliability of the data and to maintain consistency across studies.[3] Some of these, such as the number of NS judges and the proportion of NS samples apply to the identification method as well.

In studying speech production, it is common to use a combination of acoustic analysis and NS listener evaluation, and in the latter case, a combination of accentedness rating and sample identification (e.g., Abrahamsson & Hyltenstam, 2009; Birdsong, 2007; Flege et al., 1999; Munro & Derwing, 1995a; Rallo Fabra & Romero, 2012).

In addition to the methods described above, researchers have used other methods in studying speech perception and production, such as the visual world paradigm (e.g., Cutler, Weber, & Otake, 2006; Tremblay & Spinelli, 2014; Tremblay, Broersma, Coughlin, & Choi, 2016),[4] the sequence repetition or recall task (e.g., Dupoux, Peperkamp, & Sebastián-Gallés, 2001; Dupoux et al., 2008), the gating paradigm (e.g., Arciuli & Cupples, 2004; Cutler & Otake, 1999), and phoneme monitoring for studying speech perception (e.g., Bürki-Cohen, Miller, & Eimas, 2001; Cho & McQueen, 2006; Wagner, Ernestus, & Cutler, 2006), and kinematic or articulatory analysis for studying speech production (e.g., Chakraborty & Goffman, 2011; Flege, Fletcher, & Homiedan, 1988; Gick, Bernhardt, Bacsfalvi, & Wilson, 2008; Nissen, Dromey, & Wheeler, 2007).

2.5 Models of L2 Phonological Processing

Several theoretical frameworks have been developed that are related to phonological processing and development in a non-native language. They all deal with the processing of non-native phonology, focus largely on the segmental level, and recognize the important role an individual's first language plays. However, they also differ in some important ways among themselves. The speech learning model (SLM) proposed by James Flege was intended specifically as a model of phonological processing and development in L2. It offers a comprehensive conceptual framework for explaining the processes and factors involved in phonological development in L2. Thus, it has been a primary driving force in research on L2 phonology. Catherine Best's perceptual assimilation model (PAM) and Patricia Kuhl's native language magnet model (NLMM) were originally developed in the context of understanding child L1 phonological development (rather than L2 phonological processing), partly as a response to the finding that the establishment of one's L1 phonology in infants is accompanied by the loss of sensitivity to phonetic contrasts that were not instantiated in the native language (e.g., Eimas, Siqueland, Jusczyk, & Vigorito, 1971). They are highly relevant to L2 phonological development as they offer insights for explaining the difficulty L2 learners have in learning L2-specific phonetic contrasts. Finally, featural models emphasize that phonological development in L2 is affected by L1–L2 differences at the level of distinctive features rather than that of segments.

2.5.1 The Speech Learning Model (SLM)

The SLM deals with the issue of what affects the acquisition of nativelike production and perception of L2 phonology, particularly the former, at the segmental level. Expositions of the model can be found in several book chapters and numerous reports of empirical studies by its proponent James Flege and collaborators. The model is summarized in the following statements of assumptions, claims, and predictions based on Flege (1995, 1999, 2002, 2003).

The SLM has three basic assumptions (a) speech production and perception are related such that accurate production is dependent on accurate perception. Thus, according to Flege, "many L2 production errors have a perceptual basis" (1995, p. 238) (b) L1 and L2 sounds exist in a "common phonological space" (1995, p. 239), and thus they interact and influence each other, and (c) adults have the same capability in developing nativelike phonology in an L2 as children learning their first language. In Flege's words, "the mechanisms and processes used in learning the L1 sound system, including category formation, remain intact over the life span, and can be applied to L2 learning" (Flege, 1995, p. 239).

Based on these assumptions, the model makes three major claims about the development of L2 phonology. First, successful perception of the difference between an L2 sound segment and its closest L1 sound is crucial for the development of a new L2 category. When a learner is able to discern the difference between a pair of L1–L2 sounds (or between two similar L2 segments), this perceptual differentiation allows the development of a new L2 category through the process of category dissimilation. The establishment of the new L2 category in turn results in more nativelike pronunciation. However, if a pair of L1–L2 sounds are not perceptually differentiated, the L2 segment is likely to be assimilated to and treated as the closest L1 segment. Similarly, when a learner is not able to perceptually differentiate two L2 segments, they are likely to be treated as a single category. In both cases, the outcome is the formation of a composite category, one that may contain acoustic properties of both L1 and L2 segments or both L2 segments. The representation of such composite categories is the cause for inaccurate pronunciation. Second, L2 input and segmental similarity are the two major determinants for adequate perceptual differentiation. The quantity and quality of L2 input available to a learner affects how successful he or she is in perceiving the difference between two sound segments. The more or better input is available, the more likely it is for an L2 learner to see the difference between a pair of L1–L2 segments or between two L2 segments. The input factor is related to a number of other variables. The first one is the age of acquisition (AOA). Learners with lower AOA usually have more and better input than older learners do. The second is the length of residence (LOR). Learners with longer LOR tend to have more L2 input than those with shorter LOR do. The third is the amount of continued L1 use. Learners may differ in how much L1 they continue to use even while living in an L2 environment. Extensive L1 use is likely to be accompanied by reduced L2 input. In addition to input, the degree of similarity between an L2 segment and its closest L1 counterpart, or between two L2 segments, also plays a key role. Perceptual differentiation is easier in the presence of less overlap between two sound segments. And "the greater is the perceived phonetic dissimilarity of an L2 speech sound from the closest L1 sound, the more likely it is that a new category will be created for the L2 sound" (Flege, 2003, p. 329). See Section 3.2.2.1 for research evidence related to the similarity factor.

Third, the learning of an L2 will affect the representation of L1 phonetic categories. All models of non-native phonological development recognize that the perception and development of L2 sounds rely, at least initially, on the existing L1 phonetic categories. The SLM goes one step further by proposing that in the case of both category dissimilation and category assimilation, increasing L2 experience will lead to the alteration of L1 phonetic categories. Flege suggests that where a new L2 category is established through category dissimilation, "the new L2 category and the pre-existing L1 category may dissimilate from one another. If this happens, neither the L1 category nor the new L2 category will be identical to the categories possessed by monolinguals" (2003, p. 331). Where category assimilation occurs, it results in the formation of a composite category that incorporates the features of both L1 and L2 sounds. While this means inaccurate perception and production of an L2 sound, it also means that the L1 category is no longer the same as that of a monolingual speaker. This is particularly true when an L2 learner becomes more and more experienced in the new language. Increasing L2 experiences may push a composite category more and more toward the L2 category. Flege (1987) provides an example of such a case in his study of English speakers learning French and French speakers learning English. The VOT is shorter in French than in English. English speakers who had become fluent in French were found to have an English VOT that was shorter than that of monolingual English speakers. The same L2 effect was also found for French speakers learning English. See Section 3.2.3 for related research evidence.

The basic idea of the model is summarized in Figure 2.4.

The SLM makes four testable predictions: a) younger learners are more likely to develop accurate L2 phonetic representations than older learners, b) learners exposed to more and better L2 input are more likely to develop accurate L2 phonetic representations than those with more limited input, c) an L2 phonetic category that has a closer L1 counterpart is harder to establish than one without such a counterpart, and d) the learning of an L2 will affect the representation of L1 phonetic categories. Flege and colleagues have done a great deal of research testing each of these predictions, some of which will be reviewed in the next chapter.

length of residence
Age of Acq.

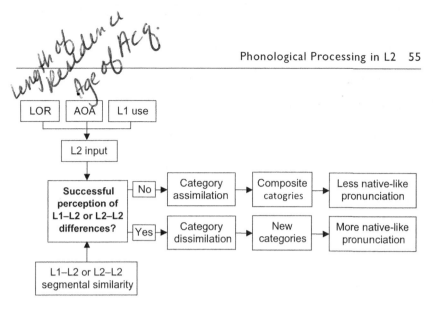

Figure 2.4 An Illustration of Flege's Speech Learning Model

The SLM also represents a different view from the critical period hypothesis (CPH) on how age affects phonological development in L2. The SLM acknowledges that individuals are less likely to develop nativelike phonology as they get older, but it differs from the CPH proposed by Lenneberg (1967) in two ways. First, it refutes the presence of a sudden decline in a learner's ability to develop nativelike pronunciation around puberty, as often suggested by the CPH. Instead, research done within this model showed a linear decline of this ability with increasing age (e.g., Flege et al., 1995a; Yeni-Komshian, Flege, & Liu, 2000). Second, it refutes the neural-plasticity explanation of this decline that is associated with the CPH. Instead, Flege argues that

> as L1 phonetic categories develop slowly through childhood and into early adolescence, they become more likely to perceptually assimilate L2 vowels and consonants. If instances of an L2 speech sound category persist in being identified as instances of an L1 speech sound, category formation for the L2 speech sound will be blocked.
>
> (2003, p. 329)

Thus, the model attributes the age effect to L1 entrenchment rather than neural plasticity.

2.5.2 The Perceptual Assimilation Model (PAM) and PAM-L2

Even though the perceptual assimilation model (PAM) proposed by Catherine Best (1993, 1994, 1995) is often discussed in close association with Flege's SPM in the L2 phonological processing literature, it should be made clear from the outset that these two models were proposed to accomplish very different goals. The SLM is intended to offer a general framework for conceptualizing the development of phonological skills by adult L2 learners, but the PAM is developed in the context of understanding how a language-specific phonological system is developed among infants while learning their native languages. The PAM examines the perception of non-native phonetic contrasts by adults not because it is interested in this phenomenon per se, but out of its belief that information obtained at the "presumed developmental end point" can illuminate how a language-specific perceptual system is developed in earlier years of life. The two models also differ in their scope of interest. The PAM focuses itself on a much more specific phenomenon than the SLM does: the perception and discrimination of non-native segmental contrasts by individuals who have little experiences in the test language, while the SLM is concerned with a broader range of topics and factors related to L2 phonological development. Thus, methodologically, research conducted within the SLM often adopted a production task, and it typically involved L2 learners who were in the process of learning the stimulus language or proficient in that language to a varying extent. PAM-related research is more likely to adopt a perceptual task and involve infants as well as adults who are not L2 learners of the stimulus language and thus had little prior exposure to it.

The PAM is based on two assumptions. First, acoustic signals carry information about how a speech sound is produced, i.e., the articulatory gestures, and it is the latter, not the former, that is the target of speech perception. According to Best,

> both infant and adult listeners detect evidence in speech about the articulatory gestures of the vocal tract that produced the signal. . . . I mean that the articulatory gestures of speech are directly perceived and not that they are inferred from, or cognitively imputed to, the superficial acoustic properties of the signal. Because the speech signal is molded by the shape and movements of the vocal tract, according to the laws of physical acoustics, evidence about those properties is necessarily present in the patterning of the speech signal.
>
> (Best, 1993, p. 292)

Second, non-native sounds are perceived on the basis of how similar and thus how assimilable they are to native sounds. As Best puts it, "mature listeners' percepts are guided by gestural similarities and dissimilarities between non-native phones and their own native phoneme categories" (1993, p. 293).

The model offers a framework for determining the level of difficulty in accurately discriminating non-native phonetic contrasts (rather than L2 phonological processing and development in general). The framework consists of two components. The first is a classification of non-native sound segments in relation to the native phonological system or in terms of how well a non-native sound

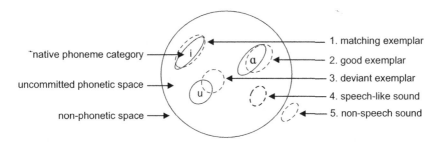

Figure 2.5 Classification of Non-Native Sounds in Relation to the Native Phonetic Space in the PAM

is assimilable to a native category (as depicted in Figure 2.5). A space metaphor is used for this purpose where all gestural properties utilized in a language are said to occupy a native phonetic space (indicated by the big solid circle in the figure). All phonetic categories of a language (small solid circles) exist in this space, but not all space is occupied. A non-native sound (dashed circles) can be considered a) to lie either outside or inside this space, b) in the latter case to occupy either a committed or uncommitted part of the space, and c) to overlap at varying degrees with a native category in a committed space, thus leading to the classification of the following five types of non-native sounds:

a) a matching exemplar whose gestural properties essentially match those of a native category (1);

b) a good exemplar that shares many but not all of the properties with a native category and thus is perceptually taken as a good token of the latter (2);

c) a deviant exemplar that shares a limited number of gestural properties with a native sound, thus with the difference between the two being clearly perceptible (3);

d) a speech-like sound that does not share any gestural property with a native sound but still sounds like a speech sound and may be perceived as a token of two or more different native categories (4); and

e) a speech sound that falls outside of the L1 phonetic space and does not sound like a speech sound (5).

The second component of the model is a set of predictions regarding how easy or difficult it is for individuals to discriminate non-native phonetic contrasts involving different types of sounds as defined above. These predictions are shown in Table 2.2 based on Table 2 in Best (1993) and on Best, McRoberts, and Goodell (2001). For example, in the case of the Two-Category type, two non-native sounds are assimilated to two different native sounds, and,

Table 2.2 Predictions Made by the PAM Regarding the Level of Difficulty in Discriminating Non-Native Contrasts

Contrast Types	Types of Sounds Involved*	Level of Difficulty
Two-Category (TC)	Each non-native phone assimilated to a different native phoneme category (1–1)	Excellent discrimination
Uncategorized-Categorized pair	One non-native phone is categorized as a native sound while the other is not (1/2/3–4)	Excellent discrimination
Category-Goodness	Both non-native phones assimilated to the same native category, but differ in discrepancy from the native phone (1–2, 2–3, or 1–3)	Good to moderate discrimination
Non-Assimilable	Both non-native phones fall outside the bounds of native phonetic space and are heard as non-speech (5–5)	Good to moderate discrimination
Uncategorizable	Both non-native phones fall within uncommitted phonetic space (4–4)	Poor to moderate discrimination
Single-Category (SC)	Both non-native phones assimilated to the same native category, but are equally distant from native phone (2–2, or 3–3)	Poor discrimination

* the numbers in the parentheses indicate the pairing of different types of L2 sounds as numbered in Figure 2.5.

as a result, they are easy to discriminate. When a pair of non-native sounds are equally similar and thus assimilated to a single native sound (the Single-Category type), their discrimination is difficult. Lying between the two ends is the Category-Goodness type where, even though both members of non-native contrast are similar to a single native category, their degree of similarity varies. These contrasts are easier than Single-Category contrasts because the different degree of discrepancy between the two members and the native category may aid discrimination.

Even though the model is developed in the context of understanding phonological development in monolingual children, the classification of the different types of non-native sounds and the predictions made by the model may be extended to adult L2 learning, as suggested by Best and Tyler (2007). In

PAM can extend to adult L2 learners

their PAM-L2, they proposed that the predictions the PAM makes about the level of difficulty in non-native contrast discrimination can also help "predict success at L2 perceptual learning" (p. 28). With success defined as the creation of a new L2-specific phonetic category, the general idea seems to be that perceptual difficulty outlined in the PAM will affect the likelihood for a new category to be established in L2 learning. Thus, for example, a new category is more likely to be created for an L2 sound in the TC contrast than in a SC contrast. They acknowledge that other factors may also play a role in the process, for example whether a sound is used in high-frequency words that form minimal pairs that are communicatively important. See Section 3.2.2.2 for empirical evidence related to the model.

2.5.3 The Native Language Magnet Model (NLMM)

Like the PAM, the NLM model (or NLMM) proposed by Patricia Kuhl (1994, 2000, 2004; Kuhl et al., 2008) is also primarily motivated by the finding of the loss of sensitivity to non-native phonetic contrasts in an infant's first year of life. Both models share the tenet that this has to do with the assimilation of non-native sounds to the established native phonetic categories. However, NLMM offers a more elaborate and comprehensive theory for how this process occurs and how language learning takes place in general.

To begin with, the NLMM sets itself apart from other views of language learning in what infants bring to the process of language learning. In contrast to the view that infants are born with a perceptual system uniquely designed for human language learning, that is, a system that is domain specific and species specific, it proposes that infants start with a more primitive general-purpose perceptual processing system which would later evolve in the process of language learning. Instead of assuming that infants are born with an innate set of phonetic categories, some of which are then selected or dropped as a result of being exposed to a particular language, the NLMM argues that phonetic categories do not preexist but emerge in the process of language learning. What is unique about infants' language learning, though, are the two driving forces, or "agents of change". The first is their ability to detect patterns and develop abstractions on the basis of the statistical properties of language input. The second is the speech directed to infants that contain exaggerated acoustic cues. Within the NLMM, the process of phonological development is seen as one in which infants are able to use this ability and exaggerated speech input to develop prototypes of phonetic categories of the language they are exposed to. A prototype is created a) based on multiple tokens of the same phoneme produced by different speakers and in different linguistic and nonlinguistic environments and b) through the process of probabilistic analysis and abstraction. The establishment of these prototypes, which is believed to occur in the first year of life, are the pivotal moments in phonological development.

Two additional processes occur with the development of phonetic proto-types, according to the model. One is the linking of auditory and motor information for the development of oral production. Unlike the PAM which argues that perception and production share the same source, i.e., the knowledge of articulatory gestures, the NLMM postulates that auditory perception skills are developed first which guides vocalization until a connection between the two is forged. The other process occurs at the neural level. The model asserts that perceptual learning is accompanied by changes at the neural level in that neural structures become committed in the learning process. According to the native language neural commitment hypothesis, "initial language exposure causes physical changes in neural tissue and circuitry that reflect the statistical and perceptual properties of language input. Neural networks become committed to patterns of native language speech" (Kuhl et al., 2008, p. 983).

Once a prototype is created, it "appears to function as a 'magnet' for other stimuli in the category" (Kuhl, 2000, p. 11853) in the sense that a non-proto-typical sound is perceived as the nearest prototype even though the two may not be identical. This is referred to as the native language magnet effect. Such

> magnet effects cause certain acoustic differences to be minimized (those near the magnet attractors) while others are maximized (those near the boundaries between two magnets). The consequence is that some of the boundaries that initially divided the space "disappear" as the perceptual space is reconfigured to incorporate a language's particular magnet placement.
>
> (Kuhl, 1994, p. 814)

In other words, physical properties of speech sounds are no longer perceived as they are but altered to fit the existing perceptual map. Thus, Kuhl characterizes the process of phonological develop as one in which "language experience warps perception" (2000, p. 11853).

The prototypes of all phonetic categories of a language, along with the space they control, are said to form a "perceptual map" of the language. One may liken this perceptual map to a political map that shows the constituent administrative units (e.g., states or cities) and their capitals and boundaries, except that the perceptual map of a language contains information about its phonetic categories, their locations (in terms of acoustic detail), and the boundaries of these categories. Phonetic prototypes are language-specific, as they are developed as a result of being exposed to a particular language. It follows that each language has its own unique perceptual map that serves as a filter in speech perception. This conception offers an explanation for the loss of sensitivity to non-native contrasts in infants: i.e., the development of a perceptual map that is specific to one's native language. With this perceptual map in place, non-native sounds have to be now perceived against this native

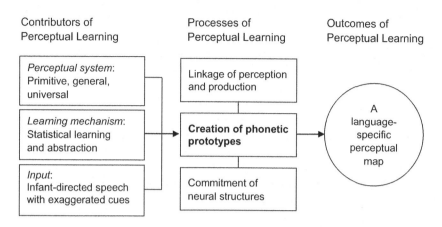

Contributors of   Processes of   Outcomes of
Perceptual Learning   Perceptual Learning   Perceptual Learning

Perceptual system: Primitive, general, universal	Linkage of perception and production	
Learning mechanism: Statistical learning and abstraction	**Creation of phonetic prototypes**	A language-specific perceptual map
Input: Infant-directed speech with exaggerated cues	Commitment of neural structures	

Figure 2.6 Contributors, Processes, and Outcomes of Perceptual Learning as Envisioned in the NLM Model

perceptual map and many contrasts not instantiated in the native language become very difficult to discriminate. Figure 2.6 is a graphic illustration of the main ideas of the model.

The NLMM does not only offer a general theory of child language learning, but also has direct implications for phonological processing and development in a second language. First, along with the SLM and the PAM, it postulates that the perception of non-native sounds is done on the basis of and thus is affected by the native perceptual system. This explains the difficulty associated with L2 speech perception. As Kuhl puts it, "once formed, language-specific filters make learning a second language much more difficult because the mapping appropriate for one's primary language is completely different from that required by other languages" (Kuhl, 2000, p. 11854). In other words, L2 learners' difficulty originates from the use of a wrong perceptual map. It follows that the essence of learning an L2 is the development of a new perceptual map that is specific to the new language. Second, the native magnet effect also suggests, as the SLM does, that an L2 sound that is more similar to an L1 sound is harder to learn than one that is less similar, as the former is more likely to be treated as the L1 sound. Thus, the level of difficulty is determined in part by the degree of phonological overlap between the two languages (Kuhl, 2004). Third, it offers a neural commitment explanation of the critical period hypothesis and child–adult differences in L2 learning. According to this model, perceptual learning leads to neural commitment or "a decline in neural flexibility" (Kuhl et al., 2008, p. 993), and the latter leads to interference and difficulty in learning an L2. Thus, what lies behind the critical period is not the age of acquisition per se, but how much learning has taken place. On this view, children are better L2 learners because their native phonetic representations are less consolidated, and their neural structures are less committed and thus more "plastic". However, Kuhl and her colleagues also suggest, as Flege does, that adult learners maintain the ability to learn an L2 (Wang & Kuhl, 2003). Finally, the model also offers insights regarding how to best help learners develop a new phonological system. On the tenet that the essence of phonological development is the creation of prototypes of L2-specific phonetic categories, effective instruction is one that can aid learners in L2 prototype formation. Specifically, instruction should aim at providing "exaggerated acoustic cues, multiple instances by many talkers, and mass listening experience" (Kuhl, 2000, p. 11855). Such input will help learners acoustically discriminate an L2 sound and its closest L1 counterpart, thus facilitating the creation of a new L2-specific prototype.

2.5.4 The Featural Models

The three models discussed so far all consider phonological processing and development at the segmental level. Analysis of L2 learners' difficulty is done through the comparison of the segmental inventories of the two languages. In contrast to these models, a number of researchers have proposed that phonological development and cross-linguistic influence may occur more at the level of distinctive features. In this view, an L2 phonetic category is difficult to learn not because this category is not instantiated in a learner's L1, but because its related phonetic feature is not employed as a distinctive feature in the learner's L1. We may collectively call these proposals featural models of L2 phonological development. One such proposal is Hancin-Bhatt's (1994) feature competition model (FCM). Similar to the other models, the FCM also assumes that L2 learners rely on their L1 phonological system in the perception of L2 segments. Drawing from works by Halle (1959), Ritchie (1968), and others, it also assumes that phonological features differ in their prominence in a language, with features that help make more phonemic distinctions being more prominent than others. The FCM postulates that different L1 features compete in L2 speech perception and the more prominent features exert more influence on the outcome of perception. Take the perception of English interdental consonants /θ/ and /ð/ by non-native speakers whose L1s do not have these segments, for example. The perceptual outcome will depend on which feature is more prominent in the learners' L1. The feature of [continuant] is highly prominent in German, so German ESL speakers are likely to keep the [continuant] feature of these two new segments and perceive them as two [+continuant] sounds /s/ and /z/, rather than two [-continuant] sounds /t/ and /d/. ESL speakers with an L1 for which [continuant] is not a prominent feature would be less likely to maintain this feature, resulting in more perception of /t/ and /d/. Hancin-Bhatt tested this model by examining the perception of these two interdentals by three groups of ESL speakers with German, Japanese, and Turkish backgrounds, respectively. The results partially supported the predictions. See Section 3.2.1 for empirical studies related to the featural models.

The idea of feature-based, rather than segment-based, transfer and development is becoming more recognized (e.g., Brown, 2000; De Jong, Hao, & Park, 2009; Flege, 1995; McAllister et al., 2002). It is present in Flege's SLM as Hypothesis 6 which states that "the phonetic category established for L2 sounds by a bilingual may differ from a monolingual's if . . . the bilingual's representation is based on different features, or feature weights, than a monolingual's" (p. 239). It is forcefully stated by Brown that

> it is the *features* contained in the learner's native grammar, not the phonological representations themselves, which constrain perception. The prediction of this position is that if a speaker's grammar lacks the feature that differentiates a given phonological contrast, then he or she will be unable to accurately perceive that contrast; conversely, the presence of the contrasting feature in the native grammar will facilitate perception of that non-native contrast, regardless of whether the particular segment is part of the inventory.
>
> (Brown, 2000, pp. 19–20)

A similar idea was put forward in the form of a feature hypothesis by McAllister et al. (2002). They proposed that "L2 features not used to signal phonological contrast in L1 will be difficult to perceive for the L2 learner and this difficulty will be reflected in the learner's production of the contrast based on this feature" (p. 230).

A featural model does not have to contradict with a segmental model of phonological transfer and development. Rather, it can be best seen as complementary to the latter.

The models of phonological development reviewed above all recognize the paramount role L1 plays. They differ in the context in which they were developed (PAM and NLM in the context of child language development vs. SLM and featural models in the context of adult L2 acquisition), in the range of phenomena they are intended to explain (e.g., more specific focus on the distinction of L2 contrasts of PAM vs. SLM as a more general theory of L2 phonological development), and in the level of analysis they put emphasis on (the focus of segments by SLM, PAM, and NLM vs. features by featural models). However, they have all served as conceptual frameworks within which questions are asked and hypotheses and predictions are formulated and empirically tested. Some of the empirical research motivated by these models will be discussed in Chapter 3.

2.6 Conclusion

This chapter provides the background knowledge for understanding L2 phonological processing research. To this end, it begins with a section on the
process of speech production and the acoustic cues used in speech perception.
This is where basic and important concepts and terms related to L2 phonological processing are explained. The chapter goes on to illustrate how languages
differ in phonology. The cross-linguistic differences described here often serve
as target structures or phenomena for studying L2 phonological processing.
The following section provides an overview of the methods used in studying
speech perception and production. The chapter ends with a summary of the
prominent models related to L2 phonological processing that motivated many
L2 phonological processing studies to be discussed in the next chapter.

Notes

1   Take myself for example. Even after having lived in an English-speaking country
    for more than 20 years, I have been misunderstood more often than not while giv-
    ing my first name over the phone. No matter how careful I am and how clear and
    precise I try to be, my pronunciation of the letter N is often understood as M by
    English NS.
2   Figure 2.1a is based on a figure for the Vowel entry of wiki at https://en.wikipedia.
    org/wiki/Vowel; Figure 2.1b is based with permission on a figure produced by Will
    Styler at his website at http://linguisticmystic.com/.
3   Two additional issues are the experience of the NS judges and the materials used.
    See Bongaerts et al. (1997) and Bongaerts et al. (2000) for the differentiation of
    experienced and inexperienced NS judges and Levi et al. (2007) for results that
    higher-frequency words could lead to high rating scores in accent rating.
4   The last two references were brought to my attention by an anonymous reviewer.

References

Abrahamsson, N. & Hyltenstam, K. (2009). Age of onset and nativelikeness in a sec-
    ond language: Listener perception versus linguistic scrutiny. *Language Learning, 59*,
    249–306.
Abu-Rabia, S. & Kehat, S. (2004). The critical period for second language pronuncia-
    tion: Is there such a thing? *Educational Psychology, 24*, 77–97.
Altenberg, E. P. (2005). The judgment, perception, and production of consonant clus-
    ters in a second language. *IRAL, 43*, 53–80.
Aoyama, K., Flege, J. E., Guion, S. G., Akahane-Yamada, R., & Yamada, T. (2004).
    Perceived phonetic dissimilarity and L2 speech learning: The case of Japanese /r/
    and English /l/ and /r/. *Journal of Phonetics, 32*, 233–250.
Arciuli, J. & Cupples, L. (2004). Effects of stress typicality during spoken word rec-
    ognition by native and nonnative speakers of English: Evidence from onset gating.
    Memory & Cognition, 32, 21–30.
Baker, W. & Trofimovich, P. (2006). Perceptual paths to accurate production of L2
    vowels: The role of individual differences. *IRAL, 44*, 231–250.

Baker, W., Trofimovich, P., Flege, J. E., Mack, M., & Halter, R. (2008). Child-adult differences in second-language phonological learning: The role of cross-language similarity. *Language and Speech, 51*, 317–342.

Behrman, A. & Akhund, A. (2013). The influence of semantic context on the perception of Spanish-accented American English. *Journal of Speech, Language, and Hearing Research, 56*, 1567–1578.

Bent, T., Kewley-Port, D., & Ferguson, S. H. (2010). Across-talker effects on non-native listeners' vowel perception in noise. *The Journal of the Acoustical Society of America, 128*, 3142–3151.

Best, C. T. (1993). Emergence of language-specific constraints in perception of non-native speech: A window on early phonological development. In B. de Boysson-Bardies (Ed.), *Developmental neurocognition: Speech and face processing in the first year of life* (pp. 289–304). Dordrecht: Kluwer.

Best, C. T. (1994). The emergence of native-language phonological influences in infants: A perceptual assimilation model. In J. C. Goodman & H. C. Nusbaum (Eds.), *The development of speech perception: The transition from speech sounds to spoken words* (pp. 167–224). Cambridge, MA: The MIT Press.

Best, C. T. (1995). A direct realist view of cross-language speech perception: Standing at the crossroads. In W. Strange (Ed.), *Speech perception and linguistic experience: Issues in cross-language research* (pp. 171–204). Baltimore: York Press.

Best, C. T., McRoberts, G., & Goodell, E. (2001). Discrimination of non-native consonant contrasts varying in perceptual assimilation to the listener's native phonological system. *Journal of the Acoustical Society of America, 109*, 775–794.

Best, C. T. & Tyler, M. D. (2007). Nonnative and second language speech perception: Commonalities and complementaries. In O. S. Bohn & M. J. Munro (Eds.), *Language experience in second language speech learning* (pp. 13–34). Amsterdam: John Benjamins.

Birdsong, D. (2007). Nativelike pronunciation among late learners of French as a second language. In M. J. Munro & O. S. Bohn (Eds.), *Second language speech learning: The role of language experience in speech perception and production* (pp. 99–116). Amsterdam: John Benjamins.

Blicher, D. L., Diehl, R. L., & Cohen, L. B. (1990). Effects of syllable duration on the perception of the Mandarin Tone 2/Tone 3 distinction: Evidence of auditory enhancement. *Journal of Phonetics, 18*, 37–49.

Boersma, P. & Weenink, D. (2016). *Praat: Doing phonetics by computer* [Computer program]. Version 6.0.10. Retrieved from www.fon.hum.uva.nl/praat/ (Accessed on January 1, 2016).

Bohn, O. S. & Best, C. T. (2012). Native-language phonetic and phonological influences on perception of American English approximants by Danish and German listeners. *Journal of Phonetics, 40*, 109–128.

Bongaerts, T., Mennen, S., & Slik, F. V. D. (2000). Authenticity of pronunciation in naturalistic second language acquisition: The case of very advanced late learners of Dutch as a second language. *Studia Linguistica, 54*, 298–308.

Bongaerts, T., Planken, B., & Schils, E. (1995). Can late starters attain a native accent in a foreign language? A test of the critical period hypothesis. In D. Singleton & Z. Lengyel (Eds.), *The age factor in second language acquisition* (pp. 30–50). Clevedon: Multilingual Matters.

Bongaerts, T., Van Summeren, C., Planken, B., & Schils, E. (1997). Age and ultimate attainment in the pronunciation of a foreign language. *Studies in Second Language Acquisition, 19*, 447–465.

Bradlow, A. R. (1995). A comparative acoustic study of English and Spanish vowels. *Journal of the Acoustical Society of America, 97*, 1916–1924.

Bradlow, A. R., Pisoni, D. B., Akahane-Yamada, R., & Tohkura, Y. I. (1997). Training Japanese listeners to identify English /r/ and /l/: IV. Some effects of perceptual learning on speech production. *The Journal of the Acoustical Society of America, 101*, 2299–2310.

Broersma, M. (2010). Perception of final fricative voicing: Native and nonnative listeners' use of vowel duration. *The Journal of the Acoustical Society of America, 127*, 1636–1644.

Brown, C. (2000). The interrelation between speech perception and phonological acquisition from infant to adult. In J. Archibalk (Ed.), *Second language acquisition and linguistic theory* (pp. 4–63). Malden, MA: Blackwell.

Burda, A. N., Scherz, J. A., Hageman, C. F., & Edwards, H. T. (2003). Age and understanding speakers with Spanish or Taiwanese accents. *Perceptual and Motor Skills, 97*, 11–20.

Bürki-Cohen, J., Grosjean, F., & Miller, J. L. (1989). Base-language effects on word identification in bilingual speech: Evidence from categorical perception experiments. *Language and Speech, 32*, 355–371.

Bürki-Cohen, J., Miller, J. L., & Eimas, P. D. (2001). Perceiving non-native speech. *Language and Speech, 44*, 149–169.

Caramazza, A. & Yeni-Komshian, G. H. (1974). Voice onset time in two French dialects. *Journal of Phonetics, 2*, 239–245.

Cebrian, J. (2006). Experience and the use of non-native duration in L2 vowel categorization. *Journal of Phonetics, 34*, 372–387.

Chakraborty, R. & Goffman, L. (2011). Production of lexical stress in non-native speakers of American English: Kinematic correlates of stress and transfer. *Journal of Speech, Language, and Hearing Research, 54*, 821–835.

Chang, C. B. (2012). Rapid and multifaceted effects of second-language learning on first-language speech production. *Journal of Phonetics, 40*, 249–268.

Chang, C. B. & Mishler, A. (2012). Evidence for language transfer leading to a perceptual advantage for non-native listeners. *The Journal of the Acoustical Society of America, 132*, 2700–2710.

Cho, T. & McQueen, J. M. (2006). Phonological versus phonetic cues in native and non-native listening: Korean and Dutch listeners' perception of Dutch and English consonants. *The Journal of the Acoustical Society of America, 119*, 3085–3096.

Chung, H., Kong, E. J., Edwards, J., Weismer, G., Fourakis, M., & Hwang, Y. (2012). Cross-linguistic studies of children's and adults' vowel spaces. *The Journal of the Acoustical Society of America, 131*, 442–454.

Clements, G. N. (2003). Feature economy in sound systems. *Phonology, 20*, 287–333.

Cooper, N., Cutler, A., & Wales, R. (2002). Constraints of lexical stress on lexical access in English: Evidence from native and non-native listeners. *Language and Speech, 45*, 207–228.

Coster, D. C. & Kratochvil, P. (1984). Tone and stress discrimination in normal Beijing dialect speech. *New papers on Chinese language use: Contemporary China papers, 18,* 119–132 (Australian National University, Canberra).

Cutler, A. (2005). Lexical stress. In D. B. Pisoni & R. E. Remez (Eds.), *The handbook of speech perception* (pp. 264–289). Oxford, UK: Blackwell.

Cutler, A. & Otake, T. (1999). Pitch accent in spoken-word recognition in Japanese. *The Journal of the Acoustical Society of America, 105,* 1877–1888.

Cutler, A., Weber, A., & Otake, T. (2006). Asymmetric mapping from phonetic to lexical representations in second-language listening. *Journal of Phonetics, 34,* 269–284.

Dalbor, J. B. (1969). *Spanish pronunciation: Theory and practice.* New York: Holt, Rinehart and Winston.

Darcy, I. & Krüger, F. (2012). Vowel perception and production in Turkish children acquiring L2 German. *Journal of Phonetics, 40,* 568–581.

Davidson, L. (2006). Phonology, phonetics, or frequency: Influences on the production of non-native sequences. *Journal of Phonetics, 34,* 104–137.

Davidson, L. (2010). Phonetic bases of similarities in cross-language production: Evidence from English and Catalan. *Journal of Phonetics, 38,* 272–288.

De Jong, K. J., Hao, Y. C., & Park, H. (2009). Evidence for featural units in the acquisition of speech production skills: Linguistic structure in foreign accent. *Journal of Phonetics, 37,* 357–373.

De Jong, K. J., Silbert, N. H., & Park, H. (2009). Generalization across segments in second language consonant identification. *Language Learning, 59,* 1–31.

Dupoux, E., Peperkamp, S., & Sebastián-Gallés, N. (2001). A robust method to study stress 'deafness'. *The Journal of the Acoustical Society of America, 110,* 1606–1618.

Dupoux, E., Sebastián-Gallés, N., Navarrete, E., & Peperkamp, S. (2008). Persistent stress 'deafness': The case of French learners of Spanish. *Cognition, 106,* 682–706.

Eimas, P. D., Siqueland, E. R., Jusczyk, P., & Vigorito, J. (1971). Speech perception in infants. *Science, 171*(3968), 303–306.

Escudero, P., Benders, T., & Lipski, S. C. (2009). Native, non-native and L2 perceptual cue weighting for Dutch vowels: The case of Dutch, German, and Spanish listeners. *Journal of Phonetics, 37,* 452–465.

Escudero, P. & Williams, D. (2011). Perceptual assimilation of Dutch vowels by Peruvian Spanish listeners. *The Journal of the Acoustical Society of America, 129,* EL1–EL7.

Fant, G. (1973). *Speech sounds and features.* Cambridge, MA: MIT Press.

Flege, J. E. (1987). The production of 'new' and 'similar' phones in a foreign language: Evidence for the effect of equivalence classification. *Journal of Phonetics, 15,* 47–65.

Flege, J. E. (1991). Age of learning affects the authenticity of voice-onset time (VOT) in stop consonants produced in a second language. *The Journal of the Acoustical Society of America, 89,* 395–411.

Flege, J. E. (1995). Second-language speech learning: Theory, findings, and problems. In W. Strange (Ed.), *Speech perception and linguistic experience: Issues in cross-language research* (pp. 233–272). Baltimore, MD: York Press.

Flege, J. E. (1999). Age of learning and second-language speech. In D. Birdsong (Ed.), *Second language acquisition and the critical period hypothesis* (pp. 101–132). Hillsdale, NJ: Lawrence Erlbaum.

Flege, J. E. (2002). Interactions between the native and second-language phonetic systems. In P. Burmeister, T. Piske, & A. Rohde (Eds.), *An integrated view of language development: Papers in honor of Henning Wode* (pp. 217–244). Trier, Germany: Wissenschaftlicher Verlag.

Flege, J. E. (2003). Assessing constraints on second-language segmental production and perception. In A. Meyer & N. Schiller (Eds.), *Phonetics and phonology in language comprehension and production, differences and similarities* (pp. 319–355). Berlin: Mouton de Gruyter.

Flege, J. E., Birdsong, D., Bialystok, E., Mack, M., Sung, H., & Tsukada, K. (2006). Degree of foreign accent in English sentences produced by Korean children and adults. *Journal of Phonetics, 34*, 153–175.

Flege, J. E. & Fletcher, K. L. (1992). Talker and listener effects on degree of perceived foreign accent. *The Journal of the Acoustical Society of America, 91*, 370–389.

Flege, J. E., Fletcher, S. G., & Homiedan, A. (1988). Compensating for a bite block in /s/ and /t/ production: Palatographic, acoustic, and perceptual data. *The Journal of the Acoustical Society of America, 83*, 212–228.

Flege, J. E., Frieda, E. M., & Nozawa, T. (1997). Amount of native-language (L1) use affects the pronunciation of an L2. *Journal of Phonetics, 25*, 169–186.

Flege, J. E. & MacKay, I. R. (2004). Perceiving vowels in a second language. *Studies in Second Language Acquisition, 26*, 1–34.

Flege, J. E., Munro, M. J., & MacKay, I. R. (1995a). Factors affecting degree of perceived foreign accent in a second language. *Journal of the Acoustical Society of America, 97*, 3125–3134.

Flege, J. E., Munro, M. J., & MacKay, I. R. (1995b). Effects of age of second-language learning on the production of English consonants. *Speech Communication, 16*, 1–26.

Flege, J. E., Yeni-Komshian, G. H., & Liu, S. (1999). Age constraints on second-language acquisition. *Journal of Memory and Language, 41*, 78–104.

Fox, R. A., Flege, J. E., & Munro, M. J. (1995). The perception of English and Spanish vowels by native English and Spanish listeners: A multidimensional scaling analysis. *The Journal of the Acoustical Society of America, 97*, 2540–2551.

Fry, D. B. (1955). Duration and intensity as physical correlates of linguistic stress. *Journal of the Acoustical Society of America, 27*, 765–768.

Gandour, J. (1983). Tone perception in far eastern-languages. *Journal of Phonetics, 11*, 149–175.

Gick, B., Bernhardt, B., Bacsfalvi, P., & Wilson, I. (2008). Ultrasound imaging applications in second language acquisition. In J. G. Hansen Edwards & M. L. Zampini (Eds.), *Phonology and second language acquisition* (pp. 315–328). Philadelphia: John Benjamins.

Goldstein, B. (2001). Transcription of Spanish and Spanish-influenced English. *Communication Disorders Quarterly, 23*, 54–60.

Guion, S. G., Flege, J. E., & Loftin, J. D. (2000). The effect of L1 use on pronunciation in Quichua–Spanish bilinguals. *Journal of Phonetics, 28*, 27–42.

Halle, M. (1959). *The sound pattern of Russian*. The Hague: Mouton.

Hallé, P. A., Best, C. T., & Levitt, A. (1999). Phonetic vs. phonological influences on French listeners' perception of American English approximants. *Journal of Phonetics, 27*, 281–306.

Hancin-Bhatt, B. (1994). Segment transfer: A consequence of a dynamic system. *Second Language Research, 10*, 241–269.

Hao, Y. C. (2012). Second language acquisition of Mandarin Chinese tones by tonal and non-tonal language speakers. *Journal of Phonetics, 40*, 269–279.

Hayes-Harb, R. (2005). Optimal L2 speech perception: Native speakers of English and Japanese consonant length contrasts. *Journal of Language and Linguistics, 4*, 1–29.

Hillenbrand, J., Getty, L. A., Clark, M. J., & Wheeler, K. (1995). Acoustic characteristics of American English vowels. *The Journal of the Acoustical Society of America, 97*, 3099–3111.

Ingvalson, E. M., McClelland, J. L., & Holt, L. L. (2011). Predicting native English-like performance by native Japanese speakers. *Journal of Phonetics, 39*, 571–584.

Ioup, G., Boustagui, E., El Tigi, M., & Moselle, M. (1994). Reexamining the critical period hypothesis. *Studies in Second Language Acquisition, 16*, 73–98.

Kang, K. H. & Guion, S. G. (2006). Phonological systems in bilinguals: Age of learning effects on the stop consonant systems of Korean-English bilinguals. *The Journal of the Acoustical Society of America, 119*, 1672–1683.

Klein, W., Plomp, R., & Pols, L. C. W. (1970). Vowel spectra, vowel spaces and vowel identification. *Journal of the Acoustical Society of America, 48*, 999–1009.

Kong, Y. Y. & Zeng, F. G. (2006). Temporal and spectral cues in Mandarin tone recognition. *The Journal of the Acoustical Society of America, 120*, 2830–2840.

Kuhl, P. K. (1994). Learning and representation in speech and language. *Current Opinion in Neurobiology, 4*, 812–822.

Kuhl, P. K. (2000). A new view of language acquisition. *Proceedings of the National Academy of Sciences of the United States of America, 97*, 11850–11857.

Kuhl, P. K. (2004). Early language acquisition: Cracking the speech code. *Nature Reviews Neuroscience, 5*, 831–843.

Kuhl, P. K., Conboy, B. T., Coffey-Corina, S., Padden, D., Rivera-Gaxiola, M., & Nelson, T. (2008). Phonetic learning as a pathway to language: New data and native language magnet theory expanded (NLM-e). *Philosophical Transactions of the Royal Society B, 363*, 979–1000.

Ladefoged, P. (2004). *Vowels and consonants: An introduction to the sounds of language* (2nd ed.). Oxford, UK: Blackwell.

Lee, B., Guion, S. G., & Harada, T. (2006). Acoustic analysis of the production of unstressed English vowels by early and late Korean and Japanese bilinguals. *Studies in Second Language Acquisition, 28*, 487–513.

Lenneberg, E. (1967). *Biological foundations of language.* New York: Wiley.

Levi, S. V., Winters, S. J., & Pisoni, D. B. (2007). Speaker-independent factors affecting the perception of foreign accent in a second language. *The Journal of the Acoustical Society of America, 121*, 2327–2338.

Lieberman, P. (1960). Some acoustic correlates of word stress in American English. *The Journal of the Acoustical Society of America, 32*, 451–454.

McAllister, R., Flege, J. E., & Piske, T. (2002). The influence of L1 on the acquisition of Swedish quantity by native speakers of Spanish, English and Estonian. *Journal of Phonetics, 30*, 229–258.

MacKay, I. R., Flege, J. E., Piske, T., & Schirru, C. (2001). Category restructuring during second-language speech acquisition. *The Journal of the Acoustical Society of America, 110*, 516–528.

MacKay, I. R., Meador, D., & Flege, J. E. (2001). The identification of English consonants by native speakers of Italian. *Phonetica, 58*(1–2), 103–125.

Maddieson, I. (1984). *Patterns of sounds.* Cambridge: Cambridge University Press.

Massaro, D. W., Cohen, M. M., Gesi, A., & Heredia, R. (1993). Bimodal speech perception: An examination across languages. *Journal of Phonetics, 21,* 445–478.

Meister, L. & Meister, E. (2011). Perception of the short vs. long phonological category in Estonian by native and non-native listeners. *Journal of Phonetics, 39,* 212–224.

Moyer, A. (1999). Ultimate attainment in L2 phonology. *Studies in Second Language Acquisition, 21,* 81–108.

Munro, M. J. & Derwing, T. M. (1995a). Foreign accent, comprehensibility, and intelligibility in the speech of second language learners. *Language Learning, 45,* 73–97.

Munro, M. J. & Derwing, T. M. (1995b). Processing time, accent, and comprehensibility in the perception of native and foreign-accented speech. *Language and Speech, 38,* 289–306.

Munro, M. J., Derwing, T. M., & Flege, J. E. (1999). Canadians in Alabama: A perceptual study of dialect acquisition in adults. *Journal of Phonetics, 27,* 385–403.

Näätänen, R. (2001). The perception of speech sounds by the human brain as reflected by the mismatch negativity (MMN) and its magnetic equivalent (MMNm). *Psychophysiology, 38,* 1–21.

Näätänen, R. (2002). The perception of speech sounds by the human brain as reflected by the mismatch negativity brain response. *International Congress Series, 1232,* 97–105.

Nenonen, S., Shestakova, A., Huotilainen, M., & Näätänen, R. (2003). Linguistic relevance of duration within the native language determines the accuracy of speech-sound duration processing. *Cognitive Brain Research, 16,* 492–495.

Nissen, S. L., Dromey, C., & Wheeler, C. (2007). First and second language tongue movements in Spanish and Korean bilingual speakers. *Phonetica, 64,* 201–216.

Oh, G. E., Guion-Anderson, S., Aoyama, K., Flege, J. E., Akahane-Yamada, R., & Yamada, T. (2011). A one-year longitudinal study of English and Japanese vowel production by Japanese adults and children in an English-speaking setting. *Journal of Phonetics, 39,* 156–167.

Pallier, C., Colomé, A., & Sebastián-Gallés, N. (2001). The influence of native-language phonology on lexical access: Exemplar-based versus abstract lexical entries. *Psychological Science, 12,* 445–449.

Parlato-Oliveira, E., Christophe, A., Hirose, Y., & Dupoux, E. (2010). Plasticity of illusory vowel perception in Brazilian-Japanese bilinguals. *The Journal of the Acoustical Society of America, 127,* 3738–3748.

Piske, T., MacKay, I. R., & Flege, J. E. (2001). Factors affecting degree of foreign accent in an L2: A review. *Journal of Phonetics, 29,* 191–215.

Rallo Fabra, L. R. & Romero, J. (2012). Native Catalan learners' perception and production of English vowels. *Journal of Phonetics, 40,* 491–508.

Ritchie, W. (1968). On the explanation of phonic interference. *Language Learning, 18,* 183–197.

Rogers, C. L. & Dalby, J. (2005). Forced-choice analysis of segmental production by Chinese-accented English speakers. *Journal of Speech, Language, and Hearing Research, 48,* 306–322.

Sebastián-Gallés, N., Echeverría, S., & Bosch, L. (2005). The influence of initial exposure on lexical representation: Comparing early and simultaneous bilinguals. *Journal of Memory and Language, 52*, 240–255.

Shestakova, A., Huotilainen, M., Čeponien, R., & Cheour, M. (2003). Event-related potentials associated with second language learning in children. *Clinical Neurophysiology, 114*, 1507–1512.

Sluijter, A. M. C. & van Heuven, V. J. (1996). Acoustic correlates of linguistic stress and accent in Dutch and American English. In *Proceedings of the fourth international conference on spoken language processing* (Vol. 2, pp. 630–633). Philadelphia: IEEE.

Southwood, H. & Flege, J. (1999). The validity and reliability of scaling foreign accent. *Clinical Linguistics & Phonetics, 13*, 335–349.

Strange, W. & Shafer, V. L. (2008). Speech perception in second language learners: The re-education of selective perception. In J. G. H. Edwards & M. L. Zampini (Eds.), *Phonology and second language acquisition* (pp. 153–191). Amsterdam and Philadelphia: John Benjamins.

Tajima, K., Kato, H., Rothwell, A., Akahane-Yamada, R., & Munhall, K. G. (2008). Training English listeners to perceive phonemic length contrasts in Japanese. *The Journal of the Acoustical Society of America, 123*, 397–413.

Thomson, R. I., Nearey, T. M., & Derwing, T. M. (2009). A modified statistical pattern recognition approach to measuring the crosslinguistic similarity of Mandarin and English vowels. *The Journal of the Acoustical Society of America, 126*, 1447–1460.

Tremblay, A., Broersma, M., Coughlin, C. E., & Choi, J. (2016). Effects of the native language on the learning of fundamental frequency in second-language speech segmentation. *Frontiers in Psychology, 7*. doi:10.3389/fpsyg.2016.00985

Tremblay, A. & Spinelli, E. (2014). English listeners' use of distributional and acoustic-phonetic cues to liaison in French: Evidence from eye movements. *Language and Speech, 57*, 310–337.

Tsukada, K., Birdsong, D., Bialystok, E., Mack, M., Sung, H., & Flege, J. (2005). A developmental study of English vowel production and perception by native Korean adults and children. *Journal of Phonetics, 33*, 263–290.

Vu, T. P. (1981). *The acoustic and perceptual nature of tone in Vietnamese.* Unpublished doctoral dissertation, Australian National University, Canberra.

Wagner, A., Ernestus, M., & Cutler, A. (2006). Formant transitions in fricative identification: The role of native fricative inventory. *The Journal of the Acoustical Society of America, 120*, 2267–2277.

Wang, Y. & Kuhl, P. K. (2003). Evaluating the 'critical period' hypothesis: Perceptual learning of Mandarin tones in American adults and American children at 6, 10 and 14 years of age. In *Poster presented at the 15th International Congress of Phonetic Sciences* (pp. 1537–1540). Retrieved from http://128.95.148.60/kuhl/pdf/wang_kuhl_2003.pdf (Accessed on January 1, 2016).

Whalen, D. H. & Xu, Y. (1992). Information for Mandarin tones in the amplitude contour and in brief segments. *Phonetica, 49*, 25–47.

Wilson, E. O. B. & Spaulding, T. J. (2010). Effects of noise and speech intelligibility on listener comprehension and processing time of Korean-accented English. *Journal of Speech, Language, and Hearing Research, 53*, 1543–1554.

Winters, S. & O'Brien, M. G. (2013). Perceived accentedness and intelligibility: The relative contributions of F_0 and duration. *Speech Communication, 55*, 486–507.

Yeni-Komshian, G., Flege, J. E., & Liu, S. (2000). Pronunciation proficiency in first and second languages of Korean–English bilinguals. *Bilingualism: Language and Cognition, 3*, 131–149.

Zhang, Y. & Francis, A. (2010). The weighting of vowel quality in native and non-native listeners' perception of English lexical stress. *Journal of Phonetics, 38*, 260–271.

Zhang, Y., Nissen, S. L., & Francis, A. L. (2008). Acoustic characteristics of English lexical stress produced by native Mandarin speakers. *The Journal of the Acoustical Society of America, 123*, 4498–4513.

Chapter 3

Phonological Processing in L2
Issues and Findings

3.1 Introduction

To many, a foreign accent is the most direct and most easily recognizable indication of being a non-native speaker. An accent is also the most common indication, as it often stays with a non-native speaker even when he or she has become nativelike in other aspects of language, as shown in the "Conrad phenomenon" (Scovel, 1969, 1988) and in many other individuals such as the former US Secretary of State Henry Kissinger. It is thus not surprising that phonology has been the focus of a tremendous amount of L2 processing research and for a long time. Built on the conceptual and methodological foundation laid out in experimental phonetics about speech perception and production in the 1950s and 1960s, researchers began to apply the concepts and techniques to the study of phonological processing among non-native speakers in the 1970s. Leading this effort were works such as Goto's (1971) demonstration of Japanese native speakers' difficulty with the English /l/-/r/ contrast; Dreher and Larkins's (1972) study of the relationship between speech perception and speech production; Guiora, Beit-Hallahmi, Brannon, Dull, and Scovel's (1972) examination of how language ego (or to be more specific alcohol assumption) was related to pronunciation accuracy; Caramazza, Yeni-Komshian, Zurif, and Carbone's (1973) investigation of the perception and production of voice onset times of English and French stops among monolingual and bilingual speakers; and Solomon and Ali's (1975) demonstration of NNS' less capability in using sentence intonation in understanding spoken language.

Considerable progress has been made since the 1970s. This progress is apparent, particularly in the past 20 years, in the amount of research output accumulated, in the breadth of topics covered, in the scope of non-native phonological phenomena revealed, and in the methodological advances made. It is beyond the space limit of a chapter to provide a comprehensive survey of this research. Instead, an effort is made to focus this chapter on research findings that examined the factors that affect L2 phonological processing and thus set it apart from L1 phonological processing. Two factors have received the most attention: an individual's L1 and age of acquisition. Research related to them is discussed in Section 3.2 and 3.3 respectively, followed by the discussion of research related to other factors in Section 3.4.

It should be noted from the outset that research on L2 phonological processing is closely related to acquisition issues. Almost all L2 phonological processing topics are related to the acquisition issue of whether NNS are able to develop nativelike phonology in a non-native language. Thus, this research demonstrates the close relationship between SLP and SLA particularly well.

3.2 Language Interaction

If one looks for an L2 phonological processing phenomenon that is most frequently and most consistently documented in the literature, the influence of a learner's L1 is the best candidate. L1 influence has also played a vital role in the development of phonological processing and development models. As shown in Section 2.5, all such models are developed around the premise that L2 perception and production rely on the existing L1 phonological categories or features, at least initially. This section reviews research that demonstrate language transfer and interaction in phonological processing and development in four subsections: L1 influence in the presence of new L2 phonetic phenomena, the role of the degree and pattern of L1–L2 overlap, the influence of L2 on L1, and L1–L2 interaction among simultaneous bilinguals.

3.2.1 L1 Influence: Dealing With New Phonetic Phenomena

Languages differ in their phonological structures (see Section 2.3). As a result, L2 learners have to deal with numerous new phonetic phenomena that are not instantiated in their L1. These phenomena may be a new segmental distinction such as the English liquid pair /l/ and /r/ for Japanese learners, a new feature such as Russian palatalization for English learners, or a new phonotactic structure such as English consonant clusters for Chinese learners. L1 influence is the most apparent and persistent under such circumstances. L2 learners tend to rely heavily on their L1 phonetic structures, which often results in a range of performance problems such as a low accuracy rate in perception and production, a longer RT, a non-native pattern of responses, or the reliance on incorrect cues. This review of research on L1 influence is organized around five levels of phonological representation: segmental, featural, suprasegmental, phonotactic, and lexical levels. Also included in this review are the studies that illustrated positive transfer, and the studies whose findings may also point to some universals in L2 phonological processing.

3.2.1.1 Segmental Transfer

At the segmental level, one of the earliest and best documented transfer phenomena is the difficulty that Japanese learners have in differentiating the two English liquids /l/ and /r/ due to a lack of this contrast in Japanese. Goto (1971) and Miyawaki et al. (1975) were among the first to demonstrate this difficulty. Goto used natural stimuli and tested both perception and production and Miyawaki et al. used synthetic stimuli and focused on perception alone. In both studies, Japanese NS were found to produce low accuracy scores in both perception and production. This phenomenon continued to be the focus of attention in more recent studies. For example, Ingvalson, McClelland, and Holt (2011) showed that even Japanese speakers who had lived in an English-speaking environment for many years failed to show native-like accuracy in both perception and production. Other L2-specific consonant contrasts have also been found to be difficult for L2 learners. These include French NS' discrimination of the English /d/-/ð/ contrast (Sundara, Polka, & Genesee, 2006) and the /r/-/w/ contrast (Hallé, Best, & Levitt, 1999), English NS' discrimination of Mandarin Chinese affricate–fricative contrasts (Tsao, Liu, & Kuhl, 2006), English NS' perception of Russian devoicing contrast (Dmitrieva, Jongman, & Sereno, 2010), Farsi and English NS' perception of the /k'/-/q'/ contrast of Salish, an American Indian language (Polka, 1992), to name just a few.

On the vowel front, Spanish speakers have been found to have difficulty in dealing with the Catalan contrast of /e/ and /ɛ/. Pallier, Bosch, and Sebastián-Gallés (1997) tested a group of Spanish-Catalan bilingual speakers who grew up in a bilingual environment, had an AOA of 6 years or younger, and were highly proficient in their L2 Catalan. The stimuli included seven synthetic vowel segments that were created by manipulating their F_1 only along the /e/-/ɛ/ continuum while holding F_2 constant. Seven samples were created with the F_1 of each segment increasing by 30 Hz starting from 404 Hz for Segment 1. Catalan NS showed a typical categorical perception effect in both the classification and discrimination tasks. In the discrimination task, for example, Catalan NS showed the best discrimination (approximately 90%) for a pair of segments that crossed the category boundary of /e/ and /ɛ/. Their discrimination decreased sharply on pairs of segments that were both on the same side of the boundary. The bilingual participants, however, failed to show a strong categorical perception effect, with discrimination rates varying between 60% and 75% for all pairs. L2 learners' difficulty with new L2 vowel distinctions has been documented in numerous other studies. Examples are the distinction of English vowels among Mandarin (Chen, Robb, Gilbert, & Lerman, 2001), Catalan (Cebrian, 2006; Rallo Fabra & Romero, 2012), Spanish (Escudero & Vasiliev, 2011), Dutch (Escudero, Simon, & Mitterer, 2012; Simon & D'Hulster, 2012), and Korean (Ingram & Park, 1997) ESL speakers, the distinction of German vowel contrast of /iː/-/ɪ/ and /iː/-/eː/ among Turkish NS (Darcy & Krüger, 2012), and the perception of the German /Y/-/U/ contrast by English NS (Polka, 1995).

3.2.1.2 Featural Transfer

Distinctive features such as length and stress are employed in some languages, but not in others. L2 learners have been found to have difficulty with L2 features that are not instantiated in their L1. One such feature is length (or duration). On the one hand, it has been shown that L2 speakers whose L1s do not make temporal distinctions can make use of this temporal cue in L2 speech perception under some circumstances, e.g., Russian learners of Estonian in Meister and Meister (2011) and Catalan learners of English in Cebrian (2006). On the other hand, research evidence abounds that documents L2 speakers' difficulty with length.

A classic example of perceptual difficulty is English speakers' struggle to differentiate Japanese long and short consonants and vowels (e.g., Callan, Callan, Tajima, & Akahane-Yamada, 2006; Han, 1992; Hardison & Saigo, 2010; Hirata, 2004; Hirata, Whitehurst, & Cullings, 2007; Minagawa & Kiritani, 1996; Tajima, Kato, Rothwell, Akahane-Yamada, & Munhall, 2008). Another example is Finish and Swedish ESL speakers' difficulty in utilizing the duration cue in the perception of English syllable final fricatives /s/ and /z/ such as in *peace* and *peas*. These two segments differ in the length of both the preceding vowel and the fricatives themselves. Similar distinctions are made in French but not in Finnish and Swedish. Flege and Hillenbrand (1986) tested English NS and ESL speakers from French, Finnish, and Swedish backgrounds on the voicing distinction. The participants were presented with stimuli that varied in vowel duration and fricative duration along the *peace–peas* continuum and asked to identify whether a stimulus was *peace* or *peas*. English and French speakers showed sensitivity to the manipulation of both durations, but the Finnish and Swedish groups were found to show a sensitivity to vowel duration only.

Some studies showed that NNS often differ from NS in the location of the boundary between long and short segments. Meister and Meister (2011) tested Russian-speaking learners of Estonian on Estonian vowel length distinctions. Vowel duration is a distinctive feature in Estonian, but not in Russian. The stimuli were created by manipulating the duration of a vowel (e.g., from 80 ms to 160 ms) and presenting them in isolation, in nonsense syllables, and in real words. The participants were asked to identify the vowel as being long or short. The results showed that Russian learners of Estonian had no difficulty differentiating long and short vowels. At the same time, they were found to differ in the location of the boundary between long and short vowels, which was longer for NNS than for NS (146 ms vs. 137 ms). Similarly, in identifying short and long vowels of Finnish, Russian-speaking learners of Finnish were found to have a boundary set at 135 ms, compared to 120 ms shown among Finnish NS (Ylinen, Shestakova, Alku, & Huotilainen, 2005), and Spanish ESL speakers tended to have a much shorter VOT boundary for the voiced–voiceless distinction than English NS did (Flege, 1991).

Temporal inaccuracy has also been well documented in production by NNS. For example, Flege, Munro, and Skelton (1992) compared Spanish and Mandarin ESL speakers to English NS in the production of English vowels in the syllabic context of /c_t/ vs. /c_d/. Acoustic analyses of their production showed that NNS produced a significantly shorter vowel duration in the /c_d/ context than NS, and the differences in vowel duration between the voiced and voiceless stops /d/ and /t/ context was smaller in NNS than in NS. Birdsong (2007) showed that English-speaking learners of French produced longer VOTs than French NS did in producing French voiceless stops. In Liu, Jin, and Chen (2013), Mandarin and Korean ESL speakers were found to produce a larger vowel duration difference across vowels than English NS did. Further examples include Korean ESL speakers' lack of vowel length distinction in producing Australian English (Ingram & Park, 1997) which seems to contradict with what was found in Liu, Jin, and Chen, ESL speakers' non-nativeness in duration distinction in producing stressed and unstressed vowels in English (e.g., Fokes & Bond, 1989; Lee, Guion, & Harada, 2006), and Spanish ESL speakers' temporal inaccuracy in producing English vowels and consonants (Shah, 2004).

Several studies have been done within a featural model in order to specifically test the featural transfer hypothesis. One of them was reported by McAllister, Flege, and Piske (2002). They examined the sensitivity to the Swedish quantity (or length) contrast among three groups of NNS: Estonian, English, and Spanish L1 speakers. Among the three L1s, Estonian is similar to Swedish in employing the quantity distinction as a primary phonological feature, but English and Spanish do not. However, the latter two languages are also different in that the quantity feature may serve as an acoustic cue in phonological processing in English, e.g., in the perception of vowels in stressed and unstressed syllables (even though it is not a primary cue). Words and nonwords with contrasting long and short vowels were used as critical stimuli. The participants were asked to perform both perception and production tasks in three experiments. Consistent with the featural hypothesis, Estonian speakers outperformed the other two NNS groups, and the English speakers showed better accuracy than the Spanish speakers (Experiments 1 and 2). The English speakers' advantage remained even when English and Spanish participants were matched for age, AOA, LOR, frequency of L2 use, L2 ability (Experiment 3). In light of the latter finding from English and Spanish speakers, a feature prominence hypothesis was formulated stating that "the relative importance of a feature in the L1 will determine the extent to which the feature is successfully used in producing and perceiving phonological contrasts in the L2" (p. 254). This view contrasts with one that treats a feature as a dichotomous factor, i.e., being present or absent in a learner's L1.

Two additional studies provided further evidence for a featural model. Larson-Hall (2004) also reported a study that compared the prediction made by a featural model and the SLM. They tested Japanese learners' discrimination of Russian consonants involving palatalization. A pair of Russian consonants can be differentiated on the basis of whether the middle of the tongue is raised to the palate before and after its pronunciation (i.e., palatalized), such as мат (/mat/, checkmate) and матъ (/mat^j/, mother). Palatalization is a distinctive feature in Russian but not in Japanese. In line with the prediction of a featural model, even advanced Japanese learners of Russian had difficulty with some of the contrasts. Lee et al. (2006) who tested the featural model by comparing Japanese and Korean ESL speakers' production of English vowels in stressed and unstressed syllables and by comparing their performance to those of English NS. Among the three acoustic correlates measured, i.e., F_0, duration, and intensity, no difference was found between the two NNS groups and the NS group in F_0. However, while Japanese ESL speakers were found to be very similar to NS in vowel duration and intensity differences, Korean ESL speakers were found to produce a much smaller contrast than NS did. They attributed this difference to the fact that the duration feature plays a more prominent role in Japanese than in Korean.

Even though featural transfer is well documented, research findings are not always consistent with the prediction of a feature-based model. For example, Arabic has voicing contrast such as /t/-/d/ and /k/-/g/, but for the voiced stop /b/, there is not a voiceless counterpart /p/. If a featural model is correct, Arabic ESL speakers should have little difficulty in learning /p/ because the voicing feature is instantiated in the native language. However, Arabic ESL speakers do seem to have difficulty with this phoneme in production, as reported by Flege and Port (1981). A more recent study reported by Barrios, Jiang, and Idsardi (2016) also failed to find L1 influence at the featural level. They tested Spanish ESL speakers' discrimination of two English vowel contrasts, /æ/-/ɑ/ and /i/-/ɪ/. The two pairs are similar in that one member is not used in Spanish, i.e., /æ/ and /ɪ/. The two contrasts differ, though, in whether the relevant features that differentiate them are used in Spanish. The features that distinguish the /æ/-/ɑ/ pair, i.e., [±back] and [±high], are used in Spanish, but the feature that distinguishes the /i/-/ɪ/, i.e., tense/lax, is not. A featural model would predict that Spanish ESL speakers should have less difficulty with the /æ/-/ɑ/ pair than with the /i/-/ɪ/ pair. However, the results obtained in the AX discrimination task (Experiment 1) and with the priming paradigm following Pallier, Colomé, and Sebastián-Gallés (2001) (Experiment 2) did not support this prediction.

often when talking to a baby or dog, you adapt a set of suprasegmentals that is different, use word stress exag.; rhyme a lot, etc.

3.2.1.3 Suprasegmental Transfer

Distinctive features may be segmental such as consonant or vowel length or suprasegmental such as word stress and tone. A great deal of research has documented language transfer at the suprasegmental level where a suprasegmental feature is used in L2 but not in a learner's L1. In studying the perception and production of word stress, some studies showed nativelike performance in producing stressed and unstressed syllables by advanced L2 speakers (e.g., Field, 2005; Lee et al., 2006; Nguyễn & Ingram, 2005; Zhang, Nissen, & Francis, 2008). However, non-nativeness in word stress is also common. First of all, stress pattern errors do occur in L2 production. Examples of such errors can be seen in the production of English words by Chinese, Japanese, and Spanish ESL speakers as reported by Archibald (1993, 1997) and Juffs (1990). Incorrect stress placement was also shown in Chakraborty and Goffman (2011) where Bengali ESL speakers had a tendency to produce a trochaic stress pattern (stressed+unstressed) even for iambic English words (unstressed+stressed, e.g., *buffet*, *baboon*), as a result of influence from their native language Bengali which only allows trochaic pattern.[1]

L2 speakers were also found to have difficulty in relying on stress-related cues. Dupoux, Pallier, Sebastian, and Mehler (1997) and Dupoux, Sebastián-Gallés, Navarrete, and Peperkamp (2008), for example, demonstrated a lack of sensitivity to stress distinction among NS of French, a language that has fixed word stress. NNS may also differ from NS in the specific acoustic correlates they rely on. For example, Japanese ESL speakers tended to produce a longer vowel duration for reduced vowels than NS did (Kondo, 2000). Similarly, the Mandarin ESL speakers in Zhang et al. (2008) produced a significantly higher mean F_0 than NS did in producing stressed syllables (198 Hz vs. 163 Hz), which the authors attributed to the participants' tonal language background. Further evidence of L2 speakers' difficulty with word stress can be seen in Cutler (2009) where Dutch NS transferred Dutch stress processing strategies in the recognition of English words, in Nguyễn, Ingram, and Pensalfini (2008) where Vietnamese ESL speakers were found to show reduced sensitivity to duration in the perception of English stress, and in Flege and Bohn (1989) where Spanish ESL speakers were found to be less able, in comparison to English NS, to produce reduced vowels in unstressed syllables. Difficulty with word stress also arises at the phrase level, e.g., in the distinctive production of compounds (e.g., blackberry) and phrases (e.g., black berry) (e.g., Nguyễn et al., 2008).

The perception and production of lexical tones represents another area where L1 influence is prominent. The most frequently observed indication of transfer lies in the difficulty in accurately perceiving tonal contrast. For example, when Cantonese, Japanese, and English NS were asked to identify Mandarin tones, they produced A' scores below 0.85 under most cases in So and

Best (2010). Some studies showed that identification accuracy did not seem to approximate that of NS even after training. For example, the participants in Wang, Spence, Jongman, and Sereno (1999) received eight training sessions of 40 minutes each in two weeks. They made significant improvements, but the mean accuracy was at 87%, significantly below that of NS. Similarly, in Francis, Ciocca, Ma, and Fenn (2008), Mandarin and English NS were trained on Cantonese tones for a period varying from ten to 30 days. Their accuracy in the identification accuracy remained at 80% or below (estimated from Figure 6 of the study) for low falling, low level, and low rising tones, even though this accuracy represented a significant improvement over their pre-training performance.

The transfer-based difficulty with tones can also been seen in non-categorical perception of tones and in response time patterns, as demonstrated in Hallé, Chang, and Best (2004). Their stimuli included two Mandarin syllables /pa/ and /pi/ pronounced in four tones. Eight stimuli were created for each of the following three tone contrasts, T1–T2, T2–T4, and T3–T4, such that two of them represented the two end points, e.g., T1 and T2, and the other six were intermediate stimuli along the continuum between the two end points. The eight stimuli for each contrast varied at even steps in F_0 and intensity, two acoustic features that differentiate the tones. These were presented to a group of French NS and a group of Mandarin controls who performed an AXB identification task. Mandarin NS showed a categorical perception effect in both accuracy and reaction time. Their accuracy scores peaked at the 95% accuracy at mid continuum, and their RTs were longest at mid continuum and dropped sharply at both ends. However, French NS showed a) an overall low accuracy of 74%, and b) little difference in their accuracy and RT along the continuum, thus indicating a lack of categorical perception. A similar finding was reported by Leather (1987) in the perception of Mandarin tones by Dutch and English speakers and by Yang and Liu (2012) in English monolingual children's perception of Mandarin tones.

Prior experience with a tonal language does not seem to always alleviate this difficulty. As tones are categorized differently in different languages, NS of a tonal language can have similar difficulty with another tonal language, as shown in Hao (2012). In this study, Mandarin tone perception and production were assessed among ten English NS and nine NS of Cantonese, a tonal language. They were asked to perform three tasks: a tone identification task in which they listened to 32 monosyllabic and 32 disyllabic stimuli and indicated the tone for each stimulus, a mimicking task in which they listened to and mimicked the auditory stimuli, and a reading-aloud task in which they read aloud Chinese words written in pinyin with tones indicated. Their production performance was evaluated by two Mandarin NS who had to identify the tone of the participants' output. Among the four tones, both groups did quite well with Tones 1 and 4. The accuracy rates were close to or above 90% under most circumstances. However, their accuracy rates were much lower for Tones 2 and 3, often below 70% except for the mimicking task. Cantonese speakers did not seem to enjoy any advantage over English speakers. Similarly, in So and Best's (2010) study, Cantonese NS were not better at classifying Mandarin tones than Japanese and English NS (but see Wayland & Guion, 2004; Wayland & Li, 2008; and Qin & Jongman, 2016 for a tonal L1 advantage).

3.2.1.4 Phonotactic Transfer

Phonotactic differences between languages presents challenges for L2 learners and often result in inaccuracy even among advanced L2 speakers. This has been particularly well demonstrated in the production of consonant clusters that are illegal in an individual's L1. For example, Davidson (2006) tested English NS on consonant clusters that were legal and illegal in English in a repetition task. The test materials included word-initial legal clusters such as /sn/ and /sm/, and illegal clusters such as /fm/, /zm/, /vm/. These clusters were used to construct a set of pseudo-Czech words that were presented to the English-speaking participants who were asked to repeat after the auditory stimuli. While they produced a high mean accuracy score of 97% on the legal clusters, their accuracy was 60%, 39%, and 22% on the three types of illegal clusters. They tended to insert a vowel between the two consonants. Similar findings were obtained in Davidson, Jusczyk, and Smolensky (2004), in which English NS' mean accuracy in producing Polish words with consonant clusters that were legal in English were 94%, but the mean scores for illegal items ranged from 11% to 63%. More examples of phonotactic transfer can be found in the perception and pronunciation of English consonant clusters by Spanish (Altenberg, 2005) and Mandarin Chinese (Crowther & Mann, 1992; Flege & Wang, 1989) ESL speakers.

A specific transfer-based phonotactic phenomenon in L2 processing is vowel epenthesis. Speakers of a language in which consonant clusters are not allowed or infrequent are found to insert a vowel between two consonants in production or to report hearing a vowel between two consonants in speech perception, the latter of which is referred to as perceptual illusion. This phenomenon is reported in several studies. In one of them, Dupoux, Kakehi, Hirose, Pallier, and Mehler (1999) constructed syllables such as *ebuzo* that were digitally manipulated to have 0 ms to full duration of the mid-syllable vowel /u/ (Experiment 1), or *ebzo* pronounced without the vowel (Experiment 2). They were presented to French and Japanese speakers who were asked to decide whether they heard a vowel /u/ in the middle of the syllable. While French-speaking participants reported hearing /u/ increasingly more often as the /u/ segment was getting longer, Japanese-speaking participants (whose L1 does not use consonant clusters regularly) reported hearing /u/ even when the vowel /u/ was absent in the stimuli. This vowel epenthesis by Japanese speakers were replicated in a ABX discrimination task involving similar stimuli. Japanese participants were also much less accurate than French speakers in discriminating syllables with and without a vowel between two consonants, the error rates being 32% and 5.8% for Japanese and French speakers, respectively (Experiment 3). See Dupoux, Pallier, Kakehi, and Mehler (2001); Parlato-Oliveira, Christophe, Hirose, and Dupoux (2010); and Davidson and Shaw (2012) for more studies related to vowel epenthesis resulting from L1 phonotactic influence.

3.2.1.5 L1 Influence and Use of Acoustic Cues

L1 influence can lead to the use of incorrect cues in perception, which results in low accuracy. F_3 frequency is the primary cue English native speakers use to differentiate /l/ and /r/. Iverson et al. (2003) found that Japanese ESL speakers tended to rely on F_2 in the distinction of the English /l/-/r/ contrast, rather than the F_3 cue. They suggested that "The perceptual spaces of Japanese adults are thus miss-tuned [sic] for acquiring the English /r/-/l/ contrast, making acoustic variation that is irrelevant to categorization more salient than the critical differences in F_3," (p. B53). The lack of a nativelike sensitivity to the F_3 cue among Japanese ESL speakers' perception and production of the /l/-/r/ contrast has been replicated in several subsequent studies (Lotto, Sato, & Diehl, 2004; Iverson, Hazan, & Bannister, 2005; Ingvalson et al., 2011; Ingvalson, Holt, & McClelland, 2012). A further example of using the wrong cues comes from Cutler (2009) who demonstrated that Dutch ESL speakers used suprasegmental cues in the perception of English stress, a cue not used by English NS.

L1 influence may also lead NNS to selectively rely on some cues more than others where multiple cues are used by NS. For example, in differentiating the syllable-final voicing contrast for fricatives such as /s/ and /z/, English NS use both the duration of the preceding vowel and that of the fricatives as cues, but Swedish and Finnish ESL speakers seemed to be insensitive to the fricative duration cue (Flege & Hillenbrand, 1986), and Dutch speakers were found not to use the vowel duration cue (Broersma, 2005). Individuals whose L1s place more weight on vowel duration as an important cue than English does were found to use the duration cue to a greater extent in processing English vowels than English NS did, such as the Catalan ESL speakers in Cebrian (2006) and the German ESL speakers in Flege, Bohn, and Jang (1997). On the other hand, English NS were found to rely on duration cues to a less extent than NS of Estonian for which duration is a distinctive feature (e.g., Lehiste & Fox, 1992). Mandarin speakers relied more on pitch cues rather than duration and intensity in the perception of English word stress due to their tonal language background (e.g., Yu & Andruski, 2010). A related finding is that tonal Mandarin speakers attended to pitch movement more than non-tonal Dutch speakers for the same reason (Braun & Johnson,

2011). English speakers were found to rely on pitch frequency (or height) only, rather than both pitch frequency and pitch contour, in the perception of lexical tones in Cantonese (Gandour, 1983). Russian learners of Finnish whose L1 does not use quantity cues were found to have a reduced sensitivity to vowel duration in processing Finnish as measured by both behavioral and electrophysiological data (e.g., Nenonen, Shestakova, Huotilainen, & Näätänen, 2003; Ylinen et al., 2005; Ylinen, Shestakova, Huotilainen, Alku, & Näätänen, 2006). The finding in Crowther and Mann (1992) that Japanese ESL outperformed Mandarin ESL speakers in the perception and production of the English voicing contrast for word-final stops could be attributed to the presence of the vocalic duration distinction in their native language Japanese, as the authors argued. Finally, Finnish and Russian speakers of Estonian were found not to use the pitch cue used by NS in perceiving the overlong quantity (Lippus, Pajusalu, & Allik, 2009).[2]

It should be noted that while inaccuracy in speech perception and production may be attributed to the use of incorrect acoustic cues, missing a right cue may not always lead to inaccuracy. NNS were sometimes found to be able to successfully differentiate a phonetic contrast without using the correct cues, as demonstrated in Broersma (2005), Lippus et al. (2009), and Cutler (2009). For example, the Dutch ESL speakers in Broersma did not rely on the vowel duration cue in the perception of the syllable-final voicing contrast (e.g., /f/ vs. /v/ in a CVC syllable), as NS did, but they produced a nativelike accuracy.

3.2.1.6 L1 Influence in Word Recognition

Perceptual inaccuracy at the segmental level has a direct impact on auditory word recognition. If a distinction is not made between /ε/ and /æ/, for example, an auditory stimulus such as /bεd/ may be perceived as *bad*, and the auditory stimulus /bit/ may be recognized as both *beat* and *bit*. Incorrect word recognition as a result of a lack of phonetic distinctions is explored and shown in several studies. For example, Pallier et al. (2001) demonstrated that Spanish-dominant Catalan speakers treated auditorily presented Catalan words *néta* and *neta* (*granddaughter* and *clean*) as the same words, thus producing a repetition priming effect due to a lack of distinction between /e/ and /ε/ in L1 Spanish. Cutler, Weber, and Otake (2006) showed that, while presented with the auditory stimulus *rocket*, Japanese ESL speakers fixated on the picture of a locker more often than control pictures.[3] See Bradlow and Pisoni (1999, Experiment 2) and Ingvalson et al. (2011) for similar findings. In addition to segmental distinctions, L1 phonotactic knowledge may also affect L2 word recognition, as demonstrated by Weber and Cutler (2006). They asked German ESL speakers to detect an English target word embedded in a nonword stimulus (the word spotting task). The stimuli were manipulated such that a phonotactic cue was or was not present to facilitate the detection and, in the former case, the cue may be L1 German specific,

L2 English specific, or may be shared by both languages. The results showed that German ESL speakers were both faster and more accurate in responding to stimuli with a German-specific cue, thus confirming the activation of the German phonotactic knowledge in their L2 processing.

3.2.1.7 Positive Transfer

L1 influence reported in most studies affect L2 processing and learning adversely, resulting in a reduced accuracy or other non-nativelike performance. L1–L2 differences can produce positive results, as well. An example of this positive transfer was reported by Chang and Mishler (2012). Korean and English differ regarding the releasing of the word-final stop, such as /p/ in *stop*. Releasing such stops is optional in English but in Korean such stops are obligatorily unreleased. This means that Korean NS have to rely on the spectral cues in the preceding vowels for the identification of the unreleased stops. The authors hypothesized that this strategy may be transferred from Korean to another language, resulting in a better identification of unreleased stops than English NS do. To test this idea, they tested a group of English NS and a group of Korean NS residing in the USA. The critical stimuli consisted of a set of Korean nonce words of CVCVC structure with the last consonant being /p/, /t/, /k/, or absent (Experiment 1), a set of English nonce words similar to their Korean counterparts but with English-specific consonants in the first two consonant positions (Experiment 2), a set of English real word pairs contrasting the three consonants such as *weep-wheat*, *seat-seek*, *lick-lip* and contrasting the presence and absence of them such as *keep-key*, *beet-bee*, *peek-pee* (Experiment 3). The stimuli were first recorded as released. The last stop was then removed so that the preceding vowels carried all the acoustic information of the final stops. The participants were asked to perform a four-alternative forced-choice identification task in which they decided whether the stimuli contained the consonant /p/, /t/, /k/, or "other" (Experiments 1 and 2) and a speeded AX discrimination task in which they decided whether the two stimuli were identical or different. The results showed that the Korean participants outperformed the English-speaking participants in the identification of both Korean and English stops in the first two experiments and in the discrimination of the English words that did and did not have a final stop (e.g., *keep-key*). Another example of NNS outperforming NS due to L1–L2 differences can be found in Dutch speakers' use of stress information in English word recognition reported by Cooper, Cutler, and Wales (2002).

3.2.1.8 L2 Processing Universals?

In the presence of prevalent signs of L1 influence, it is interesting to ask whether there are L2 phonological processing universals, i.e., processes or strategies adopted by L2 speakers regardless of their L1 backgrounds.

Unfortunately, this issue has not received much attention. Few studies have been specifically designed to examine universals in L2 speech perception and production. With little direct evidence available, indications of L2 processing universals may be potentially found in findings that showed similar patterns among L2 speakers of different L1 backgrounds. An example of such a finding was reported by Davidson (2010). She asked English and Catalan speakers to perform a nonword repetition task. The stimuli were nonwords that contained onset consonant-consonant (CC) or /CəC/ sequences. These sequences were manipulated across three types of consonants, stops, fricatives, and nasals, to form six types of sequences: stop-stop, stop-fricative, stop-nasal, fricative-fricative, fricative-stop, and fricative-nasal. In spite of the phonotactic differences between English and Catalan, several similarities were found among the participants. For example, fricative-initial sequences produced better accuracy than stop-initial sequences in both groups. When individual initial consonants were considered, both groups showed a similar accuracy pattern across the ten consonants involved, with sequences beginning with a voiceless consonant showing a higher accuracy than sequences beginning with a voiced consonant. Davidson argued that L2 speakers do not seem to just extend what they do in L1 to L2 (an idea that is sometimes referred to as the analogy hypothesis). Instead, they are also influenced by articulatory constraints faced by individuals. Similarities such as these offer promising areas where L2 universals may be found in future research.

One may also look for universals by identifying commonalities across studies. A good candidate for a universal in this approach is the use of duration information in speech perception in the absence of sufficient spectral cues available to L2 listeners. A number of studies have reported that NNS tended to rely on duration information in segment discrimination even if duration is not a primary acoustic cue in their native language. For example, the English NS showed a duration difference of 31 ms in producing /i/ and /ɪ/ in Flege, et al. (1997), but Mandarin ESL speakers in the study showed a greater difference (proficient speakers: 71 ms, less proficient: 67 ms), even though vowel duration is not a distinctive feature in Mandarin. Similarly, Catalan ESL speakers were also found to rely on vowel duration as a cue more than English NS in the perception of the same two English vowels in Cebrian (2006). In this study, stimuli were created along the continuum of /i/, /ɪ/, and /ɛ/ along two acoustic dimensions, 11 steps along the spectral dimension and four steps along the duration dimension, thus generating a total of 44 synthesized tokens. Catalan ESL speakers and English NS were asked to perform a three-alternative forced-choice identification task deciding whether a stimulus was /i/, /ɪ/, or /ɛ/. English NS were found to rely on spectral information in the perception of all three vowels. A prototypical /i/ on the basis of spectral information was perceived as /i/ regardless of duration, for example. Catalan speakers, however, showed a different pattern. They relied on spectral information in the perception of /ɛ/, but duration played an important role in their perception of /i/ and /ɪ/. For example, the prototypical /i/ was perceived as /i/ 90% of the time when the duration was 250 ms, but only a little over 50% of the time when the duration was 100 ms. The use of duration information for discriminating English /i/ and /ɪ/ has been found among Russian ESL speakers (Kondaurova & Francis, 2008), Spanish ESL speakers (Bohn, 1995; Escudero & Boersma, 2004), Mandarin ESL speakers (Bohn, 1995), Japanese ESL speakers (Morrison, 2002), as well. Additionally, Bohn (1995) reported the use of the duration cue in the perception of the English /ɛ/ and /æ/ by German ESL speakers, and Escudero, Benders, and Lipski (2009) showed that Spanish-Dutch bilinguals were able to produce nativelike accuracy in discriminating a new Dutch vowel contrast /aː/ and /ɑ/ by relying on duration information. All these findings shared two similarities: the L2 speakers were dealing with a vowel contrast that is not made in their L1, and they used duration information in spite of the fact that duration is not a distinctive feature for vowel distinction in their native language.

There are several possible explanations for this commonality. One is pedagogical. The present author and supposedly a majority of Chinese ESL speakers were explicitly taught to differentiate English /i/ and /ɪ/ on the basis of duration, treating /i/ as a long vowel and /ɪ/ as a short vowel (they are usually transcribed as /iː/ and /i/ in textbooks and dictionaries used in China). This is a possibility pointed out by Flege, et al. (1997), as well.

A second explanation was offered by Bohn (1995) in the form of the desensitization hypothesis. Bohn stated that "whenever spectral differences are insufficient to differentiate vowel contrasts because previous linguistic experience did not sensitize listeners to these spectral differences, duration differences will be used to differentiate the non-native vowel contrast" (pp. 294–295). To take the perception of English /i/ and /ɪ/ by Mandarin speakers as an example, since Mandarin does not employ unrounded front vowels, Mandarin speakers are insensitive to spectral differences in this acoustic space. As a result, they rely on the duration cue, instead. Two quick points should be made in this context. Even though this hypothesis was proposed in the pursuit of the theme that "first language transfer doesn't tell it all", language transfer is an intrinsic part of the proposal. In line with the theme of the study, Spanish ESL speakers were found to use the duration cue in differentiating English /i/ and /ɪ/ in spite of the fact that duration is not employed as an acoustic cue in Spanish. This finding was considered as "the most convincing argument for the [desensitization] hypothesis" and against transfer. At the same time, one has to recognize that the very reason for Spanish and Mandarin speakers to use the duration cue is the lack of a similar phonetic distinction in their native language, according to the hypothesis. Thus, one may view this result as reflecting L1 influence of a different type. Second, it is not clear in the proposal why the L2 speakers chose to rely on the duration cue in the absence of sufficient spectral cue, rather than, e.g., rely on wrong spectral cues, as in the perception of English /l/ and /r/ by Japanese speakers shown in Iverson et al. (2003). One may speculate that duration is acoustically more salient, or it is a cue "universally available" (Escudero & Boersma, 2004).

A third explanation was put forward by Escudero and Boersma (2004). They argued, in their reuse-of-blank-slates account, that since duration is not used as an acoustic cue in Spanish, duration values are not associated with any existing phonetic categories in the language. In that sense, "the Spanish perception of the duration continuum is still a blank slate" (p. 580). This allows them to be engaged in statistical learning while being exposed to English, just as infants do in learning L1, first using duration as a noncategorizing cue, but gradually developing duration-based categories of English vowels. Such process of category development is similar to how infants develop their L1 phonetic categories.

To conclude this section on L1 influence, research has shown that L1 is the most powerful determinant of speech perception and production in L2. Many L2 speech perception phenomena, such as inaccuracy in the perception of segments and identification of words, the use of incorrect cues, vowel epenthesis, can be attributed to the influence of the native language where L2 speakers have to deal with new phonological phenomena. Further evidence of the role of the L1 can also be seen in how the degree of L1–L2 overlap affects speech perception and production, which is the topic of the next section.

3.2.2 L1 Influence: The Role of the Degree or Pattern of L1–L2 Overlap

L2 segments differ in how similar they are to the closest L1 segments. Some L2 segments do not have counterparts in a learner's L1, such as the French vowel /y/ for English learners and the English interdentals /θ/ and /ð/ for Chinese learners. Even when similar sounds are present in L1, the degree of similarity may vary across segments. For example, the Cantonese /i/ and English /i/ are much more similar (F_1 being 310 ms and 370 ms, F_2 being 2368 ms and 2146 ms) than the Cantonese /u/ and English /u/ (F_1 being 353 ms and 374 ms, F_2 being 721 ms and 1668 ms), as reported by Chung et al. (2012).

Two proposals have been put forward about how the degree of L1–L2 overlap would affect L2 phonological processing and development. In the SLM (see Section 2.5.1), a higher degree of overlap is believed to have a detrimental effect on L2 learning, as it leads L2 learners to treat some L2 sounds as instances of existing L1 categories, thus preventing "adult L2 learners from establishing a phonetic category for similar but not new L2 phones" (Flege, 1987, p. 50). Thus, compared to new L2 segments that do not have a similar L1 segment, similar L2 segments are more difficult for learners. The NLMM

(Kuhl, 2000) shares a similar idea. An L2 segment that is closer to the space controlled by an L1 category is more likely to be treated as that L1 category, thus making the creation of a new category difficult. In this first proposal, L1–L2 overlap is determined on the basis of individual segments. The second proposal can be found in the PAM (see Section 2.5.2). As this model is more concerned with how NNS are able to differentiate two non-native segments (rather than the accurate perception and production of individual L2 segments), the L1–L2 overlap is assessed in this model in terms of how two L2 segments overlap with L1 categories, e.g., two L2 segments being similar to a single L1 segment or to two separate L1 segments. This section reviews empirical studies that are related to these two proposals.

3.2.2.1 Testing the SLM: The More Similar, the More Difficult?

A relatively direct approach to test the role of L1–L2 overlap from the SLM's perspective would be to identify L2 segments that do or do not have similar L1 segments and compare their perception and production accuracies among L2 learners. Two such studies were reported: Flege (1987) and Flege and Hillenbrand (1984). Both studies compared the production accuracy of two French vowels, /u/ and /y/, by English speakers of different proficiencies. The French vowel /u/ has a similar English counterpart /u/, but the second vowel /y/ does not. According to the prediction made by the SLM, English learners of French should experience L1 interference in learning /u/ but less so for /y/. The acoustic analysis of the participants' production seemed to support the prediction. Their production of /y/ was more similar to that produced by French NS, but their /u/ was somewhere between the English /u/ and the French /u/. A related finding was that both proficiency groups showed native-like performance for /y/, but only high-proficiency groups approximated nativelike performance for /u/. These results were consistent with the idea that a new L2 category is easier to create than a similar one due to a lack of L1 interference for the former.

Results reported by Escudero et al. (2012) provided further evidence. They tested the discrimination of the English /æ/-/ɛ/ contrast by two groups of NNS who spoke two dialects of Dutch, the Dutch spoken in North Holland and Flemish spoken in Belgium (which is considered as a dialect of Dutch). The examination of the acoustic values of these vowels in these languages showed different similarity patterns with English segments. For example, the English vowel /ɛ/ is closer to the Flemish /ɪ/ in both F_1 and F_2 than to the Dutch /ɪ/. The participants were asked to perform two tasks on a set of CVC syllables containing the two English vowels: to match the vowels to the closest Dutch vowels and to classify these two vowels as English vowels. In line with the prediction from an L1 influence perspective, Flemish participants considered the English /ɛ/ as the Dutch vowel /ɪ/ more often (41%) than

Dutch speakers (12%). In the English vowel classification task, the Flemish speakers were also found to incorrectly classify /ɛ/ as /ɪ/ more often (30%) than Dutch speakers (15%).

Guion, Flege, Akahane-Yamada, and Pruitt (2000) showed results both consistent and inconsistent with the predictions made by the SLM. In this study, Japanese speakers were asked to first map eight English consonants (/b/, /s/, /t/, /v/, /w/, /ɹ/, /l/, /θ/) to the Japanese consonants in an assimilation task. They were then tested in a discrimination task where English-English and English-Japanese consonant pairs served as stimuli. They found that when asked to differentiate the two English liquids /ɹ/ and /l/ and their Japanese counterpart /ɾ/, the participants were more accurate with /ɹ/ than with /l/. Considering that /l/ is considered more similar to the Japanese /ɾ/, this finding is consistent with the prediction of the SLM. On the other hand, some findings from the same study were not consistent with the model's predictions. An example was the perception of the English consonant /θ/. This consonant has no similar Japanese counterpart. This was confirmed in the study in that the Japanese speakers produced a low assimilation score and a low goodness-of-fit score in mapping it to the Japanese consonant /s/ and /ɸ/. According to the SLM, this consonant should be easier to learn than a similar one such as /s/. However, two findings in the study showed otherwise. First, the accuracy scores were low for the discrimination of both /s/ and /θ/ presented in English-English or English-Japanese pairs. Second, when the discrimination accuracies from three groups of Japanese speakers with low, medium, and high English experiences were compared, there was no significant difference in the perception accuracy of /θ/, which means that no substantial learning took place for this consonant among these participants.

A study conducted outside of the SLM did not seem to provide supporting evidence for the model either. Chen et al. (2001) compared the production of 11 English vowels by 40 Mandarin ESL speakers (minimum LOR in the USA being two years, minimum of 30% of daily use of English) and 40 English NS. These vowels were classified as familiar vowels (/i/, /e/, /u/, /o/, /ɑ/) and unfamiliar vowels (/ɪ/, /æ/, /ɛ/, /ʌ/, /ʊ/, /ɔ/) depending on whether there is a similar vowel in Mandarin. The F_1 and F_2 values of these vowels pronounced in the /hVd/ syllable by NNS and NS were measured and compared. Contrary to the prediction of the SLM, there was a greater difference between NNS and NS for the unfamiliar vowels than for the familiar vowels. These results should be taken with caution, though, because the classification of familiar and unfamiliar vowels was done subjectively rather than on any empirical ground.

A more recent study reported by Thomson, Nearey, and Derwing (2009) represented an innovative approach to quantify between-language overlap at the segmental level and showed that different degrees of overlap did seem to affect category development. They asked native speakers of Mandarin and English to produce syllables that contained seven Mandarin vowels and ten

English vowels. The acoustic information associated with these tokens were analyzed and used to develop three computer models of pattern recognition, one for each of the two languages, and the third one, the metamodel, treating all 17 vowels within a single system. The individual models produced a high accuracy in recognizing the tokens of each language separately (94% and 91% accuracy for Mandarin and English, respectively). The degree of overlap between the two sets of vowels was measured in terms of how frequently a vowel in one language was recognized as a vowel in the other language by the metamodel. For example, the Mandarin vowel /o/ was recognized as the English /o/ 30% of the time, and the English /o/ was recognized as the Mandarin /o/ 37.5% of the time. The mean of the two numbers, 33.75, became the overlap score for this pair of vowels. This method allowed them to determine the degree of overlap between the ten English vowels and the seven Mandarin vowels in a more objective way. The overlap scores ranged from 33.75 for English /o/, 30 for /ɒ/, 28.75 for /i/, and 26.25 for /ʊ/ at the high end of the overlap continuum, to 3.75 for /æ/, 2.50 for /ɛ/, 1.25 for /u/, and 0 for /ɪ/ at the low end. The vowels /e/ and /ʌ/ were in the middle with the overlap scores of 18.75 and 10.20. In the second part of the study, 22 NS of Mandarin with low English proficiency were asked to pronounce syllables containing the ten English vowels. The spectral values of their speech token were measured and tested against the metamodel. The results showed that the English vowels with less overlap with Chinese vowels were more likely to be classified as English vowels. The vowels with the highest rate of being identified as the target English vowels were /ɛ/ (77.3%), /ɪ/ (54.5%), and /æ/ (31.8%). They were all low-overlap vowels. In contrast, tokens of high-overlap vowels were often classified as Mandarin vowels than English vowels. For example, the vowel /o/ was classified as Mandarin /o/ more often (70.5%) than English /o/ (19.4%). The classification rates as Mandarin vowels were 68.2% for /ɒ/, 64.8% for /i/, and 43.2% for /ʊ/. An exception to this pattern was /ʌ/. It had a low-overlap score of 10.20 with its closest Mandarin counterpart /a/, but was classified as /a/ much more frequently (73.9%) than as itself (12.5%). Overall, these results were consistent with the view that more overlap may lead to less learning, as predicted by the SLM. As the authors stated, "when English vowel categories are statistically very similar to L1 Mandarin categories, learners tend to substitute the relevant L1 category for the L2 category. When English vowel categories are statistically less similar to L1 Mandarin categories, learning may occur" (p. 1458).

3.2.2.2 Testing the PAM: Pair Types and Difficulty Levels

Another line of research about the relationship between L1–L2 overlap and L2 speech perception is carried out within the framework of the PAM. This research is unique in several ways. First of all, instead of considering the degree of overlap between an L2 segment and its closest L1 category, as is done by Flege (1987), the focus is more on how a pair of L2 segments relate to an individual's L1 categories. Second, perceptual accuracy is determined in terms of how successful an individual is in differentiating a pair of L2 segments, rather than accurate identification or nativelike production of individual L2 segments. Finally, this research is unique methodologically in adopting a combination of perceptual assimilation and perceptual discrimination (or classification) tasks. More specifically, a study done within this approach typically includes three components: a) obtain the perceived relationship between L2 and L1 segments by asking participants to perform a perceptual assimilation task and to provide goodness-of-fit ratings, b) examine the perceptual accuracy for the L2 segments in a discrimination or classification task, and c) examine the relationship between L1–L2 overlap on speech perception by relating discrimination accuracy to assimilation patterns of L2 segments. In the first task, the participants are asked to decide which L1 segment an L2 segment is most similar to and to rate the degree of similarity or goodness-of-fit between the two, e.g., on a 1–7 scale. Data from this task provide a basis for determining how L2 segments are perceptually mapped onto the existing L1 segments, and thus provide a basis for classifying pairs of L2 segments. Pairs of L2 segments are then classified into different categories based on the model, which in turn provides the basis for predicting the difficulty level associated with the L2 segments (see Section 2.5.2 for the classification detail).

For example, if the two L2 English segments /i/ and /ɪ/ were both perceived to be the L1 Chinese segment /i/ in the perceptual assimilation task, this L2 pair represents a single-category assimilation pair, and is predicted to be very difficult to discriminate and learn in the model. If the English /u/ is perceived to be highly similar to the Chinese /u/, then the /i/-/u/ pair becomes a two-category assimilation pair (i.e., each assimilated to a different L1 segment) and is predicted to be easy to discriminate in the model. The participants' perceptual accuracy of pairs of such L2 segments is then assessed in a discrimination or classification task. These data are considered in relation to the assimilation patterns to determine if the overlap pattern affects their perception, as the model predicts.

Studies conducted within this approach provided supporting evidence for the role of L2–L1 overlap in L2 phonetic perception. One of such studies was reported by Best, McRoberts, and Goodell (2001). They tested English native speakers on three pairs of Zulu consonants. They were voiceless and voiced lateral fricatives /ɬ/ and /ɮ/, voiceless and ejective velar stops /k/ and /k'/, and plosive and implosive bilabial stops /b/ and /ɓ/. English-speaking participants were asked to listen to Zulu CV syllables, determine if the consonant sounded like an English consonant, and if it did, then write down the resembling English sound in English orthography, e.g., the letter k for the English consonant /k/.

They were also asked to provide a more detailed description of the stimuli as they perceived them.

The participants' performance in this perceptual assimilation task indicated three different patterns of phonetic overlap. All participants considered the two lateral fricatives as resembling two different English consonants, /ɮ/ as resembling /l/ or /z/, and the voiceless /ɬ/ as resembling /s/ or /ts/. Thus, there was little overlap between the two Zulu consonants in perceptual assimilation. There was more overlap in the perception of the velar stops. The voiceless Zulu /k/ was considered to resemble English /k/ by a majority of the participants, but the perception of the ejective consonant /k'/ varied a great deal among the participants even though most of them identified it as something related to the English /k/. A majority of the participants identified the two Zulu bilabial stops (/b/ and /ɓ/) as resembling the English /b/. Thus, the three pairs of Zulu consonants could be classified as three different contrast types, with /ɬ/-/ɮ/ being a Two-Category pair, /k/-/k'/ as a Category-Goodness pair, and /b/-/ɓ/ being a Single-Category pair. According to the model, they should be increasingly more difficult. The same group of participants were asked to complete an AXB discrimination task on these Zulu consonants. The results from the latter task supported the prediction by the perceptual assimilation model. The accuracy for the three pairs was 95%, 89.4%, and 65.9%, respectively, thus showing a decline in accuracy from Two-Category to Category-Goodness to Single-Category pairs.

Strange, Hisagi, Akahane-Yamada, and Kubo (2011) provided further evidence for the role of L2–L1 overlap in L2 discrimination within the PAM. They asked 21 Japanese speakers to perform a perceptual assimilation task on eight English vowels and an AXB discrimination task on 13 pairs of these vowels. They found that the overlap patterns of the L2 vowels on the basis of the participants' assimilation performance were highly predictive of their performance in the discrimination task. Similarly, Levy (2009) tested the discrimination of French vowels by English speakers who differed in the amount of French learning experiences, and considered how discrimination accuracy obtained in an AXB task related to the same participants' assimilation patterns. Consistent with the prediction of the PAM, they found that the participants' accuracy was higher for French vowels that were assimilated to two different L1 categories than those that were assimilated to the same L1 category.

Some studies only provided partial support for the PAM. Tsukada et al. (2005) examined the perception of English vowels by Korean children and adults. In the perceptual assimilation task, eight adult Korean-speaking participants were asked to identify eight English vowels presented in a disyllabic /b_bo/ nonword context. They were asked to decide which of the eight Korean vowels each of the eight English vowels resembled the most. These results revealed different patterns of overlap between the two phonetic systems. Some English vowels were perceived to resemble Korean vowels with a high consistency among the participants, e.g., the English /i/ as the Korean /i/ (100%), the English /ɑ/ as Korean /a/ (98%), and English /æ/ as Korean /a/ (86%). Some other English vowels were identified as resembling different Korean vowels, e.g., English /e/ as Korean /e/ (43%) and /ɛ/ (55%), and English /ʌ/ as Korean /a/ (56%) and /ʌ/ (35%). Several contrast types could be identified based on the assimilation data. For example, both English /ɑ/ and /æ/ were considered to resemble the Korean vowel /a/ and thus formed a Single-Category pair. Some pairs could be best considered as Two-Category type as both members were perceived to resemble two different Korean vowels, e.g., /i/ and /ɑ/. More pairs were Category-Goodness pairs. A different group of Korean-speaking participants were asked to perform a discrimination task on five pairs of English vowels: /ɛ/-/æ/, /e/-/ɛ/, /i/-/ɪ/, /ɑ/-/ʌ/, and /i/-/ɑ/. The data provided partial support for the PAM in that a Two-Category pair, /i/-/ɑ/, indeed produced the highest accuracy. However, the accuracy varied a great deal among those Category-Goodness pairs (which would be predicted to be similar in difficulty by the model), e.g., A' score being 0.5 for /ɛ/-/æ/ and approximately 0.68 for the /i/-/ɪ/ and /ɑ/-/ʌ/ contrasts (data from adults with five years of LOR).

Flege and MacKay (2004) considered the perception of English vowels by Italian speakers. The participants were asked to classify 11 English vowels presented in a /b_t/ or /k_d/ context in terms of seven Italian vowels. Some English vowels were consistently perceived to be an Italian vowel. For example, /ʌ/ was perceived to be Italian /a/ 93% of the time, and /i/ to be Italian /i/ 87% of times. Other English vowels were more ambiguous to the listeners. For example, /ɪ/ was identified as /i/ (65%) or /e/ (35%), and /ɛ/ was identified as either /e/ (47%) or /ɛ/ (53%). The identification performance provided the speech assimilation data for the classification of the English vowels into different types within the PAM. The participants were also asked to perform a discrimination task where each item consisted of three stimuli in the form of a /b_t/ or /k_d/ syllable. The participants were asked to listen to the stimuli and a) indicate whether the three stimuli were identical, and b) if one of them was perceived to be different from the other two, indicate which one was different by pressing one of the three buttons marked "1", "2", and "3". An A' score was computed as a measure of the discrimination accuracy. When the perceptual assimilation data and the discrimination accuracy data were considered together, the former seemed to predict the latter in some cases. For example, three English vowel pairs, /ɛ/-/æ/, /ɒ/-/ʌ/, and /i/-/ɪ/, were often perceived to be the same Italian vowels, i.e., /ɛ/, /a/, and /i/, respectively. Such single-category pairs were predicted to be difficult by the PAM. They indeed were among the vowel pairs that received the lowest A' scores. At the same time, the /ei/-/ɛ/ pair produced a high discrimination score in spite of their high degree of overlap (62% and 47% as Italian /e/). Another pair, /ɪ/-/ɛ/, showed a much lower degree of overlap in the assimilation data and thus should be easy according to the model, but the perceptual accuracy score for this pair was quite low. Thus, again, the impact of L2–L1 overlap on L2 vowel discrimination was clear, but the predictions made by PAM were only partially supported.

The studies reviewed in this section provide some evidence for the effect of L2–L1 overlap on L2 speech perception and production, thus confirming the predictions made in the SLM and the PAM. At the same time, they also demonstrate some challenges one faces in linking cross-language similarity to speech development. One of them is how to quantify this similarity or overlap, as pointed out by Flege, Bohn et al. (1997). Thomson et al. (2009) represents an attempt to meet the challenge, but their method is not widely used. This may be a reason why there have been only a small number of studies designed specifically to examine the relationship between L2–L1 overlap and L2 phonological processing within the framework of the SLM, even though the model is very explicit about this relationship. A reading of several reviews by Flege (1995, 2002, 2003, 2007) suggests that the French /u/-/y/ comparison may be the only phenomenon directly tested to substantiate the relationship within the SLM framework. A further challenge, from the perspective of the PAM, is how to make more precise predictions about this relationship. The finding from Tsukada et al. (2005) that the same Category-Goodness pairs can vary a great deal in perceptual accuracy and the finding from Levy (2009) that the same L2 vowels presented in different syllable contexts produced different patterns of results calls for a broader perspective on what affects perceptual accuracy, by taking into consideration other influencing factors such as phonetic contexts.

3.2.3 L2 Effect on L1

A question that arises in the presence of the well-documented L1 influence in L2 phonological processing and development is whether cross-language influence is unidirectional or bidirectional. Specifically, will learning an L2 have an impact on L1 categories? The answer is affirmative in the SLM. On the assumption that the phonetic categories of both languages share a common phonetic space, they are likely to interact with each other. As Flege (1981) stated,

> one would expect phonetic learning in a second language to affect pronunciation of a learner's first language. If the acoustic model provided by native language sounds can influence foreign language pronunciation, then foreign language sounds should, by virtue of their identification with native language sounds, exert an influence in the opposite direction.
>
> (p. 452)

This interaction would lead to an L1 category diverging away from an emerging new L2 category in the process of category dissimilation. In the case of category assimilation, an L1 category may converging to the L2 category, thus forming a merged or composite category that takes on acoustic features of both L1 and L2 categories. In both cases, the L1 categories will be no longer the same as those of a monolingual speaker. Such scenarios are anticipated in the interaction hypothesis (Flege, 1999; Baker, Trofimovich, Flege, Mack, & Halter, 2008).

One of the earliest demonstration of the impact of L2 learning on L1 categories was reported by Flege (1987). In addition to studying L2 segmental development, he also looked into how L1 categories were affected by comparing L2 learners' L1 production of VOT for English and French voiceless stops with that of monolingual L1 speakers. English voiceless stops have longer VOTs than French voiceless stops. The influence of L2 learning experience on L1 was most pronounced in the two groups of experienced L2 speakers who had lived in an L2 environment for an extended period of time (11.7 years in Paris for English NS, and 12.2 years in Chicago for French NS). The English NS living in Paris produced the English stop /t/ with a VOT 28 ms shorter than that of monolingual English NS, making it approximate the VOT value for the French /t/ more. The French NS living in Chicago, on the other hand, produced their L1 French /t/ with a significantly longer VOT than that of monolingual French speakers. For the latter group, there was little difference in VOT between the L1 French and L2 English /t/. Their phonetic categories for the English /t/ and the French /t/ seemed to have emerged into a single category, at least as far as the VOT value was concerned. These results were taken as evidence for "the 'merging' of the phonetic properties of similar L1 and L2 phones" and thus the "bi-directional" nature of language influence (p. 62).

Chang (2012) also explored this topic, or phonetic shift in his term, by testing American students studying in a Korean immersion program in South Korea. The study examined three questions: a) whether only limited L2 experience would affect acoustic properties of L1 categories, b) whether this influence would lead to convergence of L1 categories to the L2 acoustic values (assimilatory shift) or divergence away from the L2 values (dissimilatory shift), and c) whether such shift would be segment-based and thus would affect individual segments, or affect a class of segments. The target phonetic structures were English stops and vowels. Based on a comparison of the stop and vowel systems in the two languages, and on the assumption that phonetic shift would occur even in early L2 learning, three specific predictions were made. First, there would be an increase in VOT of English voiceless (but not voiced) stops due to the longer VOT of their Korean counterparts. Second, there would be a rise in F_0 onset following English stops due to the higher F_0 onset of Korean stops in the same environment. Finally, there would be a general downward shift in F_1 and F_2 values of all English vowels due to lower F_1 and F_2 values associated with Korean vowels. The speech samples were provided by 19 beginning Korean learners who were asked to read aloud

22 Korean and 23 English monosyllables, always in the order of Korean preceding English in the same test session. The speech elicitation was done five times over a span of five weeks. The analyses of the acoustic features associated with the speech samples from these participants largely confirmed the predictions at least among female learners. While the participants' VOT of Korean stops was increasing over time to approximate nativelike Korean values, the VOT values of English voiceless stops also increased by 19 ms, making their English pronunciation less nativelike. The same changes occurred with English vowels. There was a systematic shift of F_1 values of English vowels toward that of Korean vowels. These results led the author to state that

> experience in another language rapidly alters production of the native language. For the late L2 learners examined here, a few weeks of learning Korean promptly affected their English, in a manner that both generalized across segmental categories and approximated the phonetic properties of the L2.
>
> (p. 264)

A study reported by Dmitrieva et al. (2010) was also designed specifically to examine the influence of L2 learning on L1 production. They compared four monolingual Russian speakers living in Russia and seven Russian-English bilinguals living the USA. The phonological phenomenon involved was neutralization. It refers to the devoicing of word-final voicing contrasts involving stops and fricatives. For example, the pronunciation of the Russian words /kod/ (code) becomes /kot/ (cat) in neutralization. Russian and English differ in this respect in that word-final devoicing was common in Russian but less common in English. To elicit speech samples, the participants were asked to read aloud Russian words that were selected in relation to the phenomenon of neutralization. The degree of devoicing was assessed in four measures: preceding vowel duration, closure/frication duration, voicing into closure/frication duration, and release portion duration. Typically, a word-final voiced stop or fricative is produced with a longer vowel duration, a shorter closure/frication duration, a longer voicing into closure/frication duration, and a shorter release duration than a voiceless segment is. When neutralization occurs, some of these duration differences disappear. The comparison between monolingual Russian speakers and Russian speakers with English experiences showed a difference in the level of devoicing even though both groups were performing the reading task in their L1 Russian. While the monolingual group showed the expected devoicing in two of the four measures (vowel duration and voicing into closure/frication duration), the contrast between voiced and voiceless stops and fricatives remained in the bilingual speakers' pronunciation. They further found that the amount of L2 experiences affected the level of devoicing, with more experienced L2 speakers showing less nativelike devoicing in their L1. The authors attributed the bilingual group's non-nativelike devoicing in their L1 to their experiences learning an L2 for which devoicing is less common.

While L2 effects on L1 resulted in a convergence of L1 categories towards L2 categories in these studies, Flege and Eefting (1987) reported a case of divergent shift in L1. They tested Dutch learners of English (AOA: 12) in the production of English and Dutch voicing contrast between voiced and voiceless stops such as /t/ and /d/. Dutch has a shorter VOT boundary than English does, which means that the Dutch /t/ is pronounced with a shorter VOT than the English /t/ is. The participants were divided into three groups based on their L2 English proficiency. They were asked to read Dutch and English sentences and their speech samples were analyzed with a focus on the VOT of the English /t/ and Dutch /t/. The participants in all three proficiency groups were able to correctly produce the English voiceless stop with a longer VOT in English than in Dutch. However, the data showed a difference between the most proficient group and the other two less proficient group in the VOT associated with their L1 Dutch /t/. The VOT produced by the most proficient group was much shorter than that by the other two groups. The authors interpreted this result as revealing an effect of English learning on their L1 Dutch. It was taken to indicate that the most proficient group, not the other two proficiency groups, had established a separate L2 category for the English /t/ with a longer VOT, and as a result they shortened the VOT of the Dutch /t/ to keep them separate.

There is also some electrophysiological evidence for the effect of L2 learning on L1 phonology. Peltola, Tuomainen, Koskinen, and Aaltonen (2007) examined Finnish-speaking children who participated and did not participate in an English immersion program. The target segments were one Finnish vowel contrast /i/ and /e/, and three English vowel contrasts, /e/-/ɪ/, /i/-/ɪ/, and /i/-/e/. Their discrimination of these vowel contrasts was measured on the basis of MMN. As expected, the monolingual Finnish children showed a sensitivity to the Finnish contrast (as well as the English contrasts /i/-/ɪ/, and /i/-/e/). In contrast, the immersion children failed to show a sensitivity to the L1 Finnish contrast. A similar finding was obtained in Peltola et al. (2003) where adult Finnish native speakers with an advanced level of English proficiency showed less than nativelike response to the same Finnish contrast. These results led the authors to conclude that "the mother tongue system may not be completely fixed, and that language learning, whether done in classroom or in early immersion, may alter the perception of native vowels, at least temporarily" (p. 21).

Further evidence for the influence of L2 learning on L1 phonology can also be seen in the non-nativelike pronunciation of their native language Korean by Korean-English bilinguals reported by Yeni-Komshian, Flege, and Liu (2000), in the non-nativelike acoustic properties for their native language among late Korean-English bilinguals in Kang and Guion (2006), and in the effect of learning L2 Spanish on the production of L1 vowels among sequential Quichua-Spanish bilinguals reported by Guion (2003).

This mounting evidence for the impact of L2 learning on L1 phonology raises two questions. First, does the observed L2 impact represent a temporary processing strategy shift or a real and long-term change in mental representation of L1 categories? In the former scenario, the same person may show a sign of L2 impact in a bilingual or L2 environment but behave with no trace of L2 influence in a monolingual L1 environment. Sancier and Fowler (1997) showed that a bilingual individual's acoustic properties in speech production, specifically the VOT values, can fluctuate and change back and forth depending on where he or she lives. The ambient language may insert an impact on how one speaks. Grosjean's (1988, 1997) language mode hypothesis provides a theoretical basis for this possibility. Alternatively, we may suppose that the L1 categories have indeed been restructured as a result of learning an L2. As a result, the same people will behave less nativelike in their L1 even when they are in a monolingual L1 environment. Chang (2012) discussed phonetic drift as being "indicative of a fluid, multifaceted quality to language development over the lifespan" (p. 264). This may be interpreted to mean that the L2 impact on L1 is representational in nature and affects the long-term mental representations of L1 categories. Assuming that the representations of L1 categories have been changed, a related point to consider is how long this effect will last. Peltola et al. (2007) recognized the likelihood of this impact being temporary. Chang's statement can also accommodate subsequent changes back to nativelike L1 representations. A reason to consider this effect being temporary arises from the fact that in almost all these studies, the participants were residing in the L2 environment and were tested while the L2 figured prominently as a functional language. This L2 impact may be reversible when these individuals are immersed in an L1 environment. A more likely scenario of permanent change of L1 may occur among the participants tested by Pallier et al. (2003). These Korean children adopted by French families displayed little knowledge of their native language. In short, whether the L2 impact on L1 reported in these studies represents a temporary change of processing strategies or a relatively stable change in mental representations is yet to be determined.

Another issue to be considered is what factors constrain the merging of categories or phonetic shift. One such factor is the learners' age, as pointed out by Flege, Schirru, and MacKay (2003). Younger learners have less well established L1 categories, which are more susceptible to L2 influence. Another is the degree of overlap between a pair of L1–L2 segments. It is conceivable and as has been shown in Thomson et al. (2009) that an L1–L2 pair with a higher degree of overlap is more likely to merge into a single category than two segments that are more dissimilar. A third factor is the bilingual speaker's L2 proficiency or L2 experience. As shown in Flege and Eefting (1987), advanced L2 speakers are more likely to have their L1 categories affected. A fourth factor is the aspect of phonological processing involved. Phonetic shift seems less likely to occur in the use of segmentation strategies, for example, as shown by Cutler, Mehler, Norris, and Segui (1989, 1992). Bilinguals in these studies seemed to continue to rely on the segmentation strategies of their dominant language, with little influence from learning a second language. A fifth factor is cognate status. Amengual (2012) tested Spanish L1 and English L2 bilingual speakers, among other bilingual groups, on their pronunciation of the Spanish stop /t/. He found that these bilinguals were more likely to produce a longer (and thus more L2 English-like) VOT in producing cognates than in producing noncognates. Finally, the timeline of learning the two languages can play a role. Learning two languages simultaneously may create a situation that allows L1–L2 interaction to occur in a different way from sequential bilinguals, which brings up the next topic: L1–L2 interaction among simultaneous bilinguals.

3.2.4 The Case of Simultaneous Bilinguals

Simultaneous bilinguals learned their two languages from birth at the same time, often as a result of being exposed to two different languages spoken by the two parents (e.g., Cutler et al., 1989, 1992). Thus, both languages may be considered the native languages. This population provides a unique opportunity for studying how the two languages interact in phonology.

A number of studies examined phonological interaction among simultaneous bilinguals and often compared these bilinguals to sequential bilinguals. Some studies showed that the former group was more likely to keep the two phonological systems separate than the latter group. Guion (2003) examined vowel production among simultaneous and sequential Quichua-Spanish bilinguals, along with monolingual Spanish speakers. The participants were asked to listen to words presented in sentence frames and repeat them. Their production was analyzed in terms of spectral values. The results showed that the two groups of bilinguals produced different patterns, at least when front vowels were concerned, i.e., Quichua /ɪ/ and Spanish /i/, /e/. The sequential bilinguals produced their L2 Spanish vowels in a way similar to that of monolingual Spanish speakers, but their production of L1 Quichua vowel was not nativelike, presumably as a result of L2 influence. In contrast, the simultaneous bilinguals were able to keep three distinct vowel categories. Their production of these vowels was similar to those produced by monolingual speakers of these two languages. Guion explained the difference between simultaneous and early sequential bilinguals in terms of the timing of the exposure to both languages. On the assumption that phonetic categories are established within the first year of life, as shown in research by Werker and

Tees (1984), she suggested that "the finding that only the simultaneous bilinguals were able to partition the vowel space to allow three front vowels may be due to their exposure to both Quichua and Spanish vowels during the first year of life" (p. 122).

Sundara and Polka (2008) examined the discrimination of the English /d/ and French /d/ among simultaneous English-French bilingual speakers and compared their performance to that of early sequential English-French bilingual speakers. The English /d/ is alveolar and the French /d/ is dental, and they are different in several acoustic measures. The participants' perceptual accuracy was measured in an AXB discrimination task. The two groups showed different results. While early L2 learners showed poor discrimination, the simultaneous bilinguals were much more accurate in the task. These researchers suggested that while sequential bilinguals tend to create a merged category for these two similar stops, simultaneous bilinguals are able to keep the two phonological systems separate and create two separate categories for the two stops. Similarly, simultaneous bilinguals tested in Sundara, Polka, and Baum (2006) were able to produce English and French coronal stops in a language-specific way even though they relied on only a subset of acoustic features used by monolingual speakers.

Being able to keep the two systems separate does not always mean that there is no influence from each other. Fowler, Sramko, Ostry, Rowland, and Hallé (2008) tested, among others, five groups of participants on the production of English and French voiceless stops, /p/, /t/, and /k/. The participants were a monolingual French group, a monolingual English, a simultaneous French-English bilingual group, an L1 French sequential bilingual group, and an L1 English sequential bilingual group. Their production of English and French stops were elicited in a sentence reading task and analyzed in terms of VOT. Two findings emerged in the study. First, all three groups of bilingual speakers were able to produce language-specific stops with the VOT significantly longer in producing English stops than in producing French stops. Second, the simultaneous group produced the French stops with a significantly longer VOT than that of monolingual French speakers, and they produced English stops with a significantly shorter VOT than English monolingual speakers. The latter finding suggested that these simultaneous bilinguals, while being able to keep the two stop systems separate between the two languages, were nevertheless influenced by the fact that they were proficient in two languages.

To sum up the review on L1–L2 interaction on phonological processing, L1 influence occurs at all levels of phonological analysis, among different types of L2 speakers, and affects L2 performance in multiple ways. There is also increasing evidence for the influence of L2 on L1 in phonological processing. However, the nature of such influence, e.g., reflecting a temporary change in processing strategy due to L2 environment or permanent change in mental representation, is yet to be determined. Research so far has been directed toward identifying instances of language transfer and interaction. In the presence of the abundant evidence for L1–L2 interaction, particularly for L1 influence, it becomes also important to identify circumstances where L1 influence is expected but does not occur. A comparison of the conditions under which L1 influence occurs or does not occur can help better our understanding of the nature of L1 influence and the factors involved.

3.3 Age and Acquirability

Many of us who are immigrants to a new country in adulthood have seen our children growing up speaking the language of the new country with little accent while our own accent stubbornly persists. Plenty of anecdotal evidence has helped create the common sense that younger learners are better language learners. Thus, there is very little disagreement regarding the role of age in language acquisition in general, and in speech development in particular. However, researchers disagree on two issues in the context of phonological processing. The first one is whether nativelike phonology is attainable in L2 acquisition. This disagreement applies to both adults and children. The second is the exact causes underlying the child–adult differences in speech development. This section begins with a review of research that documented the role of age in phonological processing and development. It is followed by review of research on the acquirability issue and a summary of the views on the causes of the age-related differences.

3.3.1 Documenting Age-Related Differences

In studying age effects, the age variable is usually operationalized as the age of acquisition, or AOA, but age of learning is also used in some studies. It is usually defined as the age at which an individual is first exposed to a non-native language in naturalistic settings. For some individuals, i.e., the first-generation immigrants, this is the age at which they immigrated to a new country. Thus, some researchers used the term "age of immigration" to refer to the onset age (e.g., Rogers & Lopez, 2008; Rogers, DeMasi, & Krause, 2010). For those who were born in the country of the target language but were first exposed to a language other than the target language, it is the age at which they began to be exposed to the target language regularly, e.g., the age at which they went to school. AOA information is usually obtained through a language background questionnaire where the participants reported their own age of first exposure to the target language.

In a specific study, the AOA variable is usually manipulated in one of two ways. One is to divide the participants into two or more groups based on AOA. For example, it is common for a study to include a child learner group and an adult learner group (e.g., Baker & Trofimovich, 2006; Flege et al.,

2006), or an early learner group and a late learner group (e.g., Lee et al., 2006; Piske, Flege, MacKay, & Meador, 2002). Some studies may include multiple AOA groups, such as three groups in MacKay, Meador, and Flege (2001) and Archila-Suerte, Zevin, Bunta, and Hernandez (2012), four groups in Wang and Kuhl (2003), and ten groups in Flege, Munro, and MacKay (1995b). The second method is to treat AOA as a continuous variable rather than a categorical one and use statistical procedures such as regression analysis in data analysis (e.g., Archila-Suerte et al., 2012; Jia et al., 2006) to assess the role of AOA. The assessment of age effects is done by examining how the participants' performance in speech perception or production respond to the age manipulation.

Consistent with and going beyond our commonsensical impression of the role of age in speech development, research has produced compelling evidence for age-related differences in phonological processing and development across a wide range of age groups, involving different phonological processing phenomena, and under different testing circumstances. In most of such studies, younger learners outperformed older learners in both perception and production. For example, Flege and colleagues (Flege, 1991; Flege et al., 1995b; Flege, Yeni-Komshian, & Liu, 1999; Flege et al., 2006) examined production accuracy among Spanish-, Italian-, Korean-English bilinguals with different AOAs. The participants' pronunciation of English words was evaluated both acoustically and on the basis of rating scores provided by NS listeners. Younger learners were found to be more accurate than older learners in most measures in all these studies. For example, the younger Spanish ESL speakers were found to produce nativelike VOT while the VOT produced by the older learners were significantly shorter and thus more similar to that of Spanish in the 1991 study. The pronunciation was judged to be more accented by NS listeners as the AOA increased across the ten AOA groups in the 1995b and 1999 studies. Similar younger-learner advantages were also reported by MacKay, Flege, Piske, and Schirru (2001), Piske et al. (2002), Baker and Trofimovich (2006), Jia et al. (2006), Kang and Guion (2006), and Rogers et al. (2010).

Younger learners were also found to produce better performance than older learners in perception tasks. For example, Baker and Trofimovich (2006) tested Korean ESL speakers' perception of six English vowels in a forced-choice task. The early learner group (mean AOA: 9) showed an accuracy similar to that of NS, but the adult group was significantly lower in accuracy. Jia et al. (2006) also included a AOA manipulation among the participants who had lived in the USA for three–five years. The participants were asked to perform an AXB discrimination task on six vowel contrasts. A negative correlation was found between AOA and performance accuracy: younger AOA was associated with higher perceptual accuracy scores. The early-AOA advantage in perceptual accuracy was also shown in studies that involved degraded input (e.g., MacKay, Meador, & Flege, 2001; Mayo, Florentine, & Buus, 1997; Meador, Flege, & MacKay, 2000).

In addition to accuracy measures, a few studies also compared early and late learners with other dependent variables. Parlato-Oliveira et al. (2010) reported an intriguing study of age effects that made use of a cross-linguistic difference in vowel epenthesis between Japanese and Brazilian Portuguese speakers. When presented with consonant clusters e.g., *ebna*, that were not legal in the two languages, NS of these two languages tend to insert a vowel between the two consonants in perception. This phenomenon is known as vowel epenthesis and the inserted vowel is referred to as an "illusory epenthetic vowel". Earlier research showed that Japanese NS tended to insert the vowel /u/ between the consonants, thus perceiving *ebna* to be *ebuna*, while Brazilian Portuguese speakers tended to add /i/, thus perceiving *ebna* as *ebina* (e.g., Dupoux et al., 1999; Dupoux, Parlato, Frota, Hirose, & Peperkamp, 2011). They set out to test whether Japanese speakers who were exposed to Portuguese at different ages behaved more like Japanese or Portuguese monolingual speakers. To this end, they tested early (mean AOA: 6) and late (mean AOA: 30) Japanese learners of Portuguese and simultaneous Japanese-Portuguese bilinguals (along with Japanese and Portuguese monolinguals) in a perception task where they had to decide whether they heard a vowel between two consonants in VCCV syllables (e.g., *ebna*) embedded among many VCVCV fillers. They responded by choosing one of the six alternatives: /a/, /e/, /ɪ/, /o/, /u/, and no vowel. Replicating the earlier findings, Japanese monolinguals reported hearing /u/ and Portuguese monolinguals reported hearing /i/ in most cases. But more importantly, adult learners of Portuguese behaved more like Japanese monolinguals while early Portuguese learners and simultaneous bilinguals behaved more like Portuguese NS, thus confirming the role of age in relation to this unique phenomenon. Additional examples of studies demonstrating early-AOA advantages in other measures were found in discrimination patterns among early, intermediate, and late Spanish ESL speakers obtained through multidimensional scaling analysis (Archila-Suerte et al., 2012) and in the perceptual assimilation patterns among early and late Korean ESL speakers (Baker et al., 2008).

A small number of studies reported results contrary to those reviewed above. Lee et al. (2006) failed to show an age effect in most of their measures. They tested early and late Korean and Japanese ESL speakers on vowel production in stressed and unstressed syllables. Four measures were taken of the vowel pronunciation: F_0, duration, intensity, and vowel quality reduction. The participants were divided into early and late groups with mean AOA being 3.7 and 21.0 for the early and late Japanese participants and 3.9 and 21.4 for the early and late Korean participants. With the exception of duration ratio in favor of Korean ESL speakers, the early and late learners showed very similar patterns in most of the measures. Several studies reported an older-learner advantage itial L2 learning. Wang and Kuhl (2003) tested English speakers on the ception of Mandarin tones in a training study and the adult group outper-ــmed the three younger-learner groups. Sixteen Japanese-speaking children and 16 of their parents were tested twice, first six months after their arrival in the USA and again a year later in three studies, where Aoyama, Flege, Guion, Akahane-Yamada, and Yamada (2004) examined the perception and pro-duction of the /r/-/l/ distinction, Aoyama, Guion, Flege, and Yamada (2008) focused on the perception of /s/ and /θ/, the production of /f/, /s/, and /θ/, and global accentedness, and Oh et al. (2011) considered the production of English vowels. All three studies showed that older learners enjoyed an initial advantage but younger learners could catch up or outperform older learners in a long run in a naturalistic setting.

Current research has clearly demonstrated an early-age advantage in phono-logical development. However, two points should be made in relation to this finding. First, this advantage is documented through and thus only applicable to L2 learning in naturalistic settings. L2 learning in a classroom setting may turn out to be quite different, as shown in the review by Krashen, Long, and Scarcella (1979). Second, early learners' better performance over adults does not necessarily mean that early learners can achieve nativelike phonology. As can be seen in the following section, there is a great deal of inconsistency in research findings regarding nativelike phonology among early learners.

3.3.2 Documenting Nativelikeness in L2 Phonology

While most researchers recognize the advantage enjoyed by younger learners in phonological development, there is a great deal of disagreement regard-ing whether nativelike phonology is attainable among L2 learners, includ-ing young learners. Several scholars have explicitly suggested that adult L2 learners have the cognitive capability to develop nativelike phonology in a new language. Flege (1995), for example, suggested that "the mechanisms and processes used in learning the L1 sound system, including category formation, remain intact over the life span, and can be applied to L2 learning" (p. 239) and that "even adults retain the capacities used by infants and children in suc-cessfully acquiring L1 speech, including the ability to establish new phonetic categories for the vowels and consonants encountered in an L2" (Flege, 2003, p. 328). A similar view has been expressed by Birdsong (2007), Best and Tyler (2007), and Wayland and Li (2008).

Whether nativelike competence can be achieved in L2 phonology is ulti-mately an empirical issue. Empirical findings related to the topic may be clas-sified into four types: nativelikeness in early learners, nativelikeness in adult learners, lack of nativelikeness among adult learners even after extended expo-sure to an L2, and lack of nativelikeness among early learners. The first two findings have been used to support the view that nativelikeness is achievable in an L2, and the last two findings have been used to reject such a prospect. Note the difference between this review and the preceding section. The preceding section is concerned with the comparison of learners of different onset ages with each other which says little about nativelikeness, and this section is focused on the development of nativelike phonology among L2 speakers of different ages, thus comparing L2 speakers of different AOAs to NS.

3.3.2.1 Nativelike Phonology Among Early Learners

Many studies have shown nativelike performance among early learners in both perception and production. Flege (1991) measured the VOTs associated with English voiceless stop /t/, and found that early Spanish ESL speakers (AOA: 5–6) produced VOT values comparable to those by English NS. The early Korean ESL speakers (mean AOA: 9.0) were found to be as accurate as English NS in the perception (NS: 94.3%, early ESL: 95.2%) and production (NS: 96.4%, early ESL: 91.9%) of English vowels in Baker and Trofimovich (2006). In analyzing early Korean ESL speakers' (mean AOA: 3.8) pronunciation of English consonants, Kang and Guion (2006) found no significant difference between them and English NS in measures such as VOT and F_0 values. Early learners were found to be nativelike in some aspect of phonology in Rogers and Lopez (2008) and Archila-Suerte et al. (2012). It should be noted that young learners were often found to differ from NS in some measures at the same time when they outperformed older learners and approximated nativelike performance in other measures. These can be seen in auditory word recognition accuracy (Meador et al., 2000), in the perception and production of English stops by Italian ESL speakers (MacKay, Flege, Piske & Schirru, 2001), and in the discrimination of some difficult English contrast for Spanish ESL speakers (Archila-Suerte et al., 2012).

3.3.2.2 Nativelike Phonology Among Late Learners

What is particularly noteworthy is the finding that later learners or even adults can develop nativelike phonology in a new language. Several researchers have reported such cases.

Birdsong (2007) tested 22 adult French learners who had a mean AOA of 24.5 (range: 18–61) and a mean LOR of 11 years (range: 5–32) in France. They were asked to read 21 French words and three passages. Their pronunciation of the words was analyzed in terms of vowel duration of four vowels and the VOT of three voiceless stops. The recordings of the passages were also presented to three NS of French for accentedness rating. As a group, considerable differences were found between NS and NNS in all three measures, but when the data by individual participants were examined, three of the 22 participants had vowel duration comparable to that of NS on all four vowels, nine participants produced a VOT value within the NS range on all three stops, and three participants were judged to be NS of French by all three judges. Two participants were nativelike in all three measures. These results led Birdsong to conclude that "nativelike pronunciation is not out of the grasp of late L2 learners" (p. 99).

Bongaerts, Mennen, and Slik (2000) also identified a few adult L2 speakers who passed as NS by NS judges. The participants in the study included ten NS and 30 NNS of Dutch. The latter group had a mean AOA of 21 (ranging from 11 to 34). They were asked to read ten Dutch sentences and their pronunciation was judged by 21 NS listeners. Nativelike pronunciation was defined as a mean rating score within two standard deviations of the mean rating score of the NS controls. Out of the 30 NNS, two participants were judged to be nativelike based on this criterion. In discussing the results, the authors mentioned three factors that may have contributed to the nativelike pronunciation of these two L2 speakers: language experience (i.e., married to a Dutch speaker, Dutch being the only language spoken at home), a strong interest in nativelike pronunciation, and typological proximity of the speakers' L1 and L2 (L1 being German which is related to Dutch). They did not provide information about the AOA of these two speakers, which would be informative as well in consideration of the range of AOA being 11 to 34.

Several other studies also reported nativelike pronunciation among late L2 learners. These included two late French L2 learners (AOA: 11) who were judged to be nativelike in French in Schneiderman and Desmarais (1988), a small number of late Dutch ESL speakers in Bongaerts, Planken, and Schils (1995) and Bongaerts, Van Summeren, Planken, and Schils (1997), one out of 24 German L2 speakers (L1: English) in Moyer (1999), one late (AOA: 21) Arabic L2 speaker (L1: English) in Ioup, Boustagui, El Tigi, and Moselle (1994), and three Hebrew L2 speakers (AOA: 10.5, 11, and 14) based on the judging of their spontaneous production in Abu-Rabia and Kehat (2004). In all these studies, the participants' L2 production in spontaneous communication or in a reading task involving words, sentences, and passages were presented to NS listeners for accentedness rating, and more than half of the NS judges considered them nativelike in pronunciation.

3.3.2.3 Non-Native Phonology Among Late Learners With Long LOR

In sharp contrast to the findings of the aforementioned studies, many studies documented non-nativelikeness in phonology even among adult L2 speakers who had lived in the L2 environment for an extended period of time, as measured by the length of residence (LOR) in the target language. For example, the 240 Italian-English bilingual speakers tested in Flege, Munro, and MacKay (1995a, 1995b) had a minimal LOR of 14.6 years, the late learners in MacKay,

LOR = Length of Residence

Meador, and Flege (2001) had an average LOR of 28 years, the 88 participants in the "12 and older" group in Abrahamsson and Hyltenstam (2009) had a mean LOR of 21.2 years (minimally 10), and the adult participants in Parlato-Oliveira et al. (2010) had lived in Brazil for an average of 36 years at the time of testing. Given this extended exposure to the L2, it is a fair assessment that they had reached a steady state in phonological development, as pointed out by Flege, Munro, and MacKay. Yet, their perception and production of English segments were far from nativelike. For example, the adult learners in MacKay, Meador, and Flege had an error rate close to 40% in perceiving English consonants. Only four out of the 88 participants in Abrahamsson and Hyltenstam were considered nativelike by nine or all of the ten NS judges, and none of them were able to pass as nativelike in a closer examination of their perception and production.

This lack of nativelike phonology in spite of a long LOR is corroborated by the findings of the three longitudinal studies reviewed earlier (i.e., Aoyama et al., 2004, 2008; Oh et al., 2011). These studies demonstrated that under most circumstances adult L2 learners did not make significant progress in phonological development over a period of a year.

3.3.2.4 Non-Native Phonology Among Early Learners

In contrast to the studies that showed nativelike phonology among early learners, some studies that were specifically designed to assess nativelikeness of early L2 phonology showed otherwise. Among these were a series of such studies reported by a group of researchers based in Barcelona, Spain (Pallier et al., 1997; Sebastián-Gallés & Soto-Faraco, 1999; Bosch, Costa, & Sebastián-Gallés, 2000; Sebastián-Gallés, Echeverría, & Bosch, 2005). The bilingual nature of this region offers a privileged opportunity for exploring this topic because of the availability of a large number of bilingual speakers who learned their L2 at an early age and were highly proficient in both L1 and L2. These studies were designed to compare Catalan-dominant Catalan-Spanish bilinguals and Spanish-dominant Spanish-Catalan bilinguals in the perception of Catalan-specific phonetic contrasts such as /e/ and /ɛ/ that are absent in Spanish. The Spanish-Catalan bilinguals tested in these studies were all exposed to their L2 Catalan at an early age of 3 or 4, went through a bilingual education system, lived in a bilingual environment, and were highly proficient in their L2 Catalan. These studies examined different aspects of phonological processing among these earlier bilinguals. In the study reported by Pallier, Bosch, and Sebastián-Gallés, the stimuli were seven synthesized vowel segments along the Catalan /e/-/ɛ/ continuum. The segments varied in F_1 by 30 Hz while their F_0, duration, and pitch were kept constant. These stimuli were used in a two-alternative forced-choice identification task (referred to as the classification in the report) in Experiment 1, in an AX discrimination task in Experiment 2, and in a typicality judgment task in Experiment 3. Spanish-Catalan bilinguals showed a pattern very different from that of Catalan NS in all three experiments. In Experiment 1, for example, the Catalan NS showed a typical categorical perception of these two segments. Among the seven segments along the /e/-/ɛ/ continuum, they identified the first three segments mostly as /e/ and the last three segments mostly as /ɛ/, and the mid stimulus was judged to be ambiguous. Spanish-Catalan bilinguals as a group showed little difference in their classification across the seven stimuli. The non-native performance among early Spanish-Catalan bilinguals was also shown in auditory word recognition, as reported by Sebastián-Gallés et al. (2005). They asked Catalan-Spanish bilinguals and Spanish-Catalan bilinguals to perform an auditory word recognition task. The stimuli were 66 Catalan words with /e/ and 66 Catalan words with /ɛ/, and the nonwords created by replacing one segment with the other in these words. Thus, accurate performance in the LDT was dependent on the accurate perception of these two Catalan vowels. The results, measured in terms of the A' statistics, showed a significant difference between the two groups. The A' score for the Catalan-dominant bilinguals was 0.874 and 0.953 for stimuli involving /ɛ/ and /e/, respectively, but the A' score was 0.684 and 0.687 for the Spanish-dominant bilinguals.

Non-native performance in early learners has been reported of other bilingual populations. Abrahamsson and Hyltenstam (2009) tested 195 NNS of Swedish of varying AOA in the Stockholm area. The participants, who were all L1 Spanish speakers, included 107 individuals who had an AOA of 11 or younger, and a mean LOR of 23.1 years (minimal: 10 years). When the recordings of these early bilinguals were presented to ten NS of Swedish for native language and dialect identification, 66 of them were judged to be a native Swedish speaker by nine or more judges. Thirty-one of these were further tested on their phonology (and lexis and grammar). Four tests were used for this purpose. A reading-aloud task involving three Swedish words were used for analyzing the VOT of stops in production, a forced-choice identification task involving three minimal pairs was used to assess VOT perception, and an identification task involving 30 words and a repetition task involving 28 sentences were used to assess speech perception in noise. Only five of them (with an AOA of 1, 3, 4, 6, 7) passed all four tests as nativelike.

Similarly, Rinker, Alku, Brosch, and Kiefer (2010) documented non-nativelike phonology in early Turkish-German learners with both electrophysiological and behavioral data. They compared German NS children and early Turkish-German learners in the perception of German-specific vowel contrasts and vowel contrasts common to Turkish and German. The NS and bilingual children were 5 years old, all but one early bilinguals were born in Germany, they were all going to a German kindergarten. An ERP component MMN was used to assess their sensitivity to the vowel contrasts. The results showed no difference between the monolingual and bilingual children for vowel contrasts common to both languages, but for German-specific vowel contrasts, the early bilinguals showed a less robust MMN response in comparison to NS children. This finding was replicated in behavioral data reported by Darcy and Krüger (2012) who showed that early Turkish-German bilinguals were less accurate than monolingual German children in the perception of German-specific vowel contrasts.

Non-nativelike performance among early learners has also been reported in many other studies. The early Korean-English learners had accent rating scores significantly lower as a group than the NS controls in Flege, Yeni-Komshian, and Liu (1999, AOA=5 or younger) and were less accurate in discriminating English vowels in Tsukada et al. (2005, mean AOA≈9). The early learners in MacKay, Meador, and Flege (2001) had a mean AOA of 7 years, a mean LOR of 40 years. When presented with English nonwords in noise, their error rates in the identification of consonants were 35% and 38% for syllable-initial and syllable-final consonants, compared to 31% and 24% for NS. The early Spanish-English bilinguals in Højen and Flege (2006) had a mean AOA of 6 and LOR of 25 years. Their perception of English vowel contrasts was tested in a AXB discrimination task with varying inter-stimulus intervals (ISI). They showed a significantly lower accuracy for some contrasts at a 0 ms ISI.

Such conflicting findings, particularly between nativelike phonology in adult learners and non-nativelike phonology in early learners, raise the question of how to assess nativelikeness in phonology. Two issues are of paramount importance. The first is the selection of the right segments, phonetic features or contrasts for investigation. Segments or contrasts differ in the level of their difficulty for NNS (see Section 3.4.3 for more detail). For example, the NNS in Pallier et al. (2001) and Archila-Suerte et al. (2012) showed nativelike performance on some phonetic contrasts but not on those L2-specific or new contrasts. Thus, the selection of the target structure for investigation will directly affect the outcome of a study. For the assessment of nativelike phonology, more valid data come from segments and contrasts that are specific to the target language and that have proved to be difficult for the individuals from a particular L1 background. Nativelike performance involving easy segments or contrasts is of little use or value for the study of the acquirability and nativelikeness topic.

The second issue is how to define and operationalize nativelikeness in assessment. A majority of studies that have reported nativelike phonology in late or adult learners used global measures such as accentedness rating by NS as an assessment method (e.g., Abu-Rabia & Kehat, 2004; Birdsong, 2007; Bongaerts et al., 2000; Ioup et al., 1994). In this approach, participants are asked to read a few words or sentences and the recordings are given to a group of NS judges for the rating of overall accentedness. This accentedness judgment method is an intuitive and efficient one on the assumption that non-nativeness in phonology should result in perceivable accent by NS. If NS judges consider some speech samples as nonaccented, it is reasonable to conclude that the speakers have attained nativelike phonology.

However, this method has its limitations. The first is related to the first issue. When a small number of words or sentences are used, e.g., ten sentences in Bongaerts et al. (2000) and six sentences in Bongaerts et al. (1997), there is always the risk that the stimuli do not include the difficult segments or contrasts. The second is the criteria to be adopted for determining nativelikeness. For example, it is difficult to determine how many NS judges are needed and how many of them should provide a nativelike rating in order to determine the nativelike status. Ioup et al. (1994) classified Julie as nativelike in phonology based on the positive evaluation of eight out of the 13 NS judges, but the other five judges did consider her as a non-native speaker. Additionally, the ratio of non-native and native speech samples provided to the NS judges will affect the outcome of their evaluation, as shown in Flege and Fletcher (1992). Finally, NS evaluations may come into conflict with the results of acoustic analysis. For example, out of the 31 early learners who were judged to be native speakers of Swedish by NS listeners, only five were found to be nativelike in close phonetic scrutiny. This raises the question of whether accent judgment by NS should be taken as the only criterion for determining nativelike phonology (see Section 2.4.2 for more discussion of this issue).

If selecting inadequate phonetic structures and using a global measure for assessing nativelikeness may contribute to an overestimate of L2 speakers' nativelikeness, comparing L2 learners with monolingual L1 speakers faces the intrinsic problem of comparing bilinguals with monolinguals, which may result in an underestimate of nativelikeness. Given the interaction of the two language systems, the mental representations of phonetic categories in early L2 learners, no matter how proficient they are, are likely to be different from those of monolingual speakers. This difference can be detected when acoustic analysis, e.g., the comparison of VOT values, is used. This raises the question of whether monolingual speakers are adequate controls for assessing L2 speakers' nativelikeness where acoustic analysis is adopted. These methodological issues have to be kept in mind while exploring phonological acquirability issues.

3.3.3 Explaining Age-Related Differences

Researchers have suggested many explanations for age-related differences in language learning in general and in phonological development in particular. Several factors, collectively referred to as the affective factors, were suggested in the 1970s and 1980s. They included attitude, motivation, empathy, ego permeability, anxiety, and self-consciousness. Guiora et al. (1972) suggested, for example, that

> in the early stages of development the boundaries of the language ego are in a state of flux and, hence, pronunciation ability is quite malleable. . . . Once these boundaries become set, in terms of the degree to which they will be allowed to fluctuate under normal circumstances, the ability to approximate authentic pronunciation in a second language will be drastically reduced.
>
> (p. 422)

A similar view was expressed by Taylor (1974) who stated that

> the affective variables of motivation, empathy, ego-boundaries, and the desire to identify with a cultural group all seem to contribute to the uniform success of children in learning their native language. Whereas child language acquisition seems to be a means toward an end—socialization—and lack of such motivation in adults and the absence of a positive attitude toward language learning and the target language and culture may be responsible for the lack of success in most adult second language learning.
>
> (p. 33)

Similar views have been put forward by Schumann (1975) and Neufeld (1979). However, such an affective or social explanation was considered "inadequate" by some researchers (e.g., Long, 1990), and is pursued to a less extent in recent research (but see Moyer, 2007 for more recent discussion of the role of attitude).

This section outlines three neurolinguistic and cognitive approaches to the explanation of age-related differences in phonology: neurophysiological, neurocognitive, and L1 entrenchment approaches.

3.3.3.1 Neurophysiological Perspectives

Some researchers explained the age-related differences from a neurophysiological perspective. At least two specific versions of it can be identified, all attributing child–adult differences to how the brain seems to lose its plasticity with increasing age, particularly around puberty. One of these versions relates age-related differences to lateralization of the language function to the left hemisphere. Some clinical data suggests that language loss resulting from brain damage can be reversed if it occurred before puberty. When the left hemisphere is affected, the language function can be handled by the right hemisphere. However, this reversal is much less likely if brain damage occurred after puberty. In Penfield's (1965) words,

> after the age of ten or twelve, the general functional conations have been established and fixed for the speech cortex. After that, the speech center cannot be transferred to the cortex of the lesser side and set up all over again. This "nondominant" area that might have been used for speech is now occupied with the business of perception.
>
> (p. 792)

This is also the ages when foreign accents cannot be eradicated. This led some researchers to believe that lateralization is the cause of adults not being able to develop nativelike pronunciation and to the proposal of the critical period hypothesis (Lenneberg, 1967; Penfield & Roberts, 1959).

Representing this view in the SLA literature is Scovel (1969, 1988) who stated that

> the simultaneous occurrence of brain lateralization and the advent of foreign accents is too great a coincidence to be left neglected. It seems reasonable to me that the ability to master a language without a foreign accent before the age of about twelve is directly related to the fact that lateralization has not yet become permanent; similarly, it seems apparent that the *inability* of adults to master a language without a foreign accent after the age of about twelve is directly related to the fact that lateralization has become permanent.
>
> (1969, p. 252)

He further argued that it is not the lateralization itself that leads to an adult's inability to acquire nativelike pronunciation, but the plasticity of the brain that allows a child to relocate the language function to a nondominant hemisphere. However, he came short of specifying the nature of this plasticity or what is meant by brain plasticity. He also explained why foreign accents may persist while nativelike syntax is attainable. He reasoned that "sound patterns are produced by actual motor activity and are thus directly initiated by neurophysiological mechanisms. To the best of my knowledge, lexical and syntactic patterns lack any such 'neurophysiological reality'" (1969, p. 252). Scovel rejected the view that the real difference between child and adult language learning is the presence of the L1 in the case of adult learners that interferes with L2 learning, or the "interference theory" in his words by citing cases of children learning an L2 successfully. He asked "if the interference theory is at all valid, how can it account for the fact that children are able to overcome first language interference whereas adults cannot?" (p. 247).

A different version of the neurophysiological approach is to attribute child–adult differences to a reduced capability of the brain in making new connections as a result of neuron maturation. Representing this view is a proposal made by Pulvermüller and Schumann (1994). Central to this proposal is a hypothesized relationship between myelination and brain plasticity. A nerve cell, or neuron, has an axon that reaches out to those of other neurons for the transmission of information. Myelination is a process whereby the axons of neurons become wrapped up by myelin, a substance in the glial cells, for the rapid conduction of electrical signals between neurons. It is an important part of the maturation of the brain. Even though they acknowledged that "the causal links connecting myelination and plasticity loss are still unknown" (p. 710), they went ahead with the hypothesis that this myelination process may lead to the loss of synaptic plasticity such that it becomes harder for the myelinated neurons to make new connections or to strengthen existing ones. Assuming that language learning, like any other learning, is dependent on the building of new connections among neurons, myelination makes language learning more difficult. They also suggested, on the basis of the research reported in Conel (1939–1976) and others, that among the three regions of the brain, the primary sensory and motor areas mature first, followed by the language areas, and then by higher-order association areas. The maturation of the neuron in the language region reaches its full level around puberty. "Accordingly, neurons in the perisylvian language cortex are left with reduced plasticity around puberty" (p. 713). That explains why learning a language around or after puberty becomes difficult. As they stated, "gradual maturation of the perisylvian region of the cortex leads to a loss of plasticity therein, making it hard to acquire phonological and syntactic knowledge" (p. 717).

Unlike the lateralization explanation which lacks a specific account of the plasticity of the brain or how lateralization affects language learning, this proposal offers a more specific explanation at a cellular level that links language learning difficulty to neuron maturation. It is also posited to explain the different sensitive periods for different aspects of language. The maturation of the motor cortices occurs earlier, which leads to the earlier ending of the sensitive period for phonological development. The maturation occurs later for the higher-order association areas, which explains why the development of semantic and pragmatic knowledge is less affected by age.[4]

3.3.3.2 A Neurocognitive or Neuropsychological Approach

Some other researchers consider age-related difference as a result of learners of different ages adopting different cognitive strategies or processes which is an outcome of the maturation of the brain. Thus, this approach is similar to the first one in considering brain maturation as the ultimate cause of age-related differences, but it differs from the first in postulating an intermediate factor, the cognitive strategies, that links brain maturation to language learning. This approach has been taken, albeit implicitly, by those who reported on exceptionally talented language learners (e.g., Abu-Rabia & Kehat, 2004; Ioup et al., 1994; Schneiderman & Desmarais, 1988). They recognized the changes cerebral maturation brings out in how language learning is approached in late or adult learners, and attributed the success of these talented learners to their neurocognitive flexibility. A specific proposal linking neurocognitive processes to language learning at different ages was outlined in Archila-Suerte et al. (2012). The point of departure of their proposal was the difference in the timeline of maturation of the different part of the brain, similar to the view proposed by Pulvermüller and Schumann (1994). The subcortical areas that support sensorimotor and implicit learning matures early and the cortical areas that regulate higher-cognitive/explicit learning matures later. They speculated that younger learners are able to use the implicit and sensorimotor processes which are best fit for the establishment and discrimination of phonetic categories while being exposure to both L1 and L2 input. Thus, they are able to develop nativelike phonological representations in any language they are exposed to at an early age. Adult learners on the other hand have to rely on explicit and higher-cognitive processes which are only effective in developing between-category discriminations.[5] However, the proposal comes short of specifying why adult learners cannot use the implicit processes.

3.3.3.3 L1 Entrenchment

Many researchers attribute the difficulty older learners have to the presence of the established L1 phonetic categories. All models related to L2 phonological processing have emphasized the role L1 plays in L2 phonological processing and development. Two of them speak directly to the age issue, i.e., the SLM and the NLMM (see Section 2.5). Both models postulate that after the establishment of the phonetic system of one's native language, L2 sounds will be filtered through the existing L1 system, thus making it difficult to develop nativelike phonology. The relevance of age in this context is that the phonetic system of the native language is usually less well established among younger learners and thus the learning of a new phonetic system is less affected. As one gets older, his or her L1 phonetic system become more established and consolidated. As a result, it interferes with the learning of the new phonetic system more. As Flege puts it,

> as L1 phonetic categories develop slowly through childhood and into early adolescence, they become more likely to perceptually assimilate L2 vowels and consonants. If instances of an L2 speech sound category persist in being identified as instances of an L1 speech sound, category formation for the L2 speech sound will be blocked.
>
> (Flege, 2003, p. 328)

This idea has been referred to as the interaction hypothesis (e.g., Fl
Baker et al., 2008). Thus, in both the SLM and NLM model, it is no
per se, but the experiences of learning the native language that affect L
ing. Older learners are at a disadvantage in this regard because of their
experiences in the L1 that lead to a more consolidated L1 phonetic sys
Both models also share two additional views: a) there is no sudden drop of
ability to develop nativelike phonology around puberty, as predicted by th
critical period hypothesis, and b) adults also have the ability to develop new
phonetic categories.

There are also differences between the two models. The NLMM seems to
focus more on the impact of experiences in an individual's first year on subsequent speech perception while the SLM is interested in how L1 influences L2
phonology across a wider age span and more in production than in perception.
But more importantly, the two models differ in what underlies L1 entrenchment. Kuhl's proposal is rooted at the neurophysiological level. According to
her native language neural commitment hypothesis (Kuhl, 2004), early exposure to one's native language allows infants to develop a sensitivity to the
phonetic distinctions of his or her native language through statistical learning, i.e., detecting the regularities and patterns through a large number of
instances in the input. This

> results in a commitment of the brain's neural networks to the patterns
> of variation that describe a particular language. This learning promotes
> further learning of patterns that conform to those initially learned, while
> interfering with the learning of patterns that do not conform to those
> initially learned.
>
> (p. 832)[6]

A piece of evidence linking neural commitment to L1 and its interference
with L2 is reported by Kuhl and colleagues (Kuhl, Conboy, Padden, Nelson, &
Pruitt, 2005). They found that infants who were better at discriminating non-
native phonetic contrasts at 7 months showed slower L1 development in the
coming years. They suggested that a prolonged sensitivity to non-native contrasts and slower development of L1 skills in later years share the same cause: a
delayed neural commitment to the L1 phonetic patterns. There is some recent
research evidence for the language shaping of brain connectivity. Goucha,
Anwander, Stamatakis, Tyler, and Friederici (2015) hypothesized that languages differ in the specific cognitive processing it requires of a speaker. For
example, there is more morphosyntactic processing involved in German use
and more lexicosemantic processing in English use. Such different processes
are handled by different parts of the brain or require different types of connectivity. This means that language use may help shape the anatomical connec-
tivities of the brain. To test this idea, they compared brain activities involved

an, English, and Mandarin Chinese speakers.
v patterns involving different structures of
d these different languages, thus support-
the brain reflects the specific demands
ng is certainly consistent with Kuhl's native
hypothesis.

pproach to explaining L1 entrenchment. He (e.g.,
d a neurological explanation for three reasons. First,
lop nativelike phonology. Second, early learning does not
t-free pronunciation. Third, the AOA factor is often con-
other factors that may also affect the learning outcomes, such
ount of L2 input and the extent of L1 use. He considered L2 input
use as more important explanations of age-related differences. Younger
arners often have more and better L2 input and they are less likely to continue using their L1, which lead to their better phonological development. Thus, Flege's approach to L1 entrenchment is more experience based.

Similar L1 entrenchment views are also broadly recognized in the study of SLA, particularly from a cognitive perspective. In promoting an information processing approach to explaining age-related differences, Kennedy (1988) stated that

> if the L1 phonological system has been unitized before the acquisition of L2 begins, then the unitized system of the first language would resist any kind of alteration or expansion to include any new sounds from the L2. Perhaps, as is observable in the real world, learners, instead, force the new sounds to conform to the closest sound in their first language, thereby preserving the unitized system.
>
> (pp. 483–484)

Similarly, MacWhinney (2005) stated that "repeated use of L1 leads to its ongoing entrenchment. This entrenchment operates differentially across linguistic areas, with the strongest entrenchment occurring in output phonology and the least entrenchment in the area of lexicon" (p. 63).

In sum, researchers differ in how they explain age-related differences in phonological development. It should be pointed out that these different approaches do not have to be exclusive to each other. Many factors may play a role in a phenomenon as complicated as human language development. A challenge, though, lies in how to make more specific and precise predictions about what factors contribute to age-related differences under what circumstances.

3.4 Other Factors

In addition to an individual's L1 and age of acquisition, many other factors have been examined in relation to L2 phonological processing and development. These include, but are not limited to, motivation and attitude (e.g.,

Bongaerts et al., 1997; Moyer, 1999, 2007), gender (e.g., Thompson, 1991; Flege et al., 1995a), aptitude (e.g., Granena & Long, 2013), learning strategies such as self-regulation (Moyer, 2014), empathy (Berkowitz, 1989; Ibrahim, Eviatar, & Leikin, 2008), anxiety (Woodrow, 2006), musical ability (Slevc & Miyake, 2006), vocabulary size (Bundgaard-Nielsen, Best, & Tyler, 2011; Bundgaard-Nielsen, Best, Kroos, & Tyler, 2012), number of years of formal instruction (Bundgaard-Nielsen et al., 2012), talker-listener pairing (Bent & Bradlow, 2003; Bent, Kewley-Port, & Ferguson, 2010), and context of learning (study abroad vs. at home or formal vs. immersion; Levy & Law II, 2010; Pérez-Vidal, 2014; Simões, 1996). This section reviews studies that examined two learner-related factors: L2 experiences and L1 use, which have received more attention than other factors. It ends with a brief discussion of segment-related factors and the effect of training.

3.4.1 LOR, L2 Experiences, and L2 Proficiency

Many studies of L2 phonological processing examined these three related factors: the length of residence (LOR), L2 experience, or L2 proficiency. In studies where the role of LOR was explored, this variable is either treated as a categorical one or a continuum. In the former case, the participants are divided into groups based on the LOR, e.g., two groups of 3 and 5 years of LOR in Flege et al. (2006), two groups (5–11 years vs. 12–18 years) in Oyama (1982), and two LOR groups (2 vs. 10 years) in Wang, Behne, and Jiang (2008). In the latter case, the participants were not grouped based on the LOR. Instead, the LOR variable is treated as a covariate in data analysis or included in correlational or regression analysis (e.g., Bundgaard-Nielsen et al., 2012; MacKay, Meador, & Flege, 2001). Some researchers tested the same group of participants multiple times with a relatively long interval between testing. For example, there was an interval of 1.2 years in Flege et al. (2006), 1.1 years in Aoyama et al. (2008), and 1 year in Aoyama et al. (2004). Since the participants were living in the L2 environment between the two tests, one may consider such a design as a special case of LOR manipulated as a within-participant variable.

The L2 experience variable has been defined in multiple ways. It is common to define it in terms of the LOR in the L2 country. For example, the short, medium, and extended L2 experience groups in Trofimovich and Baker (2006) had a LOR of 3 months, 3 years, and 10 years. The "inexperienced" and "experienced" learner groups in Flege and Fletcher (1992) were also differentiated in terms of the LOR which was 0.7 and 14 years, respectively. Where L2 experiences were operationalized by means other than the LOR, the specific method varied a great deal. Simon and D'Hulster (2012) defined their three experience groups in terms of class placement (fourth-year English majors, first-year English majors, and non-English majors). In Sundara, Polka, and Genesee (2006) language experience referred to the presence or absence of simultaneous exposure to two languages. In Wang, Behne, Jongman, & Sereno (2004) study of hemispheric lateralization of Mandarin tone, linguistic experience refers to whether an individual had been exposed to a tonal language. Cebrian (2006) also defined experiences in terms of exposure where the "inexperienced group" were Catalan speakers living in Barcelona and with minimum exposure to English and the "experienced" group were Catalan speakers living in Canada. One of the criteria Guion, Flege, and Loftin (2000) used to define their three L2 experience groups was whether the L2 was used in their job. Levy (2009) classified her three experience groups based on a) with or without exposure, and b) with or without immersion.

The operationalization of L2 proficiency is done most frequently in two ways. One is based on class placement. For example, the beginner group included first-year English majors in Hanoi and the advanced group included graduate students studying in Australia in Nguyễn et al. (2008). Altenberg (2005) also divided the participants into beginning, intermediate, and advanced learners based on class placement. The second is the participants' performance in a language test. A variety of tests have been used for this purpose, e.g., the Woodcock Language Proficiency Battery-Revised for assessing English and Spanish proficiency in Archila-Suerte et al. (2012), the Dialang online diagnostic language testing system for assessing English proficiency in White, Melhorn, and Mattys (2010), the Test of Adolescent and Adult Language for assessing English proficiency in Chakraborty and Goffman (2011), and the Oxford Placement Test in Pinet and Iverson (2010).

These three variables, LOR, L2 experience, and L2 proficiency, are considered together because they are closely related. The LOR variable directly reflects the amount of L2 exposure and experiences learners have. This can be seen most clearly in the definition of L2 experience in terms of LOR in many studies. We can also reasonably assume that an L2 learner's proficiency is closely related to their amount of L2 exposure and experience. Thus, we can consider all these as composite "experience" factors.

Numerous studies have considered these factors in relation to phonological processing.[7] The findings are very complicated, to say the least. Many studies showed a positive relationship between them and the participants' performance in phonological processing. For example, in one of the earliest studies that examined the experience factor, Flege (1987) included three groups of L2 French speakers who differed in their French experiences. The least experienced group were college students who had a nine-month stay in France, the more experienced group included individuals who had an advanced degree in French and were French instructors at a university, and the most experienced group were those who had married French native speakers and had lived in France for an extended period of time (mean 11.7 years). They were asked to read aloud phrases and sentences that contained three French segments: /t/, /u/, and /y/. Their speech output was analyzed in terms of the acoustic values related to these segments, i.e., VOT for /t/, and F_2 for /u/ and /y/. In the /t/

data, the more and most experienced groups showed a VOT value much closer to that of NS than the least experienced group did. The same trend was present in the data for the two vowels. The results provided support for the role of experience in the area of segment production. In the area of segment perception, Wang et al. (2008) tested Chinese ESL speakers on the perception of English fricatives in a six-alternative identification task. The stimuli involved six English fricatives: /f/, /v/, /θ/, /ð/, /s/, and /z/. The materials were presented under four modality conditions (audio only, visual only, audio-visual congruent, and audio-visual incongruent) and two degradation conditions (with and without noise). The ESL participants were divided into two LOR groups with the mean number of years of LOR being 2 and 10. The long LOR groups outperformed the short LOR group for most of the measures. In two studies where three groups of Korean ESL group with varying LORs in the US (<1, 3, and 10 years) were tested, a positive relationship between LOR and perception and production of English vowel was reported by Baker and Trofimovich (2006) and between LOR and the production of stress patterns (particularly stress timing) was reported by Trofimovich and Baker (2006).

More evidence for a positive effect of experience on phonological processing can be found in Flege, Bohn et al. (1997), Guion et al. (2000), Levy (2009), Ito and Strange (2009), Dmitrieva et al. (2010), Pinet, Iverson, and Huckvale (2011), Ingvalson et al. (2011), and Simon and D'Hulster (2012). The effect of L2 proficiency on phonological processing can be found in Hardison and Saigo (2010), Chakraborty and Goffman (2011), and Archila-Suerte et al. (2012).

In the sense that a positive relationship between experience and phonological processing performance is expected, what is more interesting is the finding that these variables did not affect L2 speakers' performance. Among these studies, Flege (1988) reported no difference in pronunciation between the two groups of adult Taiwanese ESL speakers who differed in LOR (1.1 vs. 5.1 years). Flege et al. (2006) asked children and adult Korean ESL speakers to read English sentences and their pronunciation was judged by NS listeners in terms of accentedness. Both the children and adults were divided into two LOR groups, with the mean LOR being 3 and 5 years for the two groups. There was little difference found between the two LOR groups in accentedness. There was no significant difference in accentedness between the first recording and the second one 1.2 years later, which was also consistent with the lack of the LOR influence. White et al. (2010) tested Hungarian ESL speakers of three proficiency levels on the use of lexical knowledge as a segmentation strategy in a priming paradigm, and found all three groups of ESL participants were similar in being able to use lexical knowledge for segmentation. Hao (2012) compared NNS of Mandarin with a tonal language background (Cantonese) and without a tonal language background (English) in the perception and production of Mandarin tones. The two groups showed no significant difference in accuracy and error patterns. Finally, Cebrian

(2006) also showed no relationship between L2 experience and phonological processing. Specifically, she tested Catalan ESL speakers' use of temporal and spectral cues in the perception of the English lax-tense vowel contrast. The participants in the first experiment included Catalan speakers with little experience in English (the inexperienced group) and Catalan speakers who lived in Toronto (the experienced group). The two groups showed no apparent difference in their performance in the perceptual assimilation task. The participants in the second experiment included two groups of adult ESL speakers, one living in Canada (mean LOR being 25 years), the other being undergraduate English majors living in Spain. Their use of the temporal and spectral cues in the perception of the English lax-tense distinction was assessed in a vowel identification task. Both groups were found to rely on the duration cue, rather than the spectral cue as NS English speakers did, in the distinction of the contrast.

Some studies produced mixed results. In Levy (2009) where three groups of English-speaking participants differing in their French experience were tested on the perception of two French vowels /œ/ and /y/. The perception of French vowel /œ/ by English speakers showed an experience effect but not the perception of the vowel /y/. Altenberg (2005) asked Spanish ESL speakers of three different proficiency levels to a) judge if a consonant cluster was acceptable (the judgment task), b) listen to nonwords and identify the consonant at the beginning of the nonwords (the perception task), and c) perform a picture-naming task (the production task). The test materials included words and nonwords that included a consonant cluster that was legal in both English and Spanish, that was legal English but illegal in Spanish, and was illegal in both languages. The participants in the three proficiency groups showed no difference in the first and third task, but there was a proficiency effect for the second perception task. Flege and Liu (2001) tested Chinese ESL speakers on the perception of English consonants. The participants were divided into four groups on the basis of both their student status (students vs. nonstudents) and LOR (2.5 vs. 7.3 years for students and 1.7 vs. 6.6 years for nonstudents). A significant LOR effect was found only for students.

The conflicting findings for the role of experience and proficiency on phonological processing may have mixed causes. One such cause may have to do with the fact that the experience variable was easily confounded with other variables. For example, the LOR and AOA variables were confounded such that the long LOR group had lower AOA (arrival in Canada) than the short LOR group (11 vs. 21) in Wang et al. (2008). This created a biasing situation in favor of a positive relationship between LOR and performance. An opposite scenario appeared in Cebrian (2006). The two L2 experience groups not only differed in the amount of exposure and experiences, but also in the amount of formal instruction. The less experienced group had received more formal instruction than the experienced group. Thus, she commented that the lack of a difference between the more and less experienced Catalan ESL speakers may be attributed to the availability of metalinguistic knowledge among the less experienced group. Another cause of conflicting findings may arise from the inconsistency in how the experience variable is manipulated. An LOR difference of 3 vs. 5 years (Flege et al., 2006) is certainly quite different from a difference of 13 years (e.g., Flege & Fletcher, 1992). A small LOR difference may lead to the observed lack of an LOR effect, as Flege and Fletcher pointed out.

A more complicated cause may be that different types of test materials or learners may respond differently to the experience manipulation. It is difficult to imagine that different phonological structures or units (e.g., different segments or contrasts), different aspects of phonology (e.g., tone perception vs. stress production), or different phonological phenomena (e.g., the use of different cues in stress perception vs. the use of lexical knowledge in segmentation) are affected by L2 experience in similar ways. Thus, when different phonological structures, aspects, or phenomena are tested across studies, mixed findings are expected. The observation of a proficiency effect in the perception task but not in the judgment and production tasks in Altenberg (2005) is an example of how processing tasks adopted may affect the outcome. White et al. (2010) explained the observed lack of a proficiency effect by suggesting that the use of lexical knowledge in segmentation may be achieved with limited L2 proficiency. The absence of the proficiency effect in Dupoux et al. (2008) may be related to the high level of difficulty in stress perception among individuals whose L1 does not use stress as a distinctive feature, and the proficiency manipulation in the study was not powerful enough to avoid a floor effect under such a circumstance. Finally, different types of learners may respond to the experience manipulation differently, as shown in the finding that younger learners, but not adults, produced significant progress between Time 1 and Time 2 in Aoyama et al. (2004, 2008). This is so maybe because children and adult learners may display different developmental trajectories. In addition to the possibility that children may have access to more and better input than adults do, as suggested by Aoyama et al. (2004), children may have a longer developmental trajectory to reach a higher level of phonological development than adults do. Thus, they are more responsive to LOR manipulation than adults are. In the case of adults, it is more likely that "after L2 learners have spent a certain amount of time in a predominantly L2-speaking environment, increases in LOR will cease to have a further ameliorative effect on L2 pronunciation" (Piske, MacKay, & Flege, 2001, p. 210).

In sum, research on this topic suggests that we should not expect L2 experience variables to influence phonological processing in a uniform way, as this influence can be moderated by many linguistic and learner factors. Any finding regarding this topic has to be interpreted in relation to its specific experimental circumstances.

3.4.2 L1 Use

An L2 speaker may continue to use his or her L1, even while living in an L2 environment. The extent of L1 use is influenced by many factors such as the size of the L1 speaker community, the language used by the other members of the family, and the type of job one has. In research, the L1 use variable is usually manipulated based on information from participants' self-reports. This can be a general estimate in the percentage of L1 use in daily life, or a more detailed approach can be taken where a participant rates their extent of L1 use in relation to a list of daily situations (e.g., at home, at work, listening to music, talking with friends). The L1 use variable is usually treated as a categorical one such that the participants are divided into low and high L1-use groups.

Flege and colleagues have reported many studies on this topic that involved Italian ESL speakers residing in the USA. One of the earliest studies was reported by Flege, Frieda, and Nozawa (1997). They divided their Italian ESL speakers into two groups based on the amount of L1 use, 3% for the low-use group and 36% for the high-use group. The two groups were matched in terms of chronological age, AOA, LOR. They were asked to read aloud English sentences and their recordings were evaluated by 24 English NS in terms of accentedness. A significant group difference was found in the accentedness rating scores. The low-use group was considered to be less accented than the high-use group. This finding was replicated in Piske et al. (2001). Further evidence for a positive effect of less L1 use on L2 phonological processing can be found in several subsequent studies involving the same population, such as in vowel production (Flege et al., 2003; Flege & MacKay, 2004; Piske et al., 2002), in consonant perception (MacKay, Meador, & Flege, 2001), and in word recognition and repetition (Meador, Flege, & MacKay, 2000). At the same time, Flege and colleagues also reported a lack of L1 use effect in the production and perception of English consonants by Italian ESL speakers (MacKay, Flege, Piske, & Schirru, 2001; Flege, MacKay, & Meador, 1999). I am not aware of any explanation from these authors regarding why an L1 use effect was found in some studies but not in the other studies involving the same population.

The role of L1 use has also been explored among other L2 speaker populations. Guion, Flege, and Loftin (2000) reported another study that was also specifically designed to assess the role of L1 use. The participants were 30 Quichua speakers who learned Spanish as a second language at a young age (mean AOA being 6.4). A questionnaire was used to assess their extent of L1 use. It consisted of seven questions specifying language use situations such as at home and with friends. The participants had to indicate whether they usually used Quichua, used both languages equally, or usually used Spanish for those situations. They were divided into low L1 use, mid L1 use, and high L1 use groups based on their responses. The participants in these groups were matched in chronological age, AOA, and year of education. The speech samples were generated when the participants were asked to repeat sentences in Spanish and Quichua. These samples were presented, along with those generated by five Spanish NS, to NS of Quichua and Spanish who were asked to rate the accentedness of the speech samples on a 1–9 scale, with 1 being most accented. The results showed a relationship between accentedness and L1 use. The participants with more L1 use were perceived to be more accented. The mean rating scores were 6.8, 5.9, and 4.7 for the low, mid, and high L1-use groups, respectively. In contrast, there was no significant difference in the accentedness scores for their L1 Quichua among the three groups. Thus, the extent of L1 use affects L2 pronunciation, but not L1 pronunciation. Additionally, Baker and Trofimovich (2006) included the use of the participants' L1 Korean as a variable for analysis and found a significant correlation between L1 use and the participants' perception and production performance involving English vowels. In a case study reported by Abu-Rabia and Kehat (2004), the authors also attributed a participant's low accent scores to continued use of L1. In contrast, Ingvalson et al. (2011) did not find an L1 use effect while examining the production and perception of the English /r/-/l/ contrast among Japanese ESL speakers.

Attempts have been made to explain what underlies the L1 use effect. Piske, MacKay, and Flege (2001) ruled out the possibility that the L1 use effect is a result of a lack of L2 practice among the high-L1-use individuals on the basis that their participants had lived in an L2 environment in decades. Instead, on several occasions, Flege and colleague offered an input-based explanation. Assuming that L2 speakers develop composite categories that include features of L1 categories and L2 categories that are similar, according the SLM (see Section 2.5.1), the amount of input in the two languages will determine whether L1 or L2 features will dominate the composite category. Low and high L1-users are likely to differ in the amount of input they receive in the two languages, with more L1 input available to the high L1 users than to low L1 users. This means the composite category will be more likely to be an L1-dominant one. In the case of low L1-users, more L2 input will move the composite category toward the L2 end, thus leading to more nativelike perception and production (e.g., Flege & MacKay, 2004; Piske et al., 2001). Furthermore, Flege and MacKay also suggested that high L1 users may have stronger L1 representations, thus producing more interference in the formation of L2 specific categories, and they are more likely to be exposed to L1-accented L2 input, which may also affect the formation of L2 categories adversely.

3.4.3 Segment-Related Factors

In addition to L1, age of acquisition, L2 experiences, and the extent of L1 use, research has shown that L2 speakers do not find all L2 segments or contrasts equally easy or difficult. Where several segments or contrasts are involved in a study, it is almost always the case that some are harder than others. This may result from different overlap patterns between L1 and L2 categories, as reviewed in Section 3.2.2, but they cannot explain all the differences in learning difficulty across phonetic categories. For example, it has been widely documented that the second Mandarin tone or the Tone 2-Tone 3 contrast is the most difficult among Mandarin tones or tone contrasts for English speakers (e.g., Lee, Tao, & Bond, 2009). As English does not employ lexical tones, L1–L2 overlap patterns are hardly relevant in this context. It seems that there are certain intrinsic properties associated with some segmental or suprasegmental categories that make them more difficult to learn or process. We may consider such properties as structure-related factors.

Such structure-related differences in processing difficulty is well documented. For example, among the four pairs of short-long vowels of Swedish used in McAllister et al. (2002), there were two pairs of mid vowels and two pairs of nonmid vowels. NNS of Swedish whose L1s did not recognize duration as a distinctive feature (Spanish and English) showed nativelike performance on the nonmid vowels, but their performance was quite deviant from that of NS on the mid vowels. These authors attributed this difference to the fact that the spectral differences between long and short vowels were much smaller for mid vowel pairs than nonmid vowel pairs. On the assumption that spectral cues also aid in discrimination of short and long vowels among these NNS, this means that mid vowels are more difficult to discriminate because of fewer spectral cues available. Similarly, among the three English vowel contrasts tested in Peltola et al. (2007), /i/-/e/, /e/-/ɪ/, and /i/-/ɪ/, the Finnish ESL speakers showed a significant MMN only to the most distant English contrast /i/-/e/. The other two pairs elicited no significant MMN.

The perception and production of Mandarin tones by NNS offers another good example. Research has shown that the four lexical tones, or different pairings of them, are not equally difficult. Tone 2 or Tones 2–3 contrast has been found to cause more trouble than other tones or tone contrast (e.g., Gottfried & Suiter, 1997; Hao, 2012; Lee, Tao, & Bond, 2010; So & Best, 2010). In contrast, Tone 4 not only produces better identification but is also less affected by input modification (Lee et al., 2010). Researchers have attributed the differential difficulties associated with lexical tones to the acoustic properties of these tones. Lee et al. suggested, for example, that "Tone 4 has a distinct F_0 movement, which may be easier to detect perceptually" (p. 237). Hao also indicated that the greater confusion for Tone 2 and Tone 3 is related to the greater acoustic similarity between the two tones and the phenomenon of tone sandhi which further reduces the difference between the two tones.

There have been few systematic investigations into what acoustic properties make perception and production particularly difficult for L2 speakers or principled explanations for such segment or contrast-related difficulty. One potential explanation has been offered on the basis of the markedness concept.

A linguistic structure is considered marked when it is less basic, less frequent, or less natural than a related structure. The concept can also be stated as an implicational relationship such that if the presence of Structure A implies the presence of Structure B, Structure A is more marked than Structure B. Eckman (1977, 1991, 2008) proposed that a) phonological processing difficulties are not only affected by L1–L2 differences but also by the markedness relationship of the two languages involved (markedness differential hypothesis) and b) phonological processing of an interlanguage is the same as that of the native language in following universal implicational generalizations (the interlanguage structural conformity hypothesis). These proposals have generated only limited research (e.g., Eckman, 1991; Carlisle, 1997, 1998), perhaps because they are relevant to only a restricted set of phonological phenomena to which implicational universals apply.

3.4.4 Phonetic Training

Many studies have examined the effect of phonetic training on L2 phonological processing and the factors that may mediate this effect. A frequently adopted approach in this research is to identify an L2 phonological phenomenon that is difficult for NS and assess the effect of training in a pretest-training-posttest design. Frequently used target phonetic features for training included the distinction of the English /l/-/r/ contrast among Japanese learners (e.g., Bradlow, Pisoni, Akahane-Yamada, & Tohkura, 1997; Bradlow, Akahane-Yamada, Pisoni, & Tohkura, 1999; Logan, Lively, & Pisoni, 1991; Strange & Dittmann, 1984), the Japanese vowel duration contrast (e.g., Hirata et al., 2007; Kiyonaga, Ito, & Masataka, 2009), and the Thai or Chinese tone contrasts (e.g., Wang, Jongman, & Sereno, 2003; Wayland & Li, 2008). Other training studies have also considered issues such as the adaption to accented speech (e.g., Sidaras, Alexander, & Nygaard, 2009), the effect of perception training on production (e.g., Bradlow et al., 1997), and the effect on word recognition (e.g., Dufour, Nguyen, & Frauenfelder, 2010).

The findings are overall positive about the effectiveness of training in helping adult learners to improve their perceptual accuracy. In most of these studies, the trained group improved their perceptual accuracy between the pretest and the posttest (e.g., Hazan, Sennema, Iba, & Faulkner, 2005; Lively, Logan, & Pisoni, 1993; Wang et al., 1999). Where RT data were used, trainees were found to be faster in performing a task (e.g., Lively et al., 1993; Lively, Pisoni, Yamada, Tohkura, & Yamada, 1994). It also demonstrated that the training effect can be generalized to new auditory tokens and maintained for an extended period of time (e.g., for as long as three months in Bradlow et al., 1999). This research has also demonstrated that training effects may be mediated by multiple factors, including stimulus variability (e.g., Bradlow et al., 1997; Levi, Winters, & Pisoni, 2011; Lively et al., 1994; Logan et al., 1991), speaking rate variability

(Hirata et al., 2007), stimulus type (word vs. sentence stimuli, Hirata, 2004), input modality (audio only vs. audio-visual, Hazan et al., 2005), training method (enhancement training, inhibition training, training with a natural cue distribution, Kondaurova & Francis, 2010), and stimulus exaggeration and feedback (McCandliss, Fiez, Protopapas, Conway, & McClelland, 2002). For example, Lively et al. (1993) showed that it is more difficult for training to generalize to input produced by a new talker when the participants were trained with speech token from a single talker.

Against the background of the demonstration of the effectiveness of training, some studies showed that training effect can be quite limited. In training eight Japanese speakers to differentiate the English /l/-/r/ contrast, Takagi (2002) found considerable individual differences, with some showing native-like accuracy and some doing no better than chance after training. Tajima et al. (2008) compared a trained English group and a control English group in the amount of improvement in perceiving the duration contrasts in Japanese between a pretest and a posttest. The results showed comparable amount of improvement between the two tests. Given the participants' relative high accuracy in the pretest (around 80%), this finding suggested that at least when L2 speakers are already relatively high in accuracy, further improvement through training is difficult. Additionally, Dufour et al. (2010) failed to find reliable effect of phonemic training on auditory word recognition.

A further limitation of the training literature is that the findings often say very little about whether training can help produce nativelike performance. Most training studies have demonstrated the effectiveness of training in the form of improvement, but the L2 speakers in these studies were still far from reaching a nativelike accuracy after training. As these studies were not designed specifically to examine the relationship between training and native-like attainment, the non-nativelike performance could have been the results of insufficient training, inadequate training methods, or some other moderating factors.

3.5 Conclusion

This chapter reviews research that examined how L1, age, L2 experiences, L1 use, segment-related factors, and training affect phonological processing and development. Many other topics have been examined in L2 phonological processing research but are not included in this review due to space limitation. They include the relationship between L2 perception and L2 production (e.g., Zampini, 1998; Baker & Trofimovich, 2006), the role of visual input in L2 speech perception (Hardison, 1996, 2003, 2005; Hazan et al., 2005; Navarra & Soto-Faraco, 2007; Sueyoshi & Hardison, 2005), the locus of L2 learners' difficulty in phonological processing (e.g., Dupoux et al., 1997; Iverson et al., 2003), to name just a few.

Research on L2 phonological processing has also revealed a wide range of non-nativeness phenomena beyond lower accuracy in perception and production or a different RT pattern. For example, the intelligibility of NNS speech is more affected by noise compared to NS speech (e.g., Liu & Jin, 2013; Munro, 1998; Rogers, Dalby, & Nishi, 2004; Wilson & Spaulding, 2010), input degradation has a greater impact on NNS than on NS regardless of whether input degradation involved the addition of noise or reverberation (e.g., Cutler, Garcia Lecumberri, & Cooke, 2008; Rogers, Lister, Febo, Besing, & Abrams, 2006; Tabri, Chacra, & Pring, 2011) or involved the use of modified input or synthesized speech (e.g., Alamsaputra, Kohnert, Munson, & Reichle, 2006; Lee et al., 2009; Rogers & Lopez, 2008), NNS enjoy a smaller clear speech effect than NS do (Rogers et al., 2010), and NNS showed different patterns of neural responses (e.g., Peltola et al., 2003, 2007; Rinker et al., 2010; Uther, Giannakopoulou, & Iverson, 2012) and hemisphere involvement (e.g., Gandour et al., 2000; Hsieh, Gandour, Wong, & Hutchins, 2001; Klein, Zatorre, Milner, & Zhao, 2001) from NS, as well. The continued discovery of the full breadth of phonological non-nativeness phenomena will help further our understanding of what is meant by being a non-native speaker from a cognitive perspective.

Notes

1   An anonymous reviewer pointed out that even ESL speakers whose L1 only allows an iambic pattern (e.g., French) incorrectly produced word-initial stress in English (e.g., Tremblay & Owens, 2010) which contradicts a transfer-based interpretation of Chakraborty and Goffman's (2011) results.

2   Liu et al. (2013) found that Mandarin and Korean ESL speakers showed a larger duration difference across English vowels than NS did in production. They suggested that this may be a strategy used by L2 speakers to compensate for their lower spectral accuracy. This may be considered as a production parallel to the use of an incorrect cue in L2 perception in the sense that NS primarily use spectral rather than duration features to differentiate vowels in production.

3   An asymmetry was found in that a noun beginning with /l/ did not produce the same effect. See the study for their explanation of this asymmetry. Furthermore, as rightly pointed by an anonymous reviewer, the study failed to include a NS control group.

4   See Birdsong (2006) for discussion of a potential relationship between brain volume and age-related differences.

5   See DeKeyser (2012) for a similar view of implicit and explicit processes being differentially involved in younger and older learners for the learning of morphosyntax.

6   Kuhl does not seem to be very explicit about what is meant by neural commitment where the hypothesis is proposed (e.g., 2000, 2004). In support of her hypothesis, she cited evidence that processing an L2 involves a larger area of the brain than processing the native language (2004). This seems to suggest that neural commitment refers to the involvement and tuning of a particular region of the brain for processing the native language. However, she talks about dedicated neural networks more often than dedicated regions, which can also be interpreted as neural connections at the cellular level.

7   Reviewed in this section are studies that examined the effect of varying amounts of L2 experience on phonological processing. Some other studies considered the role of experience by comparing individuals with and without certain linguistic experience. See Sundara, Polka, and Genesee (2006); Hao (2012); and Wang et al. (2004) for examples.

References

Abrahamsson, N. & Hyltenstam, K. (2009). Age of onset and nativelikeness in a second language: Listener perception versus linguistic scrutiny. *Language Learning, 59*, 249–306.

Abu-Rabia, S. & Kehat, S. (2004). The critical period for second language pronunciation: Is there such a thing? *Educational Psychology, 24*, 77–97.

Alamsaputra, D. M., Kohnert, K. J., Munson, B., & Reichle, J. (2006). Synthesized speech intelligibility among native speakers and non-native speakers of English. *Augmentative and Alternative Communication, 22*, 258–268.

Altenberg, E. P. (2005). The judgment, perception, and production of consonant clusters in a second language. *IRAL, 43*, 53–80.

Amengual, M. (2012). Interlingual influence in bilingual speech: Cognate status effect in a continuum of bilingualism. *Bilingualism: Language and Cognition, 15*, 517–530.

Aoyama, K., Flege, J. E., Guion, S. G., Akahane-Yamada, R., & Yamada, T. (2004). Perceived phonetic dissimilarity and L2 speech learning: The case of Japanese /r/ and English /l/ and /r/. *Journal of Phonetics, 32*, 233–250.

Aoyama, K., Guion, S. G., Flege, J. E., & Yamada, T. (2008). The first years in an L2-speaking environment: A comparison of Japanese children and adults learning American English. *International Review of Applied Linguistics in Language Teaching, 46*, 61–90.

Archibald, J. (1993). The learnability of metrical parameters by adult speakers of Spanish. *IRAL, 31*, 129–142.

Archibald, J. (1997). The acquisition of English stress by speakers of nonaccentual languages: Lexical storage versus computation of stress. *Linguistics, 35*, 167–181.

Archila-Suerte, P., Zevin, J., Bunta, F., & Hernandez, A. E. (2012). Age of acquisition and proficiency in a second language independently influence the perception of non-native speech. *Bilingualism: Language and Cognition, 15*, 190–201.

Baker, W. & Trofimovich, P. (2006). Perceptual paths to accurate production of L2 vowels: The role of individual differences. *IRAL, 44*, 231–250.

Baker, W., Trofimovich, P., Flege, J. E., Mack, M., & Halter, R. (2008). Child-adult differences in second-language phonological learning: The role of cross-language similarity. *Language and Speech, 51*, 317–342.

Barrios, S., Jiang, N., & Idsardi, W. J. (2016). Similarity in L2 phonology: Evidence from L1 Spanish late-learners' perception and lexical representation of English vowel contrasts. *Second Language Research, 32*(3), 367–395.

Bent, T. & Bradlow, A. R. (2003). The interlanguage speech intelligibility benefit. *The Journal of the Acoustical Society of America, 114*, 1600–1610.

Bent, T., Kewley-Port, D., & Ferguson, S. H. (2010). Across-talker effects on non-native listeners' vowel perception in noise. *The Journal of the Acoustical Society of America, 128*, 3142–3151.

Berkowitz, D. (1989). The effect of cultural empathy on second-language phonological production. In M. R. Eisenstein (Ed.), *The dynamic interlanguage* (pp. 101–114). New York, NY: Planum.

Best, C. T., McRoberts, G., & Goodell, E. (2001). Discrimination of non-native consonant contrasts varying in perceptual assimilation to the listener's native phonological system. *Journal of the Acoustical Society of America, 109,* 775–794.

Best, C. T. & Tyler, M. D. (2007). Nonnative and second language speech perception: Commonalities and complementaries. In O. S. Bohn & M. J. Munro (Eds.), *Language experience in second language speech learning* (pp. 13–34). Amsterdam: John Benjamins.

Birdsong, D. (2006). Age and second language acquisition and processing: A selective overview. *Language Learning, 56*(S1), 9–49.

Birdsong, D. (2007). Nativelike pronunciation among late learners of French as a second language. In M. J. Munro & O. S. Bohn (Eds.), *Second language speech learning: The role of language experience in speech perception and production* (pp. 99–116). Amsterdam: John Benjamins.

Bohn, O. S. (1995). Crosslanguage speech production in adults: First language transfer doesn't tell it all. In W. Strange (Ed.), *Speech perception and linguistic experience: Issues in cross-language research* (pp. 279–304). Baltimore: York Press.

Bongaerts, T., Mennen, S., & Slik, F. V. D. (2000). Authenticity of pronunciation in naturalistic second language acquisition: The case of very advanced late learners of Dutch as a second language. *Studia Linguistica, 54,* 298–308.

Bongaerts, T., Planken, B., & Schils, E. (1995). Can late starters attain a native accent in a foreign language? A test of the critical period hypothesis. In D. Singleton & Z. Lengyel (Eds.), *The age factor in second language acquisition* (pp. 30–50). Clevedon: Multilingual Matters.

Bongaerts, T., Van Summeren, C., Planken, B., & Schils, E. (1997). Age and ultimate attainment in the pronunciation of a foreign language. *Studies in Second Language Acquisition, 19,* 447–465.

Bosch, L., Costa, A., & Sebastián-Gallés, N. (2000). First and second language vowel perception in early bilinguals. *European Journal of Cognitive Psychology, 12,* 189–221.

Bradlow, A. R., Akahane-Yamada, R., Pisoni, D. B., & Tohkura, Y. I. (1999). Training Japanese listeners to identify English /r/ and /l/: Long-term retention of learning in perception and production. *Perception & Psychophysics, 61,* 977–985.

Bradlow, A. R. & Pisoni, D. B. (1999). Recognition of spoken words by native and non-native listeners: Talker-, listener-, and item-related factors. *The Journal of the Acoustical Society of America, 106,* 2074–2085.

Bradlow, A. R., Pisoni, D. B., Akahane-Yamada, R., & Tohkura, Y. I. (1997). Training Japanese listeners to identify English /r/ and /l/: IV. Some effects of perceptual learning on speech production. *The Journal of the Acoustical Society of America, 101,* 2299–2310.

Braun, B. & Johnson, E. K. (2011). Question or tone 2? How language experience and linguistic function guide pitch processing. *Journal of Phonetics, 39,* 585–594.

Broersma, M. (2005). Perception of familiar contrasts in unfamiliar positions. *The Journal of the Acoustical Society of America, 117,* 3890–3901.

Bundgaard-Nielsen, R. L., Best, C. T., Kroos, C., & Tyler, M. D. (2012). Second language learners' vocabulary expansion is associated with improved second language vowel intelligibility. *Applied Psycholinguistics, 33,* 643–664.

Bundgaard-Nielsen, R. L., Best, C. T., & Tyler, M. D. (2011). Vocabulary size matters: The assimilation of second-language Australian English vowels to first-language Japanese vowel categories. *Applied Psycholinguistics, 32*, 51–67.

Callan, A. M., Callan, D. E., Tajima, K., & Akahane-Yamada, R. (2006). Neural processes involved with perception of non-native durational contrasts. *Neuroreport, 17*, 1353–1357.

Caramazza, A., Yeni-Komshian, G. H., Zurif, E. B., & Carbone, E. (1973). The acquisition of a new phonological contrast: The case of stop consonants in French-English bilinguals. *The Journal of the Acoustical Society of America, 54*, 421–428.

Carlisle, R. S. (1997). The modification of onsets in a markedness relationship: Testing the interlanguage structural conformity hypothesis. *Language Learning, 47*, 59–93.

Carlisle, R. S. (1998). The acquisition of onsets in a markedness relationship. *Studies in Second Language Acquisition, 20*, 245–260.

Cebrian, J. (2006). Experience and the use of non-native duration in L2 vowel categorization. *Journal of Phonetics, 34*, 372–387.

Chakraborty, R. & Goffman, L. (2011). Production of lexical stress in non-native speakers of American English: Kinematic correlates of stress and transfer. *Journal of Speech, Language, and Hearing Research, 54*, 821–835.

Chang, C. B. (2012). Rapid and multifaceted effects of second-language learning on first-language speech production. *Journal of Phonetics, 40*, 249–268.

Chang, C. B. & Mishler, A. (2012). Evidence for language transfer leading to a perceptual advantage for non-native listeners. *The Journal of the Acoustical Society of America, 132*, 2700–2710.

Chen, Y., Robb, M., Gilbert, H., & Lerman, J. (2001). Vowel production by Mandarin speakers of English. *Clinical Linguistics & Phonetics, 15*, 427–440.

Chung, H., Kong, E. J., Edwards, J., Weismer, G., Fourakis, M., & Hwang, Y. (2012). Cross-linguistic studies of children's and adults' vowel spaces. *The Journal of the Acoustical Society of America, 131*, 442–454.

Conel, J. L. (1939–1976). *The postnatal development of the human cerebral cortex* (Vols. 1–8). Cambridge, MA: Harvard University Press.

Cooper, N., Cutler, A., & Wales, R. (2002). Constraints of lexical stress on lexical access in English: Evidence from native and non-native listeners. *Language and Speech, 45*, 207–228.

Crowther, C. S. & Mann, V. (1992). Native language factors affecting use of vocalic cues to final consonant voicing in English. *The Journal of the Acoustical Society of America, 92*, 711–722.

Cutler, A. (2009). Greater sensitivity to prosodic goodness in non-native than in native listeners. *The Journal of the Acoustical Society of America, 125*, 3522–3525.

Cutler, A., Garcia Lecumberri, M. L., & Cooke, M. (2008). Consonant identification in noise by native and non-native listeners: Effects of local context. *The Journal of the Acoustical Society of America, 124*, 1264–1268.

Cutler, A., Mehler, J., Norris, D., & Segui, J. (1989). Limits on bilingualism. *Nature, 320*, 229–230.

Cutler, A., Mehler, J., Norris, D., & Segui, J. (1992). The monolingual nature of speech segmentation by bilinguals. *Cognitive Psychology, 24*, 381–410.

Cutler, A., Weber, A., & Otake, T. (2006). Asymmetric mapping from phonetic to lexical representations in second-language listening. *Journal of Phonetics, 34*, 269–284.

Darcy, I. & Krüger, F. (2012). Vowel perception and production in Turkish children acquiring L2 German. *Journal of Phonetics, 40*, 568–581.

Davidson, L. (2006). Phonology, phonetics, or frequency: Influences on the production of non-native sequences. *Journal of Phonetics, 34*, 104–137.

Davidson, L. (2010). Phonetic bases of similarities in cross-language production: Evidence from English and Catalan. *Journal of Phonetics, 38*, 272–288.

Davidson, L., Jusczyk, P., & Smolensky, P. (2004). The initial and final states: Theoretical implications and experimental explorations of Richness of the Base. In R. Kager, J. Pater, & W. Zonneveld (Eds.), *Constraints in phonological acquisition* (pp. 321–368). Cambridge: Cambridge University Press.

Davidson, L. & Shaw, J. A. (2012). Sources of illusion in consonant cluster perception. *Journal of Phonetics, 40*, 234–248.

DeKeyser, R. M. (2012). Age effects in second language learning. In S. Gass & A. Mackey (Eds.), *Handbook of second language acquisition* (pp. 442–460). London: Routledge.

Dmitrieva, O., Jongman, A., & Sereno, J. (2010). Phonological neutralization by native and non-native speakers: The case of Russian final devoicing. *Journal of Phonetics, 38*, 483–492.

Dreher, B. & Larkins, J. (1972). Non-semantic auditory discrimination: Foundation for second language learning. *The Modern Language Journal, 56*, 227–230.

Dufour, S., Nguyen, N., & Frauenfelder, U. H. (2010). Does training on a phonemic contrast absent in the listener's dialect influence word recognition? *The Journal of the Acoustical Society of America, 128*, EL43–EL48.

Dupoux, E., Kakehi, K., Hirose, Y., Pallier, C., & Mehler, J. (1999). Epenthetic vowels in Japanese: A perceptual illusion? *Journal of Experimental Psychology: Human Perception and Performance, 25*, 1568–1578.

Dupoux, E., Pallier, C., Kakehi, K., & Mehler, J. (2001). New evidence for prelexical phonological processing in word recognition. *Language and Cognitive Processes, 16*, 491–505.

Dupoux, E., Pallier, C., Sebastian, N., & Mehler, J. (1997). A destressing 'deafness' in French? *Journal of Memory and Language, 36*, 406–421.

Dupoux, E., Parlato, E., Frota, S., Hirose, Y., & Peperkamp, S. (2011). Where do illusory vowels come from? *Journal of Memory and Language, 64*, 199–210.

Dupoux, E., Sebastián-Gallés, N., Navarrete, E., & Peperkamp, S. (2008). Persistent stress 'deafness': The case of French learners of Spanish. *Cognition, 106*, 682–706.

Eckman, F. R. (1977). Markedness and the contrastive analysis hypothesis. *Language Learning, 27*, 315–330.

Eckman, F. R. (1991). The structural conformity hypothesis and the acquisition of consonant clusters in the interlanguage of ESL learners. *Studies in Second Language Acquisition, 13*, 23–41.

Eckman, F. R. (2008). Typological markedness and second language phonology. In J. G. H. Edwards & M. L. Zampini (Eds.), *Phonology and second language acquisition* (pp. 95–115). Amsterdam and Philadelphia: John Benjamins.

Escudero, P., Benders, T., & Lipski, S. C. (2009). Native, non-native and L2 perceptual cue weighting for Dutch vowels: The case of Dutch, German, and Spanish listeners. *Journal of Phonetics, 37*, 452–465.

Escudero, P. & Boersma, P. (2004). Bridging the gap between L2 speech perception research and phonological theory. *Studies in Second Language Acquisition, 26*, 551–585.

Escudero, P., Simon, E., & Mitterer, H. (2012). The perception of English front vowels by North Holland and Flemish listeners: Acoustic similarity predicts and explains cross-linguistic and L2 perception. *Journal of Phonetics, 40,* 280–288.

Escudero, P. & Vasiliev, P. (2011). Cross-language acoustic similarity predicts perceptual assimilation of Canadian English and Canadian French vowels. *The Journal of the Acoustical Society of America, 130,* EL277–EL283.

Field, J. (2005). Intelligibility and the listener: The role of lexical stress. *TESOL Quarterly, 39,* 399–423.

Flege, J. E. (1981). The phonological basis of foreign accent: A hypothesis. *TESOL Quarterly, 15,* 443–455.

Flege, J. E. (1987). The production of 'new' and 'similar' phones in a foreign language: Evidence for the effect of equivalence classification. *Journal of Phonetics, 15,* 47–65.

Flege, J. E. (1988). Factors affecting degree of perceived foreign accent in English sentences. *The Journal of the Acoustical Society of America, 84,* 70–79.

Flege, J. E. (1991). Age of learning affects the authenticity of voice-onset time (VOT) in stop consonants produced in a second language. *The Journal of the Acoustical Society of America, 89,* 395–411.

Flege, J. E. (1995). Second-language speech learning: Theory, findings, and problems. In W. Strange (Ed.), *Speech perception and linguistic experience: Issues in cross-language research* (pp. 233–272). Baltimore, MD: York Press.

Flege, J. E. (1999). Age of learning and second-language speech. In D. Birdsong (Ed.), *Second language acquisition and the critical period hypothesis* (pp. 101–132). Hillsdale, NJ: Lawrence Erlbaum.

Flege, J. E. (2002). Interactions between the native and second-language phonetic systems. In P. Burmeister, T. Piske, & A. Rohde (Eds.), *An integrated view of language development: Papers in honor of Henning Wode* (pp. 217–244). Trier, Germany: Wissenschaftlicher Verlag.

Flege, J. E. (2003). Assessing constraints on second-language segmental production and perception. In A. Meyer & N. Schiller (Eds.), *Phonetics and phonology in language comprehension and production, differences and similarities* (pp. 319–355). Berlin: Mouton de Gruyter.

Flege, J. E. (2007). Language contact in bilingualism: Phonetic system interactions. In J. Cole & J. I. Hualde (Eds.), *Laboratory phonology* (Vol. 9, pp. 353–382). Berlin, Germany: Walter de Gruyter.

Flege, J. E., Birdsong, D., Bialystok, E., Mack, M., Sung, H., & Tsukada, K. (2006). Degree of foreign accent in English sentences produced by Korean children and adults. *Journal of Phonetics, 34,* 153–175.

Flege, J. E. & Bohn, O. S. (1989). An instrumental study of vowel reduction and stress placement in Spanish-accented English. *Studies in Second Language Acquisition, 11,* 35–62.

Flege, J. E., Bohn, O. S., & Jang, S. (1997). Effects of experience on non-native speakers' production and perception of English vowels. *Journal of Phonetics, 25,* 437–470.

Flege, J. E. & Eefting, W. (1987). Cross-language switching in stop consonant perception and production by Dutch speakers of English. *Speech Communication, 6,* 185–202.

Flege, J. E. & Fletcher, K. L. (1992). Talker and listener effects on degree of perceived foreign accent. *The Journal of the Acoustical Society of America, 91,* 370–389.

Flege, J. E., Frieda, E. M., & Nozawa, T. (1997). Amount of native-language (L1) use affects the pronunciation of an L2. *Journal of Phonetics*, 25, 169–186.

Flege, J. E. & Hillenbrand, J. (1984). Limits on phonetic accuracy in foreign language speech production. *The Journal of the Acoustical Society of America*, 76, 708–721.

Flege, J. E. & Hillenbrand, J. (1986). Differential use of temporal cues to the /s/ – /z/ contrast by native and non-native speakers of English. *The Journal of the Acoustical Society of America*, 79, 508–517.

Flege, J. E. & Liu, S. (2001). The effect of experience on adults' acquisition of a second language. *Studies in Second Language Acquisition*, 23, 527–552.

Flege, J. E. & MacKay, I. R. (2004). Perceiving vowels in a second language. *Studies in Second Language Acquisition*, 26, 1–34.

Flege, J. E., MacKay, I. R., & Meador, D. (1999). Native Italian speakers' perception and production of English vowels. *The Journal of the Acoustical Society of America*, 106, 2973–2987.

Flege, J. E., Munro, M. J., & MacKay, I. R. (1995a). Factors affecting degree of perceived foreign accent in a second language. *Journal of the Acoustical Society of America*, 97, 3125–3134.

Flege, J. E., Munro, M. J., & MacKay, I. R. (1995b). Effects of age of second-language learning on the production of English consonants. *Speech Communication*, 16, 1–26.

Flege, J. E., Munro, M. J., & Skelton, L. (1992). Production of the word-final English /t/ – /d/ contrast by native speakers of English, Mandarin, and Spanish. *The Journal of the Acoustical Society of America*, 92, 128–143.

Flege, J. E. & Port, R. (1981). Cross-language phonetic interference: Arabic to English. *Language and Speech*, 24, 125–146.

Flege, J. E., Schirru, C., & MacKay, I. R. (2003). Interaction between the native and second language phonetic subsystems. *Speech Communication*, 40, 467–491.

Flege, J. E. & Wang, C. (1989). Native-language phonotactic constraints affect how well Chinese subjects perceive the word-final English /t/ – /d/ contrast. *Journal of Phonetics*, 17, 299–315.

Flege, J. E., Yeni-Komshian, G. H., & Liu, S. (1999). Age constraints on second-language acquisition. *Journal of Memory and Language*, 41, 78–104.

Fokes, J. & Bond, Z. S. (1989). The vowels of stressed and unstressed syllables in non-native English. *Language Learning*, 39, 341–373.

Fowler, C. A., Sramko, V., Ostry, D. J., Rowland, S. A., & Hallé, P. (2008). Cross language phonetic influences on the speech of French–English bilinguals. *Journal of Phonetics*, 36, 649–663.

Francis, A. L., Ciocca, V., Ma, L., & Fenn, K. (2008). Perceptual learning of Cantonese lexical tones by tone and non-tone language speakers. *Journal of Phonetics*, 36, 268–294.

Gandour, J. (1983). Tone perception in far eastern-languages. *Journal of Phonetics*, 11, 149–175.

Gandour, J., Wong, D., Hsieh, L., Weinzapfel, B., Van Lancker, D., & Hutchins, G. D. (2000). A cross-linguistic PET study of tone perception. *Journal of Cognitive Neuroscience*, 12, 207–222.

Goto, H. (1971). Auditory perception by normal Japanese adults of the sounds 'l' and 'r'. *Neuropsychologica*, 9, 317–323.

Gottfried, T. L. & Suiter, T. L. (1997). Effect of linguistic experience on the identification of Mandarin Chinese vowels and tones. *Journal of Phonetics, 25*, 207–231.

Goucha, T. B., Anwander, A., Stamatakis, E. A., Tyler, L. K., & Friederici, A. D. (2015). How language shapes the brain: Cross-linguistic differences in structural connectivity. In *Proceedings of 7th Annual Meeting of the Society for the Neurobiology of Language*. Retrieved from http://hdl.handle.net/11858/00-001M-0000-0028-F1EC-F (Accessed on November 12, 2016).

Granena, G. & Long, M. H. (2013). Age of onset, length of residence, language aptitude, and ultimate L2 attainment in three linguistic domains. *Second Language Research, 29*, 311–343.

Grosjean, F. (1988). Exploring the recognition of guest words in bilingual speech. *Language and Cognitive Processes, 3*, 233–274.

Grosjean, F. (1997). Processing mixed language: Issues, findings, and models. In A. M. De Groot & J. F. Kroll (Eds.), *Tutorials in bilingualism* (pp. 225–254). Mahwah, NJ: Lawrence Erlbaum.

Guion, S. G. (2003). The vowel systems of Quichua–Spanish bilinguals: Age of acquisition effects on the mutual influence of the first and second languages. *Phonetica, 60*, 98–128.

Guion, S. G., Flege, J. E., Akahane-Yamada, R., & Pruitt, J. C. (2000). An investigation of current models of second language speech perception: The case of Japanese adults' perception of English consonants. *The Journal of the Acoustical Society of America, 107*, 2711–2724.

Guion, S. G., Flege, J. E., & Loftin, J. D. (2000). The effect of L1 use on pronunciation in Quichua–Spanish bilinguals. *Journal of Phonetics, 28*, 27–42.

Guiora, A. Z., Beit-Hallahmi, B., Brannon, R. C. L., Dull, C. Y., & Scovel, T. (1972). The effects of experimentally induced changes in ego states on pronunciation ability in a second language: An exploratory study. *Comprehensive Psychiatry, 13*, 421–428.

Hallé, P. A., Best, C. T., & Levitt, A. (1999). Phonetic vs. phonological influences on French listeners' perception of American English approximants. *Journal of Phonetics, 27*, 281–306.

Hallé, P. A., Chang, Y. C., & Best, C. T. (2004). Identification and discrimination of Mandarin Chinese tones by Mandarin Chinese vs. French listeners. *Journal of Phonetics, 32*, 395–421.

Han, M. S. (1992). The timing control of geminate and single stop consonants in Japanese: A challenge for nonnative speakers. *Phonetica, 49*, 102–127.

Hao, Y. C. (2012). Second language acquisition of Mandarin Chinese tones by tonal and non-tonal language speakers. *Journal of Phonetics, 40*, 269–279.

Hardison, D. M. (1996). Bimodal speech perception by native and nonnative speakers of English: Factors influencing the McGurk effect. *Language Learning, 46*, 3–73.

Hardison, D. M. (2003). Acquisition of second-language speech: Effects of visual cues, context, and talker variability. *Applied Psycholinguistics, 24*, 495–522.

Hardison, D. M. (2005). Second-language spoken word identification: Effects of perceptual training, visual cues, and phonetic environment. *Applied Psycholinguistics, 26*, 579–596.

Hardison, D. M. & Saigo, M. M. (2010). Development of perception of second language Japanese geminates: Role of duration, sonority, and segmentation strategy. *Applied Psycholinguistics, 31*, 81–99.

Hazan, V., Sennema, A., Iba, M., & Faulkner, A. (2005). Effect of audiovisual perceptual training on the perception and production of consonants by Japanese learners of English. *Speech Communication, 47*, 360–378.

Hirata, Y. (2004). Training native English speakers to perceive Japanese length contrasts in word versus sentence contexts. *The Journal of the Acoustical Society of America, 116*, 2384–2394.

Hirata, Y., Whitehurst, E., & Cullings, E. (2007). Training native English speakers to identify Japanese vowel length contrast with sentences at varied speaking rates. *The Journal of the Acoustical Society of America, 121*, 3837–3845.

Højen, A. & Flege, J. E. (2006). Early learners' discrimination of second-language vowels. *The Journal of the Acoustical Society of America, 119*, 3072–3084.

Hsieh, L., Gandour, J., Wong, D., & Hutchins, G. D. (2001). Functional heterogeneity of inferior frontal gyrus is shaped by linguistic experience. *Brain and Language, 76*, 227–252.

Ibrahim, R., Eviatar, Z., & Leikin, M. (2008). Speaking Hebrew with an accent: Empathic capacity or other nonpersonal factors. *International Journal of Bilingualism, 12*, 195–207.

Ingram, J. C. & Park, S. G. (1997). Cross-language vowel perception and production by Japanese and Korean learners of English. *Journal of Phonetics, 25*, 343–370.

Ingvalson, E. M., Holt, L. L., & McClelland, J. L. (2012). Can native Japanese listeners learn to differentiate /r–l/ on the basis of F3 onset frequency? *Bilingualism: Language and Cognition, 15*, 255–274.

Ingvalson, E. M., McClelland, J. L., & Holt, L. L. (2011). Predicting native English-like performance by native Japanese speakers. *Journal of Phonetics, 39*, 571–584.

Ioup, G., Boustagui, E., El Tigi, M., & Moselle, M. (1994). Reexamining the critical period hypothesis. *Studies in Second Language Acquisition, 16*, 73–98.

Ito, K. & Strange, W. (2009). Perception of allophonic cues to English word boundaries by Japanese second language learners of English. *The Journal of the Acoustical Society of America, 125*, 2348–2360.

Iverson, P., Hazan, V., & Bannister, K. (2005). Phonetic training with acoustic cue manipulations: A comparison of methods for teaching English /r/ – /l/ to Japanese adults. *The Journal of the Acoustical Society of America, 118*, 3267–3278.

Iverson, P., Kuhl, P. K., Akahane-Yamada, R., Diesch, E., Tohkura, Y. I., Kettermann, A., & Siebert, C. (2003). A perceptual interference account of acquisition difficulties for non-native phonemes. *Cognition, 87*, B47–B57.

Jia, G., Strange, W., Wu, Y., Collado, J., & Guan, Q. (2006). Perception and production of English vowels by Mandarin speakers: Age-related differences vary with amount of L2 exposure). *The Journal of the Acoustical Society of America, 119*, 1118–1130.

Juffs, A. (1990). Tone, syllable structure and interlanguage phonology: Chinese learner's stress errors. *IRAL, 28*, 99–118.

Kang, K. H. & Guion, S. G. (2006). Phonological systems in bilinguals: Age of learning effects on the stop consonant systems of Korean-English bilinguals. *The Journal of the Acoustical Society of America, 119*, 1672–1683.

Kennedy, B. L. (1988). Adult versus child L2 acquisition: An information-processing approach. *Language Learning, 38*, 477–495.

Kiyonaga, Y., Ito, H., & Masataka, N. (2009). Training for special mora perception in non-native Japanese students learning Japanese. *Psychologia, 52*, 267–276.

Klein, D., Zatorre, R. J., Milner, B., & Zhao, V. (2001). A cross-linguistic PET study of tone perception in Mandarin Chinese and English speakers. *NeuroImage, 13,* 646–653.

Kondaurova, M. V. & Francis, A. L. (2008). The relationship between native allophonic experience with vowel duration and perception of the English tense/lax vowel contrast by Spanish and Russian listeners. *The Journal of the Acoustical Society of America, 124,* 3959–3971.

Kondaurova, M. V. & Francis, A. L. (2010). The role of selective attention in the acquisition of English tense and lax vowels by native Spanish listeners: Comparison of three training methods. *Journal of Phonetics, 38,* 569–587.

Kondo, Y. (2000). Production of schwa by Japanese speakers of English: An acoustic study of shifts in coarticulatory strategies from L1 to L2. In M. B. Broe & J. B. Pierrehumbert (Eds.), *Papers in laboratory phonology V: Acquisition and the lexicon* (pp. 29–39). New York: Cambridge University Press.

Krashen, S. D., Long, M. A., & Scarcella, R. C. (1979). Age, rate and eventual attainment in second language acquisition. *TESOL Quarterly, 13,* 573–582.

Kuhl, P. K. (2000). A new view of language acquisition. *Proceedings of the National Academy of Sciences of the United States of America, 97,* 11850–11857.

Kuhl, P. K. (2004). Early language acquisition: Cracking the speech code. *Nature Reviews Neuroscience, 5,* 831–843.

Kuhl, P. K., Conboy, B. T., Padden, D., Nelson, T., & Pruitt, J. (2005). Early speech perception and later language development: Implications for the 'Critical Period'. *Language Learning and Development, 1,* 237–264.

Larson-Hall, J. (2004). Predicting perceptual success with segments: A test of Japanese speakers of Russian. *Second Language Research, 20,* 33–76.

Leather, J. (1987). F0 pattern inference in the perceptual acquisition of second language tone. In A. James & J. Leather (Eds.), *Sound patterns in second language acquisition* (pp. 59–81). Dordrecht: Foris Publications.

Lee, B., Guion, S. G., & Harada, T. (2006). Acoustic analysis of the production of unstressed English vowels by early and late Korean and Japanese bilinguals. *Studies in Second Language Acquisition, 28,* 487–513.

Lee, C.-Y., Tao, L., & Bond, Z. S. (2009). Speaker variability and context in the identification of fragmented Mandarin tones by native and non-native listeners. *Journal of Phonetics 37,* 1–15.

Lee, C.-Y., Tao, L., & Bond, Z. S. (2010). Identification of acoustically modified Mandarin tones by non-native listeners. *Language and Speech, 53,* 217–243.

Lehiste, I. & Fox, R. A. (1992). Perception of prominence by Estonian and English listeners. *Language and Speech, 35,* 419–434.

Lenneberg, E. (1967). *Biological foundations of language.* New York: Wiley.

Levi, S. V., Winters, S. J., & Pisoni, D. B. (2011). Effects of cross-language voice training on speech perception: Whose familiar voices are more intelligible? *The Journal of the Acoustical Society of America, 130,* 4053–4062.

Levy, E. S. (2009). On the assimilation-discrimination relationship in American English adults' French vowel learning. *The Journal of the Acoustical Society of America, 126,* 2670–2682.

Levy, E. S. & Law II, F. F. (2010). Production of French vowels by American-English learners of French: Language experience, consonantal context, and the perception-production relationship. *The Journal of the Acoustical Society of America*, *128*, 1290–1305.

Lippus, P., Pajusalu, K., & Allik, J. (2009). The tonal component of Estonian quantity in native and non-native perception. *Journal of Phonetics*, *37*, 388–396.

Liu, C. & Jin, S. H. (2013). Intelligibility of American English vowels of native and non-native speakers in quiet and speech-shaped noise. *Bilingualism: Language and Cognition*, *16*, 206–218.

Liu, C., Jin, S. H., & Chen, C. T. (2013). Durations of American English vowels by native and non-native speakers: Acoustic analyses and perceptual effects. *Language and Speech*, *57*, 238–253.

Lively, S. E., Logan, J. S., & Pisoni, D. B. (1993). Training Japanese listeners to identify English /r/ and /l/. II: The role of phonetic environment and talker variability in learning new perceptual categories. *The Journal of the Acoustical Society of America*, *94*, 1242–1255.

Lively, S. E., Pisoni, D. B., Yamada, R. A., Tohkura, Y. I., & Yamada, T. (1994). Training Japanese listeners to identify English /r/ and /l/. III: Long-term retention of new phonetic categories. *The Journal of the Acoustical Society of America*, *96*, 2076–2087.

Logan, J. S., Lively, S. E., & Pisoni, D. B. (1991). Training Japanese listeners to identify English /r/ and /l/: A first report. *The Journal of the Acoustical Society of America*, *89*, 874–886.

Long, M. H. (1990). Maturational constraints on language development. *Studies in Second Language Acquisition*, *12*, 251–285.

Lotto, A. J., Sato, M., & Diehl, R. L. (2004). Mapping the task for the second language learner: The case of Japanese acquisition of /r/ and /l/. In J. Slifka, S. Manuel, & M. Matthies (Eds.), *From sound to sense: 50+ Years of discoveries in speech communication* (pp. C181–C186). Cambridge, MA: MIT Press.

McAllister, R., Flege, J. E., & Piske, T. (2002). The influence of L1 on the acquisition of Swedish quantity by native speakers of Spanish, English and Estonian. *Journal of Phonetics*, *30*, 229–258.

McCandliss, B. D., Fiez, J. A., Protopapas, A., Conway, M., & McClelland, J. L. (2002). Success and failure in teaching the [r]-[l] contrast to Japanese adults: Tests of a Hebbian model of plasticity and stabilization in spoken language perception. *Cognitive, Affective, & Behavioral Neuroscience*, *2*, 89–108.

MacKay, I. R., Flege, J. E., Piske, T., & Schirru, C. (2001). Category restructuring during second-language speech acquisition. *The Journal of the Acoustical Society of America*, *110*, 516–528.

MacKay, I. R., Meador, D., & Flege, J. E. (2001). The identification of English consonants by native speakers of Italian. *Phonetica*, *58*(1–2), 103–125.

MacWhinney, B. (2005). A unified model of language acquisition. In J. F. Kroll & A. M. B. De Groot (Eds.), *Handbook of bilingualism: Psycholinguistic approaches* (pp. 49–67). Oxford: Oxford University Press.

Mayo, L. H., Florentine, M., & Buus, S. (1997). Age of second-language acquisition and perception of speech in noise. *Journal of Speech, Language, and Hearing Research*, *40*, 686–693.

Meador, D., Flege, J. E., & MacKay, I. R. (2000). Factors affecting the recognition of words in a second language. *Bilingualism: Language and Cognition*, *3*, 55–67.

Meister, L. & Meister, E. (2011). Perception of the short vs. long phonological category in Estonian by native and non-native listeners. *Journal of Phonetics, 39,* 212–224.

Minagawa, Y. & Kiritani, S. (1996). Discrimination of the single and geminate stop contrast in Japanese by five different language groups. *Annual Bulletin of Research Institute of Logopedics and Phoniatrics, 30,* 23–28.

Miyawaki, K., Strange, W., Verbrugge, R., Liberman, A. L., Jenkins, J. J., & Fujimura, O. (1975). An effect of linguistic experience: The discrimination of [r] and [l] by native speakers of Japanese and English. *Perception and Psychophysics, 18,* 331–340.

Morrison, G. S. (2002). Perception of English /i/ and /I/ by Japanese and Spanish listeners: Longitudinal results. In G. S. Morrison & L. Zsoldos (Eds.), *Proceedings of the North West Linguistics Conference 2002.* Burnaby, BC, Canada: Simon Fraser University Linguistics Graduate Student Association.

Moyer, A. (1999). Ultimate attainment in L2 phonology. *Studies in Second Language Acquisition, 21,* 81–108.

Moyer, A. (2007). Do language attitudes determine accent? A study of bilinguals in the USA. *Journal of Multilingual and Multicultural Development, 28,* 502–518.

Moyer, A. (2014). Exceptional outcomes in L2 phonology: The critical factors of learner engagement and self-regulation. *Applied Linguistics, 35,* 418–440. doi:10.1093/applin/amu012

Munro, M. J. (1998). The effects of noise on the intelligibility of foreign accented speech. *Studies in Second Language Acquisition, 20,* 139–154.

Navarra, J. & Soto-Faraco, S. (2007). Hearing lips in a second language: Visual articulatory information enables the perception of second language sounds. *Psychological Research, 71,* 4–12.

Nenonen, S., Shestakova, A., Huotilainen, M., & Näätänen, R. (2003). Linguistic relevance of duration within the native language determines the accuracy of speech-sound duration processing. *Cognitive Brain Research, 16,* 492–495.

Neufeld, G. G. (1979). Towards a theory of language learning ability. *Language Learning, 29,* 227–241.

Nguyễn, T. A.-T. & Ingram, J. (2005). Vietnamese acquisition of English word stress. *TESOL Quarterly, 39,* 309–319.

Nguyễn, T. A.-T., Ingram, J., & Pensalfini, J. R. (2008). Prosodic transfer in Vietnamese acquisition of English contrastive stress patterns. *Journal of Phonetics, 36,* 158–190.

Oh, G. E., Guion-Anderson, S., Aoyama, K., Flege, J. E., Akahane-Yamada, R., & Yamada, T. (2011). A one-year longitudinal study of English and Japanese vowel production by Japanese adults and children in an English-speaking setting. *Journal of Phonetics, 39,* 156–167.

Oyama, S. (1982). The sensitive period and comprehension of speech. In S. Krashen, R. Scarcella, & M. Long (Eds.), *Child-adult differences in second language acquisition* (pp. 39–52). Rowley, MA: Newbury House.

Pallier, C., Bosch, L., & Sebastián-Gallés, N. (1997). A limit on behavioral plasticity in speech perception. *Cognition, 64,* B9–B17.

Pallier, C., Colomé, A., & Sebastián-Gallés, N. (2001). The influence of native-language phonology on lexical access: Exemplar-based versus abstract lexical entries. *Psychological Science, 12,* 445–449.

Pallier, C., Dehaene, S., Poline, J.-B., LeBihan, D., Argenti, A.-M., Dupoux, E., & Mehler, J. (2003). Brain imaging of language plasticity in adopted adults: Can a second language replace the first? *Cerebral Cortex, 13*, 155–161.

Parlato-Oliveira, E., Christophe, A., Hirose, Y., & Dupoux, E. (2010). Plasticity of illusory vowel perception in Brazilian-Japanese bilinguals. *The Journal of the Acoustical Society of America, 127*, 3738–3748.

Peltola, M. S., Kujala, T., Tuomainen, J., Ek, M., Aaltonen, O., & Näätänen, R. (2003). Native and foreign vowel discrimination as indexed by the mismatch negativity (MMN) response. *Neuroscience Letters, 352*, 25–28.

Peltola, M. S., Tuomainen, O., Koskinen, M., & Aaltonen, O. (2007). The effect of language immersion education on the preattentive perception of native and non-native vowel contrasts. *Journal of Psycholinguistic Research, 36*, 15–23.

Penfield, W. (1965). Conditioning the uncommitted cortex for language learning. *Brain, 88*, 787–798.

Penfield, W. & Roberts, L. (1959). *Speech and brain-mechanisms*. Princeton: Princeton University Press.

Pérez-Vidal, C. (Ed.). (2014). *Language acquisition in study abroad and formal instruction contexts* (Vol. 13). Amsterdam and Philadelphia: John Benjamins.

Pinet, M. & Iverson, P. (2010). Talker-listener accent interactions in speech-in-noise recognition: Effects of prosodic manipulation as a function of language experience. *The Journal of the Acoustical Society of America, 128*, 1357–1365.

Pinet, M., Iverson, P., & Huckvale, M. (2011). Second-language experience and speech-in-noise recognition: Effects of talker–listener accent similarity. *The Journal of the Acoustical Society of America, 130*, 1653–1662.

Piske, T., Flege, J. E., MacKay, I. R., & Meador, D. (2002). The production of English vowels by fluent early and late Italian-English bilinguals. *Phonetica, 59*, 49–71.

Piske, T., MacKay, I. R., & Flege, J. E. (2001). Factors affecting degree of foreign accent in an L2: A review. *Journal of Phonetics, 29*, 191–215.

Polka, L. (1992). Characterizing the influence of native language experience on adult speech perception. *Perception & Psychophysics, 52*, 37–52.

Polka, L. (1995). Linguistic influences in adult perception of non-native vowel contrasts. *The Journal of the Acoustical Society of America, 97*, 1286–1296.

Pulvermüller, F. & Schumann, J. H. (1994). Neurobiological mechanisms of language acquisition. *Language Learning, 44*, 681–734.

Qin, Z. & Jongman, A. (2016). Does second language experience modulate perception of tones in a third language? *Language and Speech, 59*, 318–338.

Rallo Fabra, L. R. & Romero, J. (2012). Native Catalan learners' perception and production of English vowels. *Journal of Phonetics, 40*, 491–508.

Rinker, T., Alku, P., Brosch, S., & Kiefer, M. (2010). Discrimination of native and non-native vowel contrasts in bilingual Turkish–German and monolingual German children: Insight from the Mismatch Negativity ERP component. *Brain and Language, 113*, 90–95.

Rogers, C. L., Dalby, J., & Nishi, K. (2004). Effects of noise and proficiency on intelligibility of Chinese-accented English. *Language and Speech, 47*, 139–154.

Rogers, C. L., DeMasi, T. M., & Krause, J. C. (2010). Conversational and clear speech intelligibility of /bVd/ syllables produced by native and non-native English speakers. *The Journal of the Acoustical Society of America, 128*, 410–423.

Rogers, C. L., Lister, J. J., Febo, D. M., Besing, J. M., & Abrams, H. B. (2006). Effects of bilingualism, noise, and reverberation on speech perception by listeners with normal hearing. *Applied Psycholinguistics, 27,* 465–485.

Rogers, C. L. & Lopez, A. S. (2008). Perception of silent-center syllables by native and non-native English speakers. *The Journal of the Acoustical Society of America, 124,* 1278–1293.

Sancier, M. L. & Fowler, C. A. (1997). Gestural drift in a bilingual speaker of Brazilian Portuguese and English. *Journal of Phonetics, 25,* 421–436.

Schneiderman, E. I. & Desmarais, C. (1988). The talented language learner: Some preliminary findings. *Second Language Research, 4,* 91–109.

Schumann, J. H. (1975). Affective factors and the problem of age in second language acquisition. *Language Learning, 25,* 209–235.

Scovel, T. (1969). Foreign accents, language acquisition, and cerebral dominance. *Language Learning, 19*(3–4), 245–253.

Scovel, T. (1988). *A time to speak: A psycholinguistic inquiry into the critical period for human speech.* Rowley, MA: Newbury House.

Sebastián-Gallés, N., Echeverría, S., & Bosch, L. (2005). The influence of initial exposure on lexical representation: Comparing early and simultaneous bilinguals. *Journal of Memory and Language, 52,* 240–255.

Sebastián-Gallés, N. & Soto-Faraco, S. (1999). Online processing of native and non-native phonemic contrasts in early bilinguals. *Cognition, 72,* 111–123.

Shah, A. P. (2004). Production and perceptual correlates of Spanish-accented English. In J. Slifka, S. Manuel, & M. Matthies (Eds.), *From sound to sense: 50+ years of discoveries in speech communication* (pp. 79–84). Retrieved from www.rle.mit.edu/sound tosense/conference/ pdfs/fulltext/Friday%20Posters/FA-Shah-STS.pdf (Accessed on December 6, 2015).

Sidaras, S. K., Alexander, J. E., & Nygaard, L. C. (2009). Perceptual learning of systematic variation in Spanish-accented speech. *The Journal of the Acoustical Society of America, 125,* 3306–3316.

Simões, A. R. (1996). Phonetics in second language acquisition: An acoustic study of fluency in adult learners of Spanish. *Hispania, 79,* 87–95.

Simon, E. & D'Hulster, T. (2012). The effect of experience on the acquisition of a non-native vowel contrast. *Language Sciences, 34,* 269–283.

Slevc, L. R. & Miyake, A. (2006). Individual differences in second-language proficiency does musical ability matter? *Psychological Science, 17,* 675–681.

So, C. K. & Best, C. T. (2010). Cross-language perception of non-native tonal contrasts: Effects of native phonological and phonetic influences. *Language and Speech, 53,* 273–293.

Solomon, D. & Ali, F. A. (1975). Influence of verbal content and intonation on meaning attributions of first- and second-language speakers. *The Journal of Social Psychology, 95,* 3–9.

Strange, W. & Dittmann, S. (1984). Effects of discrimination training on the perception of /r-l/ by Japanese adults learning English. *Perception & Psychophysics, 36,* 131–145.

Strange, W., Hisagi, M., Akahane-Yamada, R., & Kubo, R. (2011). Cross-language perceptual similarity predicts categorical discrimination of American vowels by naïve Japanese listeners. *The Journal of the Acoustical Society of America, 130,* EL226–EL231.

Sueyoshi, A. & Hardison, D. M. (2005). The role of gestures and facial cues in second language listening comprehension. *Language Learning*, 55, 661–699.

Sundara, M. & Polka, L. (2008). Discrimination of coronal stops by bilingual adults: The timing and nature of language interaction. *Cognition*, 106, 234–258.

Sundara, M., Polka, L., & Baum, S. (2006). Production of coronal stops by simultaneous bilingual adults. *Bilingualism: Language and Cognition*, 9, 97–114.

Sundara, M., Polka, L., & Genesee, F. (2006). Language-experience facilitates discrimination of /d-/ in monolingual and bilingual acquisition of English. *Cognition*, 100, 369–388.

Tabri, D., Chacra, K. M. S. A., & Pring, T. (2011). Speech perception in noise by monolingual, bilingual and trilingual listeners. *International Journal of Language & Communication Disorders*, 46, 411–422.

Tajima, K., Kato, H., Rothwell, A., Akahane-Yamada, R., & Munhall, K. G. (2008). Training English listeners to perceive phonemic length contrasts in Japanese. *The Journal of the Acoustical Society of America*, 123, 397–413.

Takagi, N. (2002). The limits of training Japanese listeners to identify English /r/ and /l/: Eight case studies. *The Journal of the Acoustical Society of America*, 111, 2887–2896.

Taylor, B. P. (1974). Toward a theory of language acquisition. *Language Learning*, 24, 23–35.

Thompson, I. (1991). Foreign accents revisited: The English pronunciation of Russian immigrants. *Language Learning*, 41, 177–204.

Thomson, R. I., Nearey, T. M., & Derwing, T. M. (2009). A modified statistical pattern recognition approach to measuring the crosslinguistic similarity of Mandarin and English vowels. *The Journal of the Acoustical Society of America*, 126, 1447–1460.

Tremblay, A. & Owens, N. (2010). The role of acoustic cues in the development of (non-) target-like second language prosodic representations. *Canadian Journal of Linguistics*, 55, 85–114.

Trofimovich, P. & Baker, W. (2006). Learning second language suprasegmentals: Effect of L2 experience on prosody and fluency characteristics of L2 speech. *Studies in Second Language Acquisition*, 28, 1–30.

Tsao, F. M., Liu, H. M., & Kuhl, P. K. (2006). Perception of native and non-native affricate-fricative contrasts: Cross-language tests on adults and infants. *The Journal of the Acoustical Society of America*, 120, 2285–2294.

Tsukada, K., Birdsong, D., Bialystok, E., Mack, M., Sung, H., & Flege, J. (2005). A developmental study of English vowel production and perception by native Korean adults and children. *Journal of Phonetics*, 33, 263–290.

Uther, M., Giannakopoulou, A., & Iverson, P. (2012). Hyperarticulation of vowels enhances phonetic change responses in both native and non-native speakers of English: Evidence from an auditory event-related potential study. *Brain Research*, 1470, 52–58.

Wang, Y., Behne, D. M., & Jiang, H. (2008). Linguistic experience and audio-visual perception of non-native fricatives. *The Journal of the Acoustical Society of America*, 124, 1716–1726.

Wang, Y., Behne, D. M., Jongman, A., & Sereno, J. A. (2004). The role of linguistic experience in the hemispheric processing of lexical tone. *Applied Psycholinguistics*, 25, 449–466.

Wang, Y., Jongman, A., & Sereno, J. A. (2003). Acoustic and perceptual evaluation of Mandarin tone productions before and after perceptual training. *The Journal of the Acoustical Society of America, 113*, 1033–1043.

Wang, Y. & Kuhl, P. K. (2003). Evaluating the 'critical period' hypothesis: Perceptual learning of Mandarin tones in American adults and American children at 6, 10 and 14 years of age. In *Poster presented at the 15th International Congress of Phonetic Sciences* (pp. 1537–1540). Retrieved from http://128.95.148.60/kuhl/pdf/wang_kuhl_2003.pdf (Accessed on January 1, 2016).

Wang, Y., Spence, M. M., Jongman, A., & Sereno, J. A. (1999). Training American listeners to perceive Mandarin tones. *The Journal of the Acoustical Society of America, 106*, 3649–3658.

Wayland, R. P. & Guion, S. G. (2004). Training English and Chinese listeners to perceive Thai tones: A preliminary report. *Language Learning, 54*, 681–712.

Wayland, R. P. & Li, B. (2008). Effects of two training procedures in cross-language perception of tones. *Journal of Phonetics, 36*, 250–267.

Weber, A. & Cutler, A. (2006). First-language phonotactics in second-language listening. *Journal of the Acoustical Society of America, 119*, 597–607.

Werker, J. F. & Tees, R. C. (1984). Cross-language speech perception: Evidence for perceptual reorganization during the first year of life. *Infant Behavior and Development, 7*, 49–63.

White, L., Melhorn, J. F., & Mattys, S. L. (2010). Segmentation by lexical subtraction in Hungarian speakers of second-language English. *The Quarterly Journal of Experimental Psychology, 63*, 544–554.

Wilson, E. O. B. & Spaulding, T. J. (2010). Effects of noise and speech intelligibility on listener comprehension and processing time of Korean-accented English. *Journal of Speech, Language, and Hearing Research, 53*, 1543–1554.

Woodrow, L. (2006). Anxiety and speaking English as a second language. *Regional Language Centre (RELC) Journal, 37*, 308–328.

Yang, J. & Liu, C. (2012). Categorical perception of lexical tone in 6 to 8-year-old monolingual and bilingual children. *International Journal of Asian Language Processing, 22*, 49–62.

Yeni-Komshian, G., Flege, J. E., & Liu, S. (2000). Pronunciation proficiency in first and second languages of Korean–English bilinguals. *Bilingualism: Language and Cognition, 3*, 131–149.

Ylinen, S., Shestakova, A., Alku, P., & Huotilainen, M. (2005). The perception of phonological quantity based on durational cues by native speakers, second-language users and nonspeakers of Finnish. *Language and Speech, 48*, 313–338.

Ylinen, S., Shestakova, A., Huotilainen, M., Alku, P., & Näätänen, R. (2006). Mismatch negativity (MMN) elicited by changes in phoneme length: A cross-linguistic study. *Brain Research, 1072*, 175–185.

Yu, V. Y. & Andruski, J. E. (2010). A cross-language study of perception of lexical stress in English. *Journal of Psycholinguistic Research, 39*, 323–344.

Zampini, M. L. (1998). The relationship between the production and perception of L2 Spanish Stops. *Texas Papers in Foreign Language Education, 3*, 85–100.

Zhang, Y., Nissen, S. L., & Francis, A. L. (2008). Acoustic characteristics of English lexical stress produced by native Mandarin speakers. *The Journal of the Acoustical Society of America, 123*, 4498–4513.

Chapter 4

Word Recognition in L2

4.1 Introduction

There are two facts about lexical processing that an average person does not usually pay much attention to. The first is the size of one's vocabulary. An adult with a college education typically has a vocabulary of tens of thousands of words in his or her native language. For example, an online English vocabulary size test site estimated on the basis of over two million tests that an adult native speaker of English has a vocabulary size ranging from 20,000–35,000 words. Other estimates include 17,000 words by Zechmeister, Chronis, Cull, D'Anna, and Healy (1995), and 30,000 productive vocabularies by Levelt (1989). The second is the level of ease or automaticity involved in word recognition. It takes about 200 ms for us to recognize a word, according to Levelt (1989), and this is usually done without us making much effort. The question of how the human mind is able to identify or isolate a single word among tens of thousands of them in such a short amount of time has inspired psycholinguists to explore the mechanisms and processes involved in the recognition (in listening and reading) or retrieval (in speaking and writing) of words in language use. Research on lexical processing has grown dramatically since the 1960s. This research has also laid the foundation for studying L2 lexical processing theoretically, topically, and methodologically.

This chapter is one of the two chapters on L2 lexical processing. It reviews research on word recognition in L2 in general (while Chapter 5 deals with the processing of complex words and multiword units and semantic processing in L2). It begins with a background section that introduces the basic concepts, methods, findings related to word recognition research. The next two sections discuss two L2 word recognition topics: the structure of the L2 lexicon and the role of L1 in L2 word recognition. It is followed by a section where three additional L2 word recognition topics are discussed.

4.2 Understanding Lexical Representation and Processing

When we see a string of letters or a logograph of our native language, we can instantly tell, under most circumstances, whether it is a word or not, and, if it is, what it means. Most psycholinguists believe that we are able to do so because we all have a mental lexicon in which we store all the words we know. Within the lexicon, each word is said to have a lexical entry where we store all the information we know about a word, such its spelling, pronunciation, meaning, and part of speech. Some psycholinguists such as Levelt (1989) divide the lexical entry into two parts. The lexeme part contains the form specifications such as pronunciation, spelling, and morphology, and the lemma part is where the semantic and syntactic information is stored.

4.2.1 Characteristics of Lexical Representation

A lexical entry in the lexicon has several important characteristics. First, it contains a rich array of information about a word. Some basic attributes include spelling, pronunciation, meaning, morphological structure, and syntactic category. Semantically, for example, the word *desk* would have meanings such as being a piece of furniture in the shape similar to a table and used for reading and writing. Syntactically, it is a countable noun. In addition to such basic semantic and syntactic information, a lexical entry also contains very subtle semantic and syntactic specifications and more intricate data such as its frequency of occurrence, the sociolinguistic and textual contexts it often appears in, words that it is often associated with, its connotation, to list just a few. For example, a native speaker of English knows that *fill* can only be used in a ground-object construction such as I *filled the glass with water*, but not a figure-object construction such as **I filled the water into the glass*. In contrast, *pour* can only be used in a figure-object construction such as I *poured water into the glass*, but not in a ground-object construction such as **I poured the glass with water*, but *spray* can be used in both constructions. Native speakers of English also know the semantic similarities and differences between *real* and *true* or between *major* and *main* and the nouns they often collocate with, and they also know when to use the words *Sir* and *Mister*. All such knowledge is part of the information represented in a lexical entry.

Second, the lexical entry is believed to be an abstract representation, or a prototype, of a word we know (e.g., Becker, 1976; Levelt, Roelofs, & Meyer, 1999; Marslen-Wilson & Warren, 1994). The acoustic signal for the same word can vary dependent on the age, gender, dialect of the speaker and the sociocultural and linguistic context in which it appears. Its written form can also appear differently when hand-written by different people or printed in different fonts. Native speakers typically do not have much difficulty in recognizing an intended word in natural speech communication in spite of a great deal of variations in its specific appearances. We are able to do so because the lexical entry we store in our lexicon is abstract and, thus, flexible enough to accommodate such variations. From this perspective, lexical development can be viewed as a process of establishing a successively more abstract lexical entry for a word.

Third, the retrieval of lexical information from a lexical entry is automatic in the sense that the process is usually effortless and requires little attentional resources (see Segalowitz, 2003 for detailed discussion of the concept of automaticity). This automaticity in word recognition can be seen in the classic Stroop effect (Stroop, 1935). When individuals are asked to name colors of printed words, but not words themselves, they typically show a delay in naming items whose words and colors are not consistent, e.g., the word *red* printed in green. This delay suggests that the word is processed automatically in spite of the fact that an individual is asked to name the color only. Automatic lexical processing is also evident in masked priming effects. A prime word that is presented very briefly, e.g., for 50 ms, and is not consciously visible to an individual can affect the processing of a target word (e.g., Forster & Davis, 1984).

Fourth, lexical entries are interconnected in the lexicon and interact with each other in lexical processing. This interaction may occur among words with high degree of form overlap (e.g., *project* and *protect*), as shown in the neighborhood effect in word recognition (e.g., Andrews, 1989, 1992). Such connections may be semantic in nature and exist among words that are related in meaning. For example, if I ask you to provide the first word coming to your mind for the word *big*, you are likely to say *small*, *little*, or *large*, all words related to *big* in meaning. According to the word association data provided by Nelson, McEvoy, and Schreiber (1998), 83% of the 148 people they tested provided these three words that are related in meaning to *big*. Other connections are more associative in nature. For example, the same word association data in Nelson, McEvoy, and Schreiber (1998) showed that 25% of the English NS tested produced *grass* when they were showed the word *green*. Many multiword units such as collocations, formulas, and idioms (e.g., *narrow escape*, *on the other hand*, *hit the nail on the head*) are words connected with each other through associative connections. Words may also be linked to each other because of morphological connections, e.g., between a base word and a derivation (*happy-unhappy*) or between a component word and a compound (*tooth-toothbrush*).

Finally, it is well accepted that the lexical system is connected with a conceptual system. Each word is linked to the concept it is used to express through the semantic content in the lemma. This word-concept connection is developed while a child learns words and concepts at the same time in early language and cognitive development, and becomes well consolidated with accumulating experiences in the language. Lexical processing in a native language is characterized by a strong co-activation of concepts and words. This activation is automatic and bidirectional in the sense that a related concept becomes readily available when we think of a word and vice versa. This can be seen in the ease we experience in naming pictures which requires the activation from concepts to words and in making semantic categorization of words (e.g., *is tulip a flower?*) which involves word-to-concept activation.

4.2.2 Methods for Studying Lexical Processing

Lexical processing research has employed mostly four methods. The most widely used task is that of lexical decision. In a lexical decision task (LDT), a letter sequence (or a logograph or a combination of logographs) is displayed on a computer monitor. The stimuli typically include an equal number of words and nonwords that are presented in a random order. A participant is asked to decide whether the stimulus is a word and indicate their decision by pressing two buttons or keys, one for Yes, and the other for No. The second task is naming. Depending on the stimuli used, one can further differentiate the naming task into word naming, picture naming, color naming, digit naming. In a naming task, a participant is asked to read aloud a letter sequence or a logograph, or say the name of a stimulus. In a semantic judgment task (SJT), a participant may be asked to decide whether a displayed word refers to a natural or man-made object, or refers to a living or nonliving entity. A participant may also be asked to decide whether the object referred to by the displayed word belongs to a certain category such as furniture, weapon, or vegetable. In all these three tasks, the participants are usually asked to respond as quickly and accurately as possible. The reaction time (RT), which is usually measured as the interval between the onset of the stimulus and the producing of a response, is recorded as primary data. Error rates (ER) are also taken into consideration in data analysis. Many other tasks are also used. See Jiang (2012) for more information about lexical processing tasks.

All these tasks can be used in combination with the priming paradigm. A test item in a priming study usually consists of two elements, a prime and a target. The two elements are usually displayed sequentially with an interval of varying length. This interval is referred to as the stimulus onset asynchrony or SOA. Two versions of the priming paradigm can be differentiated on the basis of stimulus display procedure. One of them is to display the prime and the target with a relatively long SOA and both the prime and target are visible to a participant (Figure 4.1a). A potential problem with this method is that a participant may develop a certain strategy such as guessing when he or she discovers a relationship between the prime and the target, e.g., a semantic relationship in the test items *doctor-nurse*. To avoid this problem, Forster and Davis (1984) devised the masked priming paradigm where the prime is not consciously visible to or identifiable by a participant. This is achieved

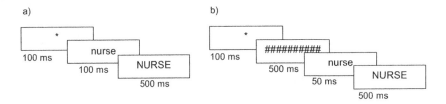

Figure 4.1 Illustration of Item Display in an Unmasked and a Masked Priming Study

by presenting the prime very briefly, e.g., 50 ms, and sandwiching it between a forward mask, e.g., a set of hash marks, and the target (which serves as the backward mask) (see Figure 4.1b). This method has the advantage of minimizing strategic effects.

The primary manipulation in a priming study is often the prime-target relation. For example, one can compare semantically related pairs and unrelated pairs (e.g., *doctor-nurse* vs. *gardener-nurse*) to study semantic priming, or morphologically related and unrelated pairs (e.g., *honeymoon-honey* vs. *classroom-honey*) to study morphological priming. The unrelated pairs are often referred to as control items. Additionally, one may also manipulate SOA to compare priming effects under masked and unmasked conditions, manipulate prime and target display modality to compare unimodal (e.g., visual-visual) and cross-modal (e.g., auditory prime-visual target) priming effects, or manipulate the tasks (e.g., LDT vs. naming). The priming paradigm has become a major tool for studying lexical processing.

4.2.3 Lexical Processing Effects

A great deal of research has been conducted to understand the structure of the mental lexicon and the mechanisms and processes involved in lexical access. This research has helped uncover some well-documented phenomena about lexical processing. These findings represent our current knowledge about the psychology of lexical processing. They have played a significant role in developing theories about lexical processing and in understanding how lexical processing is different or similar between L1 and L2.

4.2.3.1 Frequency, Familiarity, and Age-of-Acquisition Effects

The first and most well-documented lexical processing phenomenon is probably *the frequency effect*. Words differ in how frequently they get used. We use the word *good* much more frequently than the word *hood*, for example. Individuals usually enjoy an advantage in responding to high-frequency words compared to low-frequency words. This frequency effect has been observed and measured in terms of shorter naming and lexical decision latencies (e.g., Forster & Chambers, 1973; Rubenstein, Garfield, & Millikan, 1970), shorter eye fixation times (e.g., Inhoff & Rayner, 1986), and better identification rates (e.g., Howes & Solomon, 1951) for higher-frequency than for low-frequency words. In addition to whole-word frequency, two sublexical frequencies have also been found to affect word recognition. One of them is *bigram frequency*. A bigram is a unit of two adjacent letters in a word, such as *sp* or *nt*. In a particular language, some of these two-letter combinations occur more frequently than others. For example, *th* is the most frequent bigram in English. The effect of bigram frequency has been found to be quite variable across studies. It can be inhibitory in that words with higher bigram frequency counts took longer to respond to (e.g., Rice & Robinson, 1975), facilitative (e.g., Conrad, Carreiras, Tamm, & Jacobs, 2009), or have no effect (Andrews, 1992). The second is the syllable frequency. Syllable frequency can be operationalized as the total frequency of all words sharing a syllable at a particular position (e.g., Conrad & Jacobs, 2004). For example, the frequency for the syllable *ab* would be the accumulated frequency of all words beginning with this syllable such as *absent*, *abnormal*. Syllable frequency has been found to have an inhibitory effect in that words with high syllable frequency were responded to more slowly (e.g., Carreiras, Alvarez, & Devega, 1993; Perea & Carreiras, 1998).

A phenomenon related to the frequency effect is *the familiarity effect*. Familiarity differs from frequency in that it is an individualized subjective measure. A familiarity measure is usually obtained by asking participants to rate the level of familiarity of a word to them. A high-frequency word is usually more familiar to most people, and thus, the two variables are related. This raises the question of whether an observed frequency effect is actually a familiarity effect or a mixture of two. Some researchers believe so and they put this idea to test by separating the two variables. Findings from several studies demonstrated the presence of a familiarity effect independent of word frequency (Connine, Mullennix, Shernoff, & Yelens, 1990; Kreuz, 1987; Lewellen, Goldinger, Pisoni, & Greene, 1993).

A third related phenomenon is the *age of acquisition* (or AOA) *effect*. Words differ in the age at which individuals first know them. Some words are learned at a younger age than other words. The age of acquisition and frequency are often correlated, as well, as words learned early are often of high frequency. Some scholars, e.g., Carroll and White (1973), argue that the frequency effect is actually an age-of-acquisition effect. They were the first, according to Morrison and Ellis (2000), to demonstrate that the age at which words are learned affected lexical access time. Since then a large number of studies have shown an age-of-acquisition effect in word recognition and production tasks independent of frequency (e.g., Bonin, Barry, Méot, & Chalard, 2004; Butler & Hains, 1979; Ellis & Morrison, 1998; Morrison & Ellis, 1995, 2000;

Stadthagen-Gonzalez, Bowers, & Damian, 2004). However, other studies also demonstrated that a frequency effect could also be observed when age of acquisition was controlled (Gerhand & Barry, 1998, 1999). Thus, both effects are likely to be real even though they may be confounded in an individual study when test materials are not specifically selected to separate the two variables.

4.2.3.2 Other Lexical Property Effects

Lexical properties other than frequency, familiarity, and age of acquisition have also been found to affect lexical access. One of them is *word length*. Word length has been defined in terms of the number of letters or syllables in a word (e.g., De Groot, Borgwaldt, Bos, & Van den Eijnden, 2002; Juphard, Carbonnel, Ans, & Valdois, 2006). Occasionally, it is defined as the number of phonemes or morphemes. Research showed that longer words produced longer RTs, whether length is defined in terms of number of letters or number of syllables (Butler & Hains, 1979; Chumbley & Balota, 1984; De Groot et al., 2002; Stenneken, Conrad, & Jacobs, 2007; Whaley, 1978).

A second factor is *spelling-sound regularity*. Many languages, including English, do not maintain one-on-one mapping between spelling and pronunciation. The same pronunciation can be realized in different spellings such as /f/ spelled as f or ph in English; similarly, the same letter or sequence of letters may have different pronunciations in different words, such as "ouch" pronounced differently in *touch* and *couch*. A word thus may be considered regular in spelling-sound correspondence if it is consistent with how letters are usually pronounced in a specific environment in that language (e.g., *make*) or exceptional when it is not (e.g., *have*). Some studies showed that people tend to take longer in responding to words with inconsistent or irregular spelling-sound relations (e.g., Seidenberg, 1985; Stone, Vanhoy, & Van Orden, 1997; Ziegler, Montant, & Jacobs, 1997), but the effect is not always robust (e.g., Jared, McRae, & Seidenberg, 1990).

A third factor is *neighborhood size and frequency*. Two words are neighbors of each other if they differ by only one letter but with the number of letters and letter sequence being the same. Thus, *word* and *work*, or *jump* and *lump* are neighbors, but *dear* and *hare* are not. The term neighborhood size (or neighborhood density) refers to the number of neighbors a word has. Some words have many neighbors and others have few neighbors. For example, *meat* has 13 neighbors, but *glad* has only two. Some studies showed that words with more neighbors are responded to faster than words with fewer neighbors (e.g., Andrews, 1989, 1992). This is called the neighborhood density effect. It was also shown in some studies that individuals took longer to respond to words with a high-frequency neighbor than words without high-frequency neighbors (e.g., Carreiras, Perea, & Grainger, 1997; Grainger, 1990). This is referred to as the neighborhood frequency effect.

4.2.3.3 Meaning-Related Effects

Some semantic properties of words have also been found to affect word recognition. One of such properties is *concreteness*. Some words refer to entities that can be perceived by the senses, and some do not. We can see or touch a tree, but not a concept, for example. Thus, words differ in concreteness. When other variables are controlled, people tend to respond to concrete words faster than to abstract words (e.g., James, 1975; Schwanenflugel, Harnishfeger, & Stowe, 1988). Related to concreteness is the concept of *imageability* which refers to the extent to which one can create a mental image of what is referred to by a word. Concrete words are usually more imageable than abstract words, but words of similar concreteness can differ in their imageability. Some research showed that, everything else being equal, people tended to respond to words of higher imageability faster than words of lower imageability (e.g., Balota, Cortese, Sergent-Marshall, Spieler, & Yap, 2004; Morrison & Ellis, 2000).

The number of meanings a word has also affects lexical access. Research shows that people respond to words with more meanings, e.g., *head*, faster than words with fewer meanings, e.g., *skull*, when other properties are held constant (e.g., Borowsky & Masson, 1996; Millis & Button, 1989; Hino & Lupker, 1996). A related variable is the number of associates. When the recognition of a word automatically activates another, the latter is referred to as an associate of the former. Words differ in the number of associates they have. For example, *corpse* has three, and *cost* has 14 in Nelson et al. (1998) word association norms. Individuals have been found to respond to words with more associates faster than words with fewer associates (Balota et al., 2004; Duñabeitia, Avilés, & Carreiras, 2008).

4.2.3.4 Nonword-Related Effects

Nonwords (also referred to as nonce words or pseudowords) are letter strings or logograms that do not form a word, e.g., *balertty*. Three lexical processing effects are related to nonwords. The first is the *lexicality effect.* Individuals usually accept a word faster than they reject a nonword, which is a well-replicated finding (e.g., Scarborough, Cortese, & Scarborough, 1977; Stenneken et al., 2007). This term has also been used to refer to the finding that it is easier to detect a letter in a word than in a nonword (e.g., Hildebrandt, Caplan, Sokol, & Torreano, 1995). The second is the *nonword legality effect.* A nonword may be considered legal if the letter sequence follows orthographic rules of the language (e.g., *brone*) or illegal if they do not (e.g., *zfot*). Research showed that it takes less time to reject illegal nonwords than legal nonwords (e.g., Coltheart, Davelaar, Jonasson, & Besner, 1977). The third one is the *pseudohomophones* effect. A pseudo-homophone is a nonword that sounds like a real word. *Brane* is one because it sounds like *brain*. Rubenstein, Lewis, and Rubenstein (1971) found that their participants took longer to reject pseudohomophones than to reject other non-pseudohomophonic nonwords (e.g., *brone*). The finding was replicated in Coltheart et al. (1977) and Seidenberg, Petersen, MacDonald, and Plaut (1996).

4.2.3.5 Priming Effects

A number of priming effects have been observed in lexical processing research. A priming effect refers to either a facilitation or inhibition in recognizing a word as a result of having previously encountered the same word or another word. One such effect is the repetition priming effect. Individuals show a better performance in responding to a target word that was shown previously. The form priming effect has been observed when a target word is preceded by a form-related prime, e.g., groject/project (e.g., Forster, Davis, Schoknecht, & Carter, 1987). Priming effects can also be obtained on morphologically related prime-target pairs such as inflectional (e.g., *vowed-vow*), derivational (*worker-work*), and compound (*honeymoon-honey*) words (e.g., Fiorentino & Fund-Reznicek, 2009; Grainger, Colé, & Segui, 1991; Marslen-Wilson, Bozic, & Randall, 2008; Shoolman & Andrews, 2003). Finally, semantically or associatively related words can produce facilitative priming effect, as well (See Lucas, 2000 for a meta-analysis).

4.2.3.6 Context Effects

Word recognition has been shown to be influenced by linguistic context in various ways. For examples, words were responded to faster in naming (e.g., West, Stanovich, Feeman, & Cunningham, 1983) or LDT (e.g., Becker, 1980; Eisenberg & Becker, 1982) when they appeared in a congruent sentence context than in a neutral or incongruent context. It also took less time to recognize a word when it appeared in a later part of a sentence when more contextual information was available than in an early part of a sentence (Marslen-Wilson & Tyler, 1980). When the stimuli were ambiguous, sentence context played a significant role in determining what word was identified (e.g., Connine, Blasko, & Hall, 1991). Individuals were also found to need less information for identifying a word when context was available (Grosjean, 1980). There is also electrophysiological evidence showing that context effects occur early in the word recognition process (e.g., Sereno, Brewer, & O'Donnell, 2003).

4.3 The L2 Lexicon

While learning a second language, an L2 learner develops a mental lexicon for the language in which all L2 words are stored. Assuming that this L2 lexicon is separated from the L1 lexicon, one may ask whether there are differences in how lexical entries are represented and how the lexicon is structured between the two languages. This section reviews two lines of research related to this question: the importance of form-based connections in the L2 lexicon and the episodic L2 lexicon.

4.3.1 Importance of Form-Based Connections

There are at least two lines of evidence suggesting that form-based connections play a more important role in the L2 lexicon than in the L1 lexicon. The first one comes from word association studies. The word association task (WAT), originally used to study child lexicosemantic and cognitive development in psychology (e.g., Ervin, 1961; McNeill, 1966), has been one of the most frequently used tasks to study the L2 lexicon. In a WAT, a participant is presented with a stimulus word and asked to provide a response word. The task may be timed or untimed, it may be discrete (writing down the first word coming to the mind) or continuous (writing down a predetermined number of words or as many words as possible in a given duration of time), it can be done within the same modality (e.g., visual stimulus-written response) or across modalities (e.g., aural stimulus-written response), it can be done within or between languages, and the response can be either free (any word coming to the mind) or controlled (the words that meet a predetermined criterion, e.g., beginning with the letter f or the name of a piece of furniture). The most frequently used version of the WAT in L2 research is the untimed discrete free word association (WA) done in the visual modality, with occasional variations in some aspect, such as the use of the aural-oral (e.g., Wolter, 2001), continuous (e.g., Zareva, 2007), and timed versions (e.g., Fitzpatrick & Izura, 2011).

It is conceivable that a perceived stimulus word can elicit a number of competing response words. The use of the WAT in the L2 context is based on the assumption that an individual's responses to stimulus words are indications of how words are interconnected in the L2 lexicon and the strength of such interconnections. Thus, by examining these responses and by comparing them to those produced by NS, we can infer how words are linked and organized in the L2 lexicon and how such organization is similar to or different from that of the L1 lexicon.

One of the earliest attempts to examine L2 lexical organization by means of a WAT was reported by Meara (1978). He tested a group of 76 English-speaking learners of French with 100 high-frequency French words in a free WAT. The participants were asked to write down the first word coming to their mind. Two methods of response classification and comparison were adopted. One was to classify them as syntagmatic, paradigmatic, and clang responses, a method widely used in early L1 word association studies. The first refers to a response word that is not in the same word class as the stimulus word, such as *soft* in response to *cloth* (thus forming a stimulus-response pair of *cloth-soft*, same below). Paradigmatic responses are words in the same class as the response word, such as *dog-cat*. Clang responses are words that are similar in pronunciation or spelling but have no semantic relationship, such as *sheep-sheet*. In the second classification method, which we may refer to as the nativelikeness method, a response from NNS was classified as one of the three categories: a) also a primary response provided by French NS, b) not a primary response but among the responses by French NS, or c) not among the responses by NS. The results showed some similarities between NNS and NS. For example, both groups produced a high proportion of paradigmatic responses. However, there were also a great deal of discrepancies. In terms of the nativelikeness of the responses (the second classification), the NNS were found to produce a relatively low percentage of NL responses. The percentage of responses for the three categories were 23%, 40%, and 37%, respectively. That is, 37% of the responses from NNS were not responses from NS. Particularly noteworthy in the present context was the finding that these non-nativelike responses were mostly orthographically similar clang responses, contrasting with NS who produced few clang responses. Meara also noted the findings that some NS primary responses were completely absent from NNS, and that NNS produced a low proportion of syntagmatic responses. Meara interpreted these differences as indicating that the L1 lexicon was primarily organized on the principle of meaning, but there is more reliance on form in the organization of the L2 lexicon. However, he was cautious not to consider this as the only interpretation.

There was a reemergence of interest in this line of research in the 2000s, led by Wolter (2001). In this study, Wolter tested 13 Japanese ESL speakers and nine NS of English in an aural-oral discrete free WAT. The stimulus words included two lists of English words. The first list consisted of 45 English words of relatively high frequency intended for both NS and NNS. The second list included 45 low-frequency words used for NS only. Each list contained an equal number of nouns, verbs, and adjectives. A word knowledge test was also given to assess the participants' familiarity with each stimulus word on a scale of 1–5. The participants' responses were classified using the traditional three-way (syntagmatic-paradigmatic-clang) system. The use of the words in a wide frequency range, particularly the low-frequency words for NS, in combination of the word knowledge test represented a unique feature of the study and allowed the examination of the relationship between familiarity and word association performance. The overall analysis of the data from the first list showed two differences between NS and NNS: NS produced more paradigmatic responses while NNS produced more syntagmatic responses, and NNS produced more clang responses than NS. However, when the low-frequency words and the familiarity were taken into consideration, the two groups were quite similar with regard to the clang responses: both NS and NNS produced a high proportion of clang responses on words that were not familiar to them, and the proportion dropped significantly on familiar words for both groups. These latter results were interpreted as indicating a similarity in the structure of the lexicon in L1 and L2.

The discovery of the relationship between familiarity and WA response pattern is an important finding. However, the finding that both NS and NNS produced more clang responses to less familiar words does not necessarily mean that the L1 and L2 lexicons are similar in organization. Instead, the finding suggests that both NS and NNS may adopt similar strategies while performing the WAT. When the meaning of a word is known, they produce meaning-related responses (either syntagmatic or paradigmatic), but when the meaning is not familiar, they produce more form-related responses. The adoption of this shared strategy is not surprising because in the absence of any semantic information, word form becomes the primary or only lexical property that links a word with another. The similarity shown in Wolter (2001) does not necessarily contradict with the conclusion that form-based connections play a more important role in L2 lexical representation, as words in the L2 lexicon are usually of lower frequencies to L2 speakers which affects how they are interconnected.

Several subsequent studies have replicated the finding that L2 speakers produced more form-related responses (Fitzpatrick, 2006; Fitzpatrick & Izura, 2011; Namei, 2004). In the study reported by Fitzpatrick (2006), for example, 40 NNS and 40 English NS were tested with 60 words selected from the different frequency sublists of the Academic Word List (Coxhead, 2000). The participants were asked to write down the first word coming to their minds for each stimulus word. The responses were classified as meaning-based, form-based, and position-based (or collocational), and erratic associations. She found that while both NNS and NS produced more meaning-related response, NNS speakers produced significantly more form-based responses than NS and NS produced significantly more position-based responses.

It should be pointed out in this context that findings from L2 word association studies are very inconsistent. There seems to be a study that showed an opposite pattern for every result reported. Here are some examples. Zareva and Wolter (2012) and Zareva (2007) showed that both NS and NNS produced more paradigmatic responses than syntagmatic responses, but NNS in Wolter (2001) and both NS and NNS in Nissen and Henriksen (2006) showed an opposite pattern. The NNS participants in Wolter (2001) produced a high 35% of form-related or clang responses, so did the participants in Namei (2004, 26% and 16% for the Persian bilingual third and sixth graders, for example), but it was only 0.3% in Nissen and Henriksen (2006) and completely absent in Zareva (2007) and Zareva and Wolter (2012). Finally, in both Fitzpatrick (2006) and Fitzpatrick and Izura (2011), NS produced more collocational or position-based responses than NNS, but in Zareva and Wolter (2012), the pattern was opposite. This inconsistency has its methodological causes, as word association studies varied a great deal in the types of stimulus words selected (e.g., in terms of frequency and part of speech), the procedure adopted (e.g., modality and timing), and particularly the method used to classify responses. All these factors, particularly the last one, can affect the results directly.

While the findings from the word association studies have to be interpreted with cause, there is another line of evidence corroborating with them in showing a more prominent form-based principle of lexical organization. This evidence comes from the orthographic priming effects in L2 morphological priming studies.

To determine whether complex words are represented holistically or in a decomposed manner, a morphological priming paradigm is often adopted to test if a complex word such as *butterfly* would prime its component word such as *butter*. The observation of such a morphological priming effect is often taken as evidence for decomposition. To determine whether the observed morphological priming effect was morphological in nature or due to ortho-graphic overlap, a control comparison is often included in such studies, by including prime-target pairs that overlap in orthography but not in morphol-ogy, e.g., *restaurant-rest*. A morphological priming effect is considered mor-phological in nature only if orthographically related pairs do not produce a priming effect under the same experimental conditions. In studies involving L1 speakers, prime-target pairs that only had orthographic overlap usually did not produce a priming effect. For example, Rastle, Davis, Marslen-Wilson, and Tyler (2000) used orthographically similar but morphologically unrelated prime-target pairs such as *rubber-rub*; Gonnerman, Seidenberg, and Andersen (2007) used pairs such as *spinach-spin*; Longtin, Segui, and Hallé (2003) used French pairs such as *abricot-abri*. None of these studies showed an orthographic priming effect among L1 speakers.

Results from multiple studies involving L2 speakers showed a different pattern in that they often produced an orthographic priming effect. In one of these studies, Diependaele, Duñabeitia, Morris, and Keuleers (2011) used three types of prime-target pairs (each with their own control condition): morphologically related and semantically related (e.g., *viewer-view*), morpho-logically decomposable but semantically unrelated (e.g., *corner-corn* where *-er* is a legitimate suffix even though it is not in this word), and orthographically similar but morphologically and semantically unrelated (e.g., *freeze-free*). They tested English NS (Experiment 1), Spanish ESL speakers (Experi-ment 2), and Dutch ESL speakers (Experiment 3) with the same set of mate-rials. For orthographic condition which is the focus of the present discussion, there was a nonsignificant priming effect of 1 ms among English NS, but both ESL speaker groups showed a reliable orthographic priming effect (14 ms in both cases). Li, Jiang, and Gor (2017) reported a similar finding. They included an orthographic condition where the target overlapped with the first syllable of the prime in orthography but not in morphology or meaning, such as *restaurant-rest*. This condition was intended as a control condition and no priming effect was expected. However, a robust orthographic priming effect of 74 ms was observed of the NNS while English NS showed no such effect. In a third study, Heyer and Clahsen (2015) attempted to specifically assess the orthographic priming effect among L2 speakers. They tested advanced German ESL speakers on two types of prime-target pairs. They were either morphologically related such as *darkness-dark*, or only orthographically similar such as *country-count*. English NS showed a reliable morphological priming effect but no orthographic priming effect, but the German ESL participants showed a priming effect for both types of prime-target pairs. Finally, the latest finding of an orthographic priming effect (e.g., *freeze-free*) among L2 speakers in the absence of such an effect among NS under the same experimental conditions was reported by Li, Taft, and Xu (2017).

Two points are worth mentioning about this surprising orthographic priming effect observed among L2 speakers. First, it was observed when NS showed no such effect with the same set of materials and under the same experimental condition. Thus, it reflects a unique feature of lexical representation and processing among L2 speakers, rather than the artifact of experimental materials and procedure. It suggests that form-relatedness may play a more important role in L2 than in L1 lexical organization. Second, this effect was observed under the masked priming condition where the prime was not consciously visible to the participants in all these studies. Thus, if L2 speakers' unique performance in the word association studies is an outcome of both subconscious and conscious processes, the masked orthographic priming reflects an automatic process in lexical processing rather than the employment of a conscious and deliberate strategy by L2 speakers.

The findings of more form-related responses in word association and the orthographic priming effect among L2 speakers suggest that lexical form seems to play an important role in the organization of the L2 lexicon. This begs the question of why this happens. Two potential explanations may be offered. The first is the attention given to lexical forms in the process of L2 learning, particularly among classroom learners. Word form accuracy often figures prominently in the learning process, as it is the most basic and fundamental part of vocabulary acquisition early on. Both teachers and learners make a conscious and deliberate effort to achieve form accuracy in spelling and pronunciation. This attention on form may go well beyond the initial exposure to a new word as form confusion is quite common in L2 learning (e.g., Meara, 1983). The second explanation may be found in a relatively weak connection between lexical form and meaning in L2 (e.g., Kroll & Stewart, 1994; Jiang, 2000). L1 word learning usually involves the simultaneous development of lexical form and meaning. This results in a strong connection between the two. L2 words are often learned after the establishment of a semantic system. There is less semantic development taking place in the process. Thus, the connections are much weaker between lexical forms and meaning (see for example Costa et al., 2014; Dufour & Kroll, 1995; Keatley, Spinks, & de Gelder, 1994; Sholl, Sankaranarayanan, & Kroll, 1995 for related evidence), which may also lead to a form prominence in L2 lexical representation.

Even though the proposal was made by Meara (1978) four decades ago, more and converging evidence becomes available only recently for the idea that lexical form seems to play a more important role in the organization of the L2 lexicon. How this unique aspect of the L2 lexicon affects lexical processing in a broader context is yet to be explored.

4.3.2 The Episodic L2 Lexicon

Within the conception of a two-memory system of Tulving (1972, 1983), individuals have a semantic memory system and an episodic memory system. The two systems differ in both the content itself and in how the content is retrieved. The semantic system is defined as "a mental thesaurus, organized knowledge a person possesses about words and other verbal symbols, their meaning and referents, about relations among them" (Tulving, 1972, p. 386). The retrieval of information from the semantic information is usually automatic and subconscious. In contrast, the episodic system receives and stores information about episodes or events. It records snapshots of what happens in an individual's life. Furthermore, individuals are more likely to have a higher level of conscious awareness associated with what is represented in or retrieved from the episodic memory. For example, the word *museum*, including its spelling, pronunciation, and meaning, is stored in the semantic memory. Its meaning is automatically activated when we see the word, but the details of your last visit to a museum, such as the weather, the location, the trip there, what was seen there, are part of the episodic memory. Recalling these details is usually a conscious process. As the lexical system is part of the semantic memory and we are more concerned with lexical organization, we are contrasting lexical and episodic systems (rather than semantic and episodic memories) in the present discussion.

In experimental settings, lexical and episodic memories can be differentiated and tapped by means of different tasks. In an LDT where a person is asked to decide whether a letter string constitutes a word or not, one has to search the lexical system for making a decision. In an episodic recognition task (ERT), such as those used in Forster (1985) and Neely and Durgunoğlu (1985), a participant was first presented with a set words to be remembered or responded to in a study phase. Subsequently, in a test phase, he or she is asked to decide whether a word is one of those seen previously in the study phase. To perform this task successfully, one has to search the episodic system.

There is evidence showing that lexical information obtained differently ended up in different systems. It was found that semantically related word pairs such as *doctor-nurse* produced semantic priming effect in an LDT, but not in an ERT. However, when pairs of unrelated words such as *city-grass* were memorized to form associative pairs, they produced priming effects in an ERT, but not in an LDT (e.g., Carroll & Kirsner, 1982; Dagenbach, Horst, & Carr, 1990; Neely & Durgunoğlu, 1985). The latter finding suggested that consciously learned lexical knowledge is stored in an episodic system.

In comparison to the L1 lexical system, two aspects of the L2 lexical system distinguish itself. First, unlike the L1 system that is developed subconsciously in childhood, an L2 system, under most circumstances, is learned consciously. L2 learners are usually consciously aware of both the words they are learning and the learning process. Second, the L1 system is closely connected with the conceptual system because the two systems are developed simultaneously, but the L2 system is usually developed without substantial conceptual development. Instead, L2 words are either linked to their L1 translations or existing concepts. As a result, the connections between L2 word form and meanings may be considerably weaker than those between L1 words and concepts. Strong word form-meaning connections have been shown to be critical for words to be represented lexically. Dagenbach, Carr, and Barnhardt (1990) showed, for example, that newly learned words could produce a repetition or semantic priming effect when and only when the meanings were learned such that they became recallable, not just recognizable. For these two reasons, i.e., the conscious learning process and a weak form-meaning connection, the L2 system may have more of an episodic characteristic associated with its representation even though it can function as a lexical system.

The first piece of evidence for the episodic nature of L2 lexical representation was obtained in a study reported by Jiang and Forster (2001). The immediate concern of the study was the asymmetry in translation priming, i.e., translation priming being observed from L1 to L2, but not from L2 to L1 (e.g., Gollan, Forster, & Frost, 1997; Jiang, 1999). This asymmetry raised the question of why a strong L2-to-L1 lexical link, which has been assumed to exist and used to explain a faster translation time in L2-to-L1 translation than the reverse in the revised hierarchical model (RHM, Kroll & Stewart, 1994), did not produce a translation priming effect from L2 to L1 in an LDT adopted by Gollan et al. (1997) and Jiang (1999). We hypothesized that these lexical links were formed in a process of conscious learning and may be represented in the episodic memory. To test this idea, we switched the task from lexical decision to episodic recognition. Indeed, robust priming effects were found from L2 to L1 in an ERT, thus confirming the episodic nature of L2–L1 lexical links or the L2 lexical system in general.

Further evidence for the episodic L2 hypothesis was reported more recently by Witzel and Forster (2012). In addition to replicating the findings of Jiang and Forster (2001), they examined the repetition effect in L2 in an ERT. Note that in order to set up an ERT, a set of words has to be shown to the participants in the training phase. In the test phase, both previously shown words ("old" items) and "new" words (words familiar to the participants but were not shown in the training phase) are presented for the participants to decide if they are among those shown in the training phase. In previous research, a repetition priming effect has been found for the "old" words only, not for "new" words (e.g., Forster, 1985; Rajaram & Neely, 1992). This makes sense as only previously shown words have established episodic traces for the priming effect to occur. Witzel and Forster reasoned that if the L2 lexical system was represented episodically, both "old" and "new" items should produce a repetition priming effect in an ERT. This was indeed what they found. While NS of English showed a repetition priming effect only for the "old" items (the repetition priming effects being 55 ms and 5 ms for the "old" and "new" items), L2 speakers showed a reliable repetition priming effect for both "old" and "new" items (71 ms and 32 ms, respectively). A repetition priming effect for "new" items in L2 provides a more direct piece of evidence for the episodic L2 hypothesis.

Finally, even though some previous research was not conducted to explore the episodic nature of L2 representation, the findings are consistent with the idea. One of such findings is the better recall rates associated with L2. The first indications of this finding came from earlier bilingual recall studies (e.g., Doob, 1957; Lambert, Ignatow, & Krauthamer, 1968; McCormack, Brown, & Ginis, 1979). Under several different experimental circumstances, bilinguals were found to produce better recall performance in their L2 than in L1. For example, Lambert et al. (1968) asked English-French bilinguals to recall words presented to them earlier. When L1 English words and L2 French words were presented separately, the recall rates were higher in L2 than in L1. A better recall rate in L2 than L1 was also reported by Nekrasova (2009) recently.

Another finding was reported Segalowitz and de Almeida (2002). They asked English-French bilinguals to complete three tasks in their two languages: the relatedness task (judging the semantic relatedness of a pair of words), the simple classification task (judging whether a verb referred to motion or psychological state), and the arbitrary classification task. In the last task, the participants had to first learn which set, A or B, a word belonged to. In the test phase, they had to decide whether a word belonged to Set A or Set B based on their previous learning. The results in the simple classification task was intuitive: the participants produced a faster RT and a low error rate (ER) in their L1 than in L2 (RT: 1039 ms vs. 1397 ms; ER: 3.2% vs. 11.6%). The results from the arbitrary classification task was just the opposite. The bilinguals' performance was more accurate in L2 than in L1.

The L2 advantage in the arbitrary classification task in Segalowitz and de Almeida (2002) and the better recall performance in L2 in the other studies make perfect sense within the conception of the episodic L2 hypothesis. Unlike the simple classification task which taps the semantic memory system, the arbitrary classification task and the recall task are essentially episodic memory tasks. Episodic memory traces were established in the learning phase when the participants familiarized themselves with a set of words or learned which set a word belonged to. Their performance in the test phase was driven by these episodic traces. If we assume that the L2 lexical system is episodic in nature, their better performance in L2 is not surprising. It may be due to their highly developed memorization and retrieval skills associated with an episodic system, their less interference from the semantic system in working with L2, or both.

To conclude this section, there is considerable evidence to suggest that form-based connections may play a more important role in the organization of the L2 lexicon than in the organization of the L1 lexicon and there may be a strong episodic memory component associated with L2 lexical representation. Both phenomena may be a result of the same causes: the conscious and deliberate nature of the learning processes associated with L2 and weak connections between L2 lexical form and meaning. The prominence of form-based connections and the episodic characteristic may represent two unique aspects of the L2 lexicon, and thus are worth further exploration. For example, it is interesting to consider how other lexical processing phenomena may be linked to these two characteristics and how they relate to the circumstances of L2 learning (e.g., naturalistic vs. classroom) and learner factors such as age of acquisition and L2 proficiency.

4.4 Word Recognition in L2: The Role of L1

A major difference between L1 and adult L2 acquisition is that the latter takes place in the presence of an established lexical system. A great deal of evidence has accumulated showing how the recognition of L2 words is influenced by both the lexical properties of the learner's L1 and the word recognition skills learners have developed in L1. In the former case, L2 speakers were found to transfer their L1-specific processing strategies to L2 word recognition, and in the latter case, L2 word recognition and reading skills were found to correlate with or to be predictable by L2 learners' level of development of word decoding and reading skills in L1.

4.4.1 Transfer of Processing Strategies: Phonology vs. Orthography

Languages differ in what their written forms represent. In an alphabetic language, the written symbols, such as letters, are used to represent speech sounds or phonemes. Sometimes, a further distinction is made between an alphabetic language and a syllabic language. A written symbol of the latter represents a syllable rather than a phoneme, e.g., Korean, but both types are alphabetic in the sense that written forms are used to represent sounds. In a logographic language, such as Chinese, however, the written form represents morphemes or meanings directly, at least in principle.

Languages can also differ in the degree of consistency or regularity in their letter-phoneme correspondence. There is little letter-phoneme correspondence in a logographic language. Such languages are said to have a deep orthography. Alphabetic languages can differ in the consistency of letter-phoneme mapping. Languages such as Russian and Italian have a high degree of letter-phoneme correspondence in that a letter almost always represents the same phoneme, and a phoneme is almost always represented by the same letter. These languages are said to have a shallow orthography. Languages such as English and French have less consistent letter-phoneme correspondence. The letter "a" can represent different phonemes in different English words, e.g., /æ/ in *cat*, /ɔ/ in *want*, and /ə/ in *about*. These languages are said to have a deeper orthography than languages such as Russian and Italian. Orthographic depth can be best viewed as a continuum, with logographic languages like Chinese occupying its deep end and highly regular languages such as Russian and Italian at the shallow end, and many other languages such as English and French fall between the two.

In visual word recognition, the visual input provides two types of information about a word, i.e., its spelling or orthography and its pronunciation or phonology. An issue involved in visual word recognition research is whether individuals rely on orthographic or phonological information more in visual word recognition. According to the Orthographic Depth Hypothesis proposed by Katz and Frost (1992), both phonology and orthography are involved, but orthographic depth determines which of the two plays a dominant role. Speakers of orthographically shallow languages rely more on phonology, and speakers of a deep-orthography language such as Chinese rely more on orthography.[1]

Within the framework of this hypothesis, L2 speakers whose L1 and L2 differ in orthographic depth provide a good testing ground for examining whether L2 learners transfer processing strategies from L1 to L2 in visual word recognition. For example, will L2 speakers whose L1 is shallow rely more on phonology while processing a language of deeper orthography? Many studies have been conducted to explore this issue. For example, Chitiri, Sun, Willows, and Taylor (1992) showed that native speakers of Greek, a shallow language, use phonological information more than English native speakers did in processing English words. These studies can be classified into three categories: a) studies that intended to test if indeed phonology played less important role in L2 processing by logographic L1 speakers, as compared to alphabetic L1 learners, b) studies that intended to explore if orthography played a more important role in L2 processing by logographic L1 speakers than by learners with an alphabetic L1, and c) studies that intended to explore both effects. These studies are reviewed below in this order.

A number of studies showed that logographic L1 speakers relied on pho-nology to a lesser extent than alphabetic L1 speakers while processing an L2. In two studies reported by Koda (1989, 1990), the use of word recognition strategies was assessed by examining the extent to which making phonologi-cal information unavailable would affect L2 speakers' performance. In both studies, the manipulation of the availability of phonological information was achieved by using pronounceable and nonpronounceable stimuli. In the 1989 study, the participants were first shown a series of nonwords and then asked to identify a probe stimulus. The stimuli included pronounceable (e.g., *cais, keis*) and nonpronounceable (e.g., *kjwz, wngz*) nonwords and the focus was on the participants' recall accuracy for the two types of stimuli. In the 1990 study, the participants were asked to read two passages and their reading speed and recall accuracy were assessed. The names of the main characters in the stories were either pronounceable nonwords or Sanskrit symbols whose pronunciation was not known to the participants. In both studies, Japanese, Arabic, and Spanish ESL speakers were tested, with the former representing a logographic L1 group and the latter two alphabetic groups. The rationale underlying the design of the two studies was that if L2 speakers transferred their L1 word processing strategies to L2 processing, Japanese ESL speakers who were assumed to rely on orthographic information more in L1 processing should be less affected by the use of nonpronounceable stimuli, and as a result, they should show less dif-ference between the pronounceable and nonpronounceable conditions than the other two groups. The results supported this prediction in both studies.

Subsequent studies have further demonstrated this tendency of using less phonology among logographic L1 speakers. Holm and Dodd (1996) showed ESL speakers from Hong Kong had less phonological awareness than those from Vietnam. Mori (1998) tested English-speaking and Chinese/Korean-speaking learners of Japanese on a pseudocharacter recognition task with pseudocharacters that had or did not have a phonological radical, and found that Chinese/Korean learners were less affected by this phonological manip-ulation than the English-speaking participants. Muljani, Koda, and Moates (1998) showed that native speakers of Indonesia, an alphabetic language, showed a sensitivity to letter-phoneme congruency in producing faster RT in LDT to congruent than incongruent English words but no such difference was found among Chinese ESL speakers. In comparing Chinese and Korean ESL speakers' English word naming and category judgment performance, Wang and Koda (2005) found that Korean ESL speakers outperformed Chinese speakers in naming accuracy or judgment speed and accuracy, showing their advantage of having an alphabetic L1. They also made more regularization errors in naming low-frequency exceptional words than the Chinese group, showing a stronger tendency in relying on spelling-sound rules. In Hamada and Koda (2008), Chinese and Korean ESL speakers were compared in per-forming a pseudoword naming task and in word learning. Korean ESL speakers again outperformed Chinese speakers in both accuracy and naming latencies. Furthermore, pseudoword recognition performance was correlated with word learning outcomes only among Korean ESL speakers.

On the flip side of the issue, two studies were designed to test whether logographic language speakers indeed relied more on orthographic information than alphabetic L1 speakers in processing an alphabetic L2. Akamatsu asked Chinese and Japanese ESL speakers on the one hand and Persian ESL speakers on the other to name English words (1999) or read passages for comprehension (2003). The stimuli included words with and without case alternation (e.g., read vs. ReAd). The use of an orthographic processing strategy was determined by comparing the participants' performance in the regular and case-altered conditions. She reasoned that if logographic L1 speakers relied more on orthographic information than alphabetic L1 speakers, they would be more affected by case alternation in terms of their naming or reading latencies. This was confirmed in both studies.

In considering both phonology and orthography in a single study, Wade-Woolley (1999) tested Russian (alphabetic L1) and Japanese (logographic L1) ESL speakers on a variety of tasks measuring their general English proficiency (including vocabulary and reading comprehension), working memory, and phonological and orthographic awareness. Phonological awareness was assessed in a phoneme deletion task in which a participant first listened to and repeated a pseudoword such as *smeck*. He or she was subsequently asked to say the pseudoword without a predesignated phoneme, e.g., /s/ in this example. Two tasks were used to assess the participants' orthographic knowledge. In the pseudoword choice task, the stimuli consisted of pairs of pseudowords that were equally pronounceable but differed in orthographic permissibility, such as *filv* and *filk* (*filv* being less permissible because the letter v seldom appears at the end of an English word). These pseudoword pairs were presented to the participants who had to decide which one of the two was more likely to be a real English word. Both accuracy and RT were emphasized. The second task was the spelling recognition subtest of the Peabody Individual Achievement Test (Markwardt, 1989). The participants listened to a word and then had to identify it among four stimuli, one being the word just heard and the other three being similar to the target word both orthographically and phonologically. The results showed that even though the two groups were matched in overall English proficiency and working memory, Japanese ESL speakers outperformed the Russian speakers on the orthographic tasks and the Russian speakers outperformed the Japanese speakers on the phonological task. Wade-Woolley suggested that learners' L1s affected the processing strategies they adopted but this did not affect both groups in reaching a comparable level of proficiency in L2 word recognition and reading.

Similarly, Wang, Koda, and Perfetti (2003) contrasted logographic Chinese and alphabetic Korean ESL speakers' use of phonological and orthographic information in a semantic category judgment task. In performing the task, the participants had to decide whether a word belonged to a particular category (e.g., rose for flower). They manipulated the stimuli such that some nonexemplars were phonologically similar to a real exemplar. Among these phonologically similar items, some were also orthographically similar and the others were orthographically dissimilar. For example, *feat* was similar to the real exemplar of *feet* for the body part category in both phonology and orthography, but *rows* was similar to the exemplar *rose* for the flower category in phonology only (i.e., *rose* and *rows* were considered very different spelling). They were matched with nonexemplar control words that were dissimilar to the real exemplar in both phonology and orthography (e.g., *fees* and *robs* for the two examples above). By comparing the participants' RT and AC in correctly rejecting the nonexemplars in the critical and control conditions, they intended to determine the extent to which phonology or orthography was involved in word processing. For example, an individual would take longer and/or make more errors in rejecting *feat* as an exemplar for the body part category than the control word *fees* if phonology played a role in the process. The results showed that Korean ESL speakers made more errors in rejecting phonologically similar nonexemplars than their controls, but Chinese did not show such a difference. The Chinese-speaking participants, however, made more errors on orthographically similar items than orthographically dissimilar items. There results suggested that phonology seemed to affect lexical processing among Korean ESL speakers but orthography affected Chinese ESL speakers more.[2] More reliance on orthography than on phonology in L2 reading among logographic L1 learners has also been demonstrated in Haynes and Carr (1990), Jackson, Lu, and Ju (1994), and Chikamatsu (1996).

There seems to be relatively consistent evidence in support of the role individuals' L1 orthography plays in L2 visual word recognition. L2 speakers with a deep L1 orthography tended to rely on orthography more and on phonology less than those with a shallow L1 orthography. It should be noted that this research has focused on the comparison of L2 speakers of different L1 backgrounds in using the two types of information. There is little research to compare the extent to which the two types of information are used by the same group of participants. For example, we don't know whether L2 speakers with a deep-orthography L1 rely on orthography more than phonology or L2 speakers with a shallow-orthography L1 rely on phonology more than orthography.

4.4.2 Transfer of Word Recognition and Reading Skills

Another approach to examining transfer is to determine whether there is a correlation in word recognition and reading skills between L1 and L2 or if the level of development in L1 lexical processing skills correctly predicts the level of development in L2. Such correlations and predictability are often interpreted as evidence for transfer, albeit in a less direct way. Much of this research is motivated by the idea that accuracy in phonological representation is at the heart of linguistic development, including the development of word recognition and reading skills (Baddeley, 1986), and by the linguistic coding deficit hypothesis proposed by Sparks and Ganschow (1991, 1993; Sparks, 1995). According to the latter, "FL learning difficulties are based on native language difficulties . . . and that the phonological code is the locus of learning difficulties for most poor FL learners" (Sparks & Ganschow, 1991, p. 289). This research was also based on findings in monolingual reading studies that phonological skills are closely related to the development of visual word recognition and reading in children (e.g., McDougall, Hulme, Ellis, & Monk, 1994; Rack, Hulme, Snowling, & Wightman, 1994; Siegel, 1993; Wagner & Torgesen, 1987). Consequently, this research is characterized methodologically by the assessment of phonological skills, including, if not particularly, phonological awareness, in L1 on the one hand and of the development of phonological, orthographic, reading skills, and sometimes overall L2 proficiency on the other hand in order to determine whether the former is correlated with or predictive of the latter.

Among the first to study and demonstrate this relationship were Durgunoğlu, Nagy, and Hancin-Bhatt (1993). They tested a group of 31 Spanish-English bilingual first graders on multiple tests to assess their development in Spanish and English oral proficiency, Spanish and English vocabulary, letter identification, phonological awareness, and English word and pseudoword naming. Within this design, there were six independent variables: Spanish and English oral proficiencies, letter identification performance, word recognition performance in Spanish and English, and phonological awareness in Spanish. The two dependent variables were accuracy in the English pseudoword and word naming tasks (which were referred to as the transfer tests in the study). Cross-language transfer was determined by examining the relationship between the independent and dependent variables through multiple regression analyses. To assess their level of phonological awareness, the participants were asked to perform three tasks all in Spanish. One was a segmenting task in which a participant was asked to divide a monosyllabic word (e.g., *fin*) into phonemes (*f-i-n*) or a disyllabic word (e.g., *foto*) into syllables (*fo-to*). The second was a blending task in which the participant was presented with two or more components (phonemes or syllables) of a word (e.g., *p-e-z*) and asked to say the complete word by combining them (*pez*). The third was a matching task in which a participant listened to a target word (e.g., *ganas*) along with three additional words (e.g., *gota, luna, bota*) and decide which of those three words shared the initial phoneme, for example, with the target word. Two tests were used to assess the participants' lexical processing skills in L2 English (the dependent measures). In the first pseudoword naming task, the participants listened to the components of pseudowords such as *fub* and *mox*, and were asked to separate them into onsets and rhymes. The written form of these components was then presented to the participants who were asked to combine them and read the combined pseudowords aloud. In the word naming task, these elements were combined to form real English words such as *fox*. These new combinations were presented to the participants on index cards and they listened to their pronunciation and had to read them aloud. A series of multiple regression analyses were done to determine the relationship between the independent and dependent variables. When all six independent variables were used in the analysis, they explained 62% and 77% of the variance of the performance in the two naming tasks. However, two variables, Spanish word recognition and phonological awareness, were found to have the strongest correlation with the dependent variables. In a separate analysis, these two variables explained 57% and 74% of the variance for the two naming tests. Further analyses showed that the two variables each contributed to the naming outcomes independently.

The effect of phonological awareness in L1 on L2 word recognition does not only apply to languages that are both alphabetic, as shown by Gottardo, Yan, Siegel, and Wade-Woolley (2001). They tested children from Grade 1 through Grade 8 who were Cantonese speaking learners of English on multiple Chinese and English tests that measured their development in general reading proficiency, phonological and orthographic awareness, and syntactic processing. To assess their phonological awareness in English, for example, the participants were asked to complete a rhyme detection test, a phoneme detection test, a phoneme deletion test, a rapid automatized naming test, and a pseudoword repetition test. Phonological awareness in Chinese was assessed with rhyme detection, tone detection, rapid automatized naming, and pseudoword repetition tasks. The results of the study revealed two important relationships: a correlation between the participants' L1 and L2 phonological skills and a correlation between their phonological skills in both languages and their L2 reading development.

A large number of studies on this topic have appeared since the 1990s, mostly involving school children learning a second language. Almost all of them showed a relationship between L1 phonological development and L2 word recognition and reading skills (e.g., Dickinson, McCabe, Clark-Chiarelli, & Wolf, 2004; Dufva & Voeten, 1999; Kahn-Horwitz, Shimron, & Sparks, 2005, 2006; Lindsey, Manis, & Bailey, 2003; McBride-Chang et al., 2008; Meschyan & Hernandez, 2002; Sparks, Ganschow, Artzer, Siebenhar, & Plageman, 1998; Sparks, Patton, Ganschow, Humbach, & Javorsky, 2006; Sparks, Humbach, & Javorsky, 2008; Verhoeven, 2007; see Durgunoğlu, 2002 for a review of earlier studies), but some studies revealed limitations in such transfer or language-specific processing features (e.g., Bialystok, McBride-Chang, & Luk, 2005; McBride-Chang et al., 2008). See Koda (2005) and Koda and Zehler (2008) for more detailed treatment of the topic.

Additionally, Fender (2003) demonstrated similar transfer of word recognition skills among adult L2 speakers. She compared visual word recognition in English by proficiency-matched Japanese and Arabic ESL speakers in a LDT. The Japanese group was found to be significantly faster and more accurate than the Arabic group. She attributed this difference to better developed L1 orthographic and visual word recognition skills among the Japanese ESL speakers.

4.4.3 Commonalities and Universalities in L1 and L2 Word Recognition

While L1 influence in L2 word recognition is well documented, research has also shown that lexical processing in L1 and L2 shares a great deal of commonalities and L2 word recognition among speakers of different L1 backgrounds is similar in many respects.

First of all, many lexical processing effects observed among NS have also been found among NNS. For example, the frequency effect has been well documented in L2 word recognition (e.g., Jiang, 1999; Ko, Wang, & Kim, 2011; Wang & Koda, 2005. See Section 4.5.2 for related discussion). As a matter of fact, among the eight lexical variables examined in De Groot et al. (2002), frequency was found to account for the most variance in LDT latencies in both L1 and L2. The age-of-acquisition effect has also been reported among both NS and NNS (e.g., Assink, van Well, & Knuijt, 2003; Izura & Ellis, 2004). Similar to NS, NNS have also been found to show a length effect (e.g., Lemhöfer et al., 2008) and a neighborhood density effect (e.g., Stamer & Vitevitch, 2012). Another example is the regularity effect in naming. L1 speakers have been found to name words with a regular spelling-sound relationship faster than exceptional words and this regularity effect occurs more with low-frequency words than high-frequency words. The same regularity effect has also been observed of L2 speakers, regardless of their L1 backgrounds. For example, Chinese, Japanese, and Persian ESL speakers in Akamatsu (2002) and Chinese and Korean ESL speakers in Wang and Koda (2005) all named regular English words faster and/or with higher accuracy than irregular words.

In studies that were designed specifically to compare L1 and L2 word recognition, a great deal of overlap was found, as well. For example, De Groot et al. (2002) tested Dutch-English bilinguals in both L1 Dutch and L2 English in three tasks, LDT, standard naming, and delayed naming. Their RTs in the tasks were analyzed in relation to lexical variables such as frequency, length, semantics (as measured by imageability, context availability, and definition accuracy), phonology (such as syllable onset, number of three-consonant clusters, sound intensity), neighborhood, and cognate status. Several similarities were clear from the data. The top two predictors of the variance of the LDT data were frequency and meaning in both L1 and L2, word length explained 14% and 15% of variance in Dutch and English standard naming, respectively, phonology-related variables explained a large amount of variance in naming tasks but not in LDT in both languages, and where there was a significant correlation between the RT data and a specific lexical variable in L1 Dutch, a significant correlation was found in L2 English as well.

Similarly, to examine how learners' L1 backgrounds may or may not affect word recognition in L2 and compare word recognition in L1 and L2, Lemhöfer et al. (2008) tested French, German, and Dutch ESL speakers and English NS in an English word recognition study using the progressive demasking technique first used by Grainger and Segui (1990). A total of 1025 English words were used as stimuli. Multiple regression analyses were performed to examine the relationship between the participants' performance (i.e., RT) and a set of linguistic variables. These variables included L2 English lexical variables such as word frequency, morphological family size (number of complex words a word appears in), word length, English orthographic neighborhood (both size and frequency), bigram frequency, number of meanings, syntactic ambiguity (whether a word has one or multiple parts of speech), concreteness, familiarity, meaningfulness, and cross-language variables such as cross-language orthographic neighborhood, and cross-language cognates and homographs. The four languages involved differed in orthographic depth with German being most shallow followed by Dutch, French, and English. Thus, this design allowed them to assess the extent to which a learner's L1 background would affect L2 word recognition in relation to these variables. The results showed a great deal of overlap between NS and NNS and between NNS of different L1 backgrounds. For example, the variables that were found not to be reliably predictable of NNS' performance were found to have little predictability on NS' performance, and a majority of the predictor variables for NNS were also predictors for NS. The regression analysis also showed a great deal of overlap in performance among the three NNS groups, as shown in the percentage of variations of one group that could be accounted for by another (56%–62%). The results were interpreted to mean that "the nonnative participants used very similar reading strategies in their common second language, English" (p. 24).

Furthermore, in line with the idea of the presence of universals in L1 and L2 word recognition, some studies failed to observe the expected transfer effects. For example, Jackson, Chen, Goldsberry, Kim, and Vanderwerff (1999) tested ESL speakers from Hong Kong, Taiwan, and Korea in a passage reading task. The three groups differed in two ways: a) Korean ESL speakers had an alphabetic L1 background but the other groups had a logographic background, and b) ESL students from Taiwan, but not from Hong Kong, used *zhuyin fuhao* in learning Chinese in childhood. It is a system similar to an alphabet to indicate the pronunciation of Chinese characters. To assess the extent to which the participants relied on orthography in L2 reading, several different versions of passages were prepared. A normal text with which students were familiar served as a baseline in assessing the participants' performance. Additionally, the following four variants of the text were created: the second version had words presented in mixed cases (e.g., *JaPaN iS a CoUnTrY*), the third version had pseudohomophones (e.g., *Toodai a strange thing okkerred*), the fourth version had many long words, and the fifth version had complex syntax. Case mixing, the use of pseudohomophones and long words were all intended to reduce orthographic familiarity of the words. The participants' reliance on orthographic information in reading was determined by comparing their performance in reading these alternate versions and the normal version. If L1 backgrounds affected the degree of reliance on orthography in L2 reading, one would expect these orthographic manipulations to affect ESL speakers from Hong Kong and Taiwan more than those from Korea and to affect the Hong Kong group more than the Taiwan group due to their L1 backgrounds and L1 learning experiences. The participants' performance, as assessed in terms of silent reading time, log transformed reading time, and oral reading quality, did not support such predictions.

ESL speakers from different L1 backgrounds were found to show no difference in word recognition strategies in Akamatsu (2002), as well. She tested Chinese, Japanese, and Persian ESL speakers in a word naming task. These participants represented ESL speakers with a logographic (Chinese and Japanese) and an alphabetic (Persian) L1 background. The test materials included English words that differed in frequency (high vs. low) and regularity (regular vs. exceptional, e.g., *fate* vs. *have*) thus creating four conditions. If L1 did not play a role, the three groups should produce similar findings. Specially, based on previous research (e.g., Seidenberg, 1985), they should all name regular words faster than exceptional words but this regularity effect should be enhanced for low-frequency items. If L1 played a role, Persian ESL speakers were expected to show a stronger regularity effect and perform the naming task faster than the other two groups due to the similarity between their L1 and English. The logographic groups should show no regularity effect if they primarily adopted an orthographic processing strategy. The results showed that the three groups produced the same pattern of performance. They all showed a regularity effect for low-frequency words but not for high-frequency words, and the Persian ESL group showed no advantage in naming latencies.

To conclude this review of L2 word recognition research, there is compelling evidence for L1 influence in L2 word recognition both in terms of processing strategies and literacy skill development. Where L2 speakers' L1 and L2 differ in the depth of orthography, their use of phonological and orthographic information in visual word recognition tends to be affected by the characteristics of their L1, and the development of phonological awareness in L1 has also been found to correlate with an individual's word recognition skills in L2. At the same time, research also demonstrates a great deal of similarities in L1 and L2 lexical processing. This is not surprising as L2 word recognition should also involve basic processes and mechanisms that are universal in word recognition. Where expected L1 influence was not observed (e.g., Akamatsu, 2002; Jackson et al., 1999), one may hypothesize that the experimental design did not provide a means sensitive or powerful enough to reveal L1 influence. Alternatively, these findings may offer a window of opportunity for studying the circumstances under which L1 influence would or would not occur and thus warrant close scrutiny.

4.5 Word Recognition in L2: Other Issues

In addition to L1 influence, research on L2 word recognition has produced some several other inspiring findings. This section reviews research related to the following three findings: the automatic activation of L1 translations in L2 word recognition, a larger frequency effect in L2, and lexical integration of unfamiliar words.

4.5.1 Automatic Activation of L1 Translations in L2 Word Recognition

There is an emerging interest in the topic of whether L1 translations are automatically activated or even involved in L2 word recognition. Note that L1 activation and L1 transfer are two distinct issues. The transfer of processing strategies and skills from L1 to L2 does not imply that L1 translations are directly involved in L2 word recognition. Such influence can occur at a more abstract level without the activation of L1 translations. Thus, transfer research does not speak directly to this issue. At the same time, the activation of L1 translation in L2 word recognition does not necessarily mean that it would affect L2 word recognition. Instead, it can be a by-product of L2 word recognition.

The concept of L1 translation activation in L2 word recognition is not new, though. In conceptualizing how the two languages of a bilingual speaker are linked, it has been suggested by Weinreich (1953) in his definition of subordinate bilingualism and by Potter, So, von Eckardt, and Feldman (1984) in their statement of the word association hypothesis that at the early stage of L2 learning, an L2 word may be directly linked with its L1 translation rather than the related semantic representation. Based on such proposals, L2 word recognition requires the activation of L1 translations.

There is some evidence that seems to support this view. For example, L2 learners were found to deliberately translate L2 words into L1 translations in L2 reading (e.g., Kern, 1994; Upton & Lee-Thompson, 2001), but this is more likely to be a result of a learner trying to comprehend the meaning of a sentence or text rather than occurring at the word recognition stage. Additionally, Jiang (2002, 2004) demonstrated that when two L2 words shared the same L1 translation, e.g., *standard* and *criterion* sharing *biaozhun* for Chinese-English bilinguals, L2 speakers responded to such L2 words faster and rated them as more related in a semantic judgment task than L2 words that did not share the same L1 translation. While this finding seems to indicate the involvement of L1 translations, the same-translation effect may also occur at the semantic level, a position I took. In the latter scenario, the effect is a result of two same-translation words being directly linked to the same L1 concepts, which facilitates the positive decision in a semantic judgment task.

Further and more compelling indications of the involvement of L1 translations in L2 word recognition were found in two studies that explored the processing of L2 compound words. In both Ko et al. (2011) and Cheng, Wang, and Perfetti (2011), Korean or Chinese ESL speakers were asked to perform a LDT on English compound words such as *classroom* and *honeymoon*. Translation lexicality was manipulated such that the word-for-word translation of an L2 compound may or may not be a real word in L1. For example, the word-for-word Chinese translation for the English compound *toothbrush* is *yashua* which is the real word for the same object in Chinese, but when the English compound *schoolbook* is translated into Chinese as *xiaoshu*, it is not a legitimate Chinese word (its correct translation being *keben*, or lesson book). Bilinguals were found to respond to the former type of compounds faster or with more accuracy than the latter type in these studies. This finding seemed to suggest that in L2 compound recognition, a word-for-word translation was automatically performed. If the resulting translation was not a legitimate compound in L1, a delay or an incorrect response occurred. A caveat for interpreting this finding as evidence for automatic activation of L1 translation in L2 word recognition is that translation lexicality effect was found not only in L2 processing but in both directions in Cheng, Wang, and Perfetti. Whether this bidirectional finding had to do with the fact that the participants in this study were children learning both languages at the same time or can be extended to adult unbalanced bilinguals is yet to be determined.

Several recent studies were intended to directly and specifically test if L1 translations are involved in L2 word recognition. Thierry and Wu (2007) tested English monolinguals, Chinese-English bilinguals, and Chinese monolinguals on four types of English or Chinese word pairs in a semantic judgment task in which the participants had to decide if two words were related in meaning. The four conditions differed in whether or not the Chinese translations were related in meaning and in whether the disyllabic translations shared a Chinese character. For example, the Chinese translations for the related pair *mail-post*, 邮政-邮件, shared the same first character, but the translations for the related pair *wife-husband*, 妻子-丈夫, did not. Similarly, the translations of the unrelated pair *train-ham*, 火车-火腿, shared the first character, but the translation for the unrelated pair *apple-table*, 苹果-桌子, did not. In responding to these English word pairs, both the English NS and Chinese-English bilingual groups showed a main effect of semantic relatedness, i.e., a faster response to the related pairs than to the unrelated pairs, but there was no effect of repeated characters. However, the participants' ERP data revealed a different pattern. While both NS and NNS groups showed a N400 effect while responding to related and unrelated pairs, Chinese-English bilinguals also showed a N400 for repeated/nonrepeated manipulation with the unrelated items generating a greater negative amplitude around 400 ms after the onset of the second word. Monolingual Chinese speakers completed the same task on Chinese translations. In addition to the behavioral evidence of a semantic relatedness advantage, they showed two ERP effects, one being the N400 semantic effect and the other being the P2 effect for character repetition. In the latter case, there was a greater positive-going amplitude for nonrepeated pairs around 200 ms after the onset of the stimuli, an effect that has been associated with repetition priming. In considering the ERP data from both the Chinese-English bilinguals and Chinese monolinguals, they suggested that L1 translations were automatically activated in L2 word recognition, as indicated by the reduced N400 for the repeated items, and this activation occurred post-lexically, i.e., after the recognition of the L2 words. The latter conclusion was based on the lack of an P2 effect among Chinese-English bilinguals. Two subsequent studies replicated the finding of automatic translation and showed that it was the phonological repetition, not orthographic repetition, of the translations that produced the effect (Wu & Thierry, 2010, 2012).

A similar behavioral finding was reported by Zhang, van Heuven, and Conklin (2011) who tested Chinese-English bilinguals and English NS on English word pairs that shared or did not share a character in their Chinese translations. The critical stimuli involved unrelated English word pairs such as *east* and *thing*. The latter word of the pair in this example is typically translated into 东西 (*dongxi*, literally east-west). Thus, for Chinese-English bilinguals, the otherwise unrelated pair shared the same character in their Chinese translations. By adopting the masked priming paradigm, the study was intended to examine if a hidden repetition priming effect could be observed on such stimuli, which would help explore if automatic translation occurs in L2 word recognition. To this end, the participants were asked to perform a primed LDT with stimuli in four conditions illustrated with the above example: *east-thing* (first character repetition), *down-thing* (control), *west-thing* (second character repetition), *side-thing* (control). In the second experiment, the priming direction was reversed (e.g., *thing-east*). A hidden repetition priming effect was found among Chinese-English bilinguals in both priming directions but only when the first character was repeated. This finding was again interpreted as evidence for automatic activation of L1 translations in L2 word recognition. However, when we obtained and examined the stimuli from the first author, we discovered that many items whose Chinese translations were considered to be opaque compounds were actually transparent compounds. As a result, the repetition condition contained many semantically related pairs such as *father-parent*, *big-size*, *number-math*, *watch-show*, *clock-hour*, *land-earth*.

More recently, we examined the topic from a different approach. We reasoned that if L1 translations are automatically activated in a monolingual L2 word recognition task, the frequency of these translations would have an impact on the participants' performance. For sociocultural and linguistic reasons, a word in one language and its translation in another may differ dramatically in frequency. This allows one to manipulate the frequency of both the L2 words and their L1 translations. For example, the English words *research* and *repeat* both have a frequency of 33 per million, according to Brysbaert and New (2009), but their Chinese translation, *yanjiu* and *chongfu*, have a frequency of 1001 and 49 per million, respectively, according to the frequency dictionary published by Beijing Language Institute (1986). Thus, we tested Chinese-English bilinguals and NS controls in a LDT with English words that were matched for frequency and other lexical properties but differed in the frequency of their Chinese translations. A translation frequency effect was found among the first group in that they responded to the English words with high-frequency Chinese translations significantly faster than those with low-frequency translations (Jiang, Guo, & Li, 2013). This result suggested that the activation of L1 translations were involved in and affected L2 word recognition.

The automatic activation of L1 translation in L2 word recognition became a topic of interest only recently. While there is evidence in support of such activation, little is known about the circumstances under which such activation occurs, e.g., its relationship to L2 speakers' proficiency. More importantly, it is not clear what role L1 translations play in the L2 word recognition process. Their activation may be post-lexical as a by-product of L2 word recognition, as Thierry and Wu (2007) suggested. Alternatively, L2 word recognition may entail a verification process whereby an activated candidate is checked against its L1 translation, as suggested by Jiang et al. (2013) (see Becker, 1976, 1980 and Paap, Newsome, McDonald, & Schvaneveldt, 1982 for the concept of verification in word recognition). In the latter case, the activation of L1 translations can be better seen as an integral part of L2 word recognition.

4.5.2 A Larger Frequency Effect in L2

While a reliable frequency effect has been observed in both L1 and L2 word recognition, L2 word recognition research has revealed an intriguing phenomenon: when the same set of stimuli were used, NNS tended to produce a larger frequency effect than NS. This phenomenon was already visible in some studies before it became a topic for investigation. For example, in exploring task-related and word-related variables in L1 and L2 word recognition, De Groot et al. (2002) showed that frequency had a stronger association with the participants' performance and explained more variations in L2 English than in L1 Dutch in both LDT and naming. In asking French-Dutch and Dutch-French bilinguals to name high- and low-frequency words, van Wijnendaele and Brysbaert (2002) found that both groups produced a stronger frequency effect in L2 than in L1. The same pattern surfaced in a study reported by Harrington (2006) and another study reported by Assink et al. (2003) who were primarily concerned with the age-of-acquisition effects in L1 and L2 but also included a frequency manipulation. In Lemhöfer et al. (2008), written word frequency was significantly correlated with the NNS' performance but not with NS' performance (but see Frenck-Mestre, 1993 Experiment 2 for a counterexample).

Duyck, Vanderelst, Desmet, and Hartsuiker (2008) were among the first to put the spotlight on this issue by designing a study to specifically compare the size of the frequency effect among NS and NNS. They tested Dutch-English bilinguals in a LDT with Dutch and English words that were different in frequency but matched for some other lexical variables. The participants showed a frequency of 46 ms and 103 ms in L1 Dutch and L2 English respectively. In Experiment 2, English NS were tested with the same set of English words and produced a frequency effect of 52 ms. Thus, a larger frequency effect in NNS than NS was confirmed both within the same group of participants and with the same set of materials.

Further evidence for a larger frequency effect in L2 is found in several additional studies. In Gollan et al. (2011), monolingual English speakers, Spanish and Dutch ESL speakers were tested in a LDT on high- and low-frequency English words (Experiment 2). The Dutch group who performed the task significantly more slowly than the English NS produced a larger frequency effect than NS. However, it should be noted that no such frequency and group interaction was found in eye tracking data when the participants were asked to process words in sentence contexts (Experiment 3). Whitford and Titone (2012) tested L1 dominant English-French and French-English bilinguals in a passage reading test while monitoring their eye movements. The variables under examination were passage language (L1 vs. L2), target word frequency (high vs. low), current exposure to L2 (high vs. low). The eye tracking data revealed the same pattern of differential frequency effect sizes in L1 and L2. In the gaze duration data, for example, a three-way interaction was found between language, frequency, and exposure. The frequency effect was greater in L2 than in L1. Furthermore, the effect was smaller for high-exposure participants than for the low-exposure group.

In an attempt to examine how the frequency effect revealed itself at different frequency bands among NS and NNS, we selected 16 words from five frequency bands, 500–2000, 300–399, 100–199, 50–70, 10–12 such that their average frequencies were 928, 346, 139, 58, 11 per million, respectively. We tested 18 NS and 33 NNS in a LDT, the latter consisting of 12 ESL speakers with an alphabetic L1 and 21 Chinese ESL speakers (Jiang & Botana, 2009). The study produced three findings. First, the overall frequency effects were 61 ms for the NS group and 151 ms for the NNS groups, thus confirming the larger frequency in NNS. Second, the frequency effect size was almost identical for alphabetic and logographic ESL speakers (152 ms and 150 ms respectively) even though their mean RT was quite different (653 ms and 746 ms respectively, NS=556 ms). Third, the effect revealed itself at different bands differently among NS and NNS. NS showed no frequency effect between the two highest frequency conditions (534 ms vs. 530 ms), and a small difference of 17 ms between the two lowest frequency conditions (578 ms vs. 595 ms). The biggest frequency effect in NS, in the amount of 33 ms, occurred between the 139 and 58 frequency conditions. In contrast, NNS showed an increasingly larger frequency effect as the word frequency decreased, with the effect being in the amount of 10 ms, 28 ms, 41 ms, and 72 ms with decreasing frequencies. These results suggested that a large amount of exposure to L1 words may have helped reduce the impact of frequency on word recognition at both the high and low ends of the frequency range among NS, but without such overexposure, the relationship between the frequency effect size and word frequency is more linear among NNS.

A parallel finding has been found in word production when picture naming was used as the experimental task. Gollan, Montoya, Cera, and Sandoval (2008) tested English NS and English-Spanish bilinguals with pictures whose names differed in frequency. English was the dominant language for the bilinguals even though Spanish may be their first language. These participants produced a significantly larger frequency effect in picture naming RT and ER in Spanish than in English. The frequency effect in Spanish was also larger than that of English monolinguals. A subsequent study (Gollan et al., 2011, Experiment 1) replicated the finding and showed that the same phenomenon occurred in picture naming in sentence context, as well. A similar difference was found between monolinguals and bilinguals in Ivanova and Costa (2008).

It is clear from these studies that a larger frequency effect in L2 than in L1 is a ubiquitous phenomenon. It has been found in studies using different research paradigms (LDT, word naming, progressive demasking, eye tracking) and in both visual word recognition and word production.

Different explanations have been proposed to account for the phenomenon. One explanation offered by Duyck et al. (2008) was that frequency is likely to have a smaller impact on high-frequency words than on low-frequency words because additional encounters with a word would not be able to further speed up the recognition process to the same extent in high-frequency words as in low-frequency words. For example, 20 more additional encounters with a word that has been recognized ten times previously may affect recognition time significantly but not with a word that has been recognized 1000 times. In other words, there is a ceiling effect involved in the relationship between word recognition time and high-frequency words but not between word recognition time and low-frequency words. As the subjective frequencies of L2 words are likely to be lower than L1 words, a larger frequency effect is expected. We may refer to this as the learning curve explanation. A similar view was voiced by Lemhöfer et al. (2008) when they stated that

> small changes in the number of times or ways a word is encountered have the largest consequences when the degree of experience with the given word is low, which tends to be the case for L2 words more than for words from one's mother tongue.
>
> (p. 27)

Another explanation within the rank hypothesis of Murray and For-ster (2004) was discussed in both Duyck et al. (2008) and Gollan et al. (2008). This explanation is based on two assumptions: a) word recognition time is determined by the position, or the rank, of a word in a search set (the rank hypothesis), and b) words in both languages are represented in a single lexicon. According to this explanation, L2 words are likely to be positioned toward the lower end of a search set, due to the low subjective frequency. This means that there are more lower-frequency L1 words sepa-rating high- and low-frequency L2 words, thus increasing the search time for the low-frequency L2 words. While this explanation may work with bilinguals whose two languages share the same script and thus are stored in an integrated lexicon, it is less capable of explaining the larger frequency effect in L2 among bilinguals whose two languages do not share the same script and thus are less likely to be represented in a single lexicon or search set (Jiang & Botana, 2009).

Two further explanations were tested in Diependaele, Lemhöfer, and Brys-baert (2013). The first is the language competition hypothesis. A bilingual is likely to know more words than a monolingual. This means a word is likely to have more form-related words in the bilingual lexicon than in a mono-lingual lexicon. Furthermore, for an unbalanced bilingual, the stronger L1 is more likely to affect the recognition of weaker L2 words. Thus, in word rec-ognition, L2 words are likely to face more competition than L1 words. This increased competition leads to the larger frequency effect in bilinguals than in monolinguals and a larger frequency effect in L2 than in L1.[3] This hypothesis would make two predictions. First, the frequency effect size is affected by the number of languages an individual knows and the level of proficiency in these languages. Knowing more languages or a target language being less proficient would result in a larger frequency effect. Second, the frequency effect size is affected by how orthographically similar the two or more languages are. A higher degree of similarity would lead to increased competition and thus a larger frequency effect.

The second is the lexical entrenchment hypothesis. Due to L2 learners' limited experiences in L2, L2 words are believed to have a lesser degree of lexical entrenchment or weak or less precise mental representations. This is particularly true for low-frequency L2 words. A low-frequency word may be still quite familiar to a NS, but can be quite unfamiliar to an L2 speaker, while a high-frequency word is highly familiar to both L1 and L2 speakers. Thus, one may envision a larger gap in subjective frequency between high- and low-frequency words in L2 than in L1, which results in a larger frequency effect in L2. Within this hypothesis, the amount of experience and thus the level of lexical proficiency or entrenchment is considered the only factor that determines the size of the frequency effect. Thus, contrary to the language competition hypothesis, the number of languages known, the relative proficiency of each known language, and the similarity between the known languages do not affect frequency effect sizes according to this hypothesis.

To test these alternative hypotheses, Diependaele et al. (2013) reanalyzed data from Lemhöfer et al. (2008) which provided measures of both lexical recognition time and the proficiency of four groups of participants. The focus of the analysis was to determine the relationship between proficiency and frequency effect size and how this relationship was similar or different between monolinguals and bilinguals and between bilinguals whose L1 and L2 differed in similarity. Their analysis first replicated the results in Lemhöfer et al. (2008), i.e., a larger frequency effect in bilinguals than in monolinguals. But more importantly, when the participants' proficiency scores were entered in the formula, it became a better predictor than language background (L1 vs. L2) for the variance in frequency effect. When proficiency was taken into account, the difference between monolinguals and bilinguals in frequency effect size disappeared. Furthermore, this relationship between proficiency and frequency effect was found to be highly similar among monolinguals and bilinguals and among bilinguals of different L1 backgrounds. These results support the idea that it is the differential lexical proficiency rather than anything else, e.g., language nativeness per se, that leads to the observed differences in frequency effect size in L1 and L2.

It is worthwhile to point out in this context that a greater lexical effect in L2 than in L1 has also been observed in areas other than the frequency effect. For example, in De Groot et al. (2002), three variables, semantics, length, and cognate status, affected Dutch-English bilinguals' performance in L2 more than in L1. Specifically, semantic variables affected L2 naming but not L1 naming, and length and cognate status affected LDT times in L2 but not in L1. In Lemhöfer et al. (2008), morphological family size affected L2 processing but not L1 processing. Similar to the larger frequency effect in L2, certain lexical processing effects seem to be magnified or inflated in L2 processing. Some of these differences seem to be proficiency-related, as suggested by De Groot et al. A weaker L2 is likely to be more affected by a stronger L1 than the reverse, thus leading to the observation of a cognate effect in L2 only. The length effect observed in L2 English was found to occur only among low-frequency words, and thus is also proficiency-related. Sometimes, bilinguals were also found to perform a task better in their L2 than in L1. For example, Segalowitz and Almeida (2002) found that bilinguals performed the semantic classification task better in L1 than in L2 but they performed the arbitrary classification task better in L2 than in L1. They referred to this as the L2-better-than-L1 effect. The cognitive mechanisms underlying such stronger effects or better performance in L2 are surely an interesting topic for future exploration.

4.5.3 The Integration of Unfamiliar Words

When a new word is being learned, learning can mean at least two different things: the creation of a new lexical entry that contains some lexical information, and the integration of the new entry into the existing lexical system. Leach and Samuel (2007) refer to these as lexical configuration and lexical engagement, respectively. In their conception, the former is a process of establishing the "factual information" about a word, e.g., how a word is spelled and pronounced and what it means. Lexical engagement refers to the interaction of the new word with the other members of the lexicon. Following Leach and Samuel, one may define lexical integration as a process whereby a newly established lexical entry begins to interact with the other members of the lexicon.

Research on vocabulary acquisition in L2 and lexical development in psycholinguistics have traditionally been concerned primarily with lexical creation rather than lexical integration. However, there is an emerging line of research, first begun in psycholinguistics, that explored the process of lexical integration of new words. In these studies, lexical integration was determined by examining whether or how soon newly learned words would influence the processing of existing words or vice versa. Such influence was taken as evidence of lexical interaction and integration. One of the earliest such studies was reported by Gaskell and Dumay (2003). Their study was based on the earlier finding that form-related words competed with each other in spoken word recognition. In Goldinger, Luce, and Pisoni (1989), for example, the presence of a form-related prime word resulted in a lower rate of target identification in a primed auditory word identification task. In Luce and Pisoni (1998), words with more neighbors were responded to more slowly in both LDT and naming. They reasoned that if newly learned words were integrated into the lexicon, they should interfere with the recognition of form-related existing words. To explore this issue, they created nonword auditory stimuli based on real words, e.g., *cathedruke* based on *cathedral*. They trained the participants until they reached a high level of accuracy in recognizing the new forms. They then asked the participants to perform an LDT on the base words (without showing the novel words). When the LDT was given immediately after training, no effect was found on these base words as compared to the control condition (Experiment 1). However, when testing took place overnight after training on five consecutive days, an interference was observed from Day 3. The participants responded to real words whose form-related nonwords were learned in the training sections more slowly than to control words (Experiment 2). This slower response was taken as evidence for the influence from the newly learned words and thus the lexical integration of the latter.

Several subsequent studies produced similar findings. Bowers, Davis, and Hanley (2005) also created form-related nonwords out of real words, e.g., *banara* out of *banana*. They trained the participants on the nonwords by asking them to type them, and then tested them on the base words in a semantic judgment task. The testing showed a small interference effect on the first day, but on Day 2 a robust interference effect was found in that the participants responded to the base words much more slowly than to the control words. Similar interference from the new learned words on existing words was also demonstrated in two more recent studies. Tamminen and Gaskell (2013) trained the participants on a set of nonwords by matching them to a set of definitions. They then asked the participants to perform an LDT, on Day 2 and Day 8, where the newly learned forms served as primes and semantically related words served as targets. A small but significant semantic priming effect was observed under both unmasked and masked conditions.

Kapnoula, Packard, Gupta, and McMurray (2015) explored the same issue by means of the visual world paradigm. The to-be-learned nonwords were created by means of splicing auditory stimuli of real words and nonwords. For example, three stimuli were first recorded: *bait*, *bake*, and *bape*, the first two being real words and the last a nonword. Three stimuli were then created by combining the last segment /t/ in *bait* with the first two segments /beɪ/ from the three original recordings. The vowel /eɪ/ in the base recordings carried the acoustic information of the following segment, /t/, /k/, or /p/, respectively, due to coarticulation. If we indicate this influence from the final consonant by means of a subscript, the three new spliced stimuli are /beɪ$_t$t/, /beɪ$_k$t/, and /beɪ$_p$t/. The three resulting stimuli differed in the vowel /beɪ/ having acoustic features matching the resulting word bate in /beɪ$_t$t/, having acoustic features from a different word *bake* in /beɪ$_k$t/, and having acoustic features from a nonword in /beɪ$_p$t/, thus creating three conditions: matching splice, competing word splice, and nonword splice. Based on previous research, it was predicted that the second stimulus, /beɪ$_k$t/, would take longer to process than the third one, /beɪ$_p$t/, as the vowel in the second stimulus carries the acoustic information of a competing real word *bake* while the vowel in the third stimulus does not (note that *bape* is a nonword). The study took advantage of this phenomenon and tested whether the third stimuli would also produce an interference after *bape* was trained as a new word. If a newly trained word was integrated into the lexicon and interacted with its members, an inhibition should be observed. A lack of interference could be taken as evidence for a lack of integration. The interference was assessed in terms of the rate of eye fixation on a picture. In the test session, four pictures were presented on a computer monitor, one being related to *bate* and the others being not. Four conditions were created in terms of the auditory stimuli: matching splice (e.g., /beiₜt/), competing word splice (e.g., /beiₖt/), nonword splice (/beiₚt/) with and without training. It was predicted that hearing a matching stimulus should lead to a higher percentage of looks to the *bate* picture. Hearing the competing word stimulus should result in a lower percentage of looks. Hearing a nonword splice should have little impact on looks if no training took place, but it would lead to lower percentage of looks after training. These predictions were supported by the results. Most importantly, a trained nonword splice behaved similarly to a word splice in producing a lower percentage of looks to the related picture. What is particularly noteworthy about this study is that the results were obtained in testing that took place immediately after training, without overnight consolidation, which has been suggested to be critical for lexical integration to occur by Gaskell and Dumay (2003). Their results were taken as evidence demonstrating the "immediate lexical integration of novel word forms", as the title of their report indicates.

In addition to these studies that assessed lexical integration by examining how newly learned words affect existing words, there is also evidence for such lexical integration in that existing words can also affect the processing of newly learned words (e.g., Vitevitch, Storkel, Francisco, Evans, & Goldstein, 2014) and that newly learned words can affect the processing of each other (e.g., Magnuson, Tanenhaus, Aslin, & Dahan, 2003).

The evidence, however, is not all consistent. Qiao, Forster, and Witzel (2009) reported a study whose findings questioned the quick integration of new word forms. This study was conducted in responding to the findings reported by Bowers et al. (2005), and adopted the same test materials and the same training task. However, they assessed lexical integration by means of the prime lexicality effect (PLE), an idea similar to that of Gaskell and Dumay (2003). The PLE refers to the differential effects a form-related prime has on the recognition of a target depending on whether the prime is a word or not. A form-related nonword prime produces facilitation, but a form-related word shows no facilitation in visual word recognition (Davis & Lupker, 2006; Forster & Veres, 1998). Thus, lexical integration was assessed by examining whether newly learned word forms (e.g., *banara*) would facilitate the recognition of their base words (e.g., *banana*) in the masked priming paradigm. A facilitation would indicate their nonword status. A lack of facilitation or even inhibition would suggest that these novel words had been integrated, or lexicalized in Qiao, Forster, and Witzel's term. The training and the testing each occurred on two days. The results showed that trained nonwords behaved just like untrained nonwords on both days in producing a facilitation on the form-related targets. In a subsequent study, Qiao and Forster (2013) found that newly learned words behaved like real words only after four training sessions across four weeks.

In addition to the findings being inconsistent across these studies, it should also be noted that in all these studies, the to-be-learned novel words were made up of phonological categories of the participants' native language or orthographically similar to real words in their L1. The fact that the novel word forms consisted of sublexical units in the participants' native language may explain, at least in part, the quick integration. The question is whether these findings may generalize to the learning of L2 words. Indeed, two studies utilized L2 stimuli, and the findings were also in favor of a quick integration.

In one of these studies, Elgort (2011) tested advanced ESL speakers with English stimuli. She created 48 pseudowords by replacing a letter in a real English word, e.g., *maximize→maxidise, geometry→teometry*. The participants went through a training session where they learned the form and meaning of these pseudowords and spent a week consolidating their learning until they could both recognize and retrieve these "words" at a mean accuracy rate of 94%. Three lexical processing effects were used to assess lexical development and integration. The two effects related to lexical integration were the prime lexicality effect (Experiment 1) and the semantic priming effect (Experiment 3). The rationale underlying the use of the first was similar to that of Qiao et al. (2009): a facilitative priming effect from a newly learned word on a form-related target would be taken as a lack of lexical integration. A semantic priming effect between the pseudowords and semantically related targets would also support lexical integration. Additionally, the repetition priming effect was used to assess whether the pseudowords had achieved a lexical status (Experiment 2). Based on the previous finding that a repetition priming effect usually occurs for words, not for nonwords (e.g., Forster & Davis, 1984), a repetition priming effect observed of the learned pseudowords would indicate their lexical status.

The results from the prime lexicality effect experiment showed a nonsignificant facilitation of 20 ms for the trained pseudowords, while the untrained nonwords produced a significant priming effect of 75 ms. These results suggested that the pseudowords behaved differently from other nonwords. In the semantic priming experiment, both related words and trained pseudowords produced a reliable priming effect. These results supported a quick lexical integration of the newly and deliberately learned pseudowords. In the repetition priming experiments, pseudowords also behaved like real words in producing a reliable repetition priming effect. Thus, the results from all three experiments supported lexical creation and integration of these newly learned L2 pseudowords.

In the second study, Stamer and Vitevitch (2012) used real L2 words as stimuli. They tested English-speaking learners of Spanish as an L2 on Spanish words that were unfamiliar to them. They manipulated these unfamiliar words so that some had many neighbors and some had few. They trained the participants through the matching of new words with pictures. The learning was assessed through three tasks: picture naming as a productive task for assessing lexical configuration, referent identification as a receptive task for the same purpose, and a perceptual identification task to assess lexical integration. In the latter task, newly learned words were presented in noise for identification. To allow lexical integration to occur through overnight consolidation, the third task was given 48 to 72 hours after the initial exposure, while the first two tasks were given both immediately and 48–72 hours later. Their results showed that the participants performed better on words with many neighbors in all three tasks. This facilitative effect of neighborhood size on perceptual identification was taken to suggest that the processing of new words was influenced by the existing words, and thus their successful lexical integration.

The findings from these lexical integration studies, however, should be viewed with caution. The key issue to keep in mind is what is being assessed when it is supposed to be lexical integration. In some L1 studies, the training of novel words was done through tasks that did not involve meaning at all. For example, in Gaskell and Dumay, training was done through a phoneme monitoring task where a target phoneme was provided for each item and a participant had to decide if the auditory input contained the phoneme. After 12 exposures of each novel form, the participants were able to recognize the novel words with a high accuracy level of 91.3% in average. In Bowers et al. (2005), training was done in a typing task where the participants were asked to type the novel words presented on a screen as quickly and accurately as possible. Such trainings enabled the participants to become familiar with the forms of the novel words but did not involve any meaning at all. Furthermore, all novel word forms were neighbors of existing words. Lexical integration assessed under such circumstances was integration of new lexical forms that a) had no semantic content, b) consisted of elements (phonemes, letters, bigrams, syllables) of the participants' native languages, and c) were highly similar to real words. A quick integration is not surprising in such cases. A semantic component was present in training in some studies, e.g., Tamminen and Gaskell (2013). However, note that in this study, the accuracy in meaning recall after training was around 60% and 40% in the short (one day) and long (seven day) consolidation conditions, respectively, which meant that the participants could not remember the meanings of about half of the new words. A reliable semantic priming effect from such items under both masked and unmasked condition *is* surprising and should be replicated. Finally, in both studies that involved L2 learners (Elgort, 2011; Stamer & Vitevitch, 2012), as well as most L1 studies, the novel words that showed lexical integration were neighbors of known words. The determination of lexical integration is based on a neighborhood effect (e.g., Stamer & Vitevitch, 2011). In short, the quick integration findings obtained in these studies may have resulted from the use of unique materials and assessment methods. In a normal L2 learning situation, L2 learners are dealing with orthographically unique word forms often with few neighbors and they learn these words as fully functional linguistic units for expressing meanings. To what extent these findings apply to actual L2 word learning is yet to be seen.

4.6 Conclusion

Research on L2 lexical processing is probably the broadest in scope and the richest in the topics and phenomena it covers among all L2 processing areas. This research has helped discover both similarities and differences in lexical processing between L2 and L1. Regarding the former, many L1 lexical processing phenomena, such as the frequency effect and regularity effects in naming are present in L2 lexical processing (Section 4.4.3). What is more interesting is the finding of many differences. One of them is the use of L1 processing strategies in word recognition (Section 4.4.1). A related finding is the activation of L1 translations in L2 word recognition (Section 4.5.1). Unique L2 lexical processing phenomena also include a) a larger frequency effect in L2 than in L1 (Section 4.5.2), b) stronger form-based interconnections among L2 words as shown in more form-related responses in word association and masked orthographic priming effects (Section 4.3.1), and c) a stronger episodic characteristic associated with L2 lexical representations (Section 4.3.2). All these findings can be best characterized as preliminary findings that have yet to be further explored. For example, assuming that L1 translations are indeed automatically activated in L2 word recognition, it is not clear what role they play. Is their activation a by-product of L2 word recognition due to the L2–L1 associations formed in the initial learning of L2 words? Or is the activation an integral part of L2 word recognition? How does L2 proficiency affect this automatic activation? Similarly, we know little about why L2 words seem to be more interconnected through form similarities. Is it because of a weak connection between word form and concepts? Or is it due to the fact that L2 learners tend to pay more attention to form accuracy in L2 learning? Or both? Additionally, the idea of L2 lexical representations being episodic in nature needs to be further tested and elaborated, and different explanations offered for a larger frequency effect in L2 need to be empirically validated. All these issues represent some of the areas for future investigation in L2 visual word recognition.

Notes

1   Some research showed, though, that phonology plays a critically important role even in the processing and learning of a logographic language (e.g., Chan & Siegel, 2001; Perfetti & Zhang, 1995; Tan, Hoosain, & Siok, 1996).

2   See Yamada (2004) for a critique of the study and Wang, Koda, and Perfetti (2004) for a response.
3   It is not clear why more competition would lead to a greater frequency effect rather than affecting high- and low-frequency words similarly, thus slowing down L2 word recognition in general.

References

Akamatsu, N. (1999). The effects of first language orthographic features on word recognition processing in English as a second language. *Reading and Writing, 11*, 381–403.

Akamatsu, N. (2002). A similarity in word-recognition procedures among second language readers with different first language backgrounds. *Applied Psycholinguistics, 23*, 117–133.

Akamatsu, N. (2003). The effects of first language orthographic features on second language reading in text. *Language Learning, 53*, 207–231.

Andrews, S. (1989). Frequency and neighborhood effects on lexical access: Activation or search? *Journal of Experimental Psychology: Learning, Memory, and Cognition, 15*, 802–814.

Andrews, S. (1992). Frequency and neighborhood effects on lexical access: Lexical similarity or orthographic redundancy? *Journal of Experimental Psychology: Learning, Memory, and Cognition, 18*, 234–254.

Assink, E. M., van Well, S., & Knuijt, P. P. (2003). Age-of-acquisition effects in native speakers and second-language learners. *Memory & Cognition, 31*, 1218–1228.

Baddeley, A. D. (1986). *Working memory*. Oxford, UK: Oxford University Press.

Balota, D. A., Cortese, M. J., Sergent-Marshall, S. D., Spieler, D. H., & Yap, M. (2004). Visual word recognition of single-syllable words. *Journal of Experimental Psychology: General, 133*, 283–316.

Becker, C. A. (1976). Allocation of attention during visual word recognition. *Journal of Experimental Psychology: Human Perception and Performance, 2*, 556–566.

Becker, C. A. (1980). Semantic context effects in visual word recognition: An analysis of semantic strategies. *Memory & Cognition, 8*, 493–512.

Beijing Language Institute. (1986). *A frequency dictionary of modern Chinese*. Beijing: Beijing Language Institute Press.

Bialystok, E., McBride-Chang, C., & Luk, G. (2005). Bilingualism, language proficiency, and learning to read in two writing systems. *Journal of Educational Psychology, 97*, 580–590.

Bonin, P., Barry, C., Méot, A., & Chalard, M. (2004). The influence of age of acquisition in word reading and other tasks: A never ending story? *Journal of Memory and Language, 50*, 456–476.

Borowsky, R. & Masson, M. E. J. (1996). Semantic ambiguity effects in word identification. *Journal of Experimental Psychology: Learning, Memory, and Cognition, 22*, 63–85.

Bowers, J. S., Davis, C. J., & Hanley, D. A. (2005). Interfering neighbours: The impact of novel word learning on the identification of visually similar words. *Cognition, 97*, B45–B54.

Brysbaert, M. & New, B. (2009). Moving beyond Kučera and Francis: A critical evaluation of current word frequency norms and the introduction of a new and improved word frequency measure for American English. *Behavior Research Methods, 41*, 977–990.

Butler, B. & Hains, S. (1979). Individual differences in word recognition latency. *Memory & Cognition, 7*, 68–76.

Carreiras, M., Alvarez, C. J., & Devega, M. (1993). Syllable frequency and visual word recognition in Spanish. *Journal of Memory and Language, 32*, 766–780.

Carreiras, M., Perea, M., & Grainger, J. (1997). Effects of orthographic neighborhood in visual word recognition: Cross-task comparisons. *Journal of Experimental Psychology: Learning, Memory, and Cognition, 23*, 857–871.

Carroll, M. & Kirsner, K. (1982). Context and repetition effects in lexical decision and recognition memory. *Journal of Verbal Learning and Verbal Behavior, 21*, 55–69.

Carroll, J. B. & White, M. N. (1973). Age-of-acquisition norms for 220 picturable nouns. *Journal of Verbal Learning & Verbal Behavior, 12*, 563–576.

Chan, C. & Siegel, L. S. (2001). Semantic, visual, and phonological errors of normally-achieving and poor readers in Chinese. *Journal of Experimental Child Psychology, 80*, 25–46.

Cheng, C., Wang, M., & Perfetti, C. A. (2011). Acquisition of compound words in Chinese–English bilingual children: Decomposition and cross-language activation. *Applied Psycholinguistics, 32*, 583–600.

Chikamatsu, N. (1996). The effects of L1 orthography on L2 word recognition: A study of American and Chinese learners of Japanese. *Studies in Second Language Acquisition, 18*, 403–432.

Chitiri, H.-F., Sun, Y., Willows, D., & Taylor, I. (1992). Word recognition in second-language reading. In R. Harris (Ed.), *Cognitive processing in bilinguals* (pp. 283–297). Amsterdam: Elsevier Science Publishing.

Chumbley, J. I. & Balota, D. A. (1984). A word's meaning affects the decision in lexical decision. *Memory & Cognition, 12*, 590–606.

Coltheart, M., Davelaar, E., Jonasson, J., & Besner, D. (1977). Access to the internal lexicon. In S. Dornic (Ed.), *Attention and performance VI* (pp. 535–555). Hillsdale, NJ: Erlbaum.

Connine, C. M., Blasko, D. G., & Hall, M. (1991). Effects of subsequent sentence context in auditory word recognition: Temporal and linguistic constraints. *Journal of Memory and Language, 30*, 234–250.

Connine, C. M., Mullennix, J., Shernoff, E., & Yelens, J. (1990). Word familiarity and frequency in visual and auditory word recognition. *Journal of Experimental Psychology: Learning, Memory, and Cognition, 16*, 1084–1096.

Conrad, M., Carreiras, M., Tamm, S., & Jacobs, A. M. (2009). Syllables and bigrams: Orthographic redundancy and syllabic units affect visual word recognition at different processing levels. *Journal of Experimental Psychology: Human Perception and Performance, 35*, 461–479.

Conrad, M. & Jacobs, A. M. (2004). Replicating syllable frequency effects in Spanish in German: One more challenge to computational models of visual word recognition. *Language and Cognitive Processes, 19*, 369–390.

Costa, A., Foucart, A., Hayakawa, S., Aparici, M., Apesteguia, J., Heafner, J., & Keysar, B. (2014). Your morals depend on language. *PLoS ONE, 9*(4), e94842.

Coxhead, A. (2000). A new academic word list. *TESOL Quarterly, 34*, 213–238.

Dagenbach, D., Carr, T. H., & Barnhardt, T. M. (1990). Inhibitory semantic priming of lexical decisions due to failure to retrieve weakly activated codes. *Journal of Experimental Psychology: Learning, Memory, & Cognition, 16*, 328–340.

Dagenbach, D., Horst, S., & Carr, T. H. (1990). Adding new information to semantic memory: How much learning is enough to produce automatic priming? *Journal of Experimental Psychology: Learning, Memory, and Cognition, 16*, 581–591.

Davis, C. J. & Lupker, S. J. (2006). Masked inhibitory priming in English: Evidence for lexical inhibition. *Journal of Experimental Psychology: Human Perception and Performance, 32*, 668–687.

De Groot, A. M. B., Borgwaldt, S., Bos, M., & Van den Eijnden, E. (2002). Lexical decision and word naming in bilinguals: Language effects and task effects. *Journal of Memory and Language, 47*, 91–124.

Dickinson, D. K., McCabe, A., Clark-Chiarelli, N., & Wolf, A. (2004). Cross-language transfer of phonological awareness in low-income Spanish and English bilingual preschool children. *Applied Psycholinguistics, 25*, 323–347.

Diependaele, K., Duñabeitia, J. A., Morris, J., & Keuleers, E. (2011). Fast morphological effects in first and second language word recognition. *Journal of Memory and Language, 64*, 344–358.

Diependaele, K., Lemhöfer, K., & Brysbaert, M. (2013). The word frequency effect in first- and second-language word recognition: A lexical entrenchment account. *The Quarterly Journal of Experimental Psychology, 66*, 843–863.

Doob, L. W. (1957). The effect of language on verbal expression and recall. *American Anthropologist, 59*(1), 88–100.

Dufour, R. & Kroll, J. F. (1995). Matching words to concepts in two languages: A test of the concept mediation model of bilingual representation. *Memory and Cognition, 23*, 166–180.

Dufva, M. & Voeten, M. (1999). Native language literacy and phonological memory as prerequisites for learning English as a foreign language. *Applied Psycholinguistics, 20*, 329–348.

Duñabeitia, J. A., Avilés, A., & Carreiras, M. (2008). NoA's ark: Influence of the number of associates in visual word recognition. *Psychonomic Bulletin & Review, 15*, 1072–1077.

Durgunoğlu, A. Y. (2002). Cross-linguistic transfer in literacy development and implications for language learners. *Annals of Dyslexia, 52*, 189–204.

Durgunoğlu, A. Y., Nagy, W., & Hancin-Bhatt, B. (1993). Cross-language transfer of phonological awareness. *Journal of Educational Psychology, 85*, 453–465.

Duyck, W., Vanderelst, D., Desmet, T., & Hartsuiker, R. J. (2008). The frequency effect in second-language visual word recognition. *Psychonomic Bulletin & Review, 15*, 850–855.

Eisenberg, P. & Becker, C. A. (1982). Semantic context effects in visual word recognition, sentence processing, and reading: Evidence for semantic strategies. *Journal of Experimental Psychology: Human Perception and Performance, 8*, 739–756.

Elgort, I. (2011). Deliberate learning and vocabulary acquisition in a second language. *Language Learning, 61*, 367–413.

Ellis, A. W. & Morrison, C. M. (1998). Real age-of-acquisition effects in lexical retrieval. *Journal of Experimental Psychology: Learning, Memory, and Cognition, 24*, 515–523.

Ervin, S. (1961). Changes with age in the verbal determinants of word association. *American Journal of Psychology, 74,* 361–372.

Fender, M. (2003). English word recognition and word integration skills of native Arabic- and Japanese-speaking learners of English as a second language. *Applied Psycholinguistics, 24,* 289–315.

Fiorentino, R. & Fund-Reznicek, E. (2009). Masked morphological priming of compound constituents. *The Mental Lexicon, 4,* 159–193.

Fitzpatrick, T. (2006). Habits and rabbits: Word associations and the L2 lexicon. *EUROSLA Yearbook, 6,* 121–145.

Fitzpatrick, T. & Izura, C. (2011). Word association in L1 and L2. *Studies in Second Language Acquisition, 33,* 373–398.

Forster, K. I. (1985). Lexical acquisition and the modular lexicon. *Language and Cognitive Processes, 1,* 87–108.

Forster, K. I. & Chambers, S. M. (1973). Lexical access and naming time. *Journal of Verbal Learning and Verbal Behavior, 12,* 627–635.

Forster, K. I. & Davis, C. W. (1984). Repetition priming and frequency attenuation in lexical access. *Journal of Experimental Psychology: Learning, Memory, and Cognition, 10,* 680–698.

Forster, K. I., Davis, C. W., Schoknecht, C., & Carter, R. (1987). Masked priming with graphemically related forms: Repetition or partial activation? *The Quarterly Journal of Experimental Psychology, 39,* 211–251.

Forster, K. I. & Veres, C. (1998). The prime lexicality effect: Form-priming as a function of prime awareness, lexical status, and discrimination difficulty. *Journal of Experimental Psychology: Learning Memory and Cognition, 24,* 498–514.

Frenck-Mestre, C. (1993). Use of orthographic redundancies and word identification speed in bilinguals. *Journal of Psycholinguistic Research, 22,* 397–410.

Gaskell, M. G. & Dumay, N. (2003). Lexical competition and the acquisition of novel words. *Cognition, 89,* 105–132.

Gerhand, S. & Barry, C. (1998). Word frequency effects in oral reading are not merely age-of-acquisition effects in disguise. *Journal of Experimental Psychology: Learning, Memory, and Cognition, 24,* 267–283.

Gerhand, S. & Barry, C. (1999). Age-of-acquisition and frequency effects in speeded word naming. *Cognition, 73,* B27–B36.

Goldinger, S. D., Luce, P. A., & Pisoni, D. B. (1989). Priming lexical neighbors of spoken words: Effects of competition and inhibition. *Journal of Memory and Language, 28,* 501–518.

Gollan, T. H., Forster, K. I., & Frost, R. (1997). Translation priming with different scripts: Masked priming with cognates and noncognates in Hebrew-English bilinguals. *Journal of Experimental Psychology-Learning Memory and Cognition, 23,* 1122–1139.

Gollan, T. H., Montoya, R. I., Cera, C., & Sandoval, T. C. (2008). More use almost always means a smaller frequency effect: Aging, bilingualism, and the weaker links hypothesis. *Journal of Memory and Language, 58,* 787–814.

Gollan, T. H., Slattery, T. J., Goldenberg, D., Van Assche, E., Duyck, W., & Rayner, K. (2011). Frequency drives lexical access in reading but not in speaking: The frequency-lag hypothesis. *Journal of Experimental Psychology: General, 140,* 186–209.

Gonnerman, L. M., Seidenberg, M. S., & Andersen, E. S. (2007). Graded semantic and phonological similarity effects in priming: Evidence for a distributed connectionist approach to morphology. *Journal of Experimental Psychology: General, 136,* 323–345.

Gottardo, A., Yan, B., Siegel, L. S., & Wade-Woolley, L. (2001). Factors related to English reading performance in children with Chinese as a first language: More evidence of cross-language transfer of phonological processing. *Journal of Educational Psychology, 93,* 530–542.

Grainger, J. (1990). Word frequency and neighborhood frequency effects in lexical decision and naming. *Journal of Memory and Language, 29,* 228–244.

Grainger, J., Colé, P., & Segui, J. (1991). Masked morphological priming in visual word recognition. *Journal of Memory and Language, 30,* 370–384.

Grainger, J. & Segui, J. (1990). Neighborhood frequency effects in visual word recognition: A comparison of lexical decision and masked identification latencies. *Perception & Psychophysics, 47,* 191–198.

Grosjean, F. (1980). Spoken word recognition processes and the gating paradigm. *Perception & Psychophysics, 28,* 267–283.

Hamada, M. & Koda, K. (2008). Influence of first language orthographic experience on second language decoding and word learning. *Language Learning, 58,* 1–31.

Harrington, M. (2006). The lexical decision task as a measure of L2 lexical proficiency. *EUROSLA Yearbook, 6,* 147–168.

Haynes, M. & Carr, T. (1990). Writing system background and second language reading: A component skills analysis of English reading by native speaker-readers of Chinese. In T. H. Carr & B. A. Levy (Eds.), *Reading and its development: Component skills approaches.* San Diego: Academic Press.

Heyer, V. & Clahsen, H. (2015). Late bilinguals see a scan in scanner AND in scandal: Dissecting formal overlap from morphological priming in the processing of derived words. *Bilingualism: Language and Cognition, 18,* 543–550.

Hildebrandt, N., Caplan, D., Sokol, S., & Torreano, L. (1995). Lexical factors in the word-superiority effect. *Memory & Cognition, 23,* 23–33.

Hino, Y. & Lupker, S. J. (1996). Effects of polysemy in lexical decision and naming: An alternative to lexical access accounts. *Journal of Experimental Psychology: Human Perception and Performance, 22,* 1331–1356.

Holm, A. & Dodd, B. (1996). The effect of first written language on the acquisition of English literacy. *Cognition, 59,* 119–147.

Howes, D. H. & Solomon, R. L. (1951). Visual duration threshold as a function of word-probability. *Journal of Experimental Psychology, 41,* 401–410.

Inhoff, A. W. & Rayner, K. (1986). Parafoveal word processing during eye fixations in reading: Effects of word frequency. *Perception & Psychophysics, 40,* 431–439.

Ivanova, I. & Costa, A. (2008). Does bilingualism hamper lexical access in speech production? *Acta Psychologica, 127,* 277–288.

Izura, C. & Ellis, A. W. (2004). Age of acquisition effects in translation judgement tasks. *Journal of Memory and Language, 50,* 165–181.

Jackson, N. E., Chen, H., Goldsberry, L., Kim, A., & Vanderwerff, C. (1999). Effects of variations in orthographic information on Asian and American readers' English text reading. *Reading and Writing, 11,* 345–379.

Jackson, N. E., Lu, W.-H., & Ju, D. (1994). Reading Chinese and reading English: Similarities, differences, and second-language reading. In V. W. Berninger (Ed.),

The varieties of orthographic knowledge, Vol. I: Theoretical and developmental issues (pp. 73–110). Dordrecht, Boston, and London: Kluwer Academic Publisher.

James, C. T. (1975). The role of semantic information in lexical decisions. *Journal of Experimental Psychology: Human Perception and Performance, 1*, 130–136.

Jared, D., McRae, K., & Seidenberg, M. S. (1990). The basis of consistency effects in word naming. *Journal of Memory and Language, 29*, 687–715.

Jiang, N. (1999). Testing processing explanations for the asymmetry in masked cross-language priming. *Bilingualism: Language and Cognition, 2*, 59–75.

Jiang, N. (2000). Lexical representation and development in a second language. *Applied Linguistics, 21*(1), 47–77.

Jiang, N. (2002). Form-meaning mapping in vocabulary acquisition in a second language. *Studies in Second Language Acquisition, 24*, 617–637.

Jiang, N. (2004). Semantic transfer and its implications for vocabulary teaching in a second language. *The Modern Language Journal, 88*, 416–432.

Jiang, N. (2012). *Conducting reaction time research in second language studies.* London: Routledge.

Jiang, N. & Botana, G. P. (2009). *Frequency effects in NS and NNS word recognition.* Second Language Research Forum, Michigan State University, October 30, 2009.

Jiang, N. & Forster, K. I. (2001). Cross-language priming asymmetries in lexical decision and episodic recognition. *Journal of Memory and Language, 44*, 32–51.

Jiang, N., Guo, T., & Li, M. (2013). *Translation frequency effect in L2 word recognition: Replication and extension.* Vocab@vic, University of Wellington, New Zealand, December 19, 2013.

Juphard, A., Carbonnel, S., Ans, B., & Valdois, S. (2006). Length effect in naming and lexical decision: The multitrace memory model's account. *Current Psychology Letters 19*, vol. 2, 2006. Retrieved from http://cpl.revues.org/1005 (Accessed on May 4, 2015).

Kahn-Horwitz, J., Shimron, J., & Sparks, R. (2005). Predicting foreign language reading achievement in elementary school students. *Reading and Writing: An Interdisciplinary Journal, 18*, 527–558.

Kahn-Horwitz, J., Shimron, J., & Sparks, R. (2006). Weak and strong novice readers of English as a foreign language: Effects of first language and socioeconomic status. *Annals of Dyslexia, 56*, 161–185.

Kapnoula, E. C., Packard, S., Gupta, P., & McMurray, B. (2015). Immediate lexical integration of novel word forms. *Cognition, 134*, 85–99.

Katz, L. & Frost, R. (1992). Reading in different orthographies: The orthographic depth hypothesis. In R. Frost & L. Katz (Eds.), *Orthography, phonology, morphology, and meaning* (pp. 67–84). Amsterdam: Elsevier.

Keatley, C. W., Spinks, J. A., & de Gelder, B. (1994). Asymmetrical cross-language priming effects. *Memory and Cognition, 22*, 70–84.

Kern, R. G. (1994). The role of mental translation in second language reading. *Studies in Second Language Acquisition, 16*, 441–461.

Ko, I. Y., Wang, M., & Kim, S. Y. (2011). Bilingual reading of compound words. *Journal of Psycholinguistic Research, 40*, 49–73.

Koda, K. (1989). Effects of Ll orthographic representation on L2 phonological coding strategies. *Journal of Psycholinguistic Research, 18*, 201–222.

Koda, K. (1990). The use of Ll reading strategies in 1.2 reading. *Studies in Second Language Acquisition, 12*, 393–410.

Koda, K. (2005). *Insights into second language reading: A cross-linguistic approach.* Cambridge: Cambridge University Press.

Koda, K. & Zehler, A. M. (Eds.). (2008). *Learning to read across languages: Cross-linguistic relationships in first-and second-language literacy development.* London/New York: Routledge.

Kreuz, R. J. (1987). The subjective familiarity of English homophones. *Memory & Cognition, 15*, 154–168.

Kroll, J. F. & Stewart, E. (1994). Category interference in translation and picture naming: Evidence for asymmetric connections between bilingual memory representations. *Journal of Memory and Language, 33*, 149–174.

Lambert, W. E., Ignatow, M., & Krauthamer, M. (1968). Bilingual organization in free recall. *Journal of Verbal Learning and Verbal Behavior, 7*(1), 207–214.

Leach, L., & Samuel, A. G. (2007). Lexical configuration and lexical engagement: When adults learn new words. *Cognitive Psychology, 55*, 306–353.

Lemhöfer, K., Dijkstra, T., Schriefers, H., Baayen, R. H., Grainger, J., & Zwitserlood, P. (2008). Native language influences on word recognition in a second language: A megastudy. *Journal of Experimental Psychology: Learning, Memory, and Cognition, 34*, 12–31.

Levelt, W. J. M. (1989). *Speaking: From intention to articulation.* Cambridge, MA: MIT Press.

Levelt, W. J. M., Roelofs, A., & Meyer, A. S. (1999). A theory of lexical access in speech production. *Behavioral and Brain Sciences, 22*, 1–38.

Lewellen, M. J., Goldinger, S. D., Pisoni, D. B., & Greene, B. G. (1993). Lexical familiarity and processing efficiency: Individual differences in naming, lexical decision, and semantic categorization. *Journal of Experimental Psychology: General, 122*, 316–330.

Li, J., Taft, M., & Xu, J. (2017). The processing of English derived words by Chinese-English bilinguals. *Language Learning.* doi:10.1111/lang.12247

Li, M., Jiang, N., & Gor, K. (2017). L1 and L2 processing of compound words: Evidence from masked priming experiments in English. *Bilingualism: Language and Cognition, 20*, 384–402.

Lindsey, K. A., Manis, F. R., & Bailey, C. E. (2003). Prediction of first-grade reading in Spanish-speaking English-language learners. *Journal of Educational Psychology, 95*, 482–494.

Longtin, C. M., Segui, J., & Hallé, P. A. (2003). Morphological priming without morphological relationship. *Language and Cognitive Processes, 18*, 313–334.

Lucas, M. (2000). Semantic priming without association: A meta-analytic review. *Psychonomic Bulletin & Review, 7*, 618–630.

Luce, P. A. & Pisoni, D. B. (1998). Recognizing spoken words: The neighborhood activation model. *Ear and Hearing, 19*, 1–36.

Magnuson, J. S., Tanenhaus, M. K., Aslin, R. N., & Dahan, D. (2003). The time course of spoken word learning and recognition: Studies with artificial lexicons. *Journal of Experimental Psychology: General, 132*, 202–227.

Markwardt, F. (1989). *Peabody individual achievement test—revised.* Circle Pines, MN: American Guidance Service.

Marslen-Wilson, W., Bozic, M., & Randall, B. (2008). Early decomposition in visual word recognition: Dissociating morphology, form, and meaning. *Language and Cognitive Processes, 23*, 394–421.

Marslen-Wilson, W. & Tyler, L. K. (1980). The temporal structure of spoken language understanding. *Cognition, 8*, 1–71.

Marslen-Wilson, W. & Warren, P. (1994). Levels of perceptual representation and process in lexical access: Words, phonemes, and features. *Psychological Review, 101*, 653–675.

McBride-Chang, C., Tong, X., Shu, H., Wong, A. M. Y., Leung, K. W., & Tardif, T. (2008). Syllable, phoneme, and tone: Psycholinguistic units in early Chinese and English word recognition. *Scientific Studies of Reading, 12*, 171–194.

McCormack, P. D., Brown, C., & Ginis, B. (1979). Free recall from mixed-language lists by Greek-English and French-English bilinguals. *Bulletin of the Psychonomic Society, 14*(6), 447–448.

McDougall, S., Hulme, C., Ellis, A., & Monk, A. (1994). Learning to read: The role of short-term memory and phonological skills. *Journal of Experimental Child Psychology, 58*, 112–133.

McNeill, D. (1966). A study of word association. *Journal of Verbal Learning and Verbal Behavior, 5*, 548–557.

Meara, P. (1978). Learners' associations in French. *Interlanguage Studies Bulletin, 3*, 192–211.

Meara, P. (1983). Word associations in a foreign language. *Nottingham Linguistics Circular, 11*(2), 29–38.

Meschyan, G. & Hernandez, A. (2002). Is native-language decoding skill related to second-language learning? *Journal of Educational Psychology, 94*, 14–22.

Millis, M. L. & Button, S. B. (1989). The effect of polysemy on lexical decision time: Now you see it, now you don't. *Memory & Cognition, 17*, 141–147.

Mori, Y. (1998). Effects of first language and phonological accessibility on Kanji recognition. *The Modern Language Journal, 82*, 69–82.

Morrison, C. M. & Ellis, A. W. (1995). Roles of word frequency and age of acquisition in word naming and lexical decision. *Journal of Experimental Psychology: Learning, Memory, and Cognition, 21*, 116–153.

Morrison, C. M. & Ellis, A. W. (2000). Real age of acquisition effects in word naming and lexical decision. *British Journal of Psychology, 91*, 167–180.

Muljani, D., Koda, K., & Moates, D. R. (1998). The development of word recognition in a second language. *Applied Psycholinguistics, 19*, 99–113.

Murray, W. S. & Forster, K. I. (2004). Serial mechanisms in lexical access: The rank hypothesis. *Psychological Review, 111*, 721–756.

Namei, S. (2004). Bilingual lexical development: A Persian–Swedish word association study. *International Journal of Applied Linguistics, 14*, 363–388.

Neely, J. H. & Durgunoğlu, A. Y. (1985). Dissociative episodic and semantic priming effects in episodic recognition and lexical decision tasks. *Journal of Memory and Language, 24*, 466–489.

Nekrasova, T. M. (2009). English L1 and L2 speakers' knowledge of lexical bundles. *Language Learning, 59*, 647–686.

Nelson, D. L., McEvoy, C. L., & Schreiber, T. A. (1998). *The University of South Florida word association, rhyme, and word fragment norms.* Retrieved from www.usf.edu/FreeAssociation/ (Accessed on April 2, 2015).

Nelson, D. L., McEvoy, C. L., & Schreiber, T. A. (2004). The University of South Florida free association, rhyme, and word fragment norms. *Behavior Research Methods, Instruments, & Computers, 36*, 402–407.

Nissen, H. B. & Henriksen, B. (2006). Word class influence on word association test results. *International Journal of Applied Linguistics, 16*, 389–408.

Paap, K. R., Newsome, S. L., McDonald, J. E., & Schvaneveldt, R. W. (1982). An activation–verification model for letter and word recognition: The word-superiority effect. *Psychological Review, 89*, 573.

Perea, M. & Carreiras, M. (1998). Effects of syllable frequency and syllable neighborhood frequency in visual word recognition. *Journal of Experimental Psychology: Human Perception and Performance, 24*, 134–144.

Perfetti, C. A. & Zhang, S. (1995). Very early phonological activation in Chinese reading. *Journal of Experimental Psychology: Learning, Memory, and Cognition, 21*, 24–33.

Potter, M. C., So, K., von Eckardt, B., & Feldman, L. B. (1984). Lexical and conceptual representation in beginning and proficient bilinguals. *Journal of Verbal Learning & Verbal Behavior, 23*, 23–38.

Qiao, X. & Forster, K. I. (2013). Novel word lexicalization and the prime lexicality effect. *Journal of Experimental Psychology: Learning, Memory, and Cognition, 39*, 1064–1074.

Qiao, X., Forster, K., & Witzel, N. (2009). Is banara really a word? *Cognition, 113*, 254–257.

Rack, J., Hulme, C., Snowling, M., & Wightman, J. (1994). The role of phonology in young children learning to read words: The direct-mapping hypothesis. *Journal of Experimental Child Psychology, 57*, 42–71.

Rajaram, S. & Neely, J. H. (1992). Dissociative masked repetition priming and word frequency effects in lexical decision and episodic recognition tasks. *Journal of Memory and Language, 31*, 152–182.

Rastle, K., Davis, M. H., Marslen-Wilson, W. D., & Tyler, L. K. (2000). Morphological and semantic effects in visual word recognition: A time-course study. *Language and Cognitive Processes, 15*, 507–537.

Rice, G. A., & Robinson, D. O. (1975). The role of bigram frequency in the perception of words and nonwords. *Memory & Cognition, 3*, 513–518.

Rubenstein, H., Garfield, L., & Millikan, J. A. (1970). Homographic entries in the internal lexicon. *Journal of Verbal Learning and Verbal Behavior, 9*, 487–494.

Rubenstein, H., Lewis, S. S., & Rubenstein, M. A. (1971). Evidence for phonemic recoding in visual word recognition. *Journal of Verbal Learning and Verbal Behavior, 10*, 645–657.

Scarborough, D. L., Cortese, C., & Scarborough, H. S. (1977). Frequency and repetition effects in lexical memory. *Journal of Experimental Psychology: Human Perception and Performance, 3*, 1–17.

Schwanenflugel, P. J., Harnishfeger, K. K., & Stowe, R. W. (1988). Context availability and lexical decisions for abstract and concrete words. *Journal of Memory and Language, 27*, 499–520.

Segalowitz, N. (2003). Automaticity and second languages. In C. Doughty & M. H. Long (Eds.), *The handbook of second language acquisition* (pp. 382–408). Malden, MA: Blackwell.

Segalowitz, N. & de Almeida, R. G. (2002). Conceptual representation of verbs in bilinguals: Semantic field effects and a second-language performance paradox. *Brain and Language, 81,* 517–531.

Seidenberg, M. S. (1985). The time course of phonological code activation in two writing systems. *Cognition, 19,* 1–30.

Seidenberg, M. S., Petersen, A., MacDonald, M. C., & Plaut, D. C. (1996). Pseudohomophone effects and models of word recognition. *Journal of Experimental Psychology: Learning, Memory, and Cognition, 22,* 48–62.

Sereno, S. C., Brewer, C. C., & O'Donnell, P. J. (2003). Context effects in word recognition: Evidence for early interactive processing. *Psychological Science, 14,* 328–333.

Sholl, A., Sankaranarayanan, A., & Kroll, J. F. (1995). Transfer between picture naming and translation: A test of asymmetries in bilingual memory. *Psychological Science, 6,* 45–49.

Shoolman, N. & Andrews, S. (2003). Racehorses, reindeer, and sparrow: Using masked priming to investigate morphological influences on compound word identification. In S. Kinoshita & S. Lupker (Eds.), *Masked priming: The state of the art* (pp. 241–278). New York: Psychology Press.

Siegel, L. S. (1993). Phonological processing deficits as the basis of a reading disability. *Developmental Review, 13,* 246–257.

Sparks, R. L. (1995). Examining the linguistic coding differences hypothesis to explain individual differences in foreign language learning. *Annals of Dyslexia, 45,* 187–214.

Sparks, R. L. & Ganschow, L. (1991). Foreign language learning difficulties: Affective or native language aptitude differences? *Modern Language Journal, 75,* 3–16.

Sparks, R. L. & Ganschow, L. (1993). Searching for the cognitive locus of foreign language learning problems: Linking first and second language learning. *Modern Language Journal, 77,* 289–302.

Sparks, R. L. Ganschow, L., Artzer, M., Siebenhar, D., & Plageman, M. (1998). Differences in native language skills, foreign language aptitude, and foreign language grades among high, average, and low proficiency learners: Two studies. *Language Testing, 15,* 181–216.

Sparks, R. L., Humbach, N., & Javorsky, J. (2008). Individual and longitudinal differences among high and low-achieving, LD, and ADHD L2 learners. *Learning and Individual Differences, 18,* 29–43.

Sparks, R. L., Patton, J., Ganschow, L., Humbach, N., & Javorsky, J. (2006). Native language predictors of foreign language proficiency and foreign language aptitude. *Annals of Dyslexia, 56,* 129–160.

Stadthagen-Gonzalez, H., Bowers, J. S., & Damian, M. F. (2004). Age-of-acquisition effects in visual word recognition: Evidence from expert vocabularies. *Cognition, 93,* B11–B26.

Stamer, M. K. & Vitevitch, M. S. (2012). Phonological similarity influences word learning in adults learning Spanish as a foreign language. *Bilingualism: Language and Cognition, 15,* 490–502.

Stenneken, P., Conrad, M., & Jacobs, A. M. (2007). Processing of syllables in production and recognition tasks. *Journal of Psycholinguistic Research, 36,* 65–78.

Stone, G. O., Vanhoy, M., & Van Orden, G. C. (1997). Perception is a two-way street: Feedforward and feedback phonology in visual word recognition. *Journal of Memory and Language, 36,* 337–359.

Stroop, J. R. (1935). Studies of interference in serial verbal reactions. *Journal of Experimental Psychology*, 18, 643–662.

Tamminen, J. & Gaskell, M. G. (2013). Novel word integration in the mental lexicon: Evidence from unmasked and masked semantic priming. *The Quarterly Journal of Experimental Psychology*, 66, 1001–1025.

Tan, L. H., Hoosain, R., & Siok, W. W. (1996). Activation of phonological codes before access to character meaning in written Chinese. *Journal of Experimental Psychology: Learning, Memory, and Cognition*, 22, 865–882.

Thierry, G. & Wu, Y. J. (2007). Brain potentials reveal unconscious translation during foreign-language comprehension. *Proceedings of the National Academy of Sciences*, 104, 12530–12535.

Tulving, E. (1972). Episodic and semantic memory. In E. Tulving & W. Donaldson (Eds.), *Organization and memory* (pp. 382–403). New York: Academic Press.

Tulving, E. (1983). *Elements of episodic memory*. Oxford: Clarendon Press.

Upton, T. A. & Lee-Thompson, L. C. (2001). The role of the first language in second language reading. *Studies in Second Language Acquisition*, 23, 469–495.

Van Wijnendaele, I. & Brysbaert, M. (2002). Visual word recognition in bilinguals: Phonological priming from the second to the first language. *Journal of Experimental Psychology: Human Perception and Performance*, 28, 616–627.

Verhoeven, L. (2007). Early bilingualism, language transfer, and phonological awareness. *Applied Psycholinguistics*, 28, 425–439.

Vitevitch, M. S., Storkel, H. L., Francisco, A. C., Evans, K. J., & Goldstein, R. (2014). The influence of known-word frequency on the acquisition of new neighbors in adults: Evidence for exemplar representations in word learning. *Language, Cognition and Neuroscience*, 29(10), 1311–1316.

Wade-Woolley, L. (1999). First language influences on second language word reading: All roads lead to Rome. *Language Learning*, 49, 447–471.

Wagner, R. K. & Torgesen, J. K. (1987). The nature of phonological processing and its causal role in the acquisition of reading skills. *Psychological Bulletin*, 101, 192–212.

Wang, M. & Koda, K. (2005). Commonalities and differences in word identification skills among learners of English as a second language. *Language Learning*, 55, 71–98.

Wang, M., Koda, K., & Perfetti, C. A. (2003). Alphabetic and nonalphabetic L1 effects in English word identification: A comparison of Korean and Chinese English L2 learners. *Cognition*, 87, 129–149.

Wang, M., Koda, K., & Perfetti, C. A. (2004). Language and writing systems are both important in learning to read: A reply to Yamada. *Cognition*, 93, 133–137.

Weinreich, U. (1953). *Languages in contact: Findings and problems*. New York: Linguistic Circle of New York.

West, R. F., Stanovich, K. E., Feeman, D. J., & Cunningham, A. E. (1983). The effect of sentence context on word recognition in second- and sixth-grade children. *Reading Research Quarterly*, 19, 6–15.

Whaley, C. P. (1978). Word-nonword classification time. *Journal of Verbal Learning and Verbal Behavior*, 17, 143–154.

Whitford, V. & Titone, D. (2012). Second-language experience modulates first- and second-language word frequency effects: Evidence from eye movement measures of natural paragraph reading. *Psychonomic Bulletin & Review*, 19, 73–80.

Witzel, N. O. & Forster, K. I. (2012). How L2 words are stored: The episodic L2 hypothesis. *Journal of Experimental Psychology: Learning, Memory, and Cognition, 38,* 1608.

Wolter, B. (2001). Comparing the L1 and L2 mental lexicon: A depth of individual word knowledge model. *Studies in Second Language Acquisition, 23,* 41–69.

Wu, Y. J. & Thierry, G. (2010). Chinese–English bilinguals reading English hear Chinese. *The Journal of Neuroscience, 30,* 7646–7651.

Wu, Y. J. & Thierry, G. (2012). Unconscious translation during incidental foreign language processing. *NeuroImage, 59,* 3468–3473.

Yamada, J. (2004). An L1-script-transfer-effect fallacy: A rejoinder to Wang et al. (2003). *Cognition, 93,* 127–132.

Zareva, A. (2007). Structure of the second language mental lexicon: How does it compare to native speakers' lexical organization? *Second Language Research, 23,* 123–153.

Zareva, A. & Wolter, B. (2012). The 'promise' of three methods of word association analysis to L2 lexical research. *Second Language Research, 28,* 41–67.

Zechmeister, E. B., Chronis, A. M., Cull, W. L., D'Anna, C. A., & Healy, N. A. (1995). Growth of a functionally important lexicon. *Journal of Literacy Research, 27,* 201–212.

Zhang, T., van Heuven, W. J., & Conklin, K. (2011). Fast automatic translation and morphological decomposition in Chinese-English bilinguals. *Psychological Science, 22,* 1237–1242.

Ziegler, J. C., Montant, M., & Jacobs, A. M. (1997). The feedback consistency effect in lexical decision and naming. *Journal of Memory and Language, 37,* 533–554.

Chapter 5

Processing Complex Words, Multiword Units, and Meanings in L2

5.1 Introduction

The study of L2 word recognition reviewed in Chapter 4 deals with words as individual whole units. L2 lexical processing research has also considered the processing of complex words and multiword units such as formulas and collocations. Complex words are words with more than one morpheme. Three types of complex words are usually distinguished: inflected, derivational, and compound words, such as *walked*, *unhappy*, and *classroom*. They differ in how morphemes are combined in their creation. The inflectional and derivational words are created by adding inflectional and derivational affixes to a root, and a compound is made of two free morphemes. Several types of multiword units can be distinguished as well even though they are not always clearly defined and differentiated in the literature. They may include formulaic expressions (or simply formulas) such as *on the other hand*, lexical bundles such as *the end of the*, collocations such as *on foot* and *by car*, and idioms such as *beat around the bush*.

Investigations into these lexical units have attempted to answer a common research question: are they represented holistically or in a decomposed way? For example, is the word *unhappy* stored in our lexicon as a single unit or as two units, i.e., *un* and *happy*? Similarly, is the expression *on the other hand* stored as a whole unit or as four individual words? Other questions have also been explored such as how L2 proficiency, semantic transparency (i.e., whether the meaning of a compound is the combined meanings of its two component words, e.g., *classroom* being transparent and *honeymoon* being opaque), cross-linguistic congruency (i.e., whether an L2 collocation has a counterpart in L1) affect their representation and processing.

Furthermore, lexical processing research has examined how lexical meaning is represented and processed in an L2. This research has examined primarily two questions: to what extent L2 learners are able to develop L2-specific semantic structures rather than continue to rely on their L1 semantic system, and whether the processing of meaning in L1 and L2 is subserved by the same or different neural substrates. The processing of compounds, multiword units, and lexical meanings are the focus of this chapter.

5.2 Processing Complex Words in L2

The study of complex word processing has primarily considered two research issues: holistic representation and the role of L1. This section begins with an introductory subsection in which research questions and theoretical positions are explained and frequently used methods are described. Two additional subsections follow in which research on these two issues is reviewed.

5.2.1 Representation and Processing of Complex Words: Models and Approaches

A central issue in the psycholinguistic study of language processing is the unit of representation and processing. In the case of complex words, the issue is whether complex words are represented and processed as a whole or by their component morphemes. The separation of a complex word into its component morphemes in processing is referred to as decomposition. Thus, the issue is whether the recognition of complex words occurs with or without decomposition. Assuming decomposition occurs in the course of word recognition, a related issue is whether it occurs before or after a complex word is recognized.

Four different views can be identified regarding these issues. The first is to postulate that the recognition of complex words goes through an obligatory decomposition process whereby a complex word is divided into its component stem and affix(es) (e.g., Taft & Forster, 1975; Taft, 1994, 2004; Stockall & Marantz, 2006). Within this view, complex words do not have separate lexical representations in their whole-word forms. Instead, they are always represented in the form of their stems. Affixes used to form complex words are also represented separately. To use Taft and Forster's example, the word *lucky* is represented as *luck*, the stem, plus the affix *-y* that is represented as a separate entry in the lexicon. In word recognition, a complex word first has to be decomposed into its stem and affix(es), which are then used for lexical access. In the affix stripping model of Taft and Forster (1975; Taft, 1981), for example, affixes are first stripped of a complex word in the initial stage of word recognition and the stem is used for locating the lexical entry. In this view, a complex word is recognized through its stem, and morphological decomposition is obligatory and precedes lexical access. This view also implies that certain morphological rules must be involved in the representation and processing of complex words. This view is often referred to as the morphological decomposition hypothesis or sublexical hypothesis.

The second view is opposite to the first in both representation and processing. In this view which is often attributed to Butterworth (1983), all complex words are represented in their full forms in the lexicon. Thus, words such as *luck, lucky, unlucky,* and *luckily* all have their separate entries but are also connected with each other through morphological or semantic links. In

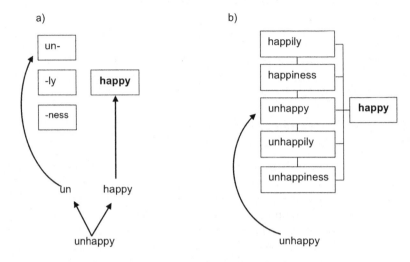

Figure 5.1 Two Opposing Views Regarding the Representation and Processing of Complex Words

processing, complex words are recognized through a direct mapping of the input with the full-form lexical representations without considering their morphological structures or constituents. This view is often referred to as the full-listing hypothesis, the whole-word representation hypothesis, or the full storage model. Some researchers acknowledge the representation of both whole-word and morphemic representations and the involvement of decomposition in complex word recognition, but they suggest that such decomposition occurs only after rather than prior to the recognition of a complex word. The supralexical model of Giraudo and Grainger (2001, 2003) represents such a view. The two opposing views are illustrated in Figure 5.1.

These two views can both accommodate some research findings, but in different ways. For example, a morphological priming effect has been repeatedly documented in that a derived word such as *unhappy* can facilitate the recognition of its stem *happy*. According to the morphological decomposition hypothesis, the derived word *unhappy* is first decomposed into two morphemes *un* and *happy*. The word is then recognized through the access of the stem *happy* prior to the onset of the target *happy*, leading to a faster access time. Within this conception, a morphological priming effect is essentially a repetition priming effect, as the same lexical entry is involved in processing the prime and the target. In a full-listing model, the effect can be explained through the spreading of activation from the derived word to the stem via lexical connections. When the prime word *unhappy* is recognized, it activates words that are morphologically linked, including the stem target *happy*. Thus, the effect is associative in nature.

A third view takes a position between the two. Known as the dual route model or hypothesis, this view recognizes that both decomposition and rule application on the one hand and full listing and direct mapping on the other are involved in the representation and processing of complex words. In one version of this view, different types of words are associated with different manners of representation and processing. In another version, both routes are involved in all types of words and engaged in a horse race (with or without interaction) and the faster route determines the outcome. An important aspect of such dual route models is the identification of factors that affect which mechanism, decomposition or direct mapping, is favored in the processing of a particular type of complex words, or which route wins in the race. One such factor is regularity of inflection. Regular affixed words such as *walked* are believed to be presented in a decomposed manner and recognized faster via rule application while irregular words such as *taught* are stored and processed in their whole-word forms (e.g., Marslen-Wilson & Tyler, 1998; Pinker, 1991; Pinker & Ullman, 2002). The second is semantic transparency. Semantically transparent words such as *punishment* favor a decompositional route while opaque words such as *casualty* are represented and processed holistically (e.g., Marslen-Wilson, Tyler, Waksler, & Older, 1994). The third factor is frequency. High-frequency words are more likely to be accessed via the whole-word route and low-frequency words via decomposition (e.g., Alegre & Gordon, 1999). A factor related to frequency is familiarity. In the Augmented Addressed Morphology model of Caramazza (Caramazza, Laudanna, & Romani, 1988; Chialant & Caramazza, 1995), for example, a complex word is recognized via both a whole-word route and a decompositional route, but the former is usually faster than the latter in the processing of familiar words. Morphological decomposition plays a more important role in recognizing unfamiliar words. Similar dual route hypothesis is also endorsed by Baayen and colleagues (e.g., Baayen, Dijkstra, & Schreuder, 1997).

The fourth view represents a connectionist perspective on the issue. Lexical representation in a connectionist model consists of a large number of basic phonological, orthographic, semantic neuron-like units. These units are interconnected and the strength of connections is weighted according to input frequency and the degree of regularity. The processing of input sends activation to the network through these units and connections. The ultimate pattern of activation determines the recognition of a word. Within such a model, the essence of word recognition, whether it is monomorphemic or multimorphemic words, relies on a single mechanism of form-meaning mapping. Morphological relationship does not have any unique status above and beyond form-meaning overlaps. Any observed morphological effects, such as morphological priming, is the outcome of phonological, orthographic, and semantic activations in the network. For example, *happily* primes *happy* not because they are morphologically linked but because of the phonological, orthographic, and semantic overlaps between them (e.g., Gonnerman, Seidenberg, & Andersen, 2007).

To study the representation and processing of complex words, researchers have adopted predominantly two approaches: the frequency effect approach and the morphological priming approach. In the former approach, three types of frequency are differentiated. The surface frequency refers to the frequency count of the complex word itself, e.g., *unhappy*. The stem frequency refers to the frequency count of the stem of a complex word, e.g., *happy* for *unhappy*. The cumulative frequency refers to the combined frequency count of all words sharing the same stem, e.g., *happy*, *unhappy*, *happily*, *unhappily*, *happiness*, *unhappiness*. By manipulating different types of frequency, one can determine if complex words are processed in their whole form or via decomposition. If complex words are represented as a whole rather than in a decomposed way, then, word recognition should be affected more by surface frequency than by stem frequency. Thus, two sets of derived words that are matched for surface frequency but differ in stem frequency, e.g., *hopeful* and *fearful*, should produce comparable RTs. On the contrary, if complex words are represented and processed by their individual morphemes, then stem and cumulative frequencies should affect the participants' performance more than surface frequency. Thus, *hopeful* should be responded to faster than *fearful* because its stem *hope* is of higher frequency than the stem *fear*. For example, Taft (1979) selected derived (Experiment 1) and inflected (Experiment 2) words of high and low stem frequencies as critical stimuli. Surface frequency and the number of affixed words were controlled. In both experiments, words with high-frequency stems were responded to faster than words with low-frequency stems, thus confirming the process of decomposition (see Sereno & Jongman, 1997 for another example).

In the morphological priming approach, two morphologically related words are used as a prime and a target, e.g., *walked-walk*, *weakness-weak*, *classroom-class*. Morphologically unrelated words are used as control primes. A morphological priming effect, e.g., a faster RT on *weak* following *weakness* than following *laziness*, is interpreted as evidence for decomposition. In this case, the priming effect is considered as an outcome of the decomposition of the prime *weakness* into two morphemes, *weak* and *ness*, which creates a condition for a repetition priming effect. However, as was pointed out earlier, the whole-word representation hypothesis can also explain the morphological priming effect via lexical connections. Thus, further manipulations are often necessary to differentiate the predictions of the two opposing views. For example, the morphological priming can be compared to repetition priming in magnitude. If inflected-stem pairs such as *walked-walk* produce the same amount of priming as repetition pairs such as *walk-walk*, the decomposition model is favored.

There is compelling evidence that morphological decomposition occurs routinely in L1 word recognition (see Amenta & Crepaldi, 2012 for a recent review). For example, stem frequency effects or cumulative stem frequency effects, which are predicted by a decompositional model, have been repeatedly observed in different languages and with different methods (e.g., Baayen et al., 1997; Colé, Beauvillain, & Segui, 1989; Juhasz, Starr, Inhoff, & Placke, 2003; Taft & Ardasinski, 2006). Morphological priming effects have been observed in a large number of studies (e.g., Marslen-Wilson et al., 1994; Rastle, Davis, Marslen-Wilson, & Tyler, 2000). Also consistent with the decompositional view was the finding that morphologically decomposable nonwords were more difficult to process than nondecomposable nonwords (e.g., Caramazza et al., 1988). Furthermore, in priming studies where repeated prime-target pairs (e.g., *boil-boil*) and inflected-stem (e.g., *boiled-boil*) or derived-stem pairs (e.g., *bitterness-bitter*) were included, morphologically related pairs were found to produce a priming effect of the same magnitude as that of the repetition condition (e.g., Silva & Clahsen, 2008). There is also considerable evidence indicating that decomposition is prelexical and obligatory. For example, when the prime is masked, morphological priming has been observed for prime-target pairs that were not morphologically related but involve a legitimate affix such as *corner-corn* and *apartment-apart*. Furthermore, morphological priming effects have been observed with very short prime exposure, e.g., 32 ms, while orthographic or semantic priming effects occurred only with longer exposure (e.g., Boudelaa & Marslen-Wilson, 2005; Rastle et al., 2000) suggesting that morphological decomposition occurs prior to the recognition of a word (see Rastle & Davis, 2008 for a review of the evidence in support of prelexical decomposition).

5.2.2 Processing Complex Words in L2: The Decomposition Debate

How complex words are represented and processed among L2 speakers is a relatively new topic. Among the approximately 20 empirical studies published in academic journals on the topic since the 2000s, a majority of them were intended to study one of the two research issues: a) the extent of morphological decomposition, and b) the influence of the native language. These two issues can be related if one assumes that the extent of morphological decomposition is affected by the morphological structures and related processing strategies of an individual's L1, but most studies have kept these two issues separate. Their primary focus was either on decomposition or on the role of L1. This subsection reviews research on decomposition while the next subsection deals with L1 influence.

In studying whether decomposition occurs to the same extent in L2 processing as in L1 processing, some researchers suggest that morphological decomposition occurs less often or to a lesser extent in L2 processing. Representing this view is Ullman's declarative/procedural model (2001, 2005). At the foundation of the model is the separation of two memory systems that are subserved by distinct neural substrates. The two neuroanatomically separate systems are believed to serve different cognitive functions. The declarative memory system is associative in nature and contains information about facts and events. The procedural memory system deals more with the learning, representation, and use of abstract rules and structural knowledge. In the context of language learning, "the declarative memory system underlies the mental lexicon, whereas the procedure memory system subserves aspects of the mental grammar" (Ullman, 2005, p. 148). Thus, an inflected word such as *walked* is likely to be treated as a whole in the declarative memory and as a combinatory item of *walk+ed* in the procedural memory. The capacity of these memory systems is linked in the model to body hormones and chemicals. Specifically, estrogen enhances declarative memory and inhibits procedural memory and dopamine is closely related to procedural memory. In this view, variations in the two memory systems both across individuals and across the life span of the same individual can be explained in terms of the differences and fluctuations of these chemicals. Applying this analysis to second language learning, Ullman argues that with the increased level of estrogen in early adulthood which results in enhanced declarative memory and attenuated procedural memory, the learning of grammatical-procedural knowledge becomes more difficult than that of lexical-declarative knowledge. Consequently,

> young adult L2 learners should tend to rely heavily on declarative memory, even for functions that depend upon the procedural system in L1. In particular, L2 learners should tend to memorize complex linguistic forms (e.g., *walked*) that can be computed compositionally by L1 speakers (e.g., *walk +-ed*).
>
> (Ullman, 2005, p. 152)

Even though this model is not specifically proposed to account for the representation and processing of complex words in L2, it has been interpreted by scholars such as Clahsen and his colleagues (e.g., Silva & Clahsen, 2008) to mean that L2 learners are more likely to treat complex words as whole forms rather than in a decomposed way.[1]

A similar position is adopted as an extension of the shallow structure hypothesis proposed by Clahsen and Felser (2006) from syntax to morphology. Similar to L2 speakers' reduced ability to use structural information in sentence processing, L2 speakers are believed to be less capable of using morphological structures in the processing of complex words (Clahsen, Balkhair, Schutter, & Cunnings, 2013).

However, an opposite prediction can also be made. Research has shown that low-frequency words are more likely to be represented and processed in a decompositional manner while high-frequency words favor a whole-word representation and processing (e.g., Alegre & Gordon, 1999). Similarly, more familiar words are believed to be processed in a whole-word form while less familiar words take the decompositional route (Caramazza et al., 1988; Chialant & Caramazza, 1995). If we assume that L2 speakers usually have less experience in L2 than in L1, and as a result, L2 words are usually less frequent or familiar to L2 speakers, then it may be predicted that a decompositional route is favored in processing L2 complex words (e.g., Portin & Laine, 2001). Lemhöfer, Koester, and Schreuder (2011) also suggested that due to typically weaker representations of L2 words, and thus, weaker whole-word representations, L2 speakers may rely on decompositional processing more.

A great deal of research has been done to explore this issue. The findings from some studies were interpreted as confirming the view that L2 speakers were less able to use morphological structures. For example, Silva and Clahsen (2008) conducted four experiments to determine if L2 users are able to process inflected and derived words in a decomposed way. The first two experiments involved inflected-stem prime-target pairs such as *boiled-boil* and the last two experiments involved derived-stem pairs that contained two suffixes, -ness and -ity, e.g., *boldness-bold, acidity-acid*. The participants were English NS and Chinese and German ESL speakers (Experiments 1, 3, 4) and Japanese ESL speakers (Experiment 2). The masked priming paradigm was adopted in all four experiments with an SOA of 60 ms for all experiments except for Experiment 2 which had an SOA of 30 ms. In all four experiments, three prime-target relations were included, identical or repetition prime (*boil-boil*), inflected or derived prime (*boiled-boil*), and an unrelated prime (*jump-boil*). The inclusion of these three conditions allowed them to determine a) if the morphological priming effect could be obtained (by comparing morphological and unrelated conditions), and b) if morphological priming was the same in magnitude to the repetition priming (by comparing repetition and morphological conditions). A full decomposition model would predict that the participants would produce as much priming in the morphological condition as in the repetition condition. However, if inflected or derived words were not decomposed, one would expect either no morphological priming effect or an effect much smaller than the repetition condition. The results from the four experiments showed that L2 speakers were different from NS. In the first two experiments, NS showed a morphological priming effect similar in magnitude to the repetition priming effect, thus, indicating full decomposition. The two ESL groups, on the other hand, showed reliable repetition priming but no morphological priming. In Experiments 3 and 4, NS showed the same pattern as in the first two experiments. NNS, however, showed a sign of partial decomposition in that they produced a morphological priming effect that was smaller than the repetition priming effect. No difference was found between the three groups of ESL speakers, suggesting that this lack of or reduced morphological priming was not influenced by L1 backgrounds. They took the findings as supporting Ullman's (2005) claim that morphological structures are less utilized in L2 processing.

Several subsequent studies were reported by Clahsen and his colleagues that provided further evidence for this L1–L2 difference. In Neubauer and Clahsen (2009), the processing of German regular and irregular particles by NS and German L2 speakers with a Polish background was examined in three tasks, acceptability judgment (AJ), lexical decision, and masked priming. In the AJ task, a participant was asked to read a context passage and a sentence in which a critical verb was shown in either its regular participle form or its irregular form. The participant's task was to rate the naturalness of the inflected form on a 1–5 scale. Previous research showed that NS of English and German preferred the regular form in the case of denominal verbs while the irregular form was preferred for underived verbs with irregular roots. For example, when the noun *fly* is used as a denominal verb to mean putting flies on something, the regular form *flied* is preferred in spite of the presence of the existing irregular verb form *flew*. Similarly in German, when the noun *Wachs* (wax) is used as a verb to mean covering something with wax, its regular participle form of *verwachst* is preferred, but in the case of the irregular verb *wachsen* (to grow), its irregular participle form of *verwachsen* is preferred. This phenomenon documented in Clahsen and Almazan (1998) and Clahsen, Hadler, and Weyerts (2004); in addition, Marcus et al. (1995) suggests that NS of these languages are sensitive to morphological structures while judging the naturalness of regular and irregular participle forms. The rating performance from NNS and NS was intended as a way to determine if NNS were similarly sensitive to morphological structures. The results replicated NS' preference for the regular form for the denominal verbs, but NNS showed no difference between regular and irregular forms of denominal verbs. The LDT was motivated by the previous finding that NS responded to high-frequency participles faster than low-frequency participles but this frequency effect occurred only for irregular verbs, suggesting a whole-word form representation for irregular words and decomposed representation for regular verbs. The purpose of the LDT experiment was to determine if NNS would show the same pattern. Eighteen regular and 18 irregular verb forms served as critical stimuli. The results showed that NS replicated previous findings in showing a frequency effect for irregular verbs only, but NNS showed a frequency effect for both types of verbs, indicating that they treated both regular and irregular verbs in a non-decomposed way. The masked priming experiment was similar to that of Silva and Clahsen (2008) except for the added variable of regularity. The findings were similar, too. Most importantly, NS showed a priming effect of comparable magnitude for the repetition and morphological conditions for the regular verbs which suggested full decomposition, but NNS showed a larger repetition priming than morphological priming. In Clahsen and Neubauer (2010), derived words were examined with the same participant population and language. NNS were again found to be different from NS in producing no morphological priming effect.

Further evidence for reduced morphological analysis in L2 processing can be found in Clahsen et al. (2013), Murphy and Hayes (2010), Jacob, Fleischhauer, and Clahsen (2013), and Bowden, Gelfand, Sanz, & Ullman (2010).

In contrast to these studies, many other studies have shown that decomposition is involved in the processing of complex words by L2 as well as L1 speakers. One line of evidence is the significant morphological priming effect for regular inflected words or derived words, contrary to the findings of Silva and Clahsen (2008), Clahsen and Neubauer (2010), and Clahsen et al. (2013). In the first such study, Basnight-Brown, et al. (2007) tested English NS and Serbian and Chinese ESL speakers in a cross-modal priming study involving both regular and irregular inflected verbs. Both groups of ESL speakers produced reliable priming effects for regular verbs. Feldman, et al. (2010) reported another study in which NNS showed priming effects for both regular and irregular inflected words. They tested Serbian ESL speakers in two paradigms: masked priming and cross-modal priming. Three types of inflected verbs were tested: regular (e.g., *billed*), length preserved irregular (e.g., *fell*), and length different irregular (e.g., *taught*). Three prime-target relationships were compared: inflected-stem, orthographic overlap, and unrelated (e.g., *billed-bill*, *billion-bill*, *careful-bill*). NNS in the study produced an overall pattern that was similar to that of NS: they showed a priming effect for both regular and irregular verbs in both paradigms.

Further morphological priming effects from L2 speakers were also reported by Gor and Cook (2010) and Gor and Jackson (2013) where adult L2 Russian speakers, Russian heritage speakers, and Russian NS all produced reliable auditory morphological priming effects on regular, semiregular, and irregular inflected verbs, by Diependaele, Duñabeitia, Morris, and Keuleers (2011) where both Spanish and Dutch ESL speakers showed a similar pattern to that of NS in showing the strongest priming effect for the transparent pairs and least priming for the orthographic pairs with the opaque pairs in the middle, and by Li, Jiang, and Gor (2017) where both NNS and NS produced reliable priming effects for both transparent and opaque compounds. The observation of comparable priming effects among NS and NNS were often interpreted to indicate similar processing strategies among NS and NNS.

In addition to the morphological priming findings, studies that employed other paradigms also showed the tendency for L2 speakers to take the decompositional route. In comparing lexical decision times on monomorphemic and inflected words that were matched for other lexical properties, Lehtonen and Laine (2003) found a monomorphic advantage for low-, medium-, and high-frequency words among NNS while NS showed this advantage for high-frequency words only. These results suggested that NNS seemed to adopt a morpheme-based processing strategy for all words regardless of their frequency. Lemhöfer et al. (2011) tested NS and NNS on long and short English compounds whose morpheme boundary consisted of a legal bigram (*da* in *headache*) or an illegal bigram (*kb* in *cookbook*). The rationale for the use of this comparison is that if individuals adopted a decompositional strategy, the illegal bigrams would provide an orthotactic cue for recognizing the two component morphemes, thus producing a faster RT for compounds with illegal bigrams than those with legal bigrams. Their NS participants produced an illegal bigram advantage in RT for long words only while NNS showed this advantage for both long and short compounds. These results led the authors to conclude that the decompositional strategy was used more extensively by L2 speakers than by L1 speakers. Additionally, NS and NNS were found to adopt similar processing strategies in a self-paced reading study involving English inflected words (Pliatsikas & Marinis, 2013) and in processing German inflected words in a lexical decision study (Strobach & Schönpflug, 2011).

The review of the literature above shows a mixed picture regarding how L2 speakers are different from or similar to NS in processing complex words. These studies can be classified into three categories in terms of their findings: studies that showed a greater preference for whole-word processing among NNS than NS, studies that showed a greater preference for decompositional processing among NNS than among NS, and studies that showed no difference between NS and NNS. It should be pointed out that these conflicting results were obtained in studies that employed different paradigms. In this sense, it is particularly noteworthy to see a half-half split among the six studies that employed the same masked priming paradigm, with three showing a morphological priming effect among NNS (Feldman et al., 2010; Diependaele et al., 2011; Li et al., 2017), and the other three failing to do so (Silva & Clahsen, 2008; Clahsen & Neubauer, 2010; Clahsen et al., 2013). It is worthwhile to pursue this line of research to understand what contributed to the contradictory findings.

5.2.3 Processing Complex Words in L2: L1 Influence

Many studies have focused more on the issue of how the L2 speakers' L1s affect the representation and processing of L2 complex words while exploring the decomposition issue. The point of departure in this research is the cross-language differences in morphological richness. Some languages, often referred to as synthetic languages, employ inflectional and derivational affixes extensively. These languages have two morphological characteristics. First, they have a high morpheme-per-word ratio in that a word often consists of multiple morphemes. To use Portin and Laine's (2001) Finnish example, the Finnish word *taloissannekin*, meaning "even in your houses", consists of the stem *talo* (house) and four suffixes indicating plural (*i*), inessive case (*ssa*), possessive (*nne*), and enclitic particle (*kin*). Second, a word can have a large number of possible forms as a result of different combinations of affixes. According to these same authors, each Finnish noun can have over two thousand possible forms and a verb may have over ten thousand possible forms. In contrast, other languages, often referred to as isolating or analytic languages, employ limited morphology. Chinese, for example, has few inflectional or derivational affixes.

It has been suggested that the extent of morphological richness may affect the representation and processing of complex words. Words in a morphologically rich language are more likely to be represented and processed in a decompositional manner rather than in their whole-word forms (Portin, Lehtonen, & Laine, 2007). This supposition finds support in experimental findings that multimorphemic words took longer to process than monomorphemic words that were matched in other lexical properties (e.g., Laine, Vainio, & Hyönä, 1999). Words in a morphologically limited language, in contrast, are more likely to be represented and processed in a whole-word form. Consistent with this assumption was the finding that there was no such processing disadvantage associated with multimorphemic words in Swedish, a morphologically limited language (Portin & Laine, 2001).

An interesting question in connection with this cross-language difference is whether an L2 speaker will transfer processing strategies from L1 to L2 when the two languages differ in morphological richness and thus in processing strategies. Portin and Laine (2001) were probably the first to explore this issue. They tested NS and L2 speakers of Swedish in a LDT. The L2 speakers were NS of Finnish. The test materials included 20 monomorphemic words, 20 bimorphemic derived words, and 20 trimorphemic inflected words as critical stimuli, along with 80 filler words and 140 nonwords. The critical stimuli were matched for surface frequency, and where possible, lemma frequency. NS of Swedish, being speakers of a language with limited morphology and thus favoring a whole-word processing strategy, were expected to show no difference among the three types of words. The focus was on Finnish-Swedish bilinguals. If they transferred their Finnish decompositional processing strategies to Swedish processing, they would be expected to show a slower response to inflected or derived words in comparison to monomorphemic words. Otherwise, no difference was expected. The most important finding in the present context was that bilinguals showed a significantly longer RT to trimorphemic inflected words than monomorphemic words while NS showed no such differences. This finding seemed to suggest that these bilinguals transferred their morpheme-based decompositional strategy from L1 Finnish to L2 Swedish. However, the authors also recognized the possibility that a decompositional processing strategy may be adopted not as a result of L1 transfer but as a more general processing strategy associated with L2 processing. This latter possibility was consistent with the finding that lower frequency words are more likely to be represented and processed in a decompositional way (e.g., Alegre & Gordon, 1999) and reflected the fact that bilinguals usually had less experiences in L2.

Four subsequent studies explored the same issue with a similar design but with additional variables of frequency, proficiency, and L1 background. Lehtonen, Niska, Wande, Niemi, and Laine (2006) added the word frequency variable. They tested adult L2 speakers of Swedish with Finnish background on monomorphemic and inflected words of high, medium, and low frequencies. The results from the NS showed a significant delay in processing inflected words than monomorphemic words, but this delay occurred only with low-frequency words. NNS, on the other hand, showed an inflection disadvantage for both low- and medium-frequency words. These results suggested that adult L2 speakers seemed to be more likely to adopt a decompositional strategy, either or both because of the influence from their morphologically rich Finnish or of the fact that they were less experienced in Swedish. Portin et al. (2007) reported a study with the same task and materials but with an added variable of L2 proficiency. The results from both the high- (Experiment 1) and low-proficiency (Experiment 2) groups showed a nativelike pattern: the inflection disadvantage was present only for low-frequency words. They concluded that adult L2 speakers can develop L2-specific processing strategies.

Two studies compared L2 speakers with different L1 backgrounds. Portin et al. (2008) tested Swedish L2 speakers with an agglutinating (Hungarian) and an isolating (Chinese) language background. They again adopted the six-condition design and used the comparison between monomorphemic and inflected words as an assessment of processing strategies. Their results provided the most compelling evidence for L1 influence thus far. While performing a LDT on Swedish monomorphemic and inflected words, Hungarian speakers showed a processing cost for inflected words that were of low- or medium-frequency. Their results indicated that they adopted a whole-word strategy for high-frequency words but a morpheme-based strategy for low- and medium-frequency words. In contract, Chinese speakers showed no processing costs for inflected words of any frequency, suggesting that they adopted a whole-word processing strategy for all words, which was consistent with the prediction made on the basis of L1 transfer.

Vainio, Pajunen, and Hyönä (2014) reported another study that compared two groups of L2 speakers, i.e., Russian and Chinese speakers of L2 Finnish, each representing a typologically similar and distant language respectively. The stimuli included three types of nouns that were either in their nominative (thus monomorphemic) form or in their partitive or genitive form (thus bimorphemic). In performing a LDT, Finnish NS replicated an earlier finding of a morphological complexity effect in that they processed the monomorphemic nominative forms faster than bimorphemic partitive and genitive forms with no reliable difference between the latter two. The two NNS groups showed a pattern both different from each other and from NS. The Russian group showed a difference between nominative and partitive conditions as well as a difference between the partitive and genitive conditions. The Chinese group, on the other hand, showed no difference between the nominative and partitive conditions. This latter result was consistent with the idea that Chinese speakers may prefer a whole-word processing strategy even while processing a morphologically very complex L2.

Before the conclusion of this section on the processing of complex words which has focused on the issues of decomposition and L1 influence, it should be pointed out that other issues have also been explored in relation morphological processing in L2. For example, Zeeuw, Schreuder, and Verhoeven (2013) compared RT and ER in processing regular and irregular past tense Dutch verbs among NS and NNS grade schoolers and found a) regularly inflected verbs were easier to process for both NS and NNS third graders, b) the regular advantage was larger in NNS than in NS, and c) no difference was found between the two types of verbs among both NS and NNS when they reached the sixth grade. Several studies considered morphology from a developmental perspective by examining how individual differences in memory capacity, linguistic distance, and the amount of exposure affected the development of morphological knowledge and awareness (e.g., Ettlinger, Bradlow, & Wong, 2014; Marsden, Williams, & Liu, 2013; Nicoladis, Song, & Marentette, 2012; Zhang, 2013).

5.3 Processing Multiword Expressions in L2

Individuals produce a large number of multiword expressions in speech and written communication. Also referred to as lexical phrases (e.g., Nattinger & DeCarrico, 1992), these sequences of words have achieved some special status either because they co-occur at a high frequency or because they seem to be bond together in one way or another. Examples of such expressions are formulaic sequences such as *as soon as* and *on the other hand* and idioms such as *miss the boat* and *hit the nail on the head*. According to some estimate, such multiword units count for more than 50% (Erman & Warren, 2000) to 70% (Wray & Perkins, 2000) of written texts. Interest in these multiword units in language acquisition and use began at least as early as the 1960s (e.g., Lyons, 1968; Murrell, 1966). By the 1970s, it had attracted a great deal of attention among both L1 and L2 researchers (e.g., Brown, 1973; Clark, 1974; Hakuta, 1974; Krashen & Scarcella, 1978). There is a reemergence of interest in this topic among SLA researchers in the 2000s, which led to the publication of numerous articles in academic journals and even more presentations at conferences in recent years. This section begins with a classification of different types of multiword expressions. It is then followed by a review of research on three topics related to this phenomenon: holistic representation of formulas and lexical bundles, the role of L1 in the representation and processing of L2 collocations, and the activation of figurative and literal meanings in L2 idiom processing.

5.3.1 Defining and Differentiating Multiword Expressions

In the literature on multiword expressions, there is a tendency to use an umbrella term to refer to different types of these expressions. This is clear from Wray's (1999, 2002) definition of formulaic sequence as

> a sequence, continuous or discontinuous, of words or other meaning elements, which is, or appears to be, prefabricated: that is, stored and retrieved whole from memory at the time of use, rather than being subject to generation or analysis by the language grammar.
>
> (Wray, 1999, p. 214)

Such a definition includes any multiword unit that is believed to be stored holistically, whether it is a collocation such as *on foot*, a formulaic expression such as *at the same time*, or an idiom such as *tie the knot*. Wolter and Gyllstad (2011) defined a collocation as "a sequence consisting of two or more words which co-occur more frequently than chance would predict based on the frequency of occurrence of the individual constituent words" (p. 434). This frequency-based definition is also broad enough to cover all multiword units. The lack of a distinction of different types of multiword units is also clear in the construction of test materials. For example, Schmitt and colleagues (Schmitt, Grandage, & Adolphs, 2004; Schmitt & Underwood, 2004; Underwood, Schmitt, & Galpin, 2004) used three types of materials in their studies under the same term formulaic sequence: formulas in their traditional sense, lexical bundles as defined by Biber, Johansson, Leech, Conrad, and Finegan (1999), and idioms. Ellis, Simpson-Vlach, and Maynard (2008) also included both structurally complete or incomplete multiword sequences in their corpus-based study and discussion of psycholinguistic reality of formulaic sequences.

For the purpose of reviewing and conducting research on this topic, it is important that different types of multiword expressions are differentiated. Treating them as a homogenous linguistic type obscures important linguistic differences among them, risks failure in appreciating the different research issues in association with different types of multiword expressions, and may lead to the development of inadequate test materials in research. For these reasons, four different types of multiword expressions are differentiated.

Formulaic sequences, or formulas for short, refer to sequences of (often three or more) words a) that recur together at a high rate of frequency, b) that form a complete syntactic and semantic unit, such as a noun phrase or a prepositional phrase, and c) whose meanings can be derived from the lexical meanings of component words. Frequency of co-occurrence, syntactic completeness, and semantic compositionality are the three defining features of formulaic sequences as used in this context. Examples of formulas thus defined are *at the same time, look forward to, day and night*. Obviously, the term is defined in a narrower sense here than in many other publications.

Lexical bundles are sequences of three or more words a) that co-occur at a high frequency, ten times or higher per million words to useBiber et al.'s (1999) criterion, and b) that do not constitute a complete syntactic or semantic unit. Note that this definition differs from that of several other researchers who treated structural incompleteness as a tendency rather than a defining characteristic. For example, according to Biber and Conrad (1999, p. 183), "lexical bundles are defined as the most frequent recurring lexical sequences; however, they are usually *not* complete structural units, and usually not fixed expressions". They estimated that about 85% of lexical bundles in conversation and 95% in academic prose were incomplete units, implying that the rest of them are complete in structure. This approach allows the inclusion of both structurally complete and incomplete units as lexical bundles. Structural completeness is used as a defining feature of lexical bundles in this context to separate them from formulas. This distinction is important for the understanding of mental representation of these multiword units, as will become clear below. Examples of lexical bundles defined on the basis of both frequency and structural completeness are *is one of the, in this chapter we* (see more in Nekrasova, 2009). In sum, formulaic sequences and lexical bundles share the same quality of being frequent in co-occurrence, but they differ in whether or not the expression forms a complete syntactic or semantic unit.

The third type is *collocations*. These are usually sequences of two words that co-occur. These expressions, such as *narrow escape, by bus, take medicine, look out, agree with, interested in*, do not have to have a high degree of co-occurrence, but they represent a conventional way of combining words in a few well-defined relationships such as adjective+noun, preposition+noun, verb+noun, verb+particle, verb+preposition, adjective+preposition pairs, as the examples above illustrate. The combination of the two component words in a collocation is conventional and arbitrary in the sense that a semantically similar word can in theory express the same idea, but would sound awkward, such as *slim escape* or *eat medicine*. The arbitrariness can also be seen in the fact that different languages use different word combinations to express the same idea. For example, *take medicine* becomes *chi yao* (eat medicine) and *black tea* becomes *hong cha* (red tea) in Chinese (see Nesselhauf, 2003 for more discussion of how collocations are defined). A distinction between collocations and formulas is necessary in the context of L2 research. As pointed out by Yamashita and Jiang (2010), formulas are largely language-specific structurally while there is a greater structural overlap in collocations between languages.

For example, English formulas such as *look forward to*, *on the contrary*, *out of order* are less likely to have a counterpart in another language that is similar in structure unless the languages are historically or typologically related. However, concepts expressed by collocations such as *strong wind*, *high salary*, *wide street*, may exist in many languages and lexicalized in similar ways. Thus, a topic such as L1 influence applies to collocations more readily than to formulas. It is not surprising that all studies that examined the role of L1 in the context of multiword expressions involved collocations (e.g., Yamashita & Jiang, 2010; Wolter & Gyllstad, 2011, 2013).

The last type is idioms. Formulas, lexical bundles, and collocations are all semantically compositional sequences of words in the sense that their meanings are composed of the meanings of their constituent words, which sets them apart from idioms. Idioms, such as *play with fire* (*to do something dangerous or risky*), *bury the hatchet* (*to end a conflict or make peace*), *kick the bucket* (*to die*), are sequences of words whose meanings are usually not entirely compositional. Admittedly, many idioms have a literal meaning, and in many idioms, the meanings of the constituent words may also contribute to their overall figurative meanings, but the figurative meaning of an idiom is not a straightforward combination of the lexical meanings of its constituent words, and equally importantly, the figurative meaning is the most frequently intended meaning in idiom use. The figurative nature of idioms differentiates them from other multiword sequences, and offers an opportunity, like no other multiword sequences do, to explore issues such as the simultaneous activation of multiple meanings or the time course of such semantic activation among NS and NNS.

The differentiation of the four types of multiword units is necessary for the recognition and appreciation of the unique characteristics of each type of multiword units, which is important for the understanding of the unique research questions they pose and for developing adequate test materials in empirical studies. At the same time, one has to recognize that the boundaries among the four types of multiword units are not always clear-cut. For example, the expressions such as *in sum* and *by contrast*, can be both formulas and collocations. Some formulaic sequences, such as *at the same time* and *once in a while* are considered idioms by some. Idioms can differ in terms of their semantic decompositionality or analyzability, as pointed out by Gibbs, Nayak, and Cutting (1989). As a result, some idioms, e.g., *play with fire*, are semantically more transparent than other idioms such as *kick the bucket*.

The renewed interest in multiword units in the 2000s, as shown and led by the publication of Wray (2002) and Schmitt (2004), was accompanied by an expansion of the scope of investigation from a more functional approach (e.g., documenting, analyzing, and classifying the uses and functions of formulas in speech and written communication) to a psycholinguistic approach that is more focused on the mental processes associated with the use of these structures. A sizable body of literature has accumulated that explores the psycholinguistics of multiword units. In the following subsections, empirical research surrounding the following questions are discussed:

a) are multiword sequences represented and processed holistically?
b) are the representation and processing of L2 collocations influenced by the native language?
c) how do figurative and literal meanings interact in the processing of idioms by NNS?

5.3.2 Holistic Representation and Processing of Multiword Units

It has long been believed in both L1 and L2 literature that multiword units such as formulas and idioms are represented and processed holistically as unanalyzed units. This belief is reflected in the expressions often used to describe these lexical units, such as *prepackaged* (Clark, 1974), *prefabricated* (Brown, 1973; Hakuta, 1974; Krashen & Scarcella, 1978), *ready-made* (Raupach, 1984), *unanalyzed* (Fillmore, 1979; Hickey, 1993), *frozen* (Hickey, 1993; Lieven, Pine, & Barnes, 1992), and *semi-preconstructed* (Sinclair, 1991). It is also clear from how formulaic expressions are defined. For example, Wray (2002) defined formulaic sequences as sequences of words "stored and retrieved whole from memory at the time of use" (p. 9). Sinclair (1991) suggested that these expressions "constitute single choices" in language use (p. 110).

According to this holistic view, these phrasal expressions are stored as single whole units that are directly addressable and retrievable from the mental lexicon. In other words, these expressions have been lexicalized. Thus, *on the contrary* is represented as a single lexical unit while a nonformulaic expression such as *on the window* is stored as three individual words which are put together online in language use. Furthermore, holistic representation and processing have been considered the reason for the efficiency and fluency in language use that are associated with the use of formulas (e.g., Conklin & Schmitt, 2008; Pawley & Syder, 1983; Millar, 2011).

This belief, however, was not put to empirical test until the 2000s. The three studies included in Schmitt (2004) represented the first attempts to explore this issue systematically and empirically. These studies employed several different methods, such as oral dictation in Schmitt et al. (2004), tracking eye movements in Underwood et al. (2004), and self-paced reading in Schmitt and Underwood (2004). They involved different types of multiword units such as formulas, lexical bundles, and idioms. The findings were not consistent. NNS participants in Schmitt, Grandage, and Adolphs were found to have difficulty in reproducing a majority of lexical clusters fluently, which was taken to suggest that most of these recurrent clusters were not stored holistically, at least among the NNS tested in the study. The eye-movement data from Underwood et al. (2004) provided partial support for holistic representation of formulas in that the NNS participants showed fewer fixations on the target words used in formulas, but there was no reliable difference in the duration of fixation on the target words used within or outside a formula. The NS and NNS participants in Schmitt and Underwood (2004) showed no difference in reading time for target words embedded in formulas and nonformulaic expressions, thus negating the holistic view.

A potential cause of the conflicting results as well as an overall pattern of unfavorable findings for the holistic view from this set of studies may have to do with the fact that they often used a mixture of different types of materials. For example, the corpus-derived expressions used by Schmitt et al. (2004) included both lexical bundles such as *I see what you* and *as shown in figure* as well as formulas. The test materials were also mixed across studies. While a large number of lexical bundles were used in Schmitt, Grandage, and Adolphs, many idioms were included in Underwood et al. (2004). Thus, it is not surprising that these studies produced different results.

In an effort to further explore the issue, Jiang and Nekrasova (2007) adopted a phrase grammaticality judgment task (GJT) and focused on formulas. They asked NS and NNS of English to judge whether or not a word string presented on a computer monitor formed a grammatical phrase. Their RT and ER were recorded as primary data. The critical stimuli were formulas such as *as soon as* and *to tell the truth* and their control expressions such as *as mean as* and *to tell the price*. The two sets of materials were matched on lexical frequency and length but differed in phrasal frequency with the formulas being considerably high in frequency than their control expressions. Additionally, a set of ungrammatical sequences were included (e.g., *corner yellow that*, *party than great*) that required a No response. The design of the study was based on the assumption that in order to perform a grammaticality judgment task on a word sequence, a syntactic analysis usually had to be performed to determine if these words in this particular order constituted a grammatical expression. However, if formulas were represented holistically, they could be located in the mental lexicon directly, and thus its grammatical status could be confirmed without performing syntactic analysis. The different processes involved in performing the GJT on formulas and nonformulaic expressions are illustrated in Figure 5.2. Bypassing the syntactic analysis process would lead to a saving in performing the task. Hence, the holistic view would predict a faster RT for formulas than for control expressions. The results confirmed the predictions. Both NS and NNS responded to formulas faster than nonformulas.

Two additional studies adopted the self-paced reading task to explore the issue, one involving idioms and the other collocations. In Conklin and Schmitt's (2008) study, NS and NNS of English were asked to read sentences that contained idioms (e.g., *take the bull by the horns*, *hit the nail on the head*)

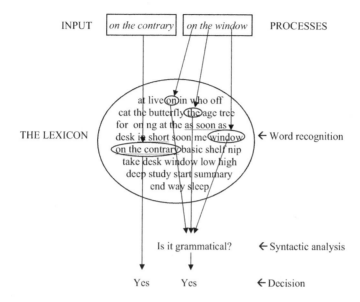

Figure 5.2 Different Processes Involved in Performing a GJT on a Formula and a Non-formulaic Expression

and non-idiomatic expressions that were constructed out of the idioms (e.g., *hit the head on the nail*). In the case of idioms, they were presented in a context that either biased an idiomatic or literal interpretation. The holistic representation was assessed by comparing the participants' reading time for the idioms (in either reading) on the one hand and that for non-idiomatic expressions on the other. The results from both NS and NNS showed that both groups were faster in reading idioms than non-idioms regardless of whether the context called for an idiomatic or literal reading, thus supporting a holistic view of idiom representation. However, it is not clear whether the expressions in the three conditions were a) matched for semantic familiarity and acceptability, and b) comparably acceptable in their contexts, both of which could have an impact on RT.[2]

In another study that adopted the self-paced reading task, Kim and Kim (2012) asked NS and NNS of English to read sentences that contained verb+particle collocations, or phrasal verbs, of different phrasal frequencies. All collocational phrases had the word *out* as the second constituent, such as *yell out*, *bail out*, and *point out*. These collocations were divided into four groups based on their phrasal frequency. The underlying assumption was that if phrasal frequency affected RT, it means that these expressions were represented holistically. The results showed a main effect of phrasal frequency for both NS and NNS. The specific pattern of the effect differed between the two groups, though. The pair-wise comparisons of the four frequency conditions showed that NS were significantly slower on the lowest-frequency set of stimuli than the other three sets. NNS responded to the highest-frequency set significantly faster than the lowest-frequency set only. There were no other pair-wise differences among NS and NNS. Based on these results, the authors suggested that NS represented and processed collocations as holistic units except for those of the lowest frequencies tested. NNS, on the other hand, seemed to process these collocations as whole units only if they were of the highest frequencies.

While these latter two studies were both considered to have confirmed the holistic view, some questions remain. First, the frequency effect observed in Kim and Kim (2012) may reflect the frequency of the verbs rather than that of the collocations. It is clear from the stimuli listed in Table 2 of that study that high-frequency collocations also contained verbs of higher frequency (*find, work, fill, point, turn, carry, reach, figure*) than those in the low-frequency collocations (*yell, test, suck, seal drain, trace, spoon, wonder*). There was no mentioning of the control of lexical properties for the verbs in these conditions. A more important issue is the interpretation of the results of both studies. In discussing the findings of Jiang and Nekrasova (2007), I provided a mechanism for linking the processing advantage observed on formulas in grammatical judgment to the holistic representation of formula: the faster RT for the formulas was a result of bypassing the syntactic analysis step in making grammatical judgment, as the grammatical status could be confirmed on the basis of the formulas being directly addressable and retrievable (as illustrated in Figure 5.2).

However, the mechanism for linking the results to the holistic view was not clear in both studies. In Kim and Kim (2012), it is not clear why a phrasal frequency effect would constitute evidence for the holistic representation of the higher-frequency expressions only. Such frequency effect can be observed of individual words, but we do not usually think that only the high-frequency words are represented holistically while the low-frequency words are stored as individual letters. The same is true of the self-paced reading results of Conklin and Schmitt (2008). While the results are consistent with the prediction of a holistic view, alternative explanations are possible, as well. One of them is a priming explanation. Individuals may take less time to read *on the head* following *hit the nail* than *on the nail* following *hit the head* because of anticipation in the former case resulted from statistical learning. There is a good chance for *hit the nail* to be followed by *on the head*. As a result, the second phrase is preactivated or primed by the first, thus resulting in some saving in processing time. This saving does not occur in processing the non-idiomatic control expression, as *hit the head* is not expected to preactivate *on the nail*. This priming effect should not be interpreted as necessarily supporting a holistic view, though. When *unhappy* primes *happy*, or *doctor* primes *nurse*, we consider this priming as indication of some type of connection existing between the two, rather than them being represented as a single unit. In this analysis, a faster reading time itself should not be equated with holistic representation and processing. This priming-effect explanation may account for the finding in Conklin and Schmitt (2008) that comparable saving was observed in processing the idioms in both their idiomatic and literal readings. If this saving was a result of holistic representation, one would expect more savings in the idiomatic than in the literal condition, as these expressions are supposedly holistically represented as idioms only.

This priming explanation of processing advantage is particularly plausible with longer expressions such as the idioms used in Conklin and Schmitt (2008) (e.g., *hit the nail on the head, take the bull by the horn*), as longer expressions leave more room for priming effects to occur. Whether it applies to shorter formulas such as those used in Jiang and Nekrasova (2007) (e.g., *on the whole, at the moment, as a result*) is yet to be determined. It is reasonable to think that there is less probability for *on the* to prime *whole*, unless the expression is holistically represented, as there are numerous possible words to follow *on the*. But this is yet to be explored. In this sense, more innovative methods are needed to provide more unequivocal evidence for the holistic representation and processing of formulas and other multiword units.

There is less evidence regarding the representation and processing of lexical bundles. For one reason, few studies have examined lexical bundles exclusively. Nekrasova (2009) attempted to explore lexical bundles, but the stimuli included many structurally complete formulas such as *at the same time, on the other hand, in the middle of, what do you think*). Tremblay et al. (2011) consider lexical bundles but they tested NS only. However, lexical bundles provide an interesting case in the study of holistic vs. decompositional representation and processing. Research has shown that a sequence of letters becomes a lexical entry in the lexicon only after some semantic content is associated with it (e.g., Forster, 1985; Dagenbach, Carr, & Barnhardt, 1990). Thus, some semantic representation (in the form of lexical meanings or propositional meanings) is critical for a linguistic expression to be represented as a lasting and independent unit in the mental lexicon. In this analysis, lexical bundles (e.g., *in this chapter we*), unlike formulas, are unlikely to be represented as whole units as they lack a semantic counterpart. In other words, frequency-driven lexical bundles defined as incomplete structural units may not have any psycholinguistic validity in terms of mental representations, contrary to what has been believed (e.g., Biber et al., 1999; Ellis et al., 2008). This is certainly an open question to be empirically explored.

To conclude this discussion of the research on the holistic representation and processing of multiword units, current research has provided limited evidence for the holistic representation of multiword units, at least in the case of formulas, idioms, and collocations. However, due to methodological issue, none of the existing evidence should be considered unequivocal. A challenge one faces in this research is to determine what constitutes compelling evidence for holistic representation and develop experimental techniques for obtaining such evidence.

5.3.3 LI Influence in Collocation Representation and Processing

Many collocations express an idea that is present across languages. Thus, a collocation in one language, such as *strong wind* or *kill time*, is likely to have a similar (but not necessarily identical) expression in another. Thus, from an L2 learner's perspective, an L2 collocation can be congruent in the sense that a word-for-word translation of the collocation also exists in the learners' L1 that has the same meaning. For example, for Chinese ESL speakers, *green tea* is a congruent English collocation because its word-for-word translation, *lücha*, (*lü*=green, *cha*=tea) makes the Chinese collocation for the same referent. An incongruent collocation is one whose word-for-word translation does not constitute a legitimate collocation with the same meaning in another language. The English expression *black tea*, for example, is an incongruent collocation to a Chinese ESL speaker because the same substance is referred to as *hong cha* (red tea) rather than *heicha* (black tea) in Chinese. The English collocation *do homework* is an incongruent one for both German and Chinese ESL speakers because in these languages, students *make homework* rather than *do homework*. When any two languages are compared, there will be a large number of congruent and incongruent collocations, which reflects the conventional and arbitrary nature of collocation formation.

This unique aspect of collocation formation creates an opportunity for studying how L2 speakers' L1 affects the learning and use of L2 collocation. Some offline studies demonstrated that cross-language congruency did affect L2 learners' learning and use of collocations. For example, in a study reported by Nesselhauf (2003), advanced German ESL speakers were found to make many more errors in writing with incongruent (42%) than congruent collocations (11%). Similar findings were also reported in many other studies (e.g., Altenberg & Granger, 2001; Biskup, 1992). However, how congruency affects the representation and processing of L2 collocation was not systematically explored in a lab setting until recently.

Yamashita and Jiang (2010) were among the first to explore this issue. They asked NS and NNS participants to perform an English phrase acceptability judgment task and recorded their RT and ER as data. The critical stimuli included 24 congruent and 24 incongruent collocations for Japanese learners of English. The 48 collocations were all acceptable in English, but the direct translations of the first set were also acceptable Japanese collocations, e.g., *quick action, great value,* but the translations of the second set did not constitute acceptable Japanese collocations, e.g., *poor value, quick death.* Lexical properties such as frequency and length were controlled. The role of L1 was assessed by comparing the participants' performance on these two different types of L2 collocations. To explore the effect of exposure and proficiency on the processing of collocations, two groups of NNS were included: those who were residing in an English-speaking country (the ESL group) and those who had never lived in an English-speaking country (the EFL group). A group of NS of English served as controls. The data from the NS showed no difference in RT and ER between the congruent and incongruent collocations. This was expected as the NS had no knowledge of Japanese and thus cross-language congruency should not affect their performance. This finding also suggested that the two sets of test materials were matched adequately. The data from the two NNS groups showed different patterns. The EFL group showed a congruency effect in both RT and ER. They responded to congruent collocations faster and with fewer errors than to incongruent collocations (RT: 1542 ms vs. 1597 ms; ER: 14.3% vs. 38.8%). The ESL group showed a congruency effect in ER only. They responded to incongruent collocations with a higher ER (19.8%) than to congruent collocations (8.3%). However, they showed no difference in RT (1388 ms vs. 1385 ms). Corroborating the ER data were the results from another study reported by Yamashita (2014) in which Japanese EFL speakers showed a higher ER on incongruent English collocations than on congruent ones in a collocation acceptability task. The ER data from both studies suggest that it takes a considerably longer time for L2 learners to develop the recognition of incongruent than congruent collocations. The RT data from the ESL group in Yamashita and Jiang showed that once L2 collocations were recognized and consolidated into the L2 lexicon, they can function as autonomous linguistic units with little influence from their L1.

Further evidence for the role of L1 in L2 collocation processing came from two studies by Wolter and Gyllstad (2011, 2013). In the 2011 study, they adopted the priming paradigm in combination with the LDT. The NS of English and Swedish ESL speakers were presented with pairs of letter strings with an SOA of 300 ms and asked to decide whether the second string was an English word or not. The critical stimuli consisted of three types of prime-target pairs shown in Example 5.1. They were verb+noun pairs that made acceptable collocations in English only and made acceptable collocations in both Swedish and English, and unrelated pairs that did not form collocations in either language. The three sets of materials were matched for a number of lexical properties and the first two sets also for the level of familiarity to the participants. They were embedded in a large number of filler items that made a total of 440 test items. A priming effect was assessed by comparing the participants' RT and ER on the two collocation conditions and the unrelated control condition. The role of L1 was determined by comparing the size of the priming effect between the congruent condition and the incongruent condition. If L1 had an impact on performance, a larger priming effect was expected for the congruent condition. The results showed that indeed there was a stronger priming effect in RT for the congruent than for the incongruent condition among ESL speakers, while English NS showed no such difference.

5.1 English-only (incongruent) collocations: *pay visit*   (n=33)

L1–L2 (congruent) collocations: *give answer*   (n=33)

Unrelated pairs: *write hope*   (n=33)

Wolter and Gyllstad (2013) adopted an acceptability judgment task similar to that of Yamashita and Jiang (2010) to explore the role of collocation frequency, L2 proficiency, and L1 in the processing of L2 collocations. The critical stimuli included five congruent and five incongruent collocations consisting of an adjective and a noun (e.g., *good news*, *free speech*) at eight frequency ranges, thus making a total of 40 congruent and 40 incongruent collocations. Eighty noncollocational adjective+noun word pairs were also used for the sake of the task. These items were presented to NS and Swedish ESL speakers who were asked to decide whether they were commonly used in English. The results showed a significant faster RT on congruent than on incongruent items among NNS (1145 ms vs. 1252 ms). No such difference was found among NS (1019 ms vs. 1012 ms).

A final study to be reviewed here is one reported by Wolter and Yamashita (2014). They tested English NS and Japanese ESL speakers in a double LDT. Two letter strings were presented to the participants who had to decide if they were both English words. Three types of word pairs were included as critical stimuli (in addition to nonword items), as shown in Example 5.2. The first set (J-only) were pairs of English words that did not form collocations in English but their Japanese translations were acceptable Japanese collocations. The second set included English collocations that were not acceptable collocations in Japanese, and the third set were word pairs that were not acceptable collocations in either language. The rationale underlying the use of these three types of word pairs was that if L1 collocational knowledge is automatically activated in L2 processing, Japanese ESL speakers should respond to the J-only items faster than the baseline items. Furthermore, they should respond to the E-only items faster than baseline items if they possessed the related collocational knowledge. The first comparison (i.e., J-only and baseline) was intended to speak directly to the purpose of exploring the role of L1 in L2 collocation processing. The result relevant to the current discussion was that there was no difference in

RT or ER between the J-only and baseline conditions. Based on the results, they concluded that L1 collocational knowledge was not activated in the processing of L2 collocations.

> 5.2 J-only: *far-eye, buy-anger* (n=54)
> E-only: low-speed, catch-breath (n=54)
> Baseline: busy-teeth, volunteer-phone (n=108)

However, a lack of an L1 effect obtained in the design of the study does not speak to the question of whether L1 collocation knowledge is involved in L2 collocation processing. Note that the issue to explore in this context is whether L1 collocation knowledge is automatically activated in and affect the processing of L2 collocation rather than in L2 word recognition or L2 processing in general. This research question requires an experimental design (in terms of experimental task and/or test materials) that involves the processing of L2 collocation. In a double LDT task, a decision is made on the basis of whether the two letter strings form words or not. Additionally, the test materials in the J-only condition were not English collocations. Even when we assume that L1 translations may be automatically activated in L2 word recognition, there is no reason to expect NNS to check whether the activated L1 words form acceptable L1 collocations when the task was a lexical decision. The collocational status is simply irrelevant to the successful performance of the LDT. A better task for the present purpose would be a collocation judgment task in which a participant has to decide whether two English words form an acceptable collocation. In this case, a negative response is required of both the J-only and baseline conditions. However, if a Japanese ESL speaker automatically checks the collocational status of the translations, it may result in a delay in reaching a negative response or in an incorrect positive response. As a result, the Japanese ESL speakers may respond to the J-only condition more slowly or with a higher ER than the baseline condition. A lack of such difference in such a collocation judgment task provides better evidence for rejecting the automatic activation of L1 collocation knowledge in L2 collocation processing.

The research findings reviewed above provide consistent evidence that L1 plays a role in the processing of L2 collocations. However, the mechanism underlying this L1 influence is yet to be explored (see Wolter & Yamashita, 2014 for related discussion). One possibility is a verification process. In the processing of L2 collocations, a bilingual may automatically check if a translation equivalent exists in L1. The existence of such an L1 collocation would facilitate the recognition process, thus giving congruent collocation a processing advantage.

5.3.4 Figurative and Literal Meanings in Idiom Processing Among NNS

A great deal of research has been done on the learning and processing of idioms by L2 speakers. Some of this research has a pedagogical focus, e.g., examining how L2 learners comprehend unknown L2 idioms and the factors that may affect their comprehension or learning process (e.g., Bulut & Celik-Yazici, 2004; Cooper, 1999; Steinel, Hulstijn, & Steinel, 2007). Other studies focused more on the mental processes involved in the processing of L2 idioms, often using L1 idiom processing as a frame of comparison. This section reviews the latter line of research, with special attention to the relationship between idiomatic and literal meanings in idiom processing, a topic that has received considerable attention in both L1 and L2 idiom processing.

Even though idioms are usually used in a figurative sense, most of them also have a literal reading. For example, while *miss the boat* is frequently used to mean missing an opportunity, the expression can also be understood literally, i.e., failing to catch a boat. The relationship between the figurative and literal meanings of idioms has been a central issue in the psycholinguistic study of L1 idiom processing since the 1970s. Researchers have examined several questions related to this issue. One of them is whether both meanings are always activated in idiom processing. Another question involves the time course of the activation of the two meanings. A third question is how the activation of figurative and literal meanings is affected by both individuals' perception of how the two types of meanings are related and the linguistic characteristics of the idioms themselves. It is beyond the scope of this section to have a comprehensive review of this research. Instead, my intention is to summarize a few influential hypotheses on the topic, thus providing a context for understanding the motivation and findings of the research done in the L2 context.

Earlier thinking on the issue was represented by the Lexical Representation Hypothesis of Swinney and Cutler (1979) and the Direct Access Hypothesis by Gibbs (1980). Both hypotheses asserted that the figurative meanings enjoyed processing advantage. They differed with regard to whether literal meaning is also activated when the context calls for the figurative meaning. Swinney and Cutler proposed that both the figurative and literal meanings are simultaneously activated when an idiom is encountered. The processing advantage associated with the figurative meaning originates from the assumption that the figurative reading is "stored and accessed as lexical items" (p. 532), thus can be assessed more efficiently, as shown in their results of faster processing of idioms over regular phrases. In Gibbs's hypothesis, however, the figurative meaning represents the conventional use of idioms and thus is always automatically computed. If the figurative meaning fits with the context, the literal meaning does not need to be computed. The latter becomes activated only when an idiom is intended for its literal meaning, or for "an unconventional use" in

Gibbs's words, e.g., in a sentence such as *the man went to the backyard and buried the hatchet near the woods*. In this scenario, both figurative and literal meanings are computed and the context-appropriate literal meaning is chosen.

These earlier hypotheses tended to treat idioms as a homogenous linguistic type. Subsequent hypotheses recognized that all idioms were not the same. They differ, for example, in the extent to which its component words contribute to their figurative meanings. These hypotheses further recognized that the processes involved in the processing of different idioms were also different. The Configuration Model proposed by Cacciari and Tabossi (1988) considers an idiom as a configuration of words that represent figurative meanings, thus the name of the hypothesis. The model contends that when idiomatic meanings are activated will depend on whether the input has a clear indication of the presence of an idiom. They referred to a word in the input with such indication as the key. Before the appearance of the key, only literal meanings are activated. Idioms can be differentiated as predictable or unpredictable depending on the location of the key in the configuration. This difference can be illustrated with the following Examples 5.3 and 5.4 from the 1988 study.

5.3 *After the excellent performance, the tennis player was in seventh heaven.*
5.4 *The girl decided to tell her boyfriend to go to the devil, once and for all.*

The idiomatic meaning becomes available early in the first example, i.e., as soon as the word *heaven* appears. In the second example, before the appearance of the word *devil*, there is no information to indicate the coming of an idiom, as the sentence can continue with many possible words, e.g., *go to the store, go to the room*. Thus, the idiom is not predictable in this context. A figurative interpretation becomes available only after the word *devil* has been recognized and integrated into the mental representation of the sentence. According to the model, where an idiom is predictable, only idiomatic meaning is activated. Where an idiom is less predictable, only the literal meaning of an incoming word (e.g., *devil* in the second example) will be activated initially. The idiomatic meaning becomes available later, after the word has been processed and indicates the presence of an idiom. The results from their cross-modal priming study provided support for this view. The word *heaven* primed the idiom-related target word *happy*, but not the literal target *saint*, but the word *devil* in the unpredictable context primed its literal target, but not its idiom-related target when the targets appeared immediately after its offset. Idiom-related priming occurred only after 300 ms.

Similarly, the idiom decomposition hypothesis proposed by Gibbs and his colleagues (Gibbs & Nayak, 1989; Gibbs, Nayak, Bolton, & Keppel, 1989; Gibbs, Nayak, & Cutting, 1989) also differentiates different types of idioms, not in terms of predictability, but in terms of analyzability or decomposability. Idioms' analyzability refers to "the degree to which their individual components independently contribute to these phrases' overall figurative interpretations" (Gibbs, Nayak, & Cutting, 1989, p. 587). Some idioms, such as *miss the boat* (miss an opportunity), are highly analyzable in that the component words, *miss* in this example, contributes directly to their figurative meanings. The meanings of these idioms are thus decomposable. Other idioms, such as *kick the bucket* (to die), are less analyzable as their figurative meanings come from none of their component words. According to the idiom decomposition hypothesis, individuals tend to perform compositional analysis while processing idioms, which activates the literal lexical meanings of the component words. In the case of decompositional idioms, this analysis facilitates the recognition of an idiom's meanings because the component words semantically contribute to the overall meaning of the idiom. This analysis, however, does not lead to the correct understanding of a nondecompositional idiom. Thus, this analysis has to be abandoned, and a figurative meaning has to be looked up in the mental lexicon. This explains why it takes longer to process nondecompositional idioms, as shown in their study. In short, idioms' decomposability affects their processing.[3]

Research on the activation of figurative and literal meanings in idiom processing among NNS did not begin until the 2000s. One of the earliest studies was reported by Matlock and Heredia (2002). They used English phrasal verbs such as *go over* which, as a phrasal verb, has an idiomatic meaning (to review) and, as a verb+preposition combination, has a literal meaning, e.g., *go over a bridge*. They constructed stimulus sentences in which the same phrase was used in its idiomatic and literal meanings as shown in Example 5.5. The participants were asked to read the sentences and then decide whether or not a subsequent sentence paraphrased the stimulus sentence correctly. The use of the paraphrase sentences served to ensure that the participants read and understand the meaning of the stimulus sentences and identify the sentences that were understood incorrectly. The primary data were their reading time on the stimulus sentences. Three groups of participants were tested: English NS, early ESL speakers, and late ESL speakers.[4] The results showed that both the NS and early L2 speaker groups read the idiomatic sentences faster than the literal sentences (NS: 4312 ms vs. 4635 ms; Early L2: 4140 ms vs. 4354 ms), but the late L2 speaker group showed no significant difference between the two conditions (6882 ms vs. 7053 ms). The results led the authors to speculate on how phrasal verbs are processed in NS and NNS of different onset ages. One possibility is that the idiomatic meaning of a phrasal verb is always activated before the literal meaning in sentence processing among NS and early L2 speakers, which is consistent with the direct access hypothesis of Gibbs

(1980). Another possibility is that both meanings are activated at the same time, but it usually takes longer to compute the literal meanings on the basis of the individual words than to activate the meaning of a holistically stored phrasal verb. Late L2 speakers, however, do not enjoy this processing advantage while processing such phrases. Instead, the literal meanings are always activated first.

5.5a   Paul went over the exam with his students.
5.5b   Paul went over the bridge with his bicycle.

A more detailed examination of the same issue was reported by Abel (2003) who additionally considered the role of decompositionality and frequency. Following the methodological approach of Titone and Connine (1994), Abel asked German ESL speakers to consider a total of 320 English idioms in terms of whether they were decomposable or nondecomposable (i.e., whether "individual words contribute to their overall figurative meanings", p. 338). They were also asked to rate their familiarity with the idioms on a 1–7 scale (7 being the most familiar). Their responses were compared with those from NS of English in Titone and Connine both in terms of all expressions used and in terms of only those 171 idioms shared between the two studies. The results showed that NNS considered more idioms as decomposable than nondecomposable (approximately 56% vs. 44%) while the NS in Titone and Connine showed an opposite pattern (42% vs. 58%). The NNS participants also rated the decomposable idioms as more familiar than nondecomposable idioms (4.9 vs. 3.0 on the 1–7 scale) and their familiarity ratings were expectedly lower than those of NS (which were 5.9 and 5.8 for decomposable and nondecomposable idioms). These results led to the development of the Dual Idiom Representation Model. According to the model, decomposable and nondecomposable idioms are represented differently at least at some developmental stage. A nondecomposable idiom such as *kick the bucket* has to be represented as a separate idiom entry in the mental lexicon from the very beginning. The comprehension of such lexicalized idioms takes place without the activation of conceptual representations of its component words as the idiom entry has its own meanings associated with it. Decomposable idioms, on the other hand, are represented and accessed via their constituent lexical entries at first. Frequent encounters of these idioms will help create their own separate idiom entries. Thus, frequency determines how a decomposable idiom, such as *miss the boat*, is represented. High-frequency idioms have a separate idiom entry in the lexicon, but low-frequency idioms are represented and accessed through their constituent words. Before an idiom entry is created, the comprehension of a decomposable idiom is achieved through the conceptual activation of its lexical entries. The term "dual" refers to the assertion that a decomposable idiom can be represented and accessed both in terms of its constituent words and as a separate idiom entry. The same frequency factor explains the differences between NS and NNS. NNS typically do not have as frequent encounters with idioms as NS do. Thus, more idioms are represented and accessed through their constituent words rather than separate idiom entries among NNS. This explains why NNS tended to judge idioms as decomposable rather than nondecomposable in the study.

Cieślicka (2006) explored the same issue in a cross-modal priming study. The participants were proficient ESL speakers studying in a Polish university at the time of testing, thus similar to those of Abel (2003). The critical stimuli included 40 idioms each embedded in a neutral sentence context that was presented auditorily. The idioms were classified as either literal (e.g., *tie the knot*, *bury the hatchet*) or non-literal (e.g., *shoot the breeze*, *have a fling*) defined in terms of the extent to which a literal interpretation is also possible of an idiomatic expression. Each sentence was accompanied by a word presented visually for a LDT. Four conditions were created in terms of idiom+target combination: a target related to the idiom's figurative meaning (*marry*), its control target (*limit*), a target related to the idiom's literal meaning (*rope*), its control target (*ripe*), as shown in Example 5.6. The visual target was presented 100 ms after the offset of either the second last or the last word of the idiom. The priming effect was computed by comparing the RT on the figurative and literal targets and their respective controls. The results showed a robust priming effect for literal targets while the figurative targets showed no reliable priming. A literal-salience resonant model was developed based on the results. According to this model, L2 learners typically become familiar with the constituent words of an idiom earlier than the idiom itself. As a result, the literal meanings of these words are likely to be more established in the mental lexicon than their figurative meanings learned later. In language processing, these literal meanings are more salient than figurative meanings in the sense that they become activated earlier and more strongly. This is believed to be true even after an idiom has become highly familiar to or automatized by an L2 speaker. Thus, learning sequence is believed to be the most important factor in this model. Regardless of familiarity and types of idioms, the literal meanings that are typically learned earlier always enjoy processing advantage.[5]

5.6 *Peter was planning to* <u>*tie the knot*</u> *later that month.*
      Critical Control

	Critical	Control
Figurative	*marry*	*limit*
Literal	*rope*	*ripe*

More recently, Siyanova-Chanturia, Conklin, and Schmitt (2011) reported a study in which NS and NNS of English were asked to read short passages for comprehension. Three conditions were created to examine the processing of idioms: a) idioms to be understood figuratively, b) idioms to be understood literally, and c) a novel expression constructed on the basis of the idiom. Example 5.7 below, which are short versions of the actual passages, illustrate the three conditions (the idiom and control expressions were underlined). These conditions were created so that a) the processing of idioms and control expressions can be compared, and b) the processing of idioms in their figurative and literal readings can be compared. The participants' eye movements were recorded in order to measure their reading times. Three measures were taken: first-pass reading time, total reading time, and fixation count. The results showed different performance patterns between NS and NNS. NS showed an idiom advantage over control expressions, but there was no significant difference between figurative and literal readings of idioms. NNS, however, showed a figurative reading disadvantage over literal readings. They were found to take longer and have more fixations while reading idioms in a figurative context than the same idioms in a literal context. No idiom processing advantage was observed over control expressions.[6] They attributed the figurative disadvantage to NNS' lack of strong consolidation of these idioms and their figurative meanings. As a result, the literal meanings are always activated first or more strongly, thus delaying their processing when the context calls for their figurative meanings.

5.7a   . . . Personally, I think you can have the highest degree from the best university in the world, but <u>at the end of the day</u> it's your contribution to the society that matters, and not the name of the university you went to at all . . . (figurative reading)

5.7b   . . . However, I still had to carry most of my stuff in small boxes from my old room to the new one. I had to make at least 50 trips so at the end of the day I was absolutely exhausted . . . (literal reading)

5.7c   . . . He's a retired man now who served in Vietnam and who's been through many things in his life, so he's got plenty of things to write about. I know that <u>at the end of the war</u> he went on to teach students at the Military Academy . . . (control expression)

Taken together, the results from the four studies suggest that NNS tend to treat idioms first as decomposable word strings that combine to activate the literal meanings based on the lexical meanings of the constituent words. The figurative readings are secondary. This represents a sharp contrast to the finding that idioms or their figurative meanings enjoy processing advantages (e.g., Gibbs, 1980; Swinney & Cutler, 1979). As pointed out by Siyanova-Chanturia et al. (2011) and demonstrated by the difference between the results from early and later L2 learners in Abel (2003), this NS–NNS difference is likely to be rooted in the differential experiences they have in the target language.

5.4 Semantic Processing in L2

Meaning is an integral part of lexical knowledge. We recognize a letter string or a logograph as a word usually because we are familiar with both the lexical form and its meaning. The study of semantic processing in an L2 constitutes a unique line of lexical processing research for its focus on how lexical meaning is represented and processed. The primary question explored in this area is how lexical meanings are represented and processed in L2 speakers.

Several characteristics can be identified from this research. First, semantic processing research is closely linked to semantic development. By examining processing data, the ultimate question to explore is whether or to what extent adult L2 speakers are able to develop a new and L2-specific semantic system while learning a new language. Second, L1 influence is the focus of attention in many studies. As L2 speakers often rely on the existing L1 semantic system in the initial stage of lexical development, semantic development often boils down to whether or to what extent L2 speakers are able to overcome L1 influence in developing the new system. Third, semantic processing research takes advantages of different semantic overlap patterns across languages. Two languages may differ in semantic structures such that a meaning is lexicalized in one language but not in another. For example, the English word *fun* does not have a ready translation in some other languages. A semantic distinction may be made in one language but not in another e.g., *criterion* and *standard* are not differentiated in Chinese. Or the same semantic space is categorized differently between two languages, e.g., the same object being referred to as a *bowl* in one language but a *plate* in another. These different patterns of semantic overlap provide opportunities for studying semantic transfer and development. Finally, this research utilizes a set of tasks different from those used in studying other lexical processing topics. Examples of such tasks are semantic classification (deciding whether a word has a concrete or abstract meaning, whether it refers to an animate or non-animate entity, or whether it designates a natural or man-made object), semantic relatedness judgment (deciding whether two words are related in meaning), and picture naming. These tasks are used because their completion requires the activation of meaning and thus can help tap semantic representation and processing.

5.4.1 L2 Semantic Processing and Development

The difficulty L2 speakers had in semantic development was already clear in some earlier offline studies. Ijaz (1986) asked advanced German and Urdu ESL speakers to complete a semantic relatedness judgment task and a sentence completion task. The target words were six English expressions, *on, upon, onto, on top of, over, above*. These words represented some semantic distinctions that were not made in the participants' L1s, such as the +/-contact distinction between *on* and *over* and +/-movement distinction between *onto* and *on* for German or Urdu speakers. The participants' performance in both tasks showed clear influence from their L1 which led Ijaz to conclude that "native language conceptual patterns appear to be powerful determinants of the meaning ascribed to L2 words and they seem to be very rigid and difficult to permeate" (p. 447). Limited semantic development and non-nativelike semantic representation were also reported in Schmitt (1998) who tracked the semantic development of four ESL speakers over an 18-month period and in Zhang (1995) who compared NNS and NS in the ranking of seven intensity words (*extremely, unusually, decidedly, quite, rather, somewhat, slightly*) and seven frequency expressions (*frequently if not always, very often, usually, frequently, about as often as not, now and then, once in a while*).

More recently, online tasks have been used to study this topic that generated RT data. In one of the earliest such studies, Jiang (2002) asked Chinese ESL speakers and English NS to perform a semantic relatedness judgment task on pairs of English words. Among the related pairs, a distinction was made between pairs that shared the same Chinese translation, e.g., *doubt-suspect, allow-permit*, and pairs that did not share the same translation, e.g., *receive-accept, artist-painter*. The two sets of L2 word pairs were matched in frequency, length, and degree of semantic relatedness. The contrast of the same- and different-translation pairs was based on the following reasoning. In performing semantic relatedness judgment, one has to a) recognize the two words, b) activate the semantic information of the words, c) compare the information, and d) reach a decision regarding relatedness based on the comparison. If semantic overlap is detected, a positive decision is made. Lack of any overlap results in a negative decision. If L2 words were mapped onto newly learned and L2-specific meanings, their translation status, i.e., having a single or two different L1 translations, should not affect their performance. However, if the stimulus words were mapped to L1 meanings, then the same-translation pairs should have a higher degree of semantic overlap than different-translation pairs. As a result, it would be easier or faster for L2 learners to detect a semantic overlap and to reach a positive decision. This would result in a faster RT for the same-translations pairs than for the different-translation pairs. This latter prediction was confirmed by the results. The Chinese ESL speakers were 99 ms faster (1075 ms vs. 1174 ms) in responding to the same-translation pairs while NS showed a nonsignificant 9 ms difference. This same-translation effect was replicated in Jiang (2004a) involving Korean ESL speakers and in Jiang (2007) where highly advanced Chinese ESL speakers were tested.

Another same-translation effect was reported by Elston-Güttler and Williams (2008). They asked German ESL speakers to complete a sentence judgment task in English. The participants were first presented with a sentence without the last word. Upon finishing reading the incomplete sentence, they pressed a button for the final word and decided if that word completed the sentence in a semantically acceptable way. The critical stimuli included sentences that ended with a word that is not semantically acceptable and thus required a No response, as shown in Example 5.8 below. Both sentences were semantically unacceptable. However, they differed in that the ending word *bubble* in Example 5.8a and an acceptable ending word *blister* shared the same German translation *Blasé* but neither *bubble* or *blister* would make the control sentence Example 5.8b acceptable. They reasoned that if L1 was involved in L2 performance, German ESL speakers should be affected by the fact that *bubble* and *blister* shared the same German translation and thus take longer or make more errors in rejecting *bubble* as an acceptable ending of the sentence, in comparison to the same word in the control sentence. To further determine whether the L1 effect occurred at the lexical or conceptual level, the degree of semantic relatedness was also manipulated by creating stimuli whose two L2 translations were highly (e.g., *pocket-bag*) or moderately (e.g., *rope-snake*) related in meaning. The hypothesis was that if L1 concepts were involved, highly related stimuli should produce more interference. On the contrary, if L1 lexical activation caused the delay or higher ER, the degree of semantic relatedness should not matter.

5.8a   *His shoes were uncomfortable due to a bubble.*
5.8b   *She was very hungry because of a bubble.*

The results were consistent with the involvement of L1 concepts in L2 processing: German ESL speakers showed a slower RT and higher ER while responding to the critical condition than to the control condition, and the stimuli of higher semantic relatedness produced more interference than the stimuli of low semantic relatedness. Thus, a similar same-translation effect was observed in this study in the form of interference in making a semantic judgment, and the effect was modulated by the degree of semantic relatedness.

In addition to the same-translation effect, non-nativeness and L1 influence in semantic processing has also been documented in the classification and naming of objects by NNS (Malt & Sloman, 2003), in the selection of appropriate Chinese verbs for video clips among Japanese and Korean learn-ers of Chinese (Saji & Imai, 2013), and in the inaccuracy in completing sentences with same-translation pairs among Chinese ESL speakers (Jiang, 2004b, 2007).

In Jiang (2004b), I proposed a comprehension-restructuring model of semantic development in L2. According to this model, the meaning of a new L2 word is typically understood within the existing L1 semantic system at first. Thus, under most circumstances, the initial form-meaning mapping occurs between an L2 word form and an L1 semantic representation, an assumption well recognized by L2 researchers (e.g., Blum & Levenston, 1978; Ellis, 1997; Giacobbe, 1992; Hall, 2002; Ringbom, 1983; Strick, 1980). From the perspec-tive of lexical development, this is the initial acquisition of the lexical form, but from the perspective of semantic development, very little acquisition or development takes place at this stage. For this reason, this stage of seman-tic development, characterized by the mapping of L2 form and L1 meaning, is referred to as the comprehension stage. The mapping of L2 form and L1 meaning results in L1 influence in L2 words use. This influence, as reflected in incorrect word choice in L2 use, is familiar to many second language teach-ers and has been well documented in empirical research as well (e.g., Biskup, 1992; Lennon, 1991; Zughoul, 1991). In Zughoul's study, for example, 73% of the 691 English lexical errors made by 128 university students could be traced to L1 influence.

As L2 speakers gain more experiences in the new language, they may notice the semantic mismatch, consciously or subconsciously, between what they know as the meaning of an L2 word and the meaning intended or under-stood by other speakers of the language. This noticing may trigger a process of semantic restructuring, the modification of the semantic specification of an L2 word in the direction of the L2-like meaning. Semantic restructuring can mean a sudden insight of a difference between the meanings of an L2 word and its L1 translation, e.g., the realization by a Chinese ESL learner, prompted by a favorable context as in my case, that a meeting can take place between two people (two people have a talk, not a meeting in Chinese). Semantic restructuring may require substantially more exposure and use of the target language under other circumstances, e.g., for a Chinese ESL speaker to dif-ferentiate *standard* and *criterion*, *real* and *true*, *complex* and *complicated*. The research reviewed in this section is consistent with the idea that semantic development is a slow and long process. Processing data suggested that L2 word forms continue to be mapped with L1 semantic structures even among advanced L2 speakers.

Before concluding this topic, some related findings from an electrophysi-ological perspective should be mentioned. Many studies have demonstrated that NNS were able to show a nativelike response pattern in semantic process-ing when electrophysiological measures were taken. Specifically, when NNS were asked to read semantically anomalous sentences, they were able to show a well-documented ERP component N400 that is associated with semantic processing. It is a negative-going potential that peaks about 400 ms after the onset of a semantic anomaly as illustrated in the sentence *for today's breakfast, I had some milk and brick* (e.g., Ardal, Donald, Meuter, Muldrew, & Luce, 1990; Hahne, 2001; Hahne & Friederici, 2001; Ojima, Nakata, & Kakigi, 2005; Osterhout, McLaughlin, Pitkänen, Frenck-Mestre, & Molinaro, 2006; Weber-Fox & Neville, 1996). The observation of a consistent N400 among NNS have been used to argue that semantic development is not subject to maturational constraints. However, it should be pointed out that a nativelike N400 in L2 semantic processing says very little about semantic development. Note that the test materials in these studies were constructed such that their translations into the participants' L1s would make semantically anomalous sentences, too. The semantic anomaly embodied in these test materials was apparent with or without substantial semantic development in L2. Thus, this ERP sensitivity should not be taken as evidence for semantic development. If NL N400 is to be used as evidence for the presence of nativelike semantic structures among NNS, test materials should be constructed such that anomalous L2 sentences become semantically acceptable when translated into L1, which has not been done so far.

5.4.2 Cerebral Involvement in Semantic Processing in L1 and L2

Prior to the study of cortical activation in semantic processing in L1 and L2 by means of brain imaging technology such as positron emission tomography (PET) and functional magnetic resonance imaging (fMRI), there was already quite some interest in knowing whether the same or different brain regions were involved in processing the two languages of a bilingual speaker (e.g., see Albert & Obler, 1978; Paradis, 1990; Vaid & Genesee, 1980 for reviews). Since the 1990s, many studies have used imaging technology to study cortical activation in bilinguals. Many of these studies were concerned with a more general issue of whether the same or different brain regions are involved in L1 and L2 processing, without a specific focus on semantic processing. This can be seen in the use of more general language tasks such as word repetition or generation (e.g., Chee, Tan, & Thiel, 1999), listening to sentences or stories (e.g., Hasegawa, Carpenter, & Just, 2002), silent description of events (e.g., Kim, Relkin, Lee, & Hirsch, 1997) that involved cognitive processes other than or more than semantic processing. Other studies considered cortical activation in semantic processing among NS and NNS and thus are more relevant to the present discussion.

Klein, Milner, Zatorre, Meyer, and Evans (1995) were among the first to examine this topic. They asked the English-French bilingual speakers to perform three experimental tasks in their L1 and L2: generating rhyme words, generating synonyms, and generating translations. The first task represented phonological processing and the latter two represented semantic processing. A word repetition task in the two languages was used as a control task. The participants' cerebral blood flow was measured by means of PET scans while they performed the tasks. They found the activation of the same left inferior frontal cortex in performing the three tasks in both languages, and concluded that their evidence was against the involvement of different neural substrates in processing L1 and L2 phonology and meaning.

Illes et al. (1999) were among the first to use fMRI to examine semantic processing in L1 and L2. They asked fluent English-Spanish bilinguals to perform two tasks in their two languages. One was to decide whether a word was an abstract or concrete noun (the semantic task). The other, which served as a control task, was to decide whether a word was presented in upper- or lower-case letters (the nonsemantic task). The cortical activation in semantic processing was assessed by subtracting activation associated with nonsemantic tasks from that with semantic tasks. The results showed that the same left inferior frontal gyrus (LIFG) was involved in the processing of meaning in both L1 and L2, which replicated the results of Klein et al. (1995). The only difference between the two studies was that a weaker activation in the right inferior frontal gyrus was also observed in Illes et al., but not in Klein et al.

Some other studies, however, showed differences in L1 and L2 semantic processing. One of such studies was reported by Wartenburger et al. (2003). They tested Italian-German bilinguals in a sentence judgment task in both languages. Among the sentences were those that were semantically anomalous, such as *Die Maus jagt die Katze* (the mouse hunts the cat), which provided data about semantic processing. Brain activities were recorded with a fMRI scanner. The results showed that there was little difference in cortical activation between L1 and L2 processing among early bilingual speakers. However, late bilinguals (onset age >6 years) showed some differences. Specifically, more bilateral activation in the inferior frontal areas was associated with semantic processing in L2 than in L1.

Some differences in cortical activation was also found by Xue, Dong, Jin, Zhang, and Wang (2004) who examined semantic processing in less proficient L2 learners. Their participants were Chinese-speaking elementary school students who had limited experiences in English. They asked these participants to perform a semantic relatedness judgment task on a pair of words in both Chinese and English. fMRI scans were obtained while they performed the task. Three findings emerged from the study. First, among the substrates that were found to be active in semantic processing, the level of activation was comparable while processing L1 and L2 in the left inferior prefrontal cortex, the fusiform cortex, the occipital cortex, and the subcortical region. Second, more activation was observed while performing the task in L2 than in L1 in the anterior cingulate area (BA32), posterior cingulated area (BA29), and the left inferior parietal lobule (BA40). Third, there was no area that was more activated while processing L1 than processing L2. See Abutalebi (2008) for a review of more studies on this topic.

The differences in findings among these studies reflect the complexities involved in mapping cortical activation to language processing in L1 and L2. Whether the same cortical regions are involved in L1 and L2 processing is not likely to be a simple Yes/No question due to language factors such as the typological relationship between the two languages involved and participant factors such as age of L2 onset, proficiency, the type of learning settings (classroom vs. naturalistic), and procedural factors such as the tasks used, as has been pointed out by many (e.g., Abutalebi, 2008; Illes et al., 1999; Roux et al., 2004; Xue et al., 2004).

5.5 Conclusion

This chapter reviews research on three topics: processing complex words, processing multiword units, and semantic processing and development in L2. There is some preliminary evidence for the decomposition of compound words (e.g., the masked morphological priming effect), for the holistic representation and processing of multiword units (e.g., formula advantage in phrase judgment), for L1 influence in L2 collocation processing (the congruency effect), and for L2 speakers' continued reliance on L1 semantic structures (the same-translation effect).

However, these findings raise many questions that are yet to be explored. One of them is what counts as unequivocal evidence for the holistic or decompositional representation and processing of lexical units. A masked priming effect from a compound to a component word (e.g., *classroom-class*) (Li et al., 2017) is consistent with the prediction of a decompositional view, but it can also be explained through the form and meaning overlap between the prime and the target. Similarly, the finding that L2 speakers were able to provide more missing words in lexical bundles than in nonlexical bundles was taken as evidence of holistic representation (Nekrasova, 2009), but all it says is that the participants were more familiar with the former than with the latter.

Second, L2 speakers were found to be able to develop an L2-specific holistic processing strategy while processing a morphologically less rich L2 (Portin et al., 2007). In light of the finding that the creation of new L2 phonological categories may affect L1 categories (see Section 3.2.3 in Chapter 3), it is interesting to explore if the development of this holistic processing strategy in L2 processing would affect the processing of the morphologically rich L1.

Third, the congruency effect in collocation processing (Wolter & Gyllstad, 2011; Yamashita & Jiang, 2010) and the same-translation effect (Elston-Güttler & Williams, 2008; Jiang, 2002, 2004a) demonstrated L1 influence in

L2 processing. It is not clear how long this effect will persist in the presence of increasing L2 proficiency. These questions represent areas for future research.

Notes

1 However, Ullman (2005) suggests at the same time that with sufficient experiences in the language, it is possible for L2 learners to use the procedural memory in the learning of structural knowledge and develop nativelike representation in L2. This makes the prediction from this model about complex L2 word representation and processing much less straightforward.
2 See Tremblay, Derwing, Libben, and Westbury (2011) for the description of a pretest to control semantic acceptability of test materials under such circumstances.
3 For other hypotheses and models, see Giora (1997) for the graded salience hypothesis, Glucksberg (1993) for the phrase-induced polysemy model, Titone and Connine (1999) for the hybrid model.
4 No explanation was provided in the article regarding how the early and late groups were differentiated.
5 See Cieślicka (2010) for similar findings in L2 production, Cieślicka (2011) for a self-paced reading study in combination with LDT showing the role of the context in suppressing irrelevant meanings, Cieślicka (2013a) for the cross-modal priming results showing compositionality did not affect NNS' preference for literal meanings, and Cieślicka (2013b) and Cieślicka and Heredia (2011) for the comparison of NS and NNS in the involvement of two hemispheres in idiom processing.
6 Note that no pretest was done to determine if the figurative and literal meanings were equally predictable in their respective context passage. However, a lack of difference between the two conditions among NS may be used as evidence of comparability in this regard.

References

Abel, B. (2003). English idioms in the first language and second language lexicon: A dual representation approach. *Second Language Research, 19,* 329–358.

Abutalebi, J. (2008). Neural aspects of second language representation and language control. *Acta Psychologica, 128,* 466–478.

Albert, M. & Obler, L. (1978). *The bilingual brain: Neurophysiological and neurolinguistic aspects of bilingualism.* New York: Academic Press.

Alegre, M. & Gordon, P. (1999). Frequency effects and the representational status of regular inflections. *Journal of Memory and Language, 40,* 41–61.

Altenberg, B. & Granger, S. (2001). The grammatical and lexical patterning of MAKE in native and non-native student writing. *Applied Linguistics, 22,* 173–195.

Amenta, S. & Crepaldi, D. (2012). Morphological processing as we know it: An analytical review of morphological effects in visual word identification. *Frontiers in Psychology, 3,* 232. doi:10.3389/fpsyg.2012.00232

Ardal, S., Donald, M. W., Meuter, R., Muldrew, S., & Luce, M. (1990). Brain responses to semantic incongruity in bilinguals. *Brain and Language, 39,* 187–205.

Baayen, R. H., Dijkstra, T., & Schreuder, R. (1997). Singulars and plurals in Dutch: Evidence for a parallel dual-route model. *Journal of Memory and Language, 37,* 94–117.

Basnight-Brown, D., Chen, L., Hua, S., Kostić, A., & Feldman, L. (2007). Monolingual and bilingual recognition of regular and irregular English verbs: Sensitivity to form similarity varies with first language experience. *Journal of Memory and Language, 57*, 65–80.

Biber, D. & Conrad, S. (1999). Lexical bundles in conversation and academic prose. In H. Hasselgard & S. Oksefjell (Eds.), *Out of corpora: Studies in honor of Stig Johansson* (pp. 181–190). Amsterdam: Rodopi.

Biber, D., Johansson, S., Leech, G., Conrad, S., & Finegan, E. (1999). *The Longman grammar of spoken and written English*. London: Longman.

Biskup, D. (1992). L1 influence on learners' renderings of English collocations: A Polish/German empirical study. In P. J. L. Arnaud & H. Béjoint (Eds.), *Vocabulary and applied linguistics* (pp. 85–93). Basingstoke, UK: Macmillan.

Blum, S. & Levenston, E. A. (1978). Universals of lexical simplification. *Language Learning, 28*, 399–415.

Boudelaa, S. & Marslen-Wilson, W. (2005). Discontinuous morphology in time: Incremental masked priming in Arabic. *Language and Cognitive Processes, 20*, 207–260.

Bowden, H., Gelfand, M., Sanz, C., & Ullman, M. (2010). Verbal inflectional morphology in L1 and L2 Spanish: A frequency effects study examining storage versus composition. *Language Learning, 60*, 44–87.

Brown, R. (1973). *A first language*. London: Allen & Unwin.

Bulut, T. & Celik-Yazici, I. (2004). Idiom processing in L2: Through rose-colored glasses. *The Reading Matrix, 4*, 105–116.

Butterworth, B. (1983). Lexical representation. In B. Butterworth (Ed.), *Language production* (Vol. 2, pp. 257–294). London: Academic Press.

Cacciari, C. & Tabossi, P. (1988). The comprehension of idioms. *Journal of Memory and Language, 27*, 668–683.

Caramazza, A., Laudanna, A., & Romani, C. (1988). Lexical access and inflectional morphology. *Cognition, 28*, 297–332.

Chee, M. W., Tan, E. W., & Thiel, T. (1999). Mandarin and English single word processing studied with functional magnetic resonance imaging. *The Journal of Neuroscience, 19*, 3050–3056.

Chialant, D. & Caramazza, A. (1995). Where is morphology and how is it processed? The case of written word recognition. *Morphological Aspects of Language Processing*, 55–76.

Cieślicka, A. B. (2006). Literal salience in on-line processing of idiomatic expressions by second language learners. *Second Language Research, 22*, 115–144.

Cieślicka, A. B. (2010). Formulaic language in L2 storage, retrieval and production of idioms. In M. Putz & L. Sicola (Eds.), *Cognitive processing in second language acquisition* (pp. 149–168). Philadelphia, PA: John Benjamins.

Cieślicka, A. B. (2011). Suppression of literal meanings in L2 idiom processing: Does context help? *Studies in Second Language Learning and Teaching*, 13–36.

Cieślicka, A. B. (2013a). Second language learners' processing of idiomatic expressions: Does compositionality matter? In K. Drozdzial-Szelest & M. Pawlak (Eds.), *Psycholinguistic and sociolinguistic perspectives on second language learning and teaching* (pp. 115–136). New York: Springer.

Cieślicka, A. B. (2013b). Do nonnative language speakers chew the fat and spill the beans with different brain hemispheres? Investigating idiom decomposability with the divided visual field paradigm. *Journal of Psycholinguistic Research, 42*, 475–503.

Cieślicka, A. B. & Heredia, R. R. (2011). Hemispheric asymmetries in processing L1 and L2 idioms: Effects of salience and context. *Brain and Language*, *116*, 136–150.

Clahsen, H. & Almazan, M. (1998). Syntax and morphology in Williams syndrome. *Cognition*, *68*, 167–198.

Clahsen, H., Balkhair, L., Schutter, J.-S., & Cunnings, I. (2013). The time course of morphological processing in a second language. *Second Language Research*, *29*, 7–31.

Clahsen, H. & Felser, C. (2006). Grammatical processing in language learners. *Applied Psycholinguistics*, *27*, 3–42.

Clahsen, H., Hadler, M., & Weyerts, H. (2004). Speeded production of inflected words in children and adults. *Journal of Child Language*, *31*, 683–712.

Clahsen, H. & Neubauer, K. (2010). Morphology, frequency, and the processing of derived words in native and non-native speakers. *Lingua*, *120*, 2627–2637.

Clark, R. (1974). Performing without competence. *Journal of Child Language*, *1*, 1–10.

Colé, P., Beauvillain, C., & Segui, J. (1989). On the representation and processing of prefixed and suffixed derived words: A differential frequency effect. *Journal of Memory and Language*, *28*, 1–13.

Conklin, K. & Schmitt, N. (2008). Formulaic sequences: Are they processed more quickly than nonformulaic language by native and nonnative speakers? *Applied Linguistics*, *29*, 72–89.

Cooper, T. C. (1999). Process of idioms by L2 learners of English. *TESOL Quarterly*, *33*, 233–262.

Dagenbach, D., Carr, T. H., & Barnhardt, T. M. (1990). Inhibitory semantic priming of lexical decisions due to failure to retrieve weakly activated codes. *Journal of Experimental Psychology: Learning, Memory, & Cognition*, *16*, 328–340.

Diependaele, K., Duñabeitia, J. A., Morris, J., & Keuleers, E. (2011). Fast morphological effects in first and second language word recognition. *Journal of Memory and Language*, *64*, 344–358.

Ellis, N. C. (1997). Vocabulary acquisition: Word structure, collocation, word-class, and meaning. In N. Schmitt & M. McCarthy (Eds.), *Vocabulary: Description, acquisition and pedagogy* (pp. 122–139). Cambridge: Cambridge University Press.

Ellis, N. C., Simpson-Vlach, R., & Maynard, C. (2008). Formulaic language in native and second language speakers: Psycholinguistics, corpus linguistics, and TESOL. *TESOL Quarterly*, *42*, 375–396.

Elston-Güttler, K. E. & Williams, J. N. (2008). First language polysemy affects second language meaning interpretation: Evidence for activation of first language concepts during second language reading. *Second Language Research*, *24*, 167–187.

Erman, B. & Warren, B. (2000). The idiom principle and the open-choice principle. *Text*, *20*, 29–62.

Ettlinger, M., Bradlow, A. R., & Wong, P. C. (2014). Variability in the learning of complex morphophonology. *Applied Psycholinguistics*, *35*, 807–831.

Feldman, L. B., Kostić, A., Basnight-Brown, D. M., Filipović-Đurđević, D., & Pastizzo, M. J. (2010). Morphological facilitation for regular and irregular verb formations in native and non-native speakers: Little evidence for two distinct mechanisms. *Bilingualism: Language and Cognition*, *13*, 119–135.

Fillmore, C. (1979). On fluency. In C. Fillmore, D. Kempler, & W. Wang (Eds.), *Individual differences in language ability and language behavior* (pp. 85–101). New York: Academic Press.

Forster, K. I. (1985). Lexical acquisition and the modular lexicon. *Language and Cognitive Processes, 1*, 87–108.

Giacobbe, J. (1992). A cognitive view of the role of L1 in the L2 acquisition process. *Second Language Research, 8*, 232–250.

Gibbs, R. W. (1980). Spilling the beans on understanding and memory for idioms in conversation. *Memory & Cognition, 8*, 149–156.

Gibbs, R. W. & Nayak, N. P. (1989). Psycholinguistic studies on the syntactic behavior of idioms. *Cognitive Psychology, 21*, 100–138.

Gibbs, R. W., Nayak, N. P., Bolton, J., & Keppel, M. (1989). Speakers' assumptions about the lexical flexibility of idioms. *Memory and Cognition, 17*, 58–68.

Gibbs, R. W., Nayak, N. P., & Cutting, C. (1989). How to kick the bucket and not decompose: Analyzability and idiom processing. *Journal of Memory and Language, 28*, 576–593.

Giora, R. (1997). Understanding figurative and literal language: The graded salience hypothesis. *Cognitive Linguistics, 8*, 183–206.

Giraudo, H. & Grainger, J. (2001). Priming complex words: Evidence for supralexical representation of morphology. *Psychonomic Bulletin and Review, 8*, 96–101.

Giraudo, H. & Grainger, J. (2003). On the role of derivational affixes in recognizing complex words: Evidence from masked priming. In R. H. Baayen & R. Schreuder (Eds.), *Morphological structure in language processing* (pp. 209–232). Berlin: Mouton de Gruyter.

Glucksberg, S. (1993). Idiom meanings and allusional content. In C. Cacciari & P. Tabossi (Eds.), *Idioms: Processing, structure, and interpretation* (pp. 3–26). New York: The Psychology Press.

Gonnerman, L. M., Seidenberg, M. S., & Andersen, E. S. (2007). Graded semantic and phonological similarity effects in priming: Evidence for a distributed connectionist approach to morphology. *Journal of Experimental Psychology: General, 136*, 323–345.

Gor, K. & Cook, S. (2010). Nonnative processing of verbal morphology: In search of regularity. *Language Learning, 60*, 88–126.

Gor, K. & Jackson, S. (2013). Morphological decomposition and lexical access in a native and second language: A nesting doll effect. *Language and Cognitive Processes, 28*, 1065–1091.

Hahne, A. (2001). What's different in second-language processing? Evidence from event-related brain potentials. *Journal of Psycholinguistic Research, 30*, 251–266.

Hahne, A. & Friederici, A. D. (2001). Processing a second language: Late learners' comprehension mechanisms as revealed by event-related brain potentials. *Bilingualism: Language and Cognition, 4*, 123–141.

Hakuta, K. (1974). Prefabricated patterns and the emergence of structure in second language acquisition. *Language Learning, 24*, 287–297.

Hall, C. J. (2002). The automatic cognate form assumption: Evidence for the parasitic model of vocabulary acquisition. *IRAL, 40*, 69–87.

Hasegawa, M., Carpenter, P. A., & Just, M. A. (2002). An fMRI study of bilingual sentence comprehension and workload. *Neuroimage, 15*, 647–660.

Hickey, T. (1993). Identifying formulas in first language acquisition. *Journal of Child Language, 20*, 27–41.

Ijaz, I. H. (1986). Linguistic and cognitive determinants of lexical acquisition in a second language. *Language Learning, 36*, 401–451.

Illes, J., Francis, W. S., Desmond, J. E., Gabrieli, J. D., Glover, G. H., Poldrack, R., Lee, C. J., & Wagner, A. D. (1999). Convergent cortical representation of semantic processing in bilinguals. *Brain and Language*, 70, 347–363.

Jacob, G., Fleischhauer, E., & Clahsen, H. (2013). Allomorphy and affixation in morphological processing: A cross-modal priming study with late bilinguals. *Bilingualism: Language and Cognition*, 16, 924–933.

Jiang, N. (2002). Form-meaning mapping in vocabulary acquisition in a second language. *Studies in Second Language Acquisition*, 24, 617–637.

Jiang, N. (2004a). Semantic transfer and its implications for vocabulary teaching in a second language. *The Modern Language Journal*, 88, 416–432.

Jiang, N. (2004b). Semantic transfer and development in adult L2 vocabulary acquisition. In P. Bogaards & B. Laufer (Eds.), *Vocabulary in a second language: Description, acquisition, and testing* (pp. 101–126). Amsterdam: Benjamins.

Jiang, N. (2007). Semantic representation and development in steady-state second language speakers. *Review of Applied Linguistics in China*, 3, 60–91.

Jiang, N. & Nekrasova, T. M. (2007). The processing of formulaic sequences by second language speakers. *The Modern Language Journal*, 91, 433–445.

Juhasz, B. J., Starr, M. S., Inhoff, A. W., & Placke, L. (2003). The effects of morphology on the processing of compound words: Evidence from naming, lexical decisions and eye fixations. *British Journal of Psychology*, 94, 223–244.

Kim, K. H., Relkin, N. R., Lee, K. M., & Hirsch, J. (1997). Distinct cortical areas associated with native and second languages. *Nature*, 388, 171–174.

Kim, S. H. & Kim, J. H. (2012). Frequency effects in L2 multi-word unit processing: Evidence from self-paced reading. *TESOL Quarterly*, 46, 831–841.

Klein, D., Milner, B., Zatorre, R. J., Meyer, E., & Evans, A. C. (1995). The neural substrates underlying word generation: A bilingual functional-imaging study. *Proceedings of the National Academy of Sciences*, 92, 2899–2903.

Krashen, S. & Scarcella, R. (1978). On routines and patterns in second language acquisition and performance. *Language Learning*, 28, 283–300.

Laine, M., Vainio, S., & Hyönä, J. (1999). Lexical access routes to nouns in a morphologically rich language. *Journal of Memory and Language*, 40, 109–135.

Lehtonen, M. & Laine, M. (2003). How word frequency affects morphological processing in monolinguals and bilinguals. *Bilingualism: Language and Cognition*, 6, 213–225.

Lehtonen, M., Niska, H., Wande, E., Niemi, J., & Laine, M. (2006). Recognition of inflected words in a morphologically limited language: Frequency effects in monolinguals and bilinguals. *Journal of Psycholinguistic Research*, 35, 121–146.

Lemhöfer, K., Koester, D., & Schreuder, R. (2011). When bicycle pump is harder to read than bicycle bell: Effects of parsing cues in first and second language compound reading. *Psychonomic Bulletin & Review*, 18, 364–370.

Lennon, P. (1991). Error and the very advanced learner. *IRAL*, 29, 31–44.

Li, M., Jiang, N., & Gor, K. (2017). L1 and L2 processing of compound words: Evidence from masked priming experiments in English. *Bilingualism: Language and Cognition*, 20, 384–402.

Lieven, E. V. M., Pine, J. M., & Barnes, H. D. (1992). Individual differences in early vocabulary development: Redefining the referential-expressive distinction. *Journal of Child Language*, 19, 287–310.

Lyons, J. (1968). *Introduction to theoretical linguistics*. Cambridge: Cambridge University Press.

Malt, B. C. & Sloman, S. A. (2003). Linguistic diversity and object naming by non-native speakers of English. *Bilingualism: Language and Cognition, 6*, 47–67.

Marcus, G. F., Brinkmann, U., Clahsen, H., Wiese, R., & Pinker, S. (1995). German inflection: the exception that proves the rule. *Cognitive Psychology, 29*, 189–256.

Marsden, E., Williams, J., & Liu, X. (2013). Learning novel morphology. *Studies in Second Language Acquisition, 35*, 619–654.

Marslen-Wilson, W. & Tyler, L. K. (1998). Rules, representations, and the English past tense. *Trends in Cognitive Sciences, 2*(11), 428–435.

Marslen-Wilson, W., Tyler, L. K., Waksler, R., & Older, L. (1994). Morphology and meaning in the English mental lexicon. *Psychological Review, 101*, 3–33.

Matlock, T. & Heredia, R. R. (2002). Understanding phrasal verbs in monolinguals and bilinguals. In R. R. Heredia & J. Altarriba (Eds.), *Bilingual sentence processing* (pp. 251–274). Amsterdam: Elsevier.

Millar, N. (2011). The processing of malformed formulaic language. *Applied Linguistics, 32*, 129–148.

Murphy, V. A. & Hayes, J. (2010). Processing English compounds in the first and second language: The influence of the middle morpheme. *Language Learning, 60*, 194–220.

Murrell, M. (1966). Language acquisition in a trilingual environment: Notes from a case-study. *Studia Linguistica, 20*, 9–34.

Nattinger, J. R. & DeCarrico, J. S. (1992). *Lexical phrases and language teaching*. Oxford, UK: Oxford University Press.

Nekrasova, T. M. (2009). English L1 and L2 speakers' knowledge of lexical bundles. *Language Learning, 59*, 647–686.

Nesselhauf, N. (2003). The use of collocations by advanced learners of English and some implications for teaching. *Applied Linguistics, 24*, 223–242.

Neubauer, K. & Clahsen, H. (2009). Decomposition of inflected words in a second language: An experimental study of German participles. *Studies in Second Language Acquisition, 31*, 403–435.

Nicoladis, E., Song, J., & Marentette, P. (2012). Do young bilinguals acquire past tense morphology like monolinguals, only later? Evidence from French-English and Chinese-English bilinguals. *Applied Psycholinguistics, 33*, 457–479.

Ojima, S., Nakata, H., & Kakigi, R. (2005). An ERP study of second language learning after childhood: Effects of proficiency. *Journal of Cognitive Neuroscience, 17*, 1212–1228.

Osterhout, L., McLaughlin, J., Pitkänen, I., Frenck-Mestre, C., & Molinaro, N. (2006). Novice learners, longitudinal designs, and event-related potentials: A means for exploring the neurocognition of second language processing. *Language Learning, 56*(s1), 199–230.

Paradis, M. (1990). Language lateralization in bilinguals: Enough already! *Brain and Language, 39*, 576–586.

Pawley, A. & Syder, F. H. (1983). Two puzzles for linguistic theory: Nativelike selection and nativelike fluency. In J. C. Richards & R. W. Schmidt (Eds.), *Language and communication* (pp. 191–225). London, UK: Longman.

Pinker, S. (1991). Rules of language. *Science, 253*, 530–535.

Pinker, S. & Ullman, M. T. (2002). The past and future of the past tense. *Trends in Cognitive Sciences, 6*, 456–463.

Pliatsikas, C. & Marinis, T. (2013). Processing of regular and irregular past tense morphology in highly proficient second language learners of English: A self-paced reading study. *Applied Psycholinguistic, 34*, 943–970.

Portin, M. & Laine, M. (2001). Processing cost associated with inflectional morphology in bilingual speakers. *Bilingualism: Language and Cognition, 4*, 55–62.

Portin, M., Lehtonen, M., Harrer, G., Wande, E., Niemi, J., & Laine, M. (2008). L1 effects on the processing of inflected nouns in L2. *Acta Psychologica, 128*, 452–465.

Portin, M., Lehtonen, M., & Laine, M. (2007). Processing of inflected nouns in late bilinguals. *Applied Psycholinguistics, 28*, 135–156.

Rastle, K. & Davis, M. H. (2008). Morphological decomposition based on the analysis of orthography. *Language and Cognitive Processes, 23*(7–8), 942–971.

Rastle, K., Davis, M. H., Marslen-Wilson, W. D., & Tyler, L. K. (2000). Morphological and semantic effects in visual word recognition: A time-course study. *Language and Cognitive Processes, 15*, 507–537.

Raupach, M. (1984). Formulae in second language speech production. In H. W. Dechert, D. Mole, & M. Raupach (Eds.), *Second language productions* (pp. 114–137). Tubingen, Germany: Gunter Narr Verlag.

Ringbom, H. (1983). Borrowing and lexical transfer. *Applied Linguistics, 4*, 207–212.

Roux, F. E., Lubrano, V., Lauwers-Cances, V., Trémoulet, M., Mascott, C. R., & Démonet, J. F. (2004). Intra-operative mapping of cortical areas involved in reading in mono- and bilingual patients. *Brain, 127*, 1796–1810.

Saji, N. & Imai, M. (2013). Evolution of verb meanings in children and L2 adult learners through reorganization of an entire semantic domain: The case of Chinese carry/hold verbs. *Scientific Studies of Reading, 17*, 71–88.

Schmitt, N. (1998). Tracking the incremental acquisition of second language vocabulary: A longitudinal study. *Language Learning, 48*, 281–317.

Schmitt, N. (Ed.). (2004). *Formulaic sequences: Acquisition, processing, and use* (Vol. 9). Philadelphia: John Benjamins.

Schmitt, N., Grandage, S., & Adolphs, S. (2004). Are corpus-derived recurrent clusters psycholinguistically valid? In N. Schmitt (Ed.), *Formulaic sequences: Acquisition, processing, and use* (pp. 127–151). Philadelphia: John Benjamins.

Schmitt, N. & Underwood, G. (2004). Exploring the processing of formulaic sequences through a self-paced reading task. In N. Schmitt (Ed.), *Formulaic sequences: Acquisition, processing, and use* (pp. 173–189). Philadelphia: John Benjamins.

Sereno, J. A. & Jongman, A. (1997). Processing of English inflectional morphology. *Memory & Cognition, 25*, 425–437.

Silva, R. & Clahsen, H. (2008). Morphologically complex words in L1 and L2 processing: Evidence from masked priming experiments in English. *Bilingualism: Language and Cognition, 11*, 245–260.

Sinclair, J. M. (1991). *Corpus, concordance, collocation.* Oxford: Oxford University Press.

Siyanova-Chanturia, A., Conklin, K., & Schmitt, N. (2011). Adding more fuel to the fire: An eye-tracking study of idiom processing by native and non-native speakers. *Second Language Research, 27*, 251–272.

Steinel, M. P., Hulstijn, J. H., & Steinel, W. (2007). Second language idiom learning in a paired-associate paradigm: Effects of direction of learning, direction of testing, idiom imageability, and idiom transparency. *Studies in Second Language Acquisition,* *29,* 449–484.

Stockall, L. & Marantz, A. (2006). A single route, full decomposition model of morphological complexity: MEG evidence. *The Mental Lexicon, 1,* 85–123.

Strick, G. J. (1980). A hypothesis for semantic development in a second language. *Language Learning, 30,* 155–176.

Strobach, T. & Schönpflug, U. (2011). Can a connectionist model explain the processing of regularly and irregularly inflected words in German as L1 and L2? *International Journal of Bilingualism, 15,* 446–465.

Swinney, D. A. & Cutler, A. (1979). The access and processing of idiomatic expressions. *Journal of Verbal Learning and Verbal Behavior, 18,* 523–534.

Taft, M. (1979). Recognition of affixed words and the word frequency effect. *Memory & Cognition, 7,* 263–272.

Taft, M. (1981). Prefix stripping revisited. *Journal of Verbal Learning and Verbal Behavior, 20,* 289–297.

Taft, M. (1994). Interactive-activation as a framework for understanding morphological processing. *Language and Cognitive Processes, 9,* 271–294.

Taft, M. (2004). Morphological decomposition and the reverse base frequency effect. *Quarterly Journal of Experimental Psychology Section A, 57,* 745–765.

Taft, M. & Ardasinski, S. (2006). Obligatory decomposition in reading prefixed words. *The Mental Lexicon, 1,* 183–199.

Taft, M. & Forster, K. I. (1975). Lexical storage and retrieval of prefixed words. *Journal of Verbal Learning and Verbal Behavior, 14,* 638–647.

Titone, D. A. & Connine, C. M. (1994). Descriptive norms for 171 idiomatic expressions: Familiarity, compositionality, predictability, and literality. *Metaphor and Symbolic Activity, 9,* 247–270.

Titone, D. A. & Connine, C. M. (1999). On the compositional and noncompositional nature of idiomatic expressions. *Journal of Pragmatics, 31*(12), 1655–1674.

Tremblay, A., Derwing, B., Libben, G., & Westbury, C. (2011). Processing advantages of lexical bundles: Evidence from self-paced reading and sentence recall tasks. *Language Learning, 61,* 569–613.

Ullman, M. T. (2001). The neural basis of lexicon and grammar in first and second language: The declarative/procedural model. *Bilingualism: Language and Cognition, 4,* 105–122.

Ullman, M. T. (2005). A cognitive neuroscience perspective on second language acquisition: The declarative/procedural model. In C. Sanz (Ed.), *Mind and context in adult second language acquisition: Methods, theory, and practice* (pp. 141–178). Washington, DC: Georgetown University.

Underwood, G., Schmitt, N., & Galpin, A. (2004). The eyes have it: An eye-movement study into the processing of formulaic sequences. In N. Schmitt (Ed.), *Formulaic sequences: Acquisition, processing, and use* (pp. 153–172). Philadelphia: John Benjamins.

Vaid, J. & Genesee, F. (1980). Neuropsychological approaches to bilingualism: A critical review. *Canadian Journal of Psychology/Revue canadienne de psychologie, 34,* 417–445.

Vainio, S., Pajunen, A., & Hyönä, J. (2014). L1 and L2 word recognition in Finnish. *Studies in Second Language Acquisition, 36,* 133–162.

Wartenburger, I., Heekeren, H. R., Abutalebi, J., Cappa, S. F., Villringer, A., & Perani, D. (2003). Early setting of grammatical processing in the bilingual brain. *Neuron*, *37*, 159–170.

Weber-Fox, C. M. & Neville, H. J. (1996). Maturational constraints on functional specializations for language processing: ERP and behavioral evidence in bilingual speakers. *Journal of Cognitive Neuroscience*, *8*, 231–256.

Wolter, B. & Gyllstad, H. (2011). Collocational links in the L2 mental lexicon and the influence of L1 intralexical knowledge. *Applied Linguistics*, *32*, 430–449.

Wolter, B. & Gyllstad, H. (2013). Frequency of input and L2 collocational processing. *Studies in Second Language Acquisition*, *35*, 451–482.

Wolter, B. & Yamashita, J. (2014). Processing collocations in a second language: A case of first language activation? *Applied Psycholinguistics*, 1–29.

Wray, A. (1999). Formulaic language in learners and native speakers. *Language Teaching*, *32*, 213–231.

Wray, A. (2002). *Formulaic language and the lexicon*. Cambridge: Cambridge University Press.

Wray, A. & Perkins, M. R. (2000). The functions of formulaic language: An integrated model. *Language & Communication*, *20*, 1–28.

Xue, G., Dong, Q., Jin, Z., Zhang, L., & Wang, Y. (2004). An fMRI study with semantic access in low proficiency second language learners. *NeuroReport*, *15*, 791–796.

Yamashita, J. (2014). Effects of instruction on Yes-No responses to L2 collocations. *Vocabulary Learning and Instruction*, *3*, 31–37.

Yamashita, J. & Jiang, N. (2010). L1 influence on the acquisition of L2 collocations: Japanese ESL users and EFL learners acquiring English collocations. *TESOL Quarterly*, *44*, 647–668.

Zeeuw, M., Schreuder, R., & Verhoeven, L. (2013). Processing of regular and irregular past-tense verb forms in first and second language reading acquisition. *Language Learning*, *63*, 740–765.

Zhang, D. (2013). Linguistic distance effect on cross-linguistic transfer of morphological awareness. *Applied Psycholinguistics*, *34*, 917–942.

Zhang, S. (1995). Semantic differentiation in the acquisition of English as a second language. *Language Learning*, *45*, 225–249.

Zughoul, M. R. (1991). Lexical choice: Towards writing problematic word lists. *IRAL*, *29*, 45–60.

Chapter 6

Sentence Processing in L2
Parsing

6.1 Introduction

If we define sentence processing broadly as a process whereby the meaning of a sentence is understood, this process consists of at least three cognitive components or stages: word recognition, parsing, and semantic integration. At the stage of word recognition, lexical information of individual words, such as meanings, syntactic properties, morphological structures, lexical associations, becomes available. Parsing is the process whereby a syntactic structure is built on the basis of the activated lexical information, morphosyntactic cues (such as word order and case marking), and an individual's syntactic knowledge. Finally, at the semantic integration stage, a mental representation of the meaning of a sentence is constructed on the basis of the information derived from the input and an individual's linguistic and real-world knowledge.

Language processing research at the sentence level, thus, may be differentiated on the basis of the component it focuses on. Some studies focused on word recognition in sentence contexts, e.g., how word recognition is influenced by sentence context (e.g., Love, Maas, & Swinney, 2003; Swinney, 1979). Other studies examined the resulting mental representation of meaning in sentence processing (e.g., Stanfield & Zwaan, 2001; Zwaan, Stanfield, & Yaxley, 2002). A majority of sentence processing studies, however, explored parsing, the process of building a syntactic structure. This is true of research in both L1 and L2.

This introductory section is divided into two subsections. The first explains sentence ambiguity and the garden-path effect, and the second summarizes models of sentence processing.

6.1.1 Sentence Ambiguity and the Garden-Path Effect

A sentence may be ambiguous in that it allows more than one interpretation. Two types of ambiguity are often differentiated: temporary ambiguity and global ambiguity. A sentence is temporarily ambiguous when it allows two interpretations in the middle of it but it also contains a subsequent disambiguating element that removes ambiguity. For example, the sentence *John remembered the answer was in the book* was ambiguous at the NP *the answer* because it can be interpreted as the direct object of the preceding verb (i.e., *remembered the answer*) or the subject of a subordinate or embedded clause (i.e., the actual sentence). The following verb *was* is the disambiguating element that helps to indicate that the second interpretation is correct, thus removing the ambiguity. A sentence is globally ambiguous when it has no disambiguating element and thus remains ambiguous even when the whole sentence is considered. For example, the sentence *the police saw the robber with binoculars* has two possible interpretations regarding who had the binoculars. Even though many readers may tend to think that it was the police who had the binoculars, structurally speaking, it is possible for the robber to have the binoculars, as well. Some of the most frequently used ambiguous structures in sentence processing research are illustrated and explained in Table 6.1 below.

Table 6.1 Types of Ambiguous Sentences Often Involved in Sentence Processing Research (the Ambiguous Element Is Underlined)

Names	Examples	Explanations
Temporary ambiguities		
a. Subject-object ambiguity	The visitor saw her friend was not feeling well.	A NP may be interpreted as the direct object of the main (or matrix) verb or the subject of the subordinate (or embedded) clause (prior to the onset of the second verb *was*).
b. Reduced relative clause (RC) ambiguity	The police interviewed at the meeting lied.	A verb may be interpreted as the predicate of the matrix clause or the beginning of a reduced RC (the ambiguity is removed with the onset of the second verb).
c. Filler-gap ambiguity	Which book do you want to take with you?	A displaced wh-expression is or is not considered as the direct object of the main verb (*want* in the example) and (the ambiguity is removed with the onset of the second verb).
Global ambiguities		
d. PP attachment ambiguity	John made the chair in the garden.	A prepositional phrase (PP) may be interpreted to modify the verb *made* or the noun *chair*.
e. Adverb attachment ambiguity	I will ask John to fix the computer tomorrow.	The adverb *tomorrow* can be interpreted to modify the main verb *ask* or the infinitive *fix*.
f. Relative clause attachment ambiguity	I really like the design of the furniture we talked about yesterday.	A relative clause may be considered to modify the first (*design*) or the second noun (*furniture*).

Such ambiguous sentences are interesting because they offer an opportunity to examine how the parser handles incoming information for the purpose of building a syntactic structure or for resolving ambiguity. Many questions can be explored about ambiguity resolution. For example, in processing a temporarily ambiguous sentence, does the parser commit to one interpretation first, or does it allow or maintain multiple interpretations at the same time? In the case of the former, what factors or strategies determine which interpretation is favored? When an incorrect analysis is initially performed, to what extent can the parser recover from it?

These questions are often explored through the observation of the garden-path effect. A temporarily ambiguous sentence that results in an initial incorrect analysis is often referred to as a garden-path sentence. One of the most frequently given examples is *the horse raced past the barn fell*. The sentence is ambiguous at the position of the verb *raced* because the verb can either be the main verb taking *the horse* as its agent or the beginning of a reduced relative clause (RRC) (thus, the sentence with a complete RC would read: *The horse that was raced past the barn fell*). Many people tend to initially interpret the first verb as the main verb, and thus have to subsequently abandon this incorrect analysis when they encounter the second verb *fell*. This reanalysis often results in a delay in processing the sentence. This delay is referred to as the garden-path effect (GPE), a term often credited to Bever (1970), along with this particular example. All three examples for illustrating temporary ambiguities in Table 6.1 are garden-path sentences.

The GPE can be assessed by comparing individuals' reading time on a garden-path sentence and its non-garden-path version. For example, in assessing the GPE in association with the subject-object ambiguity, two versions of a sentence may be created such as Examples 6.1a and 6.1b. An individual may take longer in reading the second verb *was* in 6.1a than the same word in 6.1b. This delay is referred to as the GPE. It is interpreted by some to reflect the noticing of the problem with the initial direct-object analysis of the NP *her friend* and a reanalysis of the sentence. The underlined verb in Example 6.1 is considered as the critical region as this is where the GPE should be observed. The GPE may also materialize at the following word (*not*) in a self-paced reading task (SPRT). When it happens, it is referred to as the spill-over effect.

6.1a   *The visitor saw her friend <u>was</u> not feeling well.*
6.1b   *The visitor saw that her friend <u>was</u> not feeling well.*

Another form of the GPE is known as the filled-gap effect. In using sentences such as Examples 6.2a and 6.2b, Stowe (1986) found that participants took longer to read the word *us* in 6.2a than in 6.2b. An explanation of this delay is that the parser may have initially considered the wh word *who* in 6.2a as the direct object of the verb *bring*, which has to be corrected when *us* is encountered. In contrast, this initial incorrect analysis should not occur in 6.2b.

6.2a   My *brother wanted to know who Ruth will bring us home to at Christmas.*

6.2b   My *brother wanted to know if Ruth will bring us home to Mom at Christmas.*

The GPE provides an opportunity for observing how the parser goes about building a syntactic structure. Using garden-path sentences as test materials, one can investigate under what circumstances a GPE will or will not appear, at what position of a sentence the effect will appear, what factor will affect the appearance or strength of the GPE or the success in reanalysis. Thus, the GPE has played a significant role in sentence processing research, including in the development of sentence processing models.

6.1.2 Models of Syntactic Parsing

A major debate in sentence processing research is what information is used in initial parsing. Sentence processing models can be differentiated into two general categories based on their answers to this question: modular models and interactive models. A modular model is based on the modularity theory of mind (Fodor, 1983) which postulates that the human mind consists of several separate modules. These modules are domain specific in that they handle a specific cognitive function, and they are informationally encapsulated in that only information within the module affects its function. Representing an application of the theory to sentence processing is the garden-path model (GPM) proposed by Frazier and Rayner (Frazier, 1987; Frazier & Rayner, 1982). In this model, parsing proceeds in two stages (thus the name the two-stage model for such models). The first stage generates a syntactic structure based on syntactic information alone. This initial parsing follows two universal principles: the minimal attachment principle and the late closure principle. According the former, "at points of ambiguity, the parser prefers to build the structure with the fewest number of nodes consistent with the grammar of the language" (Frazier & Rayner, 1982, p. 529). This, for example, explains the preference for treating the second NP as the object of the matrix verb rather than the subject of an embedded clause in the subject-object ambiguity (see the first example in Table 6.1), as the subject interpretation requires more nodes. According to the second principle, individuals tend to attach the incoming new element to the current phrase, i.e., keep the current phrase open as long as allowed by the grammar. This explains English native speakers' preference, while reading *I really like the design of the furniture we talked about yesterday*, for attaching the relative clause (*we talked about yesterday*) to the NP immediately preceding it, i.e., *the furniture*, rather than the first NP *the design*.

Related to these principles is the active-filler strategy or filler-driven strategy (Clifton & Frazier, 1989): the parser tends to find a gap for a displaced *wh-element* as early as possible, which explains the tendency for English speakers to treat the *wh-element* as the object of the first verb *want* while reading *which book do you want to take with you?*

In the second stage, the initial structure is then evaluated, and revised if necessary, on the basis of both syntactic and non-syntactic information. Sentence processing is serial in such models in the sense that only one structure is considered at a time. The garden-path effect in processing ambiguous sentences is explained within such models in terms of a reanalysis. With further information becoming available, the initial structure has to be abandoned or revised for an analysis consistent with the input, and this reanalysis results in a delay, and thus the GPE.

On the other side of the controversy are the interactive models that are consistent with a connectionist view of mind. Often known as constraint-based (or constraint satisfaction) models (CBM), these theories of sentence processing (e.g., MacDonald, 1994; MacDonald, Pearlmutter, & Seidenberg, 1994; Trueswell, Tanenhaus, & Garnsey, 1994) argue that all information, syntactic or non-syntactic (e.g., lexical, semantic, contextual), is immediately used in the parsing process, which generates multiple structures simultaneously. These candidate structures compete for selection, and the final interpretation is based on multiple sources of information as well. Within this model, the garden-path effect is an outcome of competition among multiple interpretations rather than reanalysis.[1] Table 6.2 summarizes the main ideas of these two different types of models.

Table 6.2 Contrasting the Garden-Path Models and the Constraint-Based Models

The Garden-Path Models (GPM)	The Constraint-Based Models (CBM)
Based on a modular view of mind.	Based on an interactive view of mind.
Only syntactic information is initially considered in parsing.	All information is considered in parsing at all times.
Sentence processing is serial in that only one interpretation is considered at a time.	Sentence processing is parallel in that multiple interpretations are considered at the same time.
Reanalysis leads to the garden-path effect.	Competition leads to the garden-path effect.

Both theories have generated a large number of empirical studies and have had a great impact on sentence processing research in L2. Empirical findings seem to exist to back up both models, as well. For example, Garnsey, Pearl-mutter, Myers, and Lotocky (1997) found that English NS did rely on lexical information of the verbs involved in analyzing syntactic structures. Thus, they showed a GPE only for sentences such as *the talented photographer accepted the money could not be spent yet* (whose main verb *accept* takes a NP as its direct object more often than a clause), but not for sentences such as *the weary traveler claimed the luggage had been stolen in Rome* (where the main verb *claim* takes a clause as its direct object more often). On the other hand, Pickering and Traxler (2003) showed that an NP was considered as the direct object of a verb even for verbs that are followed more frequently by a prepositional phrase than by a NP (e.g., *worry about the dog*). Whether parsing initially considers syntactical information only or considers all information simultaneous is an ongoing debate. This debate has also found its way in L2 parsing research.

6.2 The Role of L1 in L2 Parsing

L2 sentence processing research that employed online methods and focused on parsing did not begin until the 1990s (e.g., Juffs & Harrington, 1995, 1996; Frenck-Mestre & Pynte, 1997; Juffs, 1998a, 1998b). This research has focused primarily on two topics: the role of L1 in L2 parsing and the use of lexicose-mantic and syntactic information in parsing.[2] They are the focus of this and the following section. As research on both topics is more geared towards dem-onstrating the uniqueness of L2 parsing, it should be pointed out from the out-set that a great deal of similarities in L1 and L2 parsing were also shown in this research. For example, NNS were similar to NS in Schachter and Yip (1990), Juffs and Harrington (1995), and Juffs (2005) in showing more difficulty in processing subject-extraction sentences than object-extraction sentences, and L2 speakers have been found to produce a reliable garden-path effect involv-ing a variety of structures, such as subject-object ambiguity in Frenck-Mestre and Pynte (1997) and Juffs and Harrington (1996) and reduced relative clause in Juffs (1998a) and Rah and Adone (2010).

6.2.1 Verb Subcategorization

In studying how L2 parsing is influenced by an individual's L1, researchers have focused on two structures in particular: verb subcategorization and relative clause attachment. In relation to the former, languages differ in verb argument structure or subcategorization specifications. For example, a transitive verb in one language may be intransitive in another, as is the case with the English verb *obey* (transitive and transitive) and its French translation *obéir* (intransi-tive only) (Frenck-Mestre & Pynte, 1997). In addition to verb transitivity, verbs may differ across languages in how often they are used in a particular structure. A word in one language may take an NP as its direct object (e.g., *I heard the news*) more often than take a sentence complement (SC, e.g., *I heard the news was not true*), but its translation in another language may be just the opposite. For example, of the 20 English verbs that were judged by NS to be frequently used with a clause or sentential complement (thus SC-biased) in Dussias and Cramer Scaltz (2008), the translations of only eight of them were also frequently followed by a SC in Spanish. Nine other Spanish translations were actually used more often with a NP as a direct object (thus DO-biased), as judged by Spanish NS. Both verb transitivity and verb bias has served as linguistic phenomena in L2 parsing studies.

Research in this area showed that L2 speakers are influenced by their L1 under some circumstances and are able to overcome this influence under other circumstances. Frenck-Mestre and Pynte (1997) were among the first to explore this issue and reported both findings. They compared English-dominant and French-dominant bilinguals in reading English and French sentences that included verbs that were both similar and different in argument structure between the two languages, as shown in Examples 6.3 and 6.4. Because *obey* is transitive and *bark* is intransitive, the first English sentence involves a subject-object ambiguity (see Table 6.1), but the second sentence does not. Because the two correspondent French verbs are both intransitive, no subject-object ambiguity is involved in either French sentence. As a result, we would expect a garden-path effect for the English sentences (longer RT for reading *showed* in 6.3a than in 6.3b), but not for the French sentences.

English stimuli

6.3a   *Every time the dog obeyed the pretty little girl <u>showed</u> her approval.*
6.3b   *Every time the dog barked the pretty little girl <u>showed</u> her approval.*

French stimuli

6.4.   *Chaque fois que le chien obéissait la jolie petite fille montrait sa joie.*
6.4b   *Chaque fois que le chien aboyait la jolie petite fille montra it sa joie.*

The results from eye-movement data showed both nativelike parsing strategies among L2 speakers and the influence of L1 argument structures. In the former case, both English- and French-dominant bilinguals showed a garden-path effect in processing English sentences. This indicated that the French ESL speakers were able to treat *obey* as a transitive noun, thus overriding the influence of the intransitive use of its French translation. Similarly, both groups showed no such effect in processing French sentences, which suggested that English learners of French were also treating the French verb *obéir* as an intransitive verb. The evidence for L1 influence came primarily from the finding that the French-dominant group fixated longer on the verbs in the English sentences that were different in argument structures from French (e.g., *obey*) than verbs that were similar (e.g., *bark*) while English NS showed no such difference.

Dussias and Cramer Scaltz (2008) reported another study that showed both results. They tested Spanish-English bilinguals in an offline verb classification task and an online self-paced reading task (SPRT). In the offline task, the participants were asked to complete a sentence fragment such as *Mary believed* _____. The verbs used differed in how often they took an NP as a direct object (DO) or a clause (or sentence complement, SC) between the two languages. L1 influence was assessed by comparing how ESL speakers and English NS completed the sentences. The results showed that ESL speakers were able to complete sentences in a way consistent with English NS norming of these verbs, even where English and Spanish differed in verb bias.

In the online part of the study, Spanish-English bilinguals were asked to perform a SPRT involving sentences in six conditions, as illustrated in Examples 6.5 to 6.8 (disambiguating regions underlined). Given the first four conditions and based on earlier findings (e.g., Garnsey et al., 1997), one would expect English NS to show a garden-path effect for sentences with a DO-biased verb such as Example 6.6a (as compared to Example 6.6b), but not sentences with a SC-biased verb such as Example 6.5a. Data from English NS confirmed the prediction: they produced a garden-path effect for DO verbs only. NNS, however, showed a garden-path effect for both types of verbs. This result suggested that they had not developed or were not using L2-specific verb bias information in L2 parsing. However, while processing sentences in the last two conditions, NNS did show a sensitivity to verb bias: they responded to the disambiguating region faster when a DO-biased verb appeared in a DO sentence than in a SC sentence, and they were faster when a SC-biased verb appeared in a SC sentence than in a DO sentence. They interpreted these latter findings as indication of successful acquisition of L2-specific subcategorization knowledge.

SC Sentences

6.5a *The ticket agent admitted the mistake <u>might not</u> have been caught.*
   (SC-biased, ambiguous)
6.5b *The ticket agent admitted that the mistake <u>might not</u> have been caught.*
   (unambiguous)

6.6a   *The CIA director confirmed the rumor <u>could mean</u> a security leak.*
(DO-biased, ambiguous)
6.6b   *The CIA director confirmed that the rumor <u>could mean</u> a security leak.*
(unambiguous)

DO Sentences

6.7   *The ticket agent admitted the mistake <u>when he</u> got caught.*
6.8   *The CIA director confirmed the rumor <u>when he</u> testified before Congress.*

Some studies revealed further evidence for L1 influence. Juffs (1998b) compared ESL speakers with a Romance language background and Chinese/Korean/Japanese ESL speakers on the processing of English sentences involving verbs used in four different structures, as illustrated in Example 6.5. Predictions were made on the basis of cross-linguistic analysis of the argument structures of verbs such as *melt* and their translations in these languages. Specifically, Juffs suggested that the east Asian language groups may have more difficulty with Example 6.9a and Romance ESL speakers should have more difficulty with Example 6.9d for the same reason: an additional morphological device has to be used with these structures in their respective L1s (e.g., the word *ba* for 6.9a among Chinese speakers). There was some indication of L1 effects in the data. For example, the east Asian groups seemed to be slower than the Romance group in processing the first three structures, but the gap disappeared in processing 6.9d at least between the Romance and the Chinese groups. These results are consistent with the predictions made on the analysis of the cross-linguistic differences for such verbs and structures. Furthermore, ESL speakers with a *wh*-in-situ L1 background, (Chinese and Japanese) were found to have more difficulty in processing *wh* questions than ESL speakers whose L1 was similar to English in *wh*-movement (Spanish) in Juffs (2005) which he also attributed to L1 influence.

6.9a   First of all the cook melted the chocolate on the cake.
6.9b   *First of all the chocolate melted itself on the cake.
6.9c   First of all the chocolate melted slowly on the cake.
6.9d   First of all the cook made the chocolate melt on the cake.

Rah and Adone (2010) also interpreted their results as reflecting the effect of L1 in L2 parsing. They asked German ESL speakers to perform a SPRT on sentences such as Example 6.10. For the purpose of the present discussion, the three versions differed in that the past participle in the Example 6.10a, i.e., *seen*, represented an unambiguous beginning of a reduced relative clause (RRC) but in the other two versions, the past participle *noticed* is ambiguous as it can either begin a RRC or serve as the main verb. This means that the participants were required to construct a RRC upon seeing *seen* in processing 6.10a but not in processing the other two versions. They found that German ESL speakers were much slower in processing the past participle in 6.10a (i.e., *seen*) than that in the other versions (*noticed*), but English NS showed no such difference. They attributed this result to the fact that there is not a German counterpart for English RRCs, which made it harder for German ESL speakers to process sentences obligatorily requiring a RRC analysis.

6.10a *The brown sparrow seen by the hungry cat pecked at an insect.*
6.10b *The brown sparrow noticed on an upper branch pecked at an insect.*
6.10c *The brown sparrow noticed almost every day pecked at an insect.*

On the other hand, some studies demonstrated that L2 speakers can overcome L1 influence and develop L2-specific knowledge where L2 and L1 differ in verb subcategorization specifications. Lee, Lu, and Garnsey (2013) explore the same issue with similar materials and the same SPRT as adopted by Dussias and Cramer Scaltz (2008) but involving Korean ESL speakers of two proficiency levels. Korean is different from English in two ways. The basic word order is SVO in English but SOV in Korean. Furthermore, a complementizer (here the word *that*) is optional in English but obligatory in Korean. The purpose of the study was to determine whether Korean ESL speakers were able to develop nativelike use of verb bias information in spite of such differences. They used ten DO-biased and ten SC-biased verbs to create four conditions similar to the first four conditions in Dussias and Cramer Scaltz (2008), illustrated in Examples 6.11 and 6.12. The data from English NS replicated the earlier finding that the garden-path effect was found only for DO verbs. Korean ESL speakers showed a different pattern depending on their English proficiency. The high-proficiency group (but not the low-proficiency group) were able to produce a nativelike pattern. Note that no norming was done in the study to determine if Korean and English differed in subcategorization preference for the verbs used in the study, as was done in Dussias and Cramer Scaltz (2008). Thus, it was possible that the nativelike performance can be a result of L1 transfer. How the fact that Korean is a verb-final language relates to this possibility is yet to be determined. See Hoover and Dwivedi (1998) for another demonstration of successful adoption of NL parsing strategies by English-French bilinguals.

6.11a *The club members understood the bylaws <u>would be</u> applied to everyone.*
6.11b *The club members understood that the bylaws <u>would be</u> applied to everyone.*
6.12a *The ticket agent admitted the mistake <u>might be</u> hard to correct.*
6.12b *The ticket agent admitted that the mistake <u>might be</u> hard to correct.*

The evidence available today with regard to the extent to which adult L2 learners are able to overcome L1 influence in verb argument structure is quite limited and inconclusive at best. When both online and offline findings (such as Inagaki, 2001, 2002) are taken into consideration, it is a fair assessment that even advanced L2 speakers may (but not necessarily) continue to rely on L1 subcategorization knowledge in L2 parsing. The specific circumstances under which L2 speakers tend to continue to rely on L1 subcategorization knowledge or to successfully develop L2-specific knowledge are a worthwhile topic for future exploration.

6.2.2 Relative Clause Attachment

An ambiguity exists in relative clause (RC) attachment when a complex noun phrase (NP) is involved. As illustrated in Figure 6.1, the relative clause may be interpreted to either modify the first NP (NP1) or the second NP (NP2). These two interpretations are often referred to as high attachment and low attachment, respectively.

Two methods can be used to assess an individual's preference of the attachment. One is to ask a participant to explicitly judge and indicate whether it is the first or the second NP the RC modifies, e.g., through a questionnaire. A second method is to ask a participant to perform a reading task and measure their reading time with the use of the self-paced reading paradigm or the eye tracking paradigm. This is often done through the manipulation of

Figure 6.1 An Illustration of Two Interpretations of a Relative Clause

plural or gender marking of the NPs and the verb in the RC, as illustrated in Example 6.13 below. The difference between the first two is that the verb *be* favors a NP1 or high attachment in Example 6.13a and a NP2 or low attachment in Example 6.13b by means of number agreement. If a high attachment is preferred in parsing, individuals should read *were* in 6.13a faster than *was* in 6.13b. A preference for low attachment would result in a faster reading time for *was* in 6.13b than *were* in 6.13a. As the two conditions involve two different verb forms, 6.13c and 6.13d can be used to control this lexical variable by counterbalancing the verbs across the high- and low-attachment conditions. Thus, with such test materials, attachment preference can be determined by comparing the RT for the same verb *were* in 6.13a and 6.13c. A faster reading time for *were* in 6.13a than in 6.13c would indicate a preference for high attachment, for example. The same can be done by comparing the RT for *was* in 6.13b and 6.13d. The offline and online tasks may help explore different parsing outcomes in that the offline method provides data about the ultimate interpretation while the online method reveals attachment preference in the initial parsing.

6.13a   *Do you know the students of the professor who were at the party?*
6.13b   *Do you know the students of the professor who was at the party?*
6.13c   *Do you know the student of the professors who were at the party?*
6.13d   *Do you know the student of the professors who was at the party?*

Research has shown that languages differ in which interpretation is preferred. For example, in their seminal study, Cuetos and Mitchell (1988) demonstrated that English NS preferred the low-attachment interpretation while reading English sentences while Spanish NS preferred the high-attachment interpretation while reading Spanish sentences. Subsequent research provided further evidence for this cross-linguistic difference showing that high attachment is the preferred interpretation in French (Zagar, Pynte, & Rativeau, 1997), Dutch (Brysbaert & Mitchell, 1996), Italian (De Vincenzi & Job, 1995), Japanese (Kamide & Mitchell, 1997), and Korean (Lee & Kweon, 2004), but low attachment is preferred in processing English (Carreiras & Clifton, 1999).

This phenomenon provides a unique opportunity for exploring the role of L1 in L2 parsing. When a learner's L1 and L2 differ in RC attachment preference, will he or she transfer the L1 parsing strategy to L2 or develop L2-specific parsing preference? Frenck-Mestre (1997) reported some earliest findings. She tracked the eye movements of English and Spanish learners of French while they read French sentences with RC attachment ambiguity. The two groups of L2 learners showed a different pattern. While Spanish-speaking learners showed a preference for NP1 attachment, English-speaking participants showed a preference for NP2 attachment. These results confirmed that L2 parsing was affected by L1 processing strategies, at least among these beginning learners.

Several studies followed, and their results suggested that RC attachment is a phenomenon much less straightforward among L2 speakers than among L1 speakers. Fernández (2002) tested monolingual Spanish speakers, monolingual English speakers and Spanish-English bilingual speakers fluent in both languages in both the offline questionnaire task and the online SPRT. The test materials included 24 English and Spanish sentences in three versions as illustrated by the English sentences in Example 6.14. The first version was an ambiguous sentence which allowed both interpretations. It was used in the offline task where the participants were asked to respond to the question: *Who was divorced, the nephew or the teacher?* The second and third versions forced a high (Example 6.14b) or low (Example 6.14c) attachment through number agreement. These versions were used in the SPRT. Four findings emerged from the study. First, in the monolingual part of the study, English and Spanish monolinguals interpreted the ambiguous version in their high attachment 43% and 57% of the time respectively. This finding replicated the earlier finding that English speakers favored low attachment while Spanish favored high attachment in their respective language. Second, the online data from both groups showed a preference for low attachment while processing their respective L1, which was interpreted as an indication of the exclusive use of syntactic information in initial parsing in both languages. Third, the bilinguals showed a different pattern of preference in the offline task depending on their relative dominance of the two languages. Spanish-dominant bilinguals showed a much stronger preference for high attachment than English-dominant bilinguals in reading both English and Spanish sentences. Finally, in the online task, no preference was found in either group, according to the author, but Figure 4 in the report showed a clear difference between English- and Spanish-dominant bilinguals in processing English sentences: the former group had a 64 ms advantage for processing low-attachment sentences, while the latter group had a 113 ms advantage for processing high-attachment sentences. The two groups were similar in showing little preference in processing Spanish sentences.

6.14a Andrew had dinner yesterday with the nephew of the teacher that was divorced.

6.14b Andrew had dinner yesterday with the nephew of the teachers that was divorced.

6.14c Andrew had dinner yesterday with the nephews of the teacher that was divorced.

Another study was reported by Dussias (2003). Similar to Fernández (2002), she tested Spanish-English bilinguals in both offline and online tasks. The participants were Spanish L1-English L2 bilinguals, English L1-Spanish L2 bilinguals, and monolingual speakers of the two languages. In the offline task, 16 experimental items, along with 48 distractor and filler items, were presented to the participants in both languages in the form such as Example 6.15. The participants were asked to read the sentences and indicate their answer by circling the letter in front of the two answers.

6.15 *Peter fell in love with the daughter of the psychologist who studied in California.*
      Who studied in California?
      a. The daughter studied in California.
      b. The psychologist studied in California.

Results from the NS of the two languages replicated earlier findings in earlier studies, showing a high-attachment preference in Spanish (74%) and a low-attachment preference in English (86%). The bilingual speakers showed a less consistent pattern. Both groups of bilinguals showed a low rate of high-attachment interpretation in reading English sentences (English-Spanish: 28%, Spanish-English: 22%). In reading Spanish sentences, both groups showed a significantly lower rate of a high-attachment preference (Spanish-English: 28%, English-Spanish: 44%). These results were ambiguous as they may be subject to different interpretations. The author interpreted the results to suggest that the bilinguals had not developed L2 specific processing strategies. It was based on the lower high-attachment reading of Spanish sentence from English-Spanish bilinguals (44%) than Spanish monolinguals (74%). However, one may note that this percentage was also higher than how these same bilinguals rated English sentences (28%) or the high-attachment rate from monolingual English speakers (18%). The Spanish-English bilinguals' low rate of high-attachment preference in reading English sentences (22%) could have been interpreted as evidence that these Spanish ESL speakers had learned to adopt an English attachment preference, but this interpretation was not adopted due to the low rate of high-attachment preference in reading Spanish sentences by these same participants.

In the online part of the study, English-Spanish bilinguals, Spanish-English bilinguals, and monolingual Spanish speakers were asked to read Spanish sentences presented in four conditions, with Examples 6.16a and 6.16b being critical. The sentences were presented in three segments, as shown by the slashes in the examples. With such materials, attachment preference could be assessed by comparing the participants' reading time between the two conditions, particularly for the third segment. If a high attachment was preferred, as shown in previous studies, the second condition (6.16b) should be read faster than the first (6.16a).

6.16a *El perro mordió al cuñado de la maestra/que vivió en Chile/con su esposo.*
"The dog bit the brother-in-law of the teacher$_{FEM}$ who lived in Chile with his/her husband." (low-attachment preference)

6.16b *El perro mordió a la cuñada del maestro/que vivió en Chile/con su esposo.*
"The dog bit the sister-in-law of the teacher$_{MASC}$ who lived in Chile with his/her husband." (high-attachment preference)

The results from the NS indeed confirmed the previous finding of a preference for high-attachment in Spanish. They read the last segment of the high attachment sentences 196 ms faster than that of the low-attachment sentences. The English-Spanish bilingual showed no difference between the two conditions while the Spanish-English bilinguals read the low-attachment sentences significantly faster than high-attachment ones.

The results from both the offline and online tasks were inconsistent with the adoption of L2-spcific parsing strategies among these participants. However, they were not entirely in favor of L1 influence either, particularly in consideration of the Spanish-English bilinguals' preference for low attachment in reading both English and Spanish. There seemed to be a general tendency for L2 speakers to favor a low-attachment interpretation. Dussias (2003) suggested that this could be an outcome of bilinguals adopting a general processing principle, in this case, the principle of late closure, that was least demanding in terms of memory load.

Papadopoulou and Clahsen (2003) and Felser, Roberts, Marinis, and Gross (2003) also explored RC attachment in L2 speakers but involving the learners of Greek and English, respectively. Both studies used offline and online tasks similar to those used in Fernández (2002) and Dussias (2003) but included a comparison that was not explored in earlier L2 studies: the complex noun phrase with two NPs joined by *of* versus by *with* or their counterparts in Greek. The following examples from Felser et al.'s study illustrate this additional manipulation, with Example 6.17 used in the offline task and Example 6.18 in the online task.

6.17a *The dean liked the secretary of the professor who was reading a letter.*
6.17b *The dean liked the secretary with the professor who was reading a letter.*
6.18a *The dean liked the secretary of the professors who was reading a letter.*
6.18b *The dean liked the secretary of the professors who were reading a letter.*
6.18c *The dean liked the professors with the secretary who were reading a letter.*
6.18d *The dean liked the professors with the secretary who was reading a letter.*

The two studies produced similar findings. The offline data showed that both NS and NNS groups of participants adopted a low-attachment reading in processing sentences with the preposition *with* but there was no clear preference in processing *of* sentences. The same pattern was found in the online data. They read the verb *be* significantly faster in low-attachment sentences than in high-attachment sentences when the two NPs were joined by *with*, but there was no difference between the two versions of the *of* sentences. What is particularly relevant to the present discussion is that German and Greek ESL speakers did not seem to transfer their L1-based high-attachment preference to the processing of English *of* sentences. They attributed this lack of attachment preference to NNS' inability to use syntactic information in L2 parsing.

Even though the cross-linguistic differences in RC attachment seem to provide a unique opportunity for studying the role of L1 in L2 processing, the findings from these studies suggest that RC attachment is a more complicated phenomenon than previously thought when it is examined among bilinguals. First of all, as shown in the results from Fernández (2002) as well as Cuetos and Mitchell (1988), RC attachment preference is not a robust phenomenon to begin with (e.g., 43% and 57% of high-attachment preference for English and Spanish monolingual speakers, respectively in Fernandez). Second, some findings from these studies can be interpreted in both ways. For example, when German ESL speakers showed no attachment preference in processing English *of* sentences, as in Felser et al. (2003), one may interpret the finding as evidence of L1 transfer, showing a compromise between two languages with conflicting processing strategies, or as indicating a lack of transfer due to a marked difference between this no-preference performance and high-attachment preference shown by monolingual German speakers. Furthermore, RC attachment preference has been shown to reflect the influence of the combined experiences in both languages. Learning a second language may affect a bilingual's RC attachment in the first language, as shown in both Dussias (2003) and Dussias and Sagarra (2007). Spanish-English bilingual speakers in both studies were found to show a low-attachment preference in their L1 Spanish. This bidirectional influence makes it difficult to assess the role of L1 in L2 processing by comparing bilingual speakers' performance in L1 and L2.

6.3 Syntactic and Lexicosemantic Information in L2 Parsing

Language input contains two types of information that can aid in building a syntactic structure for a sentence. The first type is the morphosyntactic information. Word order and morphosyntactic markers (e.g., case and number marking) belong to this type. Such information works in tandem with an individual's morphosyntactic knowledge in developing a syntactic structure. The second type is the lexicosemantic information, e.g., how many arguments a verb takes and the semantic plausibility of an interpretation. Take Example 6.19 for example. When the *wh-expression* *which book* is encountered at the beginning of the sentence, the parser knows that the subsequent part of the sentence should contain a site from which the expression is displaced, most likely following a transitive verb. Under such circumstances, the displaced *wh-expression*, or a filler as it is often referred to, is said to actively look for this site, or a gap, in parsing. Such processes are driven by the syntactic information in the input and our syntactic knowledge about the language. The minimal attachment principle and the late closure principle are both suggestions of how the parser relies on syntactic information in sentence processing. This example may also illustrate a potential role lexicosemantic information plays in parsing. When the transitive verb *invite* is encountered, a potential gap becomes available for the filler *which book*. If only syntactic information is used, the parser may consider *which book* as the object of *invite*. However, an individual may realize that this analysis is semantically problematic (as one cannot invite a book), and thus wait for a more plausible gap (what occurs following *read*). This latter analysis illustrates the role semantic plausibility may play in parsing.

6.19   *Which book shall we invite the children to read first?*

L1 and L2 researchers seem to have different ideas about how these two types of information are used in parsing. As discussed in Section 6.1.2 psycholinguists working with L1s have a consensus regarding the immediate use of syntactic information in parsing, but they disagree on how lexicosemantic information affects initial parsing. L2 researchers, on the other hand, do not seem to question the use of lexicosemantic information in L2 parsing. They, instead, disagree over the extent L2 speakers are able to use syntactic information. Representing an explicitly stated view on this issue is the shallow structure hypothesis proposed by Clahsen and Felser (2006a). They suggested that L2 speakers are able to make better use of lexical and semantic information than syntactic information in sentence processing, and as a result, "the syntactic representations adult L2 learners compute for comprehension are shallower and less detailed than those of native speakers" (p. 32). Two causes of shallow processing were proposed. One was the type or nature of grammatical knowledge available to NNS. Clahsen and Felser (2006b) attributed shallow processing to the lack of "sufficiently detailed, implicit grammatical knowledge" (p. 118) that is accessible in parsing among adult L2 learners, and this adversely affects the use of universal processing strategies such as minimal attachment. Similarly, Felser and Roberts (2007) suggested that "(part of) their L2 grammatical knowledge is of a form that makes it unsuitable for use in real-time parsing, that is, it may be 'explicit' rather than 'implicit' knowledge" (p. 29). Felser and Roberts also indicated that shallow processing may be a result of having limited working memory resources among adult L2 speakers.

Even though research on the use of syntactic and lexicosemantic information preceded the proposal of the shallow structure hypothesis by Clahsen and Felser (2006a), the proposal of the hypothesis has certainly helped energize this research and bring this issue to the spotlight. Research on this topic has produced both consistent and conflicting results. The consistency lies in the demonstration of L2 speakers' ability to effectively use lexicosemantic information. The disagreement lies in whether L2 speakers are able to use syntactic information as effectively as NS.

6.3.1 The Use of Lexicosemantic Information in L2 Parsing

Among the first to compare NNS and NS in the use of syntactic and lexical information in sentence processing were Frenck-Mestre and Pynte (1997). They monitored English-French bilingual speakers' eye movements while they read French sentences that were ambiguous in prepositional phrase (PP) attachment, as shown in the following English examples (6.20 and 6.21) they used to illustrate the ambiguity and the manipulation of syntactic and lexical cues.

Structurally in both English and French, the PPs (e.g., *of espionage, on horses*) in such sentences can be used to modify the verb phrase (VP) (*accused or rejected*) or the preceding NP (*the ambassador or the manuscript*). Based on general processing principles, the VP attachment should be favored. Thus, the VP attachment versions of these two sentences, 6.20a and 6.21a, should be processed faster than the NP attachment versions, 6.20b and 6.21b. However, the two verbs in the sentences differ in that *accuse* is a ditransitive verb that can take two arguments but *reject* is a monotransitive verb that takes only one argument. If such lexical information is also taken into consideration in processing, one would expect the pattern to reverse in the second sentence. That is, the NP attachment version, 6.21b, would be processed faster than the VP attachment version, 6.21a. Assuming that NS consider both lexical and syntactic information, they are expected to read 6.20a faster than 6.20b, and 6.21b faster than 6.21a. In the case of NNS, they considered three scenarios. First, if the NNS parser was less efficient and thus could not use syntactic information as effectively as a NS could, the NP attachment of PP (6.20b and 6.21b) was favored in both sentences due to the proximation of PP to NP, or "heuristic processing". Second, if NNS relied on syntactic information only, they would prefer the VP attachment for both sentences (the a version faster than the b version for both sentences). Finally, if NNS were similar to NS in using both syntactic and lexical information, they would show a VP attachment preference for the first sentence and the NP attachment preference for the second sentence. The results showed that both NNS and NS showed a similar pattern of preference: there was a VP attachment preference for the first sentence but a NP attachment preference for the second sentence. The findings indicated that both lexical and syntactic information was effectively used in sentence processing in both NS and NNS.

6.20a   *They accused the ambassador of espionage but nothing came of it.*
6.20b   *They accused the ambassador of Indonesia but nothing came of it.*
6.21a   *He rejected the manuscript on purpose because he hated its author.*
6.21b   *He rejected the manuscript on horses because he hated its author.*

A study reported by Williams, Möbius, and Kim (2001) showed similar results. They used the filled-gap effect to assess the use of syntactic information and used verb-noun plausibility to assess the use of lexicosemantic information. In the former case, previous research has shown among NS that in processing sentences with a displaced *wh-expression* (referred to as a filler), the parser tended to actively look for and take the first available position in a sentence (referred to as a gap) for the expression, which is referred to as the active-filler strategy (Clifton & Frazier, 1989) or the filler-driven strategy (Frazier & Clifton, 1989). This sometimes results in a garden-path effect often referred to as the filled-gap effect. Take Example 6.22a for example. Following the active-filler strategy, the parser would locate a gap for the filler *which book* as soon as it becomes available, i.e., after *want*, thus treating the *wh-expression* as the direct object of *want*. When the real object *him* is encountered, the parser realizes that the gap has been incorrectly filled and thus the original analysis has to be abandoned. A gap is then correctly located after the verb *read.* The initial incorrect analysis and its correction results in a delay in processing such sentences. This delay, or the filled-gap effect, can be assessed by comparing the RTs for the word *him* in 6.22a and 6.22b. In the latter version of the sentence, the parser is less likely to take the position after *invite* as the gap for *which book* due to semantic constraints. A filled-gap effect is reflected in a longer RT for *him* in 6.22a than the same word in 6.22b.

6.22a   *Which book do you want him to read?*
6.22b   *Which book do you invite him to read?*

To assess the use of lexicosemantic information, they considered if a plausibility effect could be found in NNS as well as NS by using verbs that were or were not semantically plausible for the *wh*-expression, as shown in 6.22 above (*want a book* vs. *invite a book*). Example 6.23 provides an example to illustrate the test materials they actually used. In this example, the two versions of the sentence differed in whether or not the *wh*-expression was a plausible object for the verb. In the plausible version (6.23a), it is semantically plausible for the verb to take the *wh*-expression as its object (*fix a machine*). In the implausible version (6.23b), the verb cannot take the *wh*-expression as a plausible object (*fix a customer*).

6.23a   *Which machine did the mechanic fix the motorbike with two weeks ago?* (plausible)
6.23b   *Which customer did the mechanic fix the motorbike for two weeks ago?* (implausible)

Williams et al. (2001) asked three questions in relation to L2 processing. First, are L2 learners able to adopt a filler-driven strategy in processing *wh*-sentences which requires automatic application of syntactic knowledge? Second, will the learners' L1 affect their parsing strategies? Finally, will both NS and NNS show a sensitivity to plausibility?

To explore these issues, they tested German, Chinese, and Korean ESL speakers and English NS in two experiments. In Experiment 1, they adopted a plausibility judgment task, a modification of the stop-making-sense paradigm used in Boland, Tanenhaus, Garnsey, and Carlson (1995), and asked participants to read the sentences word by word and press a button when they felt the sentence was no longer plausible. This task produced two types of data that were useful for answering the research questions, one being the likelihood of reaching an "implausible" decision at various positions of the sentence and the other being the RT for words of interest. If NS and NNS adopted a filler-driven strategy and were sensitive to plausibility, they would consider the displaced elements *which machine* or *which customer* as the direct object of the verb, and thus be more likely to reach an "implausible" decision a) at the verb position (i.e., *fix*) in the implausible (6.23b) than in the plausible sentences (6.23a), and b) at the post-verbal NP position, i.e., *the motorbike*, in the plausible than the implausible condition, where a reanalysis was necessary. The RT data would be informative, too. If an active-filler strategy was adopted and the participants were sensitive to verb-object plausibility, one would expect them to show a delay in reading the post-verbal NP *the motorbike* in the plausible condition (6.23a) in comparison to the implausible condition (6.23b). This delay may be considered as showing more difficulty in the reanalysis of the initial attachment in the plausible condition.

The plausibility judgment results showed that both NS and NNS made more "implausible" decisions at the verb position in the implausible than the plausible condition. All groups except the Chinese group also made more "implausible" decisions at the post-verbal NP position in the plausible sentences than the implausible sentences. Both findings confirmed the use of an active-filler strategy and a sensitivity to plausibility in both NS and NNS, except for the Chinese group. The RT data provided converging evidence. All participant groups were slower in reading the post-verbal noun in the plausible condition than in the implausible condition. These findings were consistent with the view that both NS and NNS initially treated the wh-expression as the direct object of the verb and they were more likely to do so when the verb and the wh-expression were semantically plausible.

Suspecting that the results of Experiment 1 did not necessarily indicate a successful reanalysis among NNS, Williams et al. (2001) carried out a second experiment designed to specifically examine if NNS were able to recover from a garden-path effect. To this end, the participants were asked to perform an offline sentence reading task in which they read sentences and circled the word where they thought the sentence was no longer "Okay". They reasoned that if the participants considered a grammatical sentence "not Okay" more often in the plausible condition than in the implausible condition, it meant the reanalysis was not completed successfully. The results showed that indeed, NNS were more likely to judge a grammatical sentence "not Okay" in the plausible condition than in the implausible condition, suggesting that they had difficulty in successfully performing the reanalysis.

The successful use of lexicosemantic information was further confirmed in a study reported by Roberts and Felser (2011). They tested Greek ESL speakers and English NS in a SPRT on subject-object ambiguity sentences such as Examples 6.24 and 6.25. These sentences differed in the strength of the garden-path effect they may induce, with the preposed adjunct clauses in 6.25 being more likely to result in a GP effect than the structure with a complement clause such as 6.24, according to previous research. They also differed in plausibility of the second NP in relation to the preceding VP, with NP such as *the boss* and *the song* more plausible for the verb *warned* and *played*, respectively, than NPs such as *the crimes* and *the beer*.

6.24a *The inspector warned the boss would destroy very many lives.* (weak GP, plausible)

6.24b *The inspector warned the crimes would destroy very many lives.* (weak GP, implausible)

6.25a *While the band played the song pleased all the customers.* (strong GP, plausible)

6.25b *While the band played the beer pleased all the customers.* (strong GP, implausible)

The purpose of the project was to compare the plausibility effect among NS and NNS. Given the stimuli as shown above, they reasoned that if both NS and NNS adopted a filler-driven strategy and their parsing was affected by the plausibility factor, both groups should produce a longer RT at the underlined NP position for the implausible condition than for the plausible condition, and a longer RT at the underlined VP position for the plausible than the implausible condition, as a result of a great difficulty in recovering from the initial analysis for the plausible condition. Alternatively, NNS may rely on the plausibility information to a less or greater extent than NS, which can also be assessed by comparing the plausibility effect between the two groups.

The RT data showed that NNS produced the expected plausibility effect at both the NP and VP position for the weak construction and a plausibility effect at the NP position for the strong construction. In contrast, the plausibility effect was either weaker or absent for NS. They took the results as suggesting that "nonnative comprehenders may be influenced more strongly than native ones by pragmatic plausibility information during processing" (p. 322).

6.3.2 The Use of Syntactic Information in L2 Parsing

In contrast to the consistent finding regarding the use of lexicosemantic information in L2 sentence processing, there is a great deal of inconsistency across studies in whether NNS are able to use syntactic information as efficiently as NS do. Several studies have claimed to show that NNS were less able to use structural information in sentence processing, thus supporting the shallow structure hypothesis. One of these studies was reported by Marinis, Roberts, Felser, and Clahsen (2005) and conducted in response to the results of Williams et al. (2001). They argued that the finding of successful use of syntactic information by NNS, i.e., their use of the filler-driven strategy reported by Williams et al. (2001), was an outcome of the test materials used in the study. Specifically, the filled-gap effect found in the 2001 study could have reflected the process of direct word association between the wh-element (e.g., *which machine*) and the verb (e.g., *fix*). Because the postulated gap was at the same position as the direct object of the verb in the materials used by Williams, Möbius, and Kim, it was difficult to differentiate between the two explanations.

In order to avoid this problem, Marinis et al. (2005) used the intermediate gap effect discovered by Gibson and Warren (2004) as a means to explore gap filling among NNS. In Gibson and Warren's study, they used materials such as Example 6.26. The four conditions differed in that the first two versions of the sentences involved the extraction of a *wh*-element (*who*) but not the last two versions. Furthermore, there was an intermediate site for wh-movement in the first version (as indicated by the first t_i in the first version but not in the second). Gibson and Warren found that English NS were faster in reading *had pleased* in 6.26a than in 6.26b, but no such difference was found between 6.26c and 6.26d. They interpreted the finding as evidence for the presence of an intermediate gap (at the first t_i position) in the 6.26a, which made gap filling more local and thus easier.

6.26a *Extraction across a VP* (+intermediate structure):
The manager who$_i$ the consultant claimed t_i that the new proposal had pleased t_i will hire five workers tomorrow.
6.26b *Extraction across an NP* (−intermediate structure):
The manager who$_i$ the consultant's claim about the new proposal had pleased t_i will hire five workers tomorrow.
6.26c *No extraction, local subject-verb integration* (VP):
The consultant claimed that the new proposal had pleased the manager who will hire five workers tomorrow.
6.26d *No extraction, nonlocal subject-verb integration* (NP):
The consultant's claim about the new proposal had pleased the manager who will hire five workers tomorrow.

Marinis et al. (2005) argued that this intermediate gap effect provided a better test than the structures used in Williams et al. (2001), because the gap position and the direct-object position are no longer the same. They tested Chinese, Japanese, German, and Greek ESL speakers and English NS in a SPRT on stimuli similar to those of Gibson and Warren (2004) such as Example 6.27. The only difference was an added matrix clause in the last two versions to make 6.27c and 6.27d structurally as complex as 6.27a and 6.27b (compare 6.26c/d and 6.27c/d to see the difference). This was motivated by their decision to make a comparison between conditions with and without extractions as well.

6.27a *Extraction across a VP* (+intermediate gap)
The nurse who$_i$the doctor argued e'$_i$that/the rude patient/had angered e$_i$ / is refusing to work late. (slashes indicating the division of segments in display)

6.27b *Extraction across an NP* (−intermediate gap)
The nurse who$_i$ the doctor's argument about the rude patient had angered e$_i$ is refusing to work late.

6.27c *Nonextraction, local subject-verb integration* (VP)
The nurse thought the doctor argued that the rude patient had angered the staff at the hospital.

6.27d *Nonextraction, nonlocal subject-verb integration* (NP)
The nurse thought the doctor's argument about the rude patient had angered the staff at the hospital.

They made the following reasoning:

a) If the intermediate gap is used, "that" will take longer to read in 6.27a than in 6.27c because of the need of reanalysis in the former. This is the filled-gap effect.

b) The use of the intermediate gap would also lead to a faster reading time for *had angered* in 6.27a than in 6.27b because the use of an intermediate gap shortens the distance between the filler and the subcategorizer in 6.27a. And this difference should not occur in 6.27c and 6.27d. That is, there should be an interaction between extraction and the type of phrases.

c) NS were expected to show both effects outlined in b; If NNS used the same parsing strategies as NS, they should show both effects as well. The lack of such effects would indicate a failure to make use of the intermediate gap.

d) If L1 plays a role, ESL speakers with a wh-in-situ background, i.e., the Chinese and Japanese groups, should perform differently from those with an L1 that allows wh-movement.

Several findings were obtained. First, as expected, NS showed a longer RT in reading *that* in 6.27a than in 6.27c, and they were faster in reading the VP *had angered* in 6.27a than in 6.27b, and this difference did not occur in the non-extraction sentences. These results indicated that NS used the position after the first verb *argued* in 6.27a as an intermediate gap. The analysis of the NNS data showed that none of the NNS group produced a main effect of extraction at the position of *that* or *about*, and none produced an interaction between extraction and phrase type at the position of the VP *had angered*. They considered the lack of such effects among NNS as evidence for their inability in using the intermediate gap.[3]

In another study that claimed to have demonstrated shallow processing in L2 speakers, Felser and Roberts (2007) tested Greek ESL speakers in a cross-modal picture priming task in which a participant was presented with auditory input of sentences and a picture. Example 6.28 illustrates the sentences used.

6.28 *Fred chased the squirrel to which the nice monkey explained the game's₁ difficult rules₂ in the class last Wednesday.*

This structure involves a displaced *wh-expression* which is the indirect object in the relative clause, and thus should have left a trace at the position indicated by the subscript 2 in the example. This is where the gap is. Based on the earlier finding of the antecedent priming effect (e.g., Nicol & Swinney, 1989), a priming effect should be observed at this position if a word or picture was presented that is the same as or related to the antecedent, *the squirrel* in the example. The advantage of using this structure is that the gap position is different from the position immediately following the verb subcategorizer (*explained* in the example), thus avoiding the problem of any observed priming effect resulting from word association rather than gap filling, an issue raised by Marinis et al. (2005) about Williams et al.'s (2001) study.

To assess the antecedent priming effect, they displayed a picture of an object that was either mentioned (squirrel) or not mentioned (e.g., sparrow) in the sentence at two positions of the auditory input, the gap position indicated by the subscript 2 and the pre-gap position indicated by the subscript 1, thus creating a 2x2 design. The participants' task was to decide whether the picture depicted a living or nonliving thing. If an antecedent priming effect was to be observed as a result of reactivation of the antecedent, individuals should respond to the repeated picture faster than to an unrelated picture, and this effect should be found at the gap position, not at the pre-gap position, if it was a gap-filling effect.

The NNS were found to show a priming effect at both positions. They responded to the pictures in the repetition condition 53 ms and 57 ms faster than in the unrelated condition at the pre-gap and gap positions, respectively.

One may consider the priming effect at the gap position as a true gap-filling effect and thus successful use of syntactic information among NNS, but they argued otherwise. On the basis that NS tested with the same stimuli showed a priming effect only at the gap position (Roberts, Marinis, Felser, & Clahsen, 2007), they took the priming effect at both positions among NNS as indicating that "non-native comprehenders are unable to apply some of the parsing routines that are used in L1 comprehension" (p. 27), thus maintaining the shallow structure hypothesis.

Additionally, Felser et al. (2003) and Papadopoulou and Clahsen (2003) considered the issue by examining the processing of RC attachment among adult L2 English and L2 German speakers in a grammaticality judgment task (GJT) and a SPRT with sentences where the complex nouns were connected differently, i.e., with the prepositions *of* and *with* for English sentences as illustrated by Example 6.29 and with a genitive marker and preposition *me* (with) for German sentences. In both studies, the NNS produced a high accuracy rate in the former task, indicating their possession of the related linguistic knowledge. However, their performance was different from that of NS in the latter task. Specifically, they were able to produce nativelike performance for sentences with the lexical cue (*with* in English and its counterpart *me* in German) but their performance was not nativelike for sentences where such a lexical cue was not present (*of*-sentences in English and German sentences with a genitive marker), which was taken as evidence for the NNS' inability to use syntactic knowledge in parsing. For a final example, Felser, Cunnings, Batterham, & Clahsen (2012) reported an eye tracking study in which NNS were found to show a delayed use of structural information as compared to their immediate use of semantic information in processing sentences involving island constraints.

6.29a The dean liked the secretary of the professor who was reading a letter.

6.29b The dean liked the professor with the secretary who was reading a letter.

In contrast to the findings summarized above, a considerable number of studies have produced findings that NNS are able to use syntactic information in sentence processing. In addition to Frenck-Mestre and Pynte (1997) and Williams et al. (2001), more such studies have been reported by Hopp (2006), Lieberman, Aoshima, and Phillips (2006), Omaki and Schulz (2011), Witzel, Witzel, and Nicol (2012), and Dekydtspotter and Miller (2013). In one of these studies, for example, Witzel et al. (2012) tracked the participants' eye movements while they read sentences. Three structures were involved: RC attachment, adverb attachment, and coordination ambiguity, illustrated in Examples 6.30, 6.31, and 6.32 (with the critical regions underlined).

RC Attachment (Low/High Attachment)

6.30a *The son of the actress who shot herself on the set was under investigation.*
6.30b *The son of the actress who shot himself on the set was under investigation.*

Adverb Attachment (Low/High Attachment)

6.31a *Jack will meet the friend he phoned yesterday, but he doesn't want to.*
6.31b *Jack will meet the friend he phoned tomorrow, but he doesn't want to.*

Coordination Ambiguity (Unambiguous/ Temporarily Ambiguous)

6.32a *The nurse examined the mother, and the child played quietly in the corner.*
6.32b *The nurse examined the mother and the child played quietly in the corner.*

In the first structure involving RC attachment, antecedent-reflexive gender agreement determines that 6.30a and 6.30b require a low and high NP attachment, respectively. With such sentences, RC attachment preference can be determined by comparing an individual's reading time on the underlined words. One would read *herself* in 6.30a faster than *himself* in 6.30b if low attachment is preferred (assuming *himself* and *herself* takes a similar amount of reading time). The pattern would be reversed if high attachment is preferred. Similarly, high or low adverb attached (to *meeting* or *phoned*) can be assessed by comparing reading time for *yesterday* and *tomorrow* in 6.31a and 6.31b. Finally, a coordination ambiguity was present in 6.32b at the position of the NP *the child* (which can be interpreted as the direct object of the verb examined or the subject of the coordinate clause), but not in the unambiguous version 6.32a. The conjoined direct-object interpretation is consistent with the principle of minimal attachment, and has been shown to be a preferred interpretation among English NS (e.g., Frazier & Clifton, 1997). In this sense, 6.32b represents a garden-path sentence that has to be reanalyzed at the position of the second verb *played*. No such reanalysis is necessary in 6.32a due to the presence of the comma which prevents the conjoined NP interpretation.

At a result, individuals are expected to process the verb *played* faster in 6.32a than in 6.32b.

The use of the first two structures was related to the findings in Papadopoulou and Clahsen (2003) and the interpretation by these authors. The NNS in this study were found to show no interpretation preference for RC attachment for sentences without lexical cues and Papadopoulou and Clahsen interpreted this lack of preference as evidence for NNS' inability to use syntactic information. By using similar attachment structures, Witzel et al. (2012) were able to further determine whether NNS had no preference for attachment. The third structure was intended to test if NNS were able to follow the principle of minimal attachment. If they were, they should read the verb *played* in 6.32a faster than in 6.32b, which would suggest that they were able to use syntactic information. They argued that in comparison to the subject-object ambiguity structure, the use of coordination ambiguity enjoyed the advantage that it was more difficult to attribute any observed garden-path effect to lexical or subcategorizational factors.

Thirty English NS and 30 Chinese ESL speakers were tested on 96 sentences which consisted of 24 sentences for each structure and 24 fillers. The participants' first-pass reading times, go-past reading times, total reading times, and regression proportion were recorded as data (see critical regions in the above examples). The NS' performance replicated earlier findings. They showed low-attachment preference for both attachment structures and a garden-path effect for the coordination structure. NNS were nativelike in showing a preference for low attachment for the adverb attachment structure and a garden-path effect for the coordination structure. They also showed a preference for high attachment for the RC attachment structure. The most important aspect of the results was that NNS did show a reliable preference for the attachment structures, thus negating the findings from Papadopoulou and Clahsen (2003). The results were interpreted to indicate that NNS were able to use syntactic information and that their parsing was "deeper than shallow".

In sum, the research on the use of lexicosemantic and syntactic information among NNS showed consistent results across studies regarding the use of lexicosemantic information but produced conflicting results regarding the use of syntactic information in L2 processing. This research raises a number of issues to be further explored. For example, how does shallow processing apply to structures that differ in structural types and complexity and in the degree of L1–L2 overlap? If shallow processing is a result of lacking implicit grammatical knowledge, as is suggested by Clahsen and Felser (2006a, 2006b) and Felser and Roberts (2007), are adult L2 learners eventually able to develop the implicit grammatical knowledge for nativelike parsing? Or are they able to proceduralize their explicit knowledge such that it eventually becomes automatically accessible in real-time parsing? In addition to structure type and proficiency that are implicated by these questions, additional factors may affect the extent to which L2 speakers are able to utilize syntactic information in parsing. One such factor is how an L2 is learned, as demonstrated by Pliatsikas and Marinis (2013). They tested Greek ESL speakers with and without extensive naturalistic exposure employing the same test materials and tasks as used in Marinis et al. (2005) and found that the former group behaved like NS in the processing of intermediate gaps. Other factors such as working memory capacity and the age of acquisition are conceivably relevant as well and have yet to be explored.

6.4 Working Memory and L2 Sentence Processing

In addition to L1 and the type of information, some other factors have been examined in connection to both L2 parsing and L2 speakers' sensitivity to syntactic and morphosyntactic violations (see Chapter 7). These include age of acquisition (e.g., Liu, Bates, & Li, 1992; Weber-Fox & Neville, 1996) and proficiency (e.g., Coughlin & Tremblay, 2013; McDonald & Heilenman, 1992; Rossi, Gugler, Friederici, & Hahne, 2006; Sasaki, 1994; Su, 2001), and working memory. This section offers a brief discussion of how working memory capacity affects L2 sentence processing.

Working memory (WM), a term initially used by Miller, Galanter, and Pribram (1960) according to Baddeley (2003), refers to a memory system theorized by Baddelay (Baddeley & Hitch, 1974; Baddeley, 1992, 2003) for temporary storage and manipulation of information for subsequent processing. The 1974 version of the model consists of three components: the central executive, the visual-spatial sketchpad, and the phonological loop. A fourth component, the episodic buffer, was added subsequently (Baddeley, 2000). Particularly important for language processing is the phonological loop which consists of two subcomponents: "a phonological store that can hold acoustic or speech-based information for 1 to 2 seconds" and a subvocal rehearsal system that helps "maintain materials within the phonological store by subvocal repetition" and "take visually presented materials such as words or nameable pictures and register them in the phonological store by subvocalization" (Baddeley, 1992, p. 558).

In language processing research, work memory capacity is often assessed in a reading span test. One of the earlier tests was developed by Daneman and Carpenter (1980). In the test, sets of unrelated sentences such as Example 6.33 are displayed and the participants are asked to read aloud the sentences and then recall the last word of each sentence. The number of sentences in the set usually varies between two to six. The mean number of words (typically varying between two and five) or the percentage of total possible number of words successfully recalled is used as an index of one's WM capacity. To prevent individuals from focusing on remembering the last word and thus not processing the meaning of the sentences in a reading-aloud task, Waters and Caplan (1996) developed a reading span test in which a participant is asked to perform an acceptability judgment task on the sentences while trying to remember the last word. This test produces three WM measures: judgment accuracy, judgment RT, and number of words correctly recalled. They may be combined to make up a composite score for measuring WM capacity. Both these tests are widely used in sentence processing research (see Conway et al., 2005 for a review of different WM tasks).

> 6.33 *When at last his eyes opened, there was no gleam of triumph, no shade of anger. The taxi turned up Michigan Avenue where they had a clear view of the lake.*

Evidence emerged in the 1980s and 1990s suggesting that individuals differ in WM capacity and this difference affects sentence processing (e.g., Daneman & Carpenter, 1980, 1983; Just & Carpenter, 1992; King & Just, 1991). In the two studies reported by Daneman and Carpenter, for example, individuals were found to differ in the number of final words they were able to successfully recall, and WM capacity assessed this way correlated with the reading comprehension measures and affected how individuals processed ambiguous sentences. King and Just (1991) found that individuals with lower WM capacity took longer and showed poorer comprehension in reading sentences with relative clauses.

The link between WM and sentence processing lies in the amount of information (or activation in Just and Carpenter's 1992 model) one can keep available at a given time in language processing. Individuals with a larger WM capacity are able to hold and thus use more information than those with a smaller capacity. This becomes important particularly in processing ambiguous sentences, and sentences involving long-distance agreement or filler-gap dependencies. MacDonald, Just, and Carpenter (1992) demonstrated, for example, that while processing ambiguous sentences involving a reduced relative clause individuals with a larger WM capacity were able to hold both interpretations in their memory for some time while those with a smaller capacity tended to only keep the most likely interpretation in memory.[4]

How much information one can hold in one's memory temporarily for language processing purposes can conceivably affect sentence processing in L2, as well. This is particularly true for processing long or complex sentences such as those used in some L2 studies, as illustrated in Examples 6.34 and 6.35 below. Indeed, it has been long proposed that L2 speakers may have reduced WM while processing an L2 and this may affect their sentence processing. Harrington (1992) and Kilborn (1992) were among the first to explicitly link WM capacity to L2 learning and processing. Many researchers have subsequently considered reduced WM capacity as a potential cause for the differences between sentence processing in L1 and L2 (e.g., McDonald, 2006; Miyake & Friedman, 1998; Nassaji, 2002; Reyes & Hernandez, 2006). For example, Clahsen and Felser (2006a) consider reduced WM capacity as a possible explanation for why L2 syntactic processing is shallow. McDonald (2006) has also explicitly attributed adult L2 learners' difficulty in sentence processing to a smaller WM capability. Gillon Dowens, Vergara, Barber, and Carreiras (2010) also used limited WM among L2 speakers to explain their nativelike sensitivity to gender/number agreement violations within a phrase but not across phrases. The role of WM in sentence processing was also recognized in studies that treated WM capacity as a controlled variable (e.g., Leikin, 2008; Weber-Fox & Neville, 2001).[5]

6.34   *The nurse who the doctor argued that the rude patient had angered is refusing to work late* (Marinis et al., 2005).

6.35   *Everyone liked the magazine that the hairdresser read extensively and with such enormous enthusiasm about before going to the salon* (Felser et al., 2012).

Empirically, two related issues are at hand. The first is to establish that individuals have a reduced WM capacity in L2 in comparison to L1. The second is to demonstrate that the manipulation of WM capacity as an independent variable affects individuals' performance in sentence processing.

Related to the first issue, there are only a small number of published studies that explicitly compared WM capacity in L1 and L2. Osaka and Osaka (1992) tested Japanese ESL speakers who were English majors in a Japanese university with a Japanese and an ESL version of a reading span test constructed following Daneman and Carpenter (1980). The same group of participants were tested in both versions and showed a mean reading span of 3.45 (range 2 to 5) and 3.23 (range 1.5 to 5) words in L1 and L2, respectively. No statistical analysis was done regarding the reliability of the difference. Osaka, Osaka, and Groner (1993) tested German-French bilinguals in their L1 and L2. Even though their statistical analysis focused on how the participants' performance in the two languages correlated, rather than how it differed between L1 and L2, visual inspection of Figure 1 of the report clearly showed a superior performance in L1. The Japanese ESL speakers in Harrington and Sawyer's (1992) study were tested in three WM tests in both languages: the digit span, the word span, and the reading span tests. They showed significantly higher scores in their L1 Japanese than L2 English in the first two tests while their performance in the third one was comparable in L1 and L2. Better performance in an L1 WM test has also been documented in Service, Simola, Metsänheimo, and Maury (2002). These results were all obtained where L1 and L2 WM capacity was assessed with different instruments. When the same instrument was used, NS also outperformed NNS in most cases. For example, McDonald (2006) tested both NS and NNS of English in a size judgment task for assessing WM span and showed that the NS outperformed the NNS. The three groups of ESL speakers and English NS in Williams et al. (2001) were tested with the same English reading span test. The NS again did significantly better than the Korean and Chinese ESL groups, but not than the German ESL group. In Coughlin and Tremblay (2013), the French NS also outperformed the L2 French speakers in the reading span test. Thus, reduced WM capacities in L2 seemed to be supported by evidence obtained both from the same group of participants performing the task in their L1 and L2 and from NS and NNS tested with the same instrument.

The second issue, that of the role of WM in L2 sentence processing, has been explored in a number of studies.[6] Table 6.3 summarizes ten such studies with information about the topic under investigation, the method used for assessing WM capacity, the main dependent variables, and the effect of WM on participant performance. As is clear from the able, empirical evidence available thus far does not permit an unequivocal conclusion regarding this issue. Two studies are summarized below to illustrate this inconsistency in findings.

Dussias and Piñar (2010) examined the role of WM in L2 parsing among Chinese ESL speakers as well as English NS. The participants performed a SPRT in combination with grammaticality judgment on test materials such as Examples 6.36 and 6.37. These materials differed in whether the extracted wh-element (i.e., the filler) was semantically plausible or implausible for the main verb and whether the wh-element was a subject or an object in the subordinate clause. These materials allowed them to explore whether plausibility information and extraction type affected L2 parsing. These effects were assessed by comparing the participants' reading times between subject- and object-extraction sentences and between plausible and implausible sentences. Based on previous research, subject-extraction sentences should take longer than object-extraction sentences, and sentences with plausible main verb+filler combinations should take longer than sentences with implausible combinations at the post-main verb position, e.g., *killed the pedestrian* and *the pedestrian killed* in the following examples. The participants' WM capacity was assessed in a reading span

Table 6.3 A Summary of Ten Studies of L2 Sentence Processing That Included Working Memory Capacity as a Variable

Study	Topic	WM Assessment and Manipulation	Dependent Variables	Effect of WM
Miyake and Friedman (1998)	Cue preference (in the competition model)	Listening span test	Cue preference	Yes
Williams et al. (2001)	Plausibility in filler-gap dependency	RST (Daneman & Carpenter, 1980)	RT in SPRT	No
Juffs (2004)	Garden-path effect	RST (Harrington & Sawyer, 1992; Osaka & Osaka, 1992)/WST	RT in SPRT/GJT	No/ Yes
Juffs (2005)	Garden-path effect	RST (Harrington & Sawyer, 1992; Osaka & Osaka, 1992);WST	RT in SPRT/GJT	No
McDonald (2006)	Cause of L2–L1 difference in GJT	Size judgment task	GJT accuracy and RT	Yes
Felser and Roberts (2007)	L2–L1 parsing comparison	RST (Harrington & Sawyer, 1992)	RT in Alive/Not Alive picture judgment	No
Havik, Roberts, Hout, Schreuder, & Haverkort. (2009)	L2–L1 parsing comparison	RST (Daneman & Carpenter, 1980)	RT in SPRT with/ without meaning verification	Yes/ No
Sagarra and Herschensohn (2010)	Sensitivity to morphosyntactic violations	RST (Waters & Caplan, 1996)	RT in SPRT and AC in GJT	Yes
Dussias and Piñar (2010)	Plausibility in filler-gap dependency	RST (Waters & Caplan, 1996)	RT in SPRT	Yes
Foote (2011)	Sensitivity to morphosyntactic violations	RST (Waters & Caplan, 1996)	RT in SPRT	No
Coughlin and Tremblay (2013)	Sensitivity to morphosyntactic violations	RST (Waters & Caplan, 1996)	RT in SPRT	Yes

WM: working memory, RST: reading span test, WST: word span test

test that involved 80 sentences presented in sets of two–six sentences. The participants were asked to read the sentences, decide if they were acceptable grammatically and semantically, and remember and recall the last word of each sentence in a set. The number of corrected recalled words was used as a measure of their WM capacity.

6.36a *Who did the police declare killed the pedestrian?* (subject extraction—implausible)

6.36b *Who did the police declare the pedestrian killed?* (object extraction—implausible)

6.36a *Who did the police know killed the pedestrian?* (subject extraction—plausible)

6.36b *Who did the police know the pedestrian killed?* (object extraction—plausible)

In data analysis, both NS and NNS groups were further divided into high and low WM capacity groups to assess the role of WM in parsing. The results showed that only the high-capacity NNS were similar to NS in showing a) a longer RT for subject-extraction sentences than for object-extraction sentences for both plausibility conditions, and b) a plausibility effect only for subject-extraction sentences. The low-capacity NNS showed a different pattern. They produced an extraction effect only with implausible sentences, and there was no plausibility effect favoring an implausible sentence in either extraction types of sentences. The authors concluded that only high-capacity NNS were able to attend to and use the same information as NS do in sentence processing.

In a study that examined non-native speakers' sensitivity to morphosyntactic violations, Foote (2011) reported no relationship between the participants' WM capacity and their performance in the language processing task. She tested English-Spanish bilinguals on Spanish sentences with or without number or gender agreement violations in a SPRT. The participants were also given a reading span test in Spanish that was adapted from Waters and Caplan (1996, Experiment 1). The RT data obtained in the SPRT showed that late bilinguals were sensitive to both number and gender agreement violations and their sensitivity was stronger when the error involved two words adjacent to each other (the adjacent condition) than when the error involved two distant words (the distant condition). To assess the role of WM, she first calculated a sensitivity score for each participant for the adjacent and distant conditions by subtracting his or her mean RT for grammatical sentences from the same person's mean RT for ungrammatical sentences in each condition. A sensitivity reduction score was then computed by subtracting the sensitivity score for the distant condition from the sensitivity score for the adjacent condition. This score represented the extent to which an individual became less sensitive to grammatical violations due to the longer distance of the disagreement errors. These scores and the participants' reading span scores were then entered in a correlational analysis, which produced no correlation between the reading span scores and the sensitivity reduction scores for both agreement types.

One may speculate about the causes of this conflicting pattern. One lies in the different WM tests used across studies. As is clear from Table 6.3, a number of different instruments have been used which may affect the assessment outcomes. Different approaches have been taken in analyzing data, as well. One is to divide the participants into high and low WM capacity groups and assess the role of WM by examining the similarities and differences in the performance of the two groups (e.g., Dussias & Piñar, 2010; Havik et al., 2009; Williams et al., 2001). The other is to enter the participants' WM measures as an independent variable or covariate in correlational or regression analyses or ANOVA (analysis of variance) (e.g., Coughlin & Tremblay, 2013; Felser & Roberts, 2007; Foote, 2011). This may also affect the results. A trickier difference lies in the selection of a dependent variable. Due to the difference in the phenomena involved across studies, the WM effect was often assessed against different measures or phenomena, such as the plausibility effect in Dussias and Piñar (2010), the priming effect in Felser and Roberts (2007), or a sensitivity score in Foote (2011). It is possible that the WM effect may respond differently in these circumstances. Finally, there is the thorny issue of a potential confound between L2 proficiency and L2 WM measures. It has been shown in at least three studies (Coughlin & Tremblay, 2013; Sagarra & Herschensohn, 2010; Service et al., 2002) that L2 proficiency and L2 reading span scores were correlated in that those with higher L2 reading span scores were usually higher in L2 proficiency. This makes it possible that what was assessed as the impact of WM may actually be the effect of L2 proficiency.

6.5 Conclusion

The bulk of L2 parsing research has focused on two issues: the role of L1 and the use of lexicosemantic and syntactic information. As with many other topics of SLP, current research has reported conflicting findings regarding both the role of L1 (in both the areas of verb subcategorization and RC attachment) and the use of syntactic information in L2 parsing. Additionally, this research has also focused almost exclusively on sentence processing in the visual modality (except for a few such as Felser & Roberts, 2007). Studies that are designed to specifically examine unique processes involved in auditory sentence processing, or to explicitly compare auditory to visual sentence processing, are hard to find. Given the time-sensitive nature of auditory processing and more widely reported difficulty NNS have in listening than in reading, this is certainly an area that deserves more attention.

Notes

1   See Van Gompel and Pickering (2007) for an overview of sentence processing models and related research and Frazier (1995) for a rebuttal of the constraint-based models.

2   Other issues were also explored, such as prosodic and contextual constraints on ambiguity resolution (Ying, 1996) and the effect of sentence complexity and working memory in ambiguity resolution (Kim & Christianson, 2013), and sentence interpretation research within the competition model (e.g., McDonald & Heilenman, 1992; Sasaki, 1994; Su, 2001). The latter research has focused on a single linguistic phenomenon: the identification of an agent relation to mostly three cues. An effort has been made to expand the scope of linguistic phenomena that are applicable in the competition model (MacWhinney, 2005b) and to develop a unified model of L1 and L2 acquisition (MacWhinney, 2005a, 2008).

3   It should be pointed out that their analysis was not performed in close relation to the predictions. For example, to support the use of the intermediate gap, there should be a delay at Segment 3 in the Extraction-VP condition as compared to the Nonextraction-VP condition, but no such delay should occur in NP sentences (Examples 6.27b and 6.27d). However, in analyzing NS data for Segment 3, they did not separate VP conditions (*that* in Examples 35a and 35c) from NP conditions (*about* in 6.27b and 6.27d). Instead, they reported a main effect of extraction at this position. The data in their Table 2 showed that there was an extraction effect for both VP and NP sentences, which was inconsistent with their interpretation of the delay in the Extraction-VP condition as evidence for the involvement of the intermediate gap. In analyzing the NNS data, they seemed to have collapsed the Segment 3 data from Chinese and Japanese speakers, and thus ignoring the native-like pattern of the former group.

4   Some studies showed no relationship between working memory capacity and sentence processing effects in L1, e.g., Felser et al. (2012) and Sprouse, Wagers, and Phillips (2012).

5   See Traxler (2006) for words of caution regarding the role of working memory in L2 sentence processing.

6   This review focuses on the role of working memory in L2 sentence processing. Working memory has also been proposed or shown to affect L2 learning and L2 reading comprehension, e.g., Alptekin and Erçetin (2010); Ardila (2003); Atkins and Baddeley (1998); N. Ellis (1996a, 1996b); Gathercole, Service, Hitch, Adams, and Martin (1999); Harrington and Sawyer (1992); Leeser (2007); Mackey, Philp, Egi, Fujii, & Tatsumi (2002); Robinson (2002); Service (1992); and Walter (2004). See a recent review by Juffs and Harrington (2011).

References

Alptekin, C. & Erçetin, G. (2010). The role of L1 and L2 working memory in literal and inferential comprehension in L2 reading. *Journal of Research in Reading*, 33(2), 206–219.

Ardila, A. (2003). Language representation and working memory with bilinguals. *Journal of Communication Disorders*, 36, 233–240.

Atkins, P. W. B. & Baddeley, A. D. (1998). Working memory and distributed vocabulary learning. *Applied Psycholinguistics*, 19, 537–552.

Baddeley, A. D. (1992). Working memory. *Science*, 255, 556–559.

Baddeley, A. D. (2000). The episodic buffer: A new component of working memory? *Trends in Cognitive Sciences*, 4, 417–423.

Baddeley, A. D. (2003). Working memory: Looking back and looking forward. *Nature Reviews Neuroscience*, 4, 829–839.

Baddeley, A. D. & Hitch, G. J. (1974). Working memory. In G. A. Bower (Ed.), *Recent advances in learning and motivation* (Vol. 8, pp. 47–90). New York: Academic Press.

Bever, T. G. (1970). The cognitive basis for linguistic structure. In J. R. Hayes (Ed.), *Cognition and the development of language* (pp. 279–352). New York: John Wiley.

Boland, J. E., Tanenhaus, M. K., Garnsey, S. M., & Carlson, G. N. (1995). Verb argument structure in parsing and interpretation: Evidence from wh-questions. *Journal of Memory and Language, 34,* 774–806.

Brysbaert, M. & Mitchell, D. C. (1996). Modifier attachment in sentence parsing: Evidence from Dutch. *Quarterly Journal of Experimental Psychology, 49A,* 664–695.

Carreiras, M. & Clifton, C. (1999). Another word on parsing relative clauses: Eyetracking evidence from Spanish and English. *Memory & Cognition, 27,* 826–833.

Clahsen, H. & Felser, C. (2006a). Grammatical processing in language learners. *Applied Psycholinguistics, 27,* 3–42.

Clahsen, H. & Felser, C. (2006b). Continuity and shallow structures in language processing. *Applied Psycholinguistics, 27,* 107–126.

Clifton, C. & Frazier, L. (1989). Comprehending sentences with long-distance dependencies. In G. M. Carlson & M. K. Tanenhaus (Eds.), *Linguistic structure in language processing* (pp. 273–317). Dordrecht: Kluwer Academic.

Conway, A. R. A., Kane, M. J., Bunting, M. F., Hambrick, D. Z., Wilhelm, O., & Engle, R. W. (2005). Working memory span tasks: A methodological review and user's guide. *Psychonomic Bulletin & Review, 12,* 769–786.

Coughlin, C. E. & Tremblay, A. (2013). Proficiency and working memory based explanations for nonnative speakers' sensitivity to agreement in sentence processing. *Applied Psycholinguistics, 34,* 615–646.

Cuetos, F. & Mitchell, D. C. (1988). Cross-linguistic differences in parsing: Restrictions on the late-closure strategy in Spanish. *Cognition, 30,* 73–105.

Daneman, M. & Carpenter, P. A. (1980). Individual differences in working memory and reading. *Journal of Verbal Learning and Verbal Behavior, 19,* 450–466.

Daneman, M. & Carpenter, P. A. (1983). Individual differences in integrating information between and within sentences. *Journal of Experimental Psychology: Learning, Memory, and Cognition, 9,* 561–584.

Dekydtspotter, L. & Miller, A. K. (2013). Inhibitive and facilitative priming induced by traces in the processing of wh-dependencies in a second language. *Second Language Research, 29,* 345–372.

De Vincenzi, M. & Job, R. (1995). An investigation of late closure: The role of syntax, thematic structure, and pragmatics in initial interpretation. *Journal of Experimental Psychology: Learning, Memory, and Cognition, 21,* 1303–1321.

Dussias, P. E. (2003). Syntactic ambiguity resolution in L2 learners: Some effects of bilinguality on L1 and L2 processing strategies. *Studies in Second Language Acquisition, 25,* 529–557.

Dussias, P. E. & Cramer Scaltz, T. R. (2008). Spanish–English L2 speakers' use of subcategorization bias information in the resolution of temporary ambiguity during second language reading. *Acta Psychologica, 128,* 501–513.

Dussias, P. E. & Piñar, P. (2010). Effects of reading span and plausibility in the reanalysis of wh-gaps by Chinese-English L2 speakers. *Second Language Research, 26,* 443–472.

Dussias, P. E. & Sagarra, N. (2007). The effect of exposure on syntactic parsing in Spanish-English bilinguals. *Bilingualism: Language and Cognition, 10,* 101–116.

Ellis, N. C. (1996a). Sequencing in SLA. *Studies in Second Language Acquisition, 18*, 91–126.

Ellis, N. C. (1996b). Working memory in the acquisition of vocabulary and syntax: Putting language in good order. *The Quarterly Journal of Experimental Psychology: Section A, 49*, 234–250.

Felser, C., Cunnings, I., Batterham, C., & Clahsen, H. (2012). The timing of island effects in nonnative sentence processing. *Studies in Second Language Acquisition, 34*, 67–98.

Felser, C. & Roberts, L. (2007). Processing wh-dependencies in a second language: A cross-modal priming study. *Second Language Research, 23*, 9–36.

Felser, C., Roberts, L., Marinis, T., & Gross, R. (2003). The processing of ambiguous sentences by first and second language learners of English. *Applied Psycholinguistics, 24*, 453–489.

Fernández, E. M. (2002). Relative clause attachment in bilinguals and monolinguals. In R. R. Heredia & J. Altarriba (Eds.), *Bilingual sentence processing* (pp. 187–215). Amsterdam: Elsevier.

Fodor, J. A. (1983). *The modularity of mind: An essay on faculty psychology.* Cambridge, MA: MIT Press.

Foote, R. (2011). Integrated knowledge of agreement in early and late English-Spanish bilinguals. *Applied Psycholinguistics, 32*, 187–220.

Frazier, L. (1987). Sentence processing: A tutorial review. In M. Coltheart (Ed.), *Attention and performance XII: The psychology of reading* (pp. 559–586). Hillsdale, NJ: Erlbaum.

Frazier, L. (1995). Constraint satisfaction as a theory of sentence processing. *Journal of Psycholinguistic Research, 24*, 437–468.

Frazier, L. & Clifton, C. (1989). Identifying gaps in English sentences. *Language and Cognitive Processes, 4*, 93–126.

Frazier, L. & Clifton, C., Jr. (1997). Construal: Overview, motivation, and some new evidence. *Journal of Psycholinguistic Research, 26*, 277–295.

Frazier, L. & Rayner, K. (1982). Making and correcting errors during sentence comprehension: Eye movements in the analysis of structurally ambiguous sentences. *Cognitive Psychology, 14*, 178–210.

Frenck-Mestre, C. (1997). Examining second language reading: An on-line look. In A. Sorace, C. Heycock & R. Shillcock (Eds.), *Language acquisition, knowledge representation and processing: GALA 1997* (pp. 474–478). Edinburgh: HCRC.

Frenck-Mestre, C. & Pynte, J. (1997). Syntactic ambiguity resolution while reading in second and native languages. *The Quarterly Journal of Experimental Psychology A, 50*, 119–148.

Garnsey, S. M., Pearlmutter, N. J., Myers, E., & Lotocky, M. A. (1997). The contributions of verb bias and plausibility to the comprehension of temporarily ambiguous sentences. *Journal of Memory and Language, 37*, 58–93.

Gathercole, S. E., Service, E., Hitch, G. J., Adams, A. M., & Martin, A. J. (1999). Phonological short-term memory and vocabulary development: Further evidence on the nature of the relationship. *Applied Cognitive Psychology, 13*, 65–77.

Gibson, E. & Warren, T. (2004). Reading-time evidence for intermediate linguistic structure in long-distance dependencies. *Syntax, 7*, 55–78.

Gillon Dowens, M., Vergara, M., Barber, H. A., & Carreiras, M. (2010). Morphosyntactic processing in late second-language learners. *Journal of Cognitive Neuroscience, 22*, 1870–1887.

282   Sentence Processing in L2

Harrington, M. (1992). Working memory capacity as a constraint on L2 development. In R. Harris (Ed.), *Cognitive processing in bilinguals* (pp. 123–134). New York: Elsevier.

Harrington, M. & Sawyer, M. (1992). L2 working memory capacity and L2 reading skill. *Studies in Second Language Acquisition, 14,* 25–38.

Havik, E., Roberts, L., Hout, R. V., Schreuder, R., & Haverkort, M. (2009). Processing subject-object ambiguities in the L2: A self-paced reading study with German L2 learners of Dutch. *Language Learning, 59,* 73–112.

Hoover, M. & Dwivedi, V. (1998). Syntactic processing by skilled bilinguals. *Language Learning, 48,* 1–29.

Hopp, H. (2006). Syntactic features and reanalysis in near-native processing. *Second Language Research, 22,* 369–397.

Inagaki, S. (2001). Motion verbs with goal PPs in the L2 acquisition of English and Japanese. *Studies in Second Language Acquisition, 23,* 153–170.

Inagaki, S. (2002). Japanese learners' acquisition of English manner-of-motion verbs with locational/directional PPs. *Second Language Research, 18,* 3–27.

Juffs, A. (1998a). Main verb versus reduced relative clause ambiguity resolution in L2 sentence processing. *Language Learning, 48,* 107–147.

Juffs, A. (1998b). Some effects of first language argument structure and morphosyntax on second language sentence processing. *Second Language Research, 14,* 406–424.

Juffs, A. (2004). Representation, processing, and working memory in a second language. *Transactions of the Philological Society, 102,* 199–225.

Juffs, A. (2005). The influence of first language on the processing of wh-movement in English as a second language. *Second Language Research, 21,* 121–151.

Juffs, A. & Harrington, M. (1995). Parsing effects in second language sentence processing. *Studies in Second Language Acquisition, 17,* 483–516.

Juffs, A. & Harrington, M. (1996). Garden path sentences and error data in second language sentence processing. *Language Learning, 46,* 283–323.

Juffs, A. & Harrington, M. (2011). Aspects of working memory in L2 learning. *Language Teaching, 44,* 137–166.

Just, M. A. & Carpenter, P. A. (1992). A capacity theory of comprehension: Individual differences in working memory. *Psychological Review, 99,* 122–149.

Kamide, Y. & Mitchell, D. C. (1997). Relative clause attachment: Nondeterminism in Japanese parsing. *Journal of Psycholinguistic Research, 26,* 247–254.

Kilborn, K. (1992). On-line integration of grammatical information in a second language. In R. J. Harris (Ed.), *Cognitive processing in bilinguals* (pp. 337–368). Amsterdam: Elsevier.

Kim, J. H. & Christianson, K. (2013). Sentence complexity and working memory effects in ambiguity resolution. *Journal of Psycholinguistic Research, 42,* 393–411.

King, J. & Just, M. A. (1991). Individual differences in syntactic processing: The role of working memory. *Journal of Memory and Language, 30,* 580–602.

Lee, D. & Kweon, S. (2004). A sentence processing study of relative clause in Korean with two attachment sites. *Discourse and Cognition, 11,* 126–141.

Lee, E. K., Lu, D. H. Y., & Garnsey, S. M. (2013). L1 word order and sensitivity to verb bias in L2 processing. *Bilingualism: Language and Cognition, 16,* 761–775.

Leeser, M. J. (2007). Learner-based factors in L2 reading comprehension and processing grammatical form: Topic familiarity and working memory. *Language Learning, 57,* 229–270.

Leikin, M. (2008). Syntactic processing in two languages by native and bilingual adult readers: An ERP study. *Journal of Neurolinguistics, 21*, 349–373.

Lieberman, M., Aoshima, S., & Phillips, C. (2006). Nativelike biases in generation of wh-questions by nonnative speakers of Japanese. *Studies in Second Language Acquisition, 28*, 423–448.

Liu, H., Bates, E., & Li, P. (1992). Sentence interpretation in bilingual speakers of English and Chinese. *Applied Psycholinguistics, 13*, 451–484.

Love, T., Maas, E., & Swinney, D. (2003). The influence of language exposure on lexical and syntactic language processing. *Experimental Psychology, 50*, 204–216.

McDonald, J. L. (2006). Beyond the critical period: Processing-based explanations for poor grammaticality judgment performance by late second language learners. *Journal of Memory and Language, 55*, 381–401.

McDonald, J. L. & Heilenman, L. K. (1992). Changes in sentence processing as second language proficiency increases. In R. J. Harris (Ed.), *Cognitive processing in bilinguals* (pp. 325–336). Amsterdam: Elsevier.

MacDonald, M. C. (1994). Probabilistic constraints and syntactic ambiguity resolution. *Language and Cognitive Processes, 9*, 157–201.

MacDonald, M. C., Just, M. A., & Carpenter, P. A. (1992). Working memory constraints on the processing of syntactic ambiguity. *Cognitive Psychology, 24*, 56–98.

MacDonald, M. C., Pearlmutter, N. J., & Seidenberg, M. S. (1994). The lexical nature of syntactic ambiguity resolution. *Psychological Review, 101*, 676–703.

Mackey, A., Philp, J., Egi, T., Fujii, A., & Tatsumi, T. (2002). Individual differences in working memory, noticing of interactional feedback and L2 development. In P. Robinson (Ed.), *Individual differences and instructed language learning* (pp. 181–209). Philadelphia, PA: John Benjamins.

MacWhinney, B. (2005a). A unified model of language acquisition. In J. F. Kroll & A. M. B. De Groot (Eds.), *Handbook of bilingualism: Psycholinguistic approaches* (pp. 49–67). New York: Oxford University.

MacWhinney, B. (2005b). Extending the competition model. *International Journal of Bilingualism, 9*, 69–84.

MacWhinney, B. (2008). A unified model. In N. Ellis & P. Robinson (Eds.), *Handbook of cognitive linguistics and second language acquisition* (pp. 341–371). New York: Lawrence Erlbaum.

Marinis, T., Roberts, L., Felser, C., & Clahsen, H. (2005). Gaps in second language sentence processing. *Studies in Second Language Acquisition, 27*, 53–78.

Miller, G. A., Galanter, E., & Pribram, K. H. (1960). *Plans and the structure of behavior.* New York: Holt, Rinehart & Winston.

Miyake, A. & Friedman, N. (1998). Individual differences in second language proficiency: Working memory as language aptitude. In A. F. Healy & L. E. Bourne (Eds.), *Foreign language learning: Psycholinguistic studies on training and retention* (pp. 339–364). Mahwah, NJ: Lawrence Erlbaum.

Nassaji, H. (2002). Schema theory and knowledge-based processes in second language reading comprehension: A need for alternative perspectives. *Language Learning, 52*, 439–481.

Nicol, J. & Swinney, D. (1989). The role of structure in coreference assignment during sentence comprehension. *Journal of Psycholinguistic Research, 18*, 5–20.

Omaki, A. & Schulz, B. (2011). Filler-gap dependencies and island constraints in second-language sentence processing. *Studies in Second Language Acquisition, 33*, 563–588.

Osaka, M. & Osaka, N. (1992). Language-independent working memory as measured by Japanese and English reading span tests. *Bulletin of the Psychonomic Society, 30,* 287–289.

Osaka, M., Osaka, N., & Groner, R. (1993). Language-independent working memory: Evidence from German and French reading span tests. *Bulletin of the Psychonomic Society, 31,* 117–118.

Papadopoulou, D. & Clahsen, H. (2003). Parsing strategies in L1 and L2 sentence processing. *Studies in Second Language Acquisition, 25,* 501–528.

Pickering, M. J. & Traxler, M. J. (2003). Evidence against the use of subcategorisation frequency in the processing of unbounded dependencies. *Language and Cognitive Processes, 18,* 469–503.

Pliatsikas, C. & Marinis, T. (2013). Processing empty categories in a second language: When naturalistic exposure fills the (intermediate) gap. *Bilingualism Language & Cognition, 16,* 167–182.

Rah, A. & Adone, D. (2010). Processing of the reduced relative clause versus main verb ambiguity in L2 learners at different proficiency levels. *Studies in Second Language Acquisition, 32,* 79–109.

Reyes, I. & Hernandez, A. E. (2006). Sentence interpretation strategies in emergent bilingual children and adults. *Bilingualism: Language and Cognition, 9,* 51–69.

Roberts, L. & Felser, C. (2011). Plausibility and recovery from garden paths in second language sentence processing. *Applied Psycholinguistics, 32,* 299–331.

Roberts, L., Marinis, T., Felser, C., & Clahsen, H. (2007). Antecedent priming at trace positions in children's sentence processing. *Journal of Psycholinguistic Research, 36,* 175–188.

Robinson, P. (2002). Effects of individual differences in intelligence, aptitude and working memory on incidental SLA. In P. Robinson (Ed.), *Individual differences and instructed language learning* (pp. 211–251). Philadelphia, PA: John Benjamins.

Rossi, S., Gugler, M. F., Friederici, A. D., & Hahne, A. (2006). The impact of proficiency on syntactic second-language processing of German and Italian: Evidence from event-related potentials. *Journal of Cognitive Neuroscience, 18,* 2030–2048.

Sagarra, N. & Herschensohn, J. (2010). The role of proficiency and working memory in gender and number agreement processing in L1 and L2 Spanish. *Lingua, 120,* 2022–2039.

Sasaki, Y. (1994). Paths of processing strategy transfers in learning Japanese and English as foreign languages. *Studies in Second Language Acquisition, 16,* 43–72.

Schachter, J. & Yip, V. (1990). Grammaticality judgments: Why does anyone object to subject extraction? *Studies in Second Language Acquisition, 12,* 379–392.

Service, E. (1992). Phonology, working memory, and foreign-language learning. *Quarterly Journal of Experimental Psychology, 45A,* 21–50.

Service, E., Simola, M., Metsänheimo, O., & Maury, S. (2002). Bilingual working memory span is affected by language skill. *European Journal of Cognitive Psychology, 14,* 383–408.

Sprouse, J., Wagers, M., & Phillips, C. (2012). A test of the relation between working-memory capacity and syntactic island effects. *Language, 88,* 82–123.

Stanfield, R. A. & Zwaan, R. A. (2001). The effect of implied orientation derived from verbal context on picture recognition. *Psychological Science, 12,* 153–156.

Stowe, L. A. (1986). Parsing wh-constructions: Evidence for on-line gap location. *Language and Cognitive Processes, 1,* 227–245.

Su, I. R. (2001). Transfer of sentence processing strategies: A comparison of L2 learners of Chinese and English. *Applied Psycholinguistics, 22*, 83–112.

Swinney, D. (1979). Lexical access during sentence comprehension: (Re)consideration of context effects. *Journal of Verbal Learning and Verbal Behavior, 5*, 219–227.

Traxler, M. J. (2006). Commentary on Clahsen and Felser. *Applied Psycholinguistics, 27*, 95–97.

Trueswell, J. C., Tanenhaus, M., & Garnsey, S. (1994). Semantic influences on parsing. Use of thematic role information in syntactic ambiguity resolution. *Journal of Meaning and Language, 33*, 285–318.

Van Gompel, R. P. & Pickering, M. J. (2007). Syntactic parsing. In M. G. Gaskell (Ed.), *The Oxford handbook of psycholinguistics* (pp. 289–307). Oxford: Oxford University Press.

Walter, C. (2004). Transfer of reading comprehension skills to L2 is linked to mental representations of text and to L2 working memory. *Applied Linguistics, 25*, 315–339.

Waters, G. S. & Caplan, D. (1996). The measurement of verbal working memory capacity and its relation to reading comprehension. *The Quarterly Journal of Experimental Psychology: A Human Experimental Psychology, 49*, 51–75.

Weber-Fox, C. M. & Neville, H. J. (1996). Maturational constraints on functional specializations for language processing: ERP and behavioral evidence in bilingual speakers. *Journal of Cognitive Neuroscience, 8*, 231–256.

Weber-Fox, C. & Neville, H. J. (2001). Sensitive periods differentiate processing of open-and closed-class words: An ERP study of bilinguals. *Journal of Speech, Language, and Hearing Research, 44*, 1338–1353.

Williams, J., Möbius, P., & Kim, C. (2001). Native and non-native processing of English wh-questions: Parsing strategies and plausibility constraints. *Applied Psycholinguistics, 22*, 509–540.

Witzel, J., Witzel, N., & Nicol, J. (2012). Deeper than shallow: Evidence for structure-based parsing biases in second-language sentence processing. *Applied Psycholinguistics, 33*, 419–456.

Ying, H. G. (1996). Multiple constraints on processing ambiguous sentences: Evidence from adult L2 learners. *Language Learning, 46*, 681–711.

Zagar, D., Pynte, J., & Rativeau, S. (1997). Evidence for early closure attachment on first pass reading times in French. *The Quarterly Journal of Experimental Psychology: Section A, 50*, 421–438.

Zwaan, R. A., Stanfield, R. A., & Yaxley, R. H. (2002). Language comprehenders mentally represent the shapes of objects. *Psychological Science, 13*, 168–171.

Chapter 7

Sentence Processing in L2
Sensitivity to Morphosyntactic Violations

7.1 Introduction

In addition to studying L2 parsing, another line of sentence processing research emerged in the 2000s that has a different focus. These studies used sentences as test materials and sentence processing tasks such as the grammaticality judgment task (GJT), the self-paced reading task (SPRT), and eye tracking as methods for data collection. Thus, they are sentence processing studies methodologically. However, their focus was more on acquisition than on parsing, with the intention to explore whether L2 learners, particularly adult learners, are able to develop nativelike competence in grammatical morphemes such as tense, plural, and gender markers or in syntactic agreement involving these morphemes. We may refer to this line of research as the acquirability topic (as different from the parsing topic) in sentence processing research.

This topic is of paramount importance for second language acquisition and processing research, as the identification of what is and is not acquirable in L2 learning is essential in understanding how L1 and L2 learning differ. In spite of its importance, the acquirability issue has seldom been a direct and explicit topic for debate or empirical research in adult L2 research. Instead, it often surfaces or is implied in the study of two other SLA topics: the accessibility of UG in adult SLA and the critical period hypothesis. Two opposing views can be identified in the study of both topics. In UG-related research, some researchers believe that the learning of both L1 and L2 is guided by Universal Grammar (UG) and thus the processes involved are essentially the same. In this view, adults also have the ability to develop nativelike competence at least in structures that are considered part of UG (e.g., Flynn, 1989; White, 1989). Others postulate that the processes involved in adult L2 learning are fundamentally different from those underlying child L1 learning and that it is rare, if not impossible, for adults to develop nativelike competence at least in some areas of a new language (Bley-Vroman, 1989; Schachter, 1988). In relation to the critical period debate, recognizing the presence of a critical period essentially suggests that there are structures that are not acquirable in adult L2 learning (e.g., Hawkins & Chan, 1997; Johnson & Newport, 1989). Others are more inclined to reject the existence of a maturation-based critical period and tend to attribute non-nativelike performance by adult L2 learners to factors such as less than optimal input, limited level of education or L2 use, continued use of L1 (e.g., Flege, Yeni-Komshian, & Liu, 1999). In both line of research, grammatical morphemes such as tense and plural marker are used as target structures. Results from these studies are often difficult to interpret due to methodological issues, particularly the type of data collected.

7.2 Methodological Considerations for Assessing Acquisition

Effective exploration of the acquirability issue, as well as the UG-SLA and critical period topics, hinges on the employment of adequate methods for assessing acquisition. At the center of the methodological considerations is the question of what data would constitute evidence for nativelike competence involving a specific structure. The assessment of acquisition, both in the study of UG-related L2 learning and the critical period hypothesis and in studying L2 acquisition in general, has traditionally relied on accuracy data. Such data may be collected from spontaneous L2 production, picture- or video-based description or retelling, multiple choice tasks, and the GJT. L2 speakers' performance was analyzed in terms of their accuracy (% of correct use or decision) in using, choosing, and judging the target structures.

This accuracy-based approach has at least two limitations for exploring the acquirability issue. The first is the potential involvement of explicit metalinguistic knowledge. Syntactic structures such as word order and inflectional morphemes such as plural and tense markers are often explicitly taught quite early in classroom instruction. This means that most classroom learners have explicit knowledge about the form and usage of these structures. Assuming that researchers are interested in whether learners have developed native-like competence involving these structures rather than whether they have obtained explicit metalinguistic knowledge about them, every effort should be made to minimize the involvement of explicit knowledge in assessing acquisition. However, many tasks that have been used to generate such accuracy data either encourage the participants to rely on their explicit knowledge (e.g., the GJT) or are not designed to minimize the involvement of such knowledge. As has been pointed out by several researchers (e.g., DeKeyser, 2003; Jiang, 2007; Ellis, 2002), even in spontaneous production or when participants were asked to complete a task under time pressure, it is difficult to rule out the involvement of explicit knowledge. The second limitation may be referred to as the 80% problem. When a NNS shows an accuracy rate of 80% in using a particular syntactic structure or grammatical morpheme (e.g., Hinz, Krause, Rast, Shoemaker, & Watorek, 2013), it may be subject to different interpretations.

One may consider the performance as indication of acquisition as it is higher than a chance effect of 50% accuracy, e.g., in a GJT. Alternatively, one may consider such performance non-nativelike as it is significantly lower than the accuracy rate typically found among native speakers, e.g., 90%.

A methodological shift occurred in the 2000s away from the use of accuracy data. This new approach involves the employment of two different types of data, i.e., reaction time and brain response. The rationale underlying this approach is simple and straightforward: if individuals have developed native-like and automatically accessible linguistic knowledge about a structure, as NS do, they should show a sensitivity to stimuli that violate this knowledge. This sensitivity can be assessed by comparing individuals' response to grammatical and ungrammatical sentences involving a specific structure. For example, a longer response time to a word in an ungrammatical sentence than to the same word in the grammatical sentence suggests a sensitivity to the grammatical error involved. Thus, a signature methodological feature of this approach is the creation of grammatical and ungrammatical versions of the stimulus sentences for comparing participants' responses. RT data or brain responses under the grammatical and ungrammatical conditions are then compared to determine if individuals are sensitive to grammatical violations, and this sensitivity is then taken as evidence for acquisition. We may refer to this practice as the sensitivity approach to the study of L2 acquisition that contrasts with the accuracy approach in previous research.

Two parallel lines of research have emerged in the past two decades that examined NNS' sensitivity to syntactic and morphosyntactic violations, one relying on behavioral measures and the other on electrophysiological measures. Representing this approach on the behavioral front is the use of primarily two methods: the SPRT, and eye-movement tracking.[1] In both methods, a participant is asked to read sentences for comprehension. The stimuli include sentences that have a grammatical version and an ungrammatical version that differ in the target structure, as illustrated in Example7.1. The two methods differ in how data are collected. In the SPRT as first adopted in Jiang (2004) for this purpose, sentences are displayed on a computer monitor word by word or phrase by phrase. The participants are asked to read each word or fragment of the sentences and then to press a button or key to proceed to the next part. This allows the computer to record how long they take in reading each word or phrase. They are urged to read as accurately and quickly as possible. Some or all sentences are followed by a comprehension question which serves both to encourage the participants to read for meaning and provide a means for checking if they indeed do so. The participants' reading time is usually measured at three locations of both versions: the word (or phrase) before the error, the error position, the word following the error, as shown by the underlined words in 7.1. The data for the first position can be used to check if RT measure is reliable. If it is, no difference should occur at this region. The second and third positions form the critical region. This is where a difference in RT may appear if an individual is sensitive to the error. A delay in reading the critical region of the ungrammatical sentence is considered as an indication of an individual's sensitivity to the error, and thus the acquisition of nativelike competence in the target structure.

7.1a   Mary did not like any of *the rings on* sale.
7.1b   *Mary did not like any of *the ring on* sale.

In an eye tracking study, the entire sentences are presented for reading comprehension. The participants' reading time is recorded while they read, which generates a rich set of data. They include first fixation duration (the duration of the initial fixation on a region), first-pass reading time or gaze duration (sum of all time spent fixating a region before moving out to either side, but see Frenck-Mestre, 2005 for a distinction between the two), second pass reading time (the sum of fixation durations on a region after the first exit out of the region), total reading time (sum of all reading times on a region regardless of when the fixations occur), regression path time (sum of all times between the first fixation and the exit out of the region to the right), and regression rates (the proportion of trials on which there is an eye movement to an earlier part of a sentence). Individuals' sensitivity to structural anomalies is assessed by means of both reading times and regression rates. Longer reading times and higher rates of regression for the ungrammatical sentences are considered indications of a processing difficulty and thus a sensitivity to morphosyntactic violations.

On the electrophysiological front, NNS' response to structural violations has been studied by means of event-related potentials (ERP) which is an application of the electroencephalogram (EEG) technique to measuring the electrophysiological activities of the brain while an individual is performing a linguistic task (i.e., the event). This is achieved by placing electrodes on participants' scalp that detect the change of electrical voltages in various parts of the brain. In studying morphosyntactic sensitivity, electrodes are often positioned to measure brain activities in four regions: left anterior, right anterior, left posterior, right posterior, including the midline. Data analysis is usually focused on the comparison of brain responses to grammatical and ungrammatical sentences at different electrodes and at different time windows. In the latter case, variations also exist across studies, but for illustration purposes, individuals' responses can be considered in the following four time windows: 100 ms to 300 ms, 300 ms to 500 ms, 500 ms to 800 ms, and 800 ms to 1200 ms after the onset of an error in the stimuli. Similarities and differences in response patterns between NS and NNS are examined as a way to assess the development of nativelike competence among NNS (See Steinhauer, 2014 for a recent review of this method as applied to SLA research).

A signature ERP component that is closely associated with morphosyntactic anomalies is P600, first discovered by Osterhout and Holcomb (1992). It is a positive-going deflection, often broadly distributed across electrodes, that begins to show around 500 ms and peaks around 600 ms after the onset of a syntactic (e.g., phrase structure) or a morphosyntactic (e.g., gender agreement) violation. A second ERP component that is believed by some to be related to morphosyntactic processing is left anterior negativity, or LAN. This ERP component is a negative-going deflection that often occurs between 300 ms to 500 ms after the onset of a syntactic anomaly and is most pronounced on the electrodes placed on the left anterior region. When this negativity appears earlier, e.g., 100 ms to 300 ms after the onset of an error, it is often referred to as early left anterior negativity, or ELAN. The three ERP components are illustrated in Figure 7.1. In comparison to P600, left anterior negativity (including ELAN) is a much less consistent effect. These two ERP components, ELAN and P600, often together referred to as the biphasic LAN-P600 pattern, have been observed in some L1 studies (e.g., Barber & Carreiras, 2005; Chen, Shu, Liu, Zhao, & Li, 2007; Friederici, 2002), but only P600 was observed in other studies (e.g., Ainsworth-Darnell, Shulman, & Boland, 1998; Allen, Badecker, & Osterhout, 2003; Frenck-Mestre, Osterhout, McLaughlin, & Foucart, 2008).

This online approach (both behavioral and electrophysiological) is advantageous over the accuracy measure in several ways. First, data collection is done online in the sense that data are collected while the cognitive process is ongoing or unfolding. This is achieved by a) embedding the critical stimuli (e.g., words) in a larger linguistic unit (e.g., sentences), b) emphasizing response speed, and c) measuring response latencies or brain activity while the participants are in the middle of performing the linguistic task, rather than after they have completed the task (e.g., in a GJT).[2] These measures provide a more sensitive means for uncovering the retrieval and application

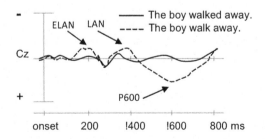

Figure 7.1 Illustration of Three ERP Components Related to Morphosyntactic Processing

of linguistic knowledge in language processing, as pointed out in Jiang (2012, pp. 8–9). Second, the measure is dichotomic in the sense that individuals either show or do not show a sensitivity to a structural violation. This helps alleviate the 80% problem. Third, productive use of an L2 often makes L2 speakers more grammar or accuracy conscious, which motivates them to rely on explicit knowledge. The use of a receptive task takes this motivation away. Thus, it is much less likely for NNS to rely on explicit knowledge while performing a reading task.

7.3 Research Findings

A large number of studies have been published to examine whether NNS are able to show a nativelike sensitivity to morphosyntactic violations. These "sensitivity" studies are reviewed in the following two subsections, with behavioral studies preceding electrophysiological studies.

7.3.1 Behavioral Studies

In one of the earliest online study of NNS' sensitivity to morphosyntactic violations, Guillelmon and Grosjean (2001) presented French noun phrases to NS and English-speaking NNS of French who had an early or late onset age for French learning. The stimuli were divided into congruent and incongruent conditions where the determiner or modifier agreed and did not agree with the noun in gender (e.g., *la jolie glace/*le joli glace*, "the nice mirror"). The participants' task was to listen to the phrase and repeat the noun as soon as possible, a task they referred to as shadowing. Based on the earlier findings from NS, they reasoned that if NNS of French had also developed nativelike knowledge about gender marking, they would behave like NS in producing a faster RT on congruent than on incongruent items. If NNS did not possess nativelike knowledge, they would show no difference. The results showed that only early learners produced a nativelike response pattern. A similar paradigm was adopted by Scherag et al. (2004) in combination with a LDT. The participants were asked to listen to German NPs that consisted of an adjective and a noun. Similar to Guillelmon and Grosjean's (2001) study, gender marking was manipulated between the adjective and the noun to create congruent and incongruent stimuli. NNS of German were found to perform differently from NS.

In the first study that adopted the SPRT for this purpose, Jiang (2004) tested Chinese ESL speakers on sentences involving number disagreement, such as Example 7.2. The NNS were found to show no difference in reading the critical region of the grammatical and ungrammatical sentences while English NS did. In order to determine whether the lack of sensitivity among NNS had resulted from the use of the SPRT itself or from a lack of sensitivity to subject-verb agreement, two additional structures were tested with the same method, one involving verb subcategorization and the other subject-verb agreement between a pronoun and a *be* verb, as shown in Examples 7.3 and 7.4 (with the slash separating grammatical and ungrammatical versions). The ESL speakers were found to show a sensitivity to both types of errors, thus ruling out the two alternative explanations.

7.2a   *The words on the <u>screen were hard</u> to recognize.*
7.2b   **The word on the <u>screen were hard</u> to recognize.*
7.3   *The teacher encouraged/*insisted the students to send the letter to the president.*
7.4   *It is clear that she/*I is open to this suggestion.*

Many subsequent studies have produced similar findings. In order to further explore whether the lack of sensitivity had to do with subject-verb agreement, Jiang (2007) used sentences that included a plural marking error but did not involve subject-verb agreement such as *Susan did not like any of the ring on sale*. Again, Chinese ESL speakers showed no sensitivity to the plural marking errors. A lack of sensitivity has also been found in the processing of English third person singular markers by Japanese ESL speakers (Shibuya & Wakabayashi, 2008; Bannai, 2011), English plural markers by Japanese speakers (Jiang, Novokshanova, Masuda, & Wang, 2011), Spanish gender markers by English speakers (Tokowicz & Warren, 2010), and Korean honorific markers by English speakers (Mueller & Jiang, 2013).

However, several other studies showed otherwise. English speakers were found to show a sensitivity to Spanish gender errors in Sagarra and Herschensohn (2010, 2011), Foote (2011), and Keating (2009), and to French gender errors in Coughlin and Tremblay (2013) and Foucart and Frenck-Mestre (2012).

Table 7.1 summarizes the information of 19 such studies on this topic. As is clear from the table, these studies involved a variety of L1–L2 combinations and participants of varying L2 proficiencies. If one considers these studies in terms of a single question of whether NNS showed nativelike sensitivity, the answer is almost a half-half split. There are 15 positive and 18 negative results (see the last column of the table). A close inspection of these studies helped reveal a few factors that may help explain this conflicting pattern. When these factors are taken into consideration, a clearer picture begins to emerge. These factors are morphological congruency, the task, and agreement distance.

The first influencing factor is morphological congruency. From the standpoint of any L2 learner, an L2 morpheme may be classified as a congruent or

Table 7.1 Summary of Behavioral Studies of Morphosyntactic Sensitivity Among NNS

References	L1:L2	Prof[1]	Structure	Additional variables	L1–L2 Similarity[2]	Task	Results: Nativelike?[3]
Guillelmon and Grosjean (2001)	English: French	A	Gender	Early/late learners	X	Primed shadowing	Yes/No
Scherag et al. (2004)	English: German	A	Gender		X	Primed LDT	No
Jiang (2004)	Chinese: English	A	Number		X	SPR	No
Jiang (2007)	Chinese: English	A	Number		X	SPR	No
Shibuya and Wakabayashi (2008)	Japanese: English	I	3rd Person singular	Missing/ overuse	X	SPR	No/Yes
Sagarra and Herschensohn (2010)	English: Spanish	I/L	Gender		X	SPR	Yes/No
Tokowicz and Warren (2010)	English: Spanish	L	Aspect/ Number/ Gender		✓/✓/x	SPR	Yes/Yes/ No
Bannai (2011)	Japanese: English	I	3rd Person singular	Missing/ overuse	X	SPR	No/Yes
Foote (2011)	English: Spanish	A	Gender/ Number		x/✓	SPR	Yes
Jiang et al. (2011)	Japanese/ Russian: English	A	Number		x/✓	SPR	No/Yes
Sagarra and Herschensohn (2011)	English: Spanish	I/L	Gender		x	SPR	Yes/No

(Continued)

Table 7.1 (Continued)

References	L1:L2	Prof[1]	Structure	Additional variables	L1–L2 Similarity[2]	Task	Results: Nativelike?[3]
VanPatten, Keating, and Leeser (2012)	English: Spanish	I	Person/Number		✓	SPR	No/No
Coughlin and Tremblay (2013)	English: French	A/I	Number		✓	SPR	Yes/No
Mueller and Jiang (2013)	English: Korean	A	Honorific		x	SPR	No
Roberts and Liszka (2013)	French/German: English	A	Aspect		✓/x	SPR	Yes/No
Keating (2009)	English: Spanish	A, I, L	Gender	+/- adjacent	x	Eye tracking	Advanced: Yes/No Others: No/No
Foucart and Frenck-Mestre (2012, Exp. 4)	English: French	A	Gender		x	Eye tracking	Yes
Sagarra and Ellis (2013)	English/Romanian: Spanish	A, L	Tense		✓	Eye tracking	Yes
Lim and Christianson (2014)	Korean: English	?	Number		x	Eye tracking	Yes

Notes:

1 prof=proficiency, A=advanced, I=intermediate, L=low, ?=no sufficient information provided.

2 x=no similar morpheme in L1, ✓=a similar morpheme present in L1.

3 yes=nativelike responses found, no=nativelike responses not found; the results before and after the slash corresponds to the conditions separated by a slash shown in the other columns of the same study.

an incongruent one depending on whether there is a similar morpheme in the L1. The English plural marker is a congruent one to Spanish and French ESL speakers because the plural meaning is also morphologically marked in these languages. The same morpheme is an incongruent for Chinese and Japanese ESL speakers because the plural meaning is not obligatorily marked with a grammatical morpheme in these languages.

The role of morphological congruency is quite clear if we consider the findings by separating congruent and incongruent morphemes. NNS were more likely to show a nativelike sensitivity when congruent morphemes were involved. For example, advanced L2 speakers in the three studies listed in Table 7.1 that included only congruent morphemes (i.e., VanPatten et al., 2012; Coughlin & Tremblay, 2013; Sagarra & Ellis, 2013) all showed a native-like sensitivity to grammatical violations. The findings from studies that only tested incongruent morphemes present a sharp contrast. There are 12 such studies in Table 7.1. Seven of them showed that NNS did not produce native-like performance when incongruent morphemes were involved. More importantly, in studies that included both congruent and incongruent morphemes, different morphemes showed a different pattern. For example, Tokowicz and Warren (2010) tested English learners of Spanish on three Spanish structures: aspect marking, number marking, and gender marking. The participants showed a nativelike sensitivity to the first two congruent structures but not to the last incongruent structure. Jiang et al. (2011) tested Russian and Japanese ESL speakers on plural violations and only Russian ESL speakers for whom the plural marker was a congruent one showed nativelike sensitivity. In the study reported by Roberts and Liszka (2013), French and German ESL speakers were tested on English aspect marking which was a congruent morpheme for French ESL speakers but not for German ESL speakers. Only French ESL speakers showed a nativelike pattern. Considered as a whole, the results from these studies suggest a morphological congruency effect: L2 speakers are more likely to show a nativelike sensitivity to morphosyntactic violations for congruent morphemes than for incongruent morphemes.

There are exceptions to this pattern. Six studies in Table 7.1 showed a nativelike sensitivity to incongruent morphemes among NNS (Foote, 2011; Foucart & Frenck-Mestre, 2012; Keating, 2009; Lim & Christianson, 2014; Sagarra & Herschensohn, 2010, 2011). Three of them employed the eye tracking method. As a matter of fact, all four studies in Table 7.1 that used this method produced nativelike performance among NNS regardless of morphological congruency. In contrast, only three out of 13 studies produced similar results on incongruent morphemes when the other methods were used. Thus, the method used seems to affect the results, as well, with nativelike sensitivity observed more often in eye tracking studies than in SLRT studies.

The third factor is distance. The elements of an agreement structure may appear adjacent to each other (e.g., *two books*) or separated by other elements (e.g., *two recently published books*). They may appear within the same phrase or across phrase or clause boundaries (e.g., *The books I borrowed are on the desk*). Thus, a distinction can be made between adjacent violations and distant violations. Agreement distance affected performance. For example, Keating (2009) tested English-speaking learners of Spanish at three proficiency levels on gender agreement between a noun and an adjective (underlined) that is within the same DP (determiner phrase), VP, or CP (complementizer phrase) of the noun, as illustrated in Examples 7.5–7.7. The agreement error involved two adjacent words in the first structure but they were distant in the second and third structures. The results showed that only the advanced group showed a sensitivity to gender violation involving two adjacent words. The same group showed no sensitivity to gender violation in the other two structures, and the intermediate and beginner groups showed no sensitivity to all three structures. Similarly, the participants in Foote (2011) showed a significant interaction between grammaticality and distance, indicating a greater sensitivity to adjacent violations than to distant violations.

7.5.   Una *casa pequeña* cuesta mucho en San Francisco.
(A *small house* costs a lot in San Francisco.)

7.6.   La *casa* es bastante *pequeña* y necesita muchas reparaciones.
(The *house* is quite *small* and needs a lot of repairs.)

7.7.   Una *casa* cuesta menos si es *pequeña* y necesita reparaciones.
(A *house* costs less if it is *small* and needs repairs.)

In sum, the following statements summarize the findings from the 19 published studies reviewed here:

a)   Adult L2 learners showed a nativelike sensitivity to agreement violations in all studies that used the eye tracking method. These violations involved both congruent and incongruent morphemes.

b)   In studies that employed the other methods, NNS are more likely to show a nativelike sensitivity to violations involving congruent morphemes (five out of six, Foote, 2011; Jiang et al., 2011; Coughlin & Tremblay, 2013; Sagarra & Ellis, 2013; Tokowicz & Warren, 2010, but not VanPatten et al., 2012) than to violations involving incongruent morphemes (three out of 13).

c)   NNS are more likely to show a nativelike sensitivity to adjacent than to distant morphosyntactic violations.

7.3.2 Electrophysiological Studies

Following the studies involving L1 speakers, researchers have used electrophysiological measures to study the development of morphosyntactic competence among L2 speakers. Sabourin and Haverkort (2003) and Tokowicz and MacWhinney (2005) were among the first to focus on morphosyntactic violations specifically. In the latter study, English-speaking learners of Spanish were tested on the following three structures in Examples 7.8–7.10. Sentences with and without errors were presented visually word by word to the participants who were asked to decide if they were grammatical. Data from nine electrodes covering left and right anterior, left and right posterior, the midline, and the central area were used for analysis in two time windows, 500 ms to 700 ms and 700 ms to 900 ms after the onset of the critical word (underlined words in the above examples). A separate GJT task was administered to assess their explicit knowledge of the structures. The participants demonstrated a P600 to the first and the third violations, but not to the second. Fourteen ERP studies are summarized in Table 7.2.[3]

7.8   *Progressive marking*
      Su abuela cocina/*cocinanda muy bien.
      "His grandmother cooks/*cooking very well."
7.9   *Number agreement in determiner+noun pairs*
      Los/*El niños están jugando.
      "The$_{plural/*singular}$ boys are playing."
7.10 *Gender agreement in determiner+noun pairs*
      Ellos fueron a una/*un fiesta.
      "They went to a$_{fem/*mas}$ party$_{fem}$."

A few methodological details should be noted before discussing the findings from electrophysiological studies. With the exception of three studies in which the stimuli were presented auditorily, supposedly at a normal speed (Mueller et al., 2005; Hahne et al., 2006; Rossi et al., 2006), most studies adopted a timed reading procedure whereby stimuli were presented visually word by word (or chunk by chunk) at a predetermined rate. The rate of presentation varied across studies, e.g., 300 ms for each word followed by a blank screen for 350 ms (hence 300+350) in Tokowicz and MacWhinney (2005), 500+200 in Chen et al. (2007), 450+150 in Frenck-Mestre et al. (2008), 250+250 in Sabourin and Stowe (2008), 500+150 in Foucart and Frenck-Mestre (2012), and 700+0 in Hahne et al. (2006). In most studies, the reading or listening task was completed in combination with a grammaticality judgment task. A participant was

Table 7.2 Summary of Electrophysiological Studies of Morphosyntactic Sensitivity Among NNS

References	L1:L2	Prof[1]	Structure	Additional Variables	Task[2]	DV[3]	Results: Nativelike?[4]
Tokowicz and MacWhinney (2005)	English: Spanish	L	Aspect/ Number/ Gender		TR+GJT	P600	Yes/No/Yes
Ojima, Nakata, and Kakigi (2005)	Japanese: English	A/L	3rd singular		TR+CQ	LAN, P600	LAN:Yes/No P600: No/No
Mueller, Hahne, Fujii, and Friederici (2005)	German: Japanese	L	Case		Listen+ GJT	LAN, P600	P600:Yes LAN: No
Rossi, Gugler, Friederici, and Hahne (2006)	Italian: German; German: Italian	A/L	Person, number		Listen+ GJT	LAN, P600	P600:Yes/Yes LAN:Yes/No
Osterhout, McLaughlin, Pitkänen, Frenck-Mestre, and Molinaro (2006)	English: French	L	Person/ Number		?	P600	Yes/No
Hahne, Mueller, and Clahsen (2006)	Russian: German	A	Tense, number	regularity	listen+ Sentence Recognition	LAN, P600	*Tense regular* LAN:Yes; P600:Yes *Tense irregular* LAN: No; P600: No *Plural regular* LAN: No; P600:Yes *Plural irregular* LAN: No; P600: No
Chen et al. (2007)	Chinese: English;	I	Number		TR+GJT	LAN, P600	LAN: No P600: No
Frenck-Mestre et al. (2008)	German: French	A	Person, number	+/-Phono realization	TR+SJT	LAN, P600	LAN: No/No P600:Yes/No

Study	prof	DV	Condition	Task	ERP	Results
Sabourin and Stowe (2008)	German/Romance: Dutch	A	Gender		TR+GJT	P600	Yes/No
Gillon Dowens, Vergara, Barber, and Carreiras (2010)	English: Spanish	A	Number, gender	+/-adjacent	TR+GJT	LAN, P600	*Number* LAN:Yes/No P600:Yes/Yes *Gender* LAN:Yes/No P600:Yes/Yes
Gillon Dowens, Guo, Guo, Barber, and Carreiras (2011)	Chinese: Spanish	I	Number/ Gender		TR+GJT	LAN, P600	LAN: No/No P600:Yes/Yes
Foucart and Frenck-Mestre (2011)	German: French	A	Gender	+/-L1–L2 similarity	TR+SJT	P600	P600:Yes/No
Foucart and Frenck-Mestre (2012)	English: French	A	Gender	N+adj/ adj+N/ N+pred adj	TR+GAJT	P600,	P600:Yes/No/No
Rossi, Kroll, and Dussias (2014)	English: Spanish	A	Number, gender	+/- high proficiency	TR+GJT	P600	*Number:Yes Gender:Yes/No*

Notes:

1 prof=proficiency, A=advanced, I=intermediate, L=low.

2 TR=timed reading, CQ=comprehension question, SJT=semantic judgment task, GAJT=general acceptability judgment task.

3 DV=dependent variable

4 Yes=nativelike responses found, No=nativelike responses not found; the results before and after the slash corresponds to the conditions separated by a slash shown in the other columns of the same study.

asked to read or listen to a sentence and then make a yes/no judgment regarding the grammatical acceptability of the stimuli. The exceptions were the use of comprehension questions in Ojima et al. (2005), a sentence recognition task in Hahne et al. (2006), and a semantic acceptability task in Frenck-Mestre et al. (2008) and Foucart and Frenck-Mestre (2011). All studies used the ERP component of P600 as a measure of NNS' sensitivity to morphosyntactic violation, and many also used LAN.

When electrophysiological evidence is considered against findings from behavioral studies, a clear difference presents itself: more ERP studies demonstrated nativelike responses among NNS than behavioral studies. Almost all ERP studies showed that NNS were able to produce nativelike sensitivity to some morphosyntax violations under some circumstances, sometimes with quantitative differences from NS, e.g., the P600 deflection peaking later or being weaker in amplitude among NNS (Rossi et al., 2006; Sabourin & Stowe, 2008). The participants in six of the seven studies that considered incongruent morphemes produced some nativelike brain responses. The only clear-cut exception was Chen et al. (2007) who tested Chinese learners of English on plural marking errors (e.g., *The price of the cars were too high). While NS showed both LAN and P600, NNS in this study produced neither deflection.

The second noticeable pattern is that, where both LAN and P600 were measured, NNS were more likely to produce a P600 than LAN. For example, English-Spanish bilinguals in Gillon Dowens et al. (2010) showed a nativelike P600 to both gender and number violations that appeared at the beginning and in the middle of a sentence, but they produced LAN only when errors occurred at the beginning. The Chinese-speaking learners of Spanish in Gillon Dowens et al. (2011) showed P600, but not LAN. High-proficiency participants in Rossi et al. (2006) showed LAN and P600 to person/number agreement violations but the low-proficiency participants only showed a delayed P600. Similarly, P600 but not LAN was observed of the participants with training in Mueller et al. (2005). The only exception is Ojima et al. (2005). They tested Japanese learners of English on semantic and morphosyntactic violations, the latter involving the third person singular -s (e.g., *Turtles moves slowly). The stimulus sentences were presented visually chunk by chunk, and the participants were asked to read the sentences and then respond to true/false statements based on the meaning of the sentences. High-proficiency NNS showed a nativelike LAN to morphosyntactic violations, but both high- and low-proficiency NNS failed to show a P600. The overall pattern shown among these studies is consistent with that involving native speakers where the P600 effect has been found to be much more consistent than the LAN effect.

ERP studies have produced conflicting results regarding the role of morphological congruency. Some findings confirmed this role. For example, both studies that failed to show nativelike P600 among NNS involved an incongruent morpheme, specifically English third person singular among Japanese ESL speakers (Ojima et al., 2005) and English plural marking among Chinese ESL speakers (Chen et al., 2007). In Gillon Dowens et al. (2010), English learners of Spanish produced a greater negativity to number violations (congruent) than to gender violations (incongruent). At the same time, several studies showed that NNS responded to incongruent morpheme violations in a way similar to NS, suggesting that morphological congruency did not affect the development of nativelike sensitivity among adult L2 learners. Such cases include English learners' response to gender violation in Spanish (Gillon Dowens et al., 2010; Rossi et al., 2014; Tokowicz & MacWhinney, 2005) and French (Osterhout et al., 2006) and Chinese-speaking participants' response to number and gender violation in Spanish (Gillon Dowens et al., 2011).

In addition to morphological congruency, L1–L2 similarity can also be defined at the level of how a rule is applied across languages when a morpheme is present in both languages. For example, French, German, and Dutch all mark gender morphologically, but the specific rules are different in these languages, with gender marking being much more similar between German and Dutch than between German and French. When L1–L2 similarity was examined at the level of specific rule application, the results from ERP studies were quite consistent: NNS were more likely to produce nativelike responses when the two languages overlap in morphosyntactic rules (Foucart & Frenck-Mestre, 2011; Sabourin & Stowe, 2008; Tokowicz & MacWhinney, 2005). For example, Tokowicz and MacWhinney (2005) tested English learners of Spanish on two congruent morphemes: progressive marking, and determiner+noun number agreement (in addition to incongruent gender marking). While aspect and number are marked in both languages, they differ in how these morphemes are used. Progressive marking is highly similar in the two languages, but number agreement applies to determiner+noun pairs only in Spanish. Thus, to English speakers, number agreement between a determiner and a noun represents a new structure. The participants were asked to read sentences presented at a predetermined rate and make a grammaticality judgment. P600 was measured at two time windows of 500–700 ms and 700–900 ms after the onset of an error. In support of the role of L1–L2 similarity, the P600 deflection was found in both time windows for progressive aspect violations but not for violations involving determiner+noun number agreement.

Some of these studies manipulated agreement distance and confirmed its role. Foucart and Frenck-Mestre (2012) tested English learners of French on gender agreement involving three structures: noun+adjective, adjective+noun, and noun+predicative adjective. The first two involved agreement between two adjacent words, but the latter a distant agreement, as shown in Examples 7.11 (an adjacent noun+adjective structure) and 7.12 (a non-adjacent noun+predicative adjective structure). While NS showed P600 to all three types of violations, NNS only showed a sensitivity to adjacent ones. See a similar finding in Gillon Dowens et al. (2010).

7.11 *Depuis une semaine, les <u>chaises</u>*fem *<u>vertes</u>*fem/*<u>verts</u>*masc *sont dans le jardin.*
(Since last week the *green chairs* are in the garden.)

7.12 *Au printemps, les <u>pommes</u>*fem *sont <u>vertes</u>*fem/*<u>verts</u>*masc *sur cet arbre.*
(In spring *apples* are *green* on this tree).

A new variable investigated in the ERP studies is phonological realization. Some grammatical morphemes are orthographically marked but phonologically silent in some languages. For example, a French verb is spelled differently when it follows a first-person singular, a second-person singular, and a second-person plural subject. e.g., *je parle, tu parles, vous parlez.* Of the three inflected verb forms, the pronunciation is the same between the first two, and the third one has a different pronunciation. Thus, a distinction can be made between morphosyntactic violations that involve a phonologically realized and a phonological silent form of a morpheme. Two studies demonstrated the role of phonological realization (Osterhout et al., 2006; Frenck-Mestre et al., 2008). In the latter study, for example, German learners of French were tested with sentences involving subject-verb person disagreement. They used sentences such as Example 7.13. The two violations illustrated in the example involved subject-verb person/number disagreement that exists in both German and French, but the first violation (*mangez*) is a phonologically realized inflected form of the verb while the second violation (*manges*) involves a phonologically silent one. In confirming the role of phonological realization, the participants were found to produce a nativelike P600 to the former type of violation but a negative deflection to the latter.

7.13 *Le matin je mange/*mangez/*manges du pain.*
(In the morning I eat bread.)

In sum, findings from electrophysiological studies largely confirmed the role of morphological congruency and violation distance, and they revealed the role of additional factors such as the cross-linguistic overlap in the application of a specific rule and phonological realization. Overall, electrophysiological data tend to favor the conclusion that NNS are able to show a nativelike sensitivity to morphosyntactic violations.

7.4 Understanding the Conflicting Findings

A consideration of the findings from both behavioral and electrophysiological approaches reveals a significant amount of inconsistencies both between these two approaches and between specific methods. Results from the studies that employed the same method diverge, too. This section outlines some potential explanations for the inconsistencies in this line of research. Four issues are considered: the methodological differences between behavioral and electrophysiological approach, the methodological difference between the SPRT and eye tracking, the proficiency factor, and the distance effect. The explanation for the role of morphological congruency is presented separately in Section 7.5.

7.4.1 Discrepancies Across Paradigms

7.4.1.1 Behavioral and ERP Studies

Data from the behavioral and electrophysiological approach showed a different pattern with a nativelike performance among NNS shown in ERP data more than behavioral data. Of the 13 behavioral studies that involved an incongruent morpheme in Table 7.1, two studies tested adjacent violations and one tested a unique participant population (Foote, 2011). All remaining ten studies showed that adult L2 learners are not able to demonstrate nativelike sensitivity to violations involving an incongruent morpheme. In contrast, of the seven published ERP studies in Table 7.2 that tested incongruent morphemes, six showed a nativelike pattern among NNS.

One way to interpret the discrepancy is to assume that the ERPs provide a more sensitive means than behavioral measures so that the former captured the morphosyntactic sensitivity missed by the latter. For example, the changes in electrical voltage on different parts of the scalp, which is the primary data in ERP studies, occurs automatically without an individual's conscious intervention, and thus are linked to the cognitive process of morphosyntactic processing in a more direct way. In contrast, the primary data in a self-paced reading task, the reading times, come from a participant's overt physical responses, in this case key or button pressing, which is extraneous to the process of language processing. The ERP method may be able to detect subtle and spontaneous brain responses that may not result in any observable differences at a behavioral level. In this sense, the ERP data provide a better assessment of NNS's sensitivity to morphosyntactic violations.

However, an alternative explanation may be found when we consider other methodological details associated with the ERP studies. All the ERP studies that showed nativelike responses to an incongruent morpheme employed the timed reading task in combination with a grammaticality judgment task. A participant was asked to read the stimulus sentences and then make a judgment regarding their grammatical accuracy or acceptability. The participants' attention was in no doubt focused on grammatical accuracy while performing the task, as required by the task. They were doing grammatical analysis rather than reading comprehension. This is certainly contradictory to the initial intention to shift from offline tasks to online tasks (e.g., Jiang, 2004) which was to direct the participants' attention away from grammatical accuracy and make the use of explicit knowledge less likely.

This raises the issue of what P600 exactly measures. Hahne and Friederici (1999; Friederici, 2002) suggested that P600 may reflect "fairly controlled later processes of reanalysis and repair" (p. 195) while early negativity reflects a first-pass automatic processes. If this is true, one may wonder if the observation of P600 among NNS was dependent on or a result from the use of the GJT. The fact that the only ERP study reviewed here that asked the participants to respond to reading comprehension questions rather than performing grammaticality judgment did not produce a P600 (Ojima et al., 2005) seems to support this possibility. Thus, an alternative explanation of the discrepancies is that because the participants were asked to perform a GJT, they were consciously engaged in grammatical analysis while reading or listening to stimulus sentences, which resulted in the noticing of morphosyntactic violations and thus the observation of P600.

Little is known about how task demand, in this case whether sentence reading is combined with a GJT or focused on comprehension, would affect the observation of P600. It is desirable to conduct ERP studies in which different tasks (e.g., GJT and reading comprehension) are used to test the same group of participants on the same structure. Such studies would help reveal whether this ERP component observed of NNS reflect the same cognitive processes as those among NS. Further research is needed to understand what this deflection means (see Gillon Dowens et al., 2010 and Molinaro, Barber, & Carreiras, 2011 for related discussion) and whether and under what circumstances it is a valid indication of the possession of nativelike knowledge among NNS.

7.4.1.2 The SPRT vs. Eye Tracking

Eye-movement recording and self-paced reading are often employed together in sentence processing studies. In most such studies, they have produced comparable results (e.g., Ferreira & Henderson, 1990; Garnsey, Pearlmutter, Myers, & Lotocky, 1997; Traxler, Pickering, & McElree, 2002). However, a striking contrast exists in the outcomes of the studies of NNS' morphosyntactic sensitivity, as the review above suggests. All four eye tracking studies demonstrated nativelike performance among NNS regardless of morphological congruency while most studies that employed the SPRT as well as priming showed the opposite findings regarding incongruent morphemes. In considering the discrepancy, one may argue that eye tracking offers a more sensitive measure of individuals' responses than self-paced reading does. First, it shares the same advantage as the electrophysiological method does in that the data are more directly tied with the reading process. Second, it provided multiple measures of a participant's responses while only a single response was recorded in self-paced reading, as pointed out by Lim and Christianson (2014). A drawback of this explanation, though, is the fact that self-paced reading has been shown to be sensitive or powerful enough to demonstrate NNS's sensitivity to other syntactic and morphosyntactic violations, such as subcategorization violations in Jiang (2004) and violations involving congruent morphemes such as in Tokowicz and Warren (2010), Jiang et al. (2011), Roberts and Liszka (2013).

I want to suggest another possibility. Successful application of any method for studying NNS' grammatical sensitivity hinges on the extent to which a participant is not paying attention to grammatical accuracy. This can be achieved by creating a situation where the application of explicit knowledge is not necessary or difficult. Jiang (2004) first adopted the self-paced reading task exactly for this reason. In a self-paced reading task, a participant is asked to read for comprehension rather than to pay attention to grammatical accuracy. The sentences are presented word by word such that stimulus sentences are never shown in their entirety for a participant to go back and forth for checking grammatical errors. And a participant is asked to read as quickly as possible. These features of the task, i.e., the receptive nature of the task, the transient nature of stimulus display, and the emphasis on comprehension and speed, combine to make the application of explicit knowledge both unnecessary and difficult.

Eye-movement recording, however, differs from self-paced reading in two important ways. One of them is that sentences are usually presented in their entirety in eye tracking studies. The second is that the participants are usually asked to read at a normal speed in eye tracking studies while they were asked to read as quickly as possible in self-paced reading. Thus, while the eye tracking paradigm has the advantages of mimicking natural reading, it also creates a condition where participants have both the time and the stimuli in front of them for them to go back and forth for checking grammatical accuracy if they desire to do so. The high regression rates reported in these studies (e.g., 55% to 60% in some conditions of Keating, 2009, 30% to 44% in many conditions in Foucart & Frenck-Mestre, 2012) indicated that they were indeed actively checking back and forth. Furthermore, in at least one eye tracking study, the participants were specifically instructed to "read the sentences silently and assess their syntactic and/or semantic acceptability" (Foucart & Frenck-Mestre, 2012, p. 243). When data were collected under a condition where the participants could or were encouraged to rely on their explicit knowledge, it is not surprising for NNS to notice the errors in the stimuli and thus show a sensitivity in some measures.

In sum, compared to data collected with a SPRT, data collected with eye tracking and electrophysiological means are more likely to be affected by participants' attention to grammatical accuracy. This may explain why more nativelike observations were made where the latter two methods were used. How task requirement and stimulus display may affect the cognitive processes under observation is certainly an area that is in need of considerable future research.

7.4.2 The Proficiency Factor

In most studies that manipulated proficiency as an independent variable, the results tended to confirm the role of proficiency in demonstrating nativelike performance among more proficient L2 speakers and a lack of such performance among less proficient participants. This is true of both behavioral studies (Coughlin & Tremblay, 2013; Keating, 2009; Sagarra & Herschensohn, 2010; Tokowicz & Warren, 2010) and electrophysiological studies (Ojima et al., 2005; Rossi et al., 2006; Rossi et al., 2014). However, a close look at the proficiency range of the participants across studies suggests that such consistent findings have to be interpreted with caution.

First of all, given the difficulty adult L2 learners have shown with grammatical morphemes, it is advantageous, in manipulating proficiency, to maintain a sufficient proficiency gap between groups, e.g., by including very advanced L2 speakers. A good example is Ojima et al. (2005) where the high-proficiency group included ESL speakers who had lived in an English-speaking country for an average of 3.7 years and used English daily and professionally. However, the participants in many of these proficiency-manipulated studies were college students. They were essentially from the same participant population, i.e., adult L2 learners who were studying the L2 in classroom at the college level. These L2 learners were placed in different proficiency groups on the basis of their test scores, course placement, or years of instruction or exposure (e.g., Coughlin & Tremblay, 2013; Keating, 2009; Rossi et al., 2014). However, in almost all of these studies, more proficient and less proficient speakers were found to show a different pattern of performance, with the former group behaving nativelike while the latter group non-nativelike. It seemed that no matter how the proficiency ranges and the criteria for grouping varied, the grouping in these studies had successfully separated those who had developed nativelike sensitivity and those who had not.

There are two potential problems with such results. First, these results seemed to suggest that nativelike sensitivity can be achieved exactly during that period of time or at the proficiency level that was used to separate the two groups. It is certainly not consistent with the long-standing difficulties adult L2 learners had demonstrated with incongruent morphemes or grammatical morphemes in general in many longitudinal and naturalistic studies (e.g.,

Franceschina, 2001; Lardiere, 1998; Long, 2003; Montrul, Foote, & Perpiñán, 2008; Sabourin, 2001).

Second, the results run into problems when findings from multiple studies are considered and compared. For example, several studies tested English-speaking learners of French or Spanish on gender agreement, and it is difficult to make sense of the results when proficiency is considered. The late English-French bilinguals in Guillelmon and Grosjean (2001) had lived in France for more than 20 years, used both English and French regularly, and rated their own oral comprehension proficiency in L1 English and L2 French as 6.8 and 6.0 on a 1–7 scale. There was every indication that these participants were highly proficient in L2 French. The participants in Sagarra and Herschensohn (2010) included fourth-year undergraduates and were rightly characterized as intermediate-level L2 Spanish speakers. The participants in Foucart and Frenck-Mestre (2012) were also English speakers studying French at a French university. It is reasonable to consider the participants in these latter two studies to be of much lower proficiency compared to those in Guillelmon and Grosjean. However, it was the participants in the latter two studies that produced nativelike performance, not those in the former. Similarly, Jiang (2004, 2007), Chen et al. (2007), and Gillon Dowens et al. (2011) all tested Chinese learners of English or Spanish on number or gender agreement. The participants in the latter two studies were all undergraduate or graduate students tested in China, and the participants in Jiang's studies were mostly graduate students living in the USA. If anything, the participants in the Jiang studies should be of higher proficiency than those third- or four-year undergraduates in Gillon Dowens et al. However, nativelike responses were observed of the participants in the latter study but not the other three. Admittedly, these studies used different methods and tested different structures. But the lack of nativelike responses among very advanced L2 speakers like those in Guillelmon and Grosjean (2001) does call for the exercise of caution in interpreting the proficiency-related findings.

Two additional issues related to proficiency are whom to test and how to assess their L2 proficiency. The study of NNS' sensitivity to morphosyntactic violations is motivated by the acquirability issue, i.e., whether adult L2 learners are able to develop nativelike competence in the area of morphosyntax in a new language. For this purpose, it is obligatory to test L2 speakers who have reached a steady state in their L2 morphosyntactic development. Testing less advanced learners always faces the risk of them developing nativelike competence with further experiences in the language in the future, thus incorrectly reaching a negative response to the question. However, few online studies have looked into this participant population so far. Longitudinal studies such as the one described in Osterhout et al. (2006) but with participants at a more advanced proficiency level may be most effective in capturing and validating the steady state. The second related issue is the long-standing challenge of how to assess a participant's L2 proficiency. A collaborative effort is needed for researchers working on this and related issues to develop and adopt a test of proficiency that is valid, sufficiently discriminative, and less time consuming than a comprehensive proficiency test so that it can be adopted in a lab setting. The use of such a test would make the proficiency-related comparison of research results across studies easier and more valid.

7.4.3 Explaining the Distance Effect

In both behavioral and ERP studies, NNS were found to be more likely to produce nativelike responses to adjacent violations than to distance violations. The cause of this distance effect is yet to be explored. One possibility is that an adjacent violation is more salient and thus easier to notice than a distant one. This explanation does not imply any differences in processing strategies in processing adjacent and distant agreement. A second possibility is that L2 learners may have stored adjective+noun or noun+adjective chunks in their memory through associative and frequency-based learning. A discrepancy between the input and these stored units can be noticed through a simple matching process. The detection of a distant violation, on the other hand, requires the application of abstract linguistic knowledge. A further possibility is that even when both types of disagreement involve the abstract structural computation, distant violations require more working memory to detect than adjacent violations do. There is some indication in support of this view in Sagarra and Herschensohn (2010). There was a correlation between the intermediate group's working memory performance and their ability to notice gender violations. All these speculations have yet to be tested.

7.5 Explaining the Morphological Congruency Effect

As the review in Section 7.3 indicates, there is compelling evidence, particularly in behavioral studies, for a morphological congruency effect among NNS in that they are more likely to produce a nativelike performance on congruent than on incongruent morphemes. Additional evidence for the morphological congruency effect is available in offline studies, as well. Jiang et al. (2011) summarized three lines of such evidence. First, several longitudinal studies documented a long-term difficulty in grammatical morphemes among highly advanced L2 speakers over an extended period of many years (Jia, 2003; Lardiere, 1998, 2007; Long, 2003; Schmidt, 1983). All these studies involved the learning and use of incongruent morphemes such as tense or plural markers by Chinese or Japanese speakers. The L2 speakers in these studies were considered highly proficient in English but showed a low accuracy rate in spontaneous production that would not improve over an extended period of time.

In contrast, one has yet to find a similar study that documented long-term difficulties involving a congruent morpheme. Second, when a study tested L2 speakers of different L1 backgrounds on a grammatical morpheme, those whose L1s had a similar morpheme consistently outperformed those whose L1s did not, even when the participants' overall L2 proficiency was matched. For example, the accuracy rates on English tense marking were above 95% and below 85% for German and Chinese ESL speakers, respectively in Hawkins and Liszka's (2003) study. Similar findings were reported by Bialystok and Miller (1999), McDonald (2000), and Sabourin, Stowe, and de Haan (2006). Finally, when the same participants were tested on multiple grammatical morphemes, they usually did better on congruent morphemes than on incongruent morphemes. For example, in a case study of Martin, a highly proficient English-Spanish bilingual speaker, Franceschina (2001) reported that among the errors he made in Spanish, 93% were related to gender agreement, an incongruent morpheme, compared to only 7% related to number marking. Bialystok (1997) and White (2003) reported similar findings.

7.5.1 Explaining the Effect: A Theoretical Proposal

What makes an incongruent morpheme particularly difficult for adult learners? An answer may lie in both the linguistic nature of grammatical morphemes and the psycholinguistic functions they serve in language processing.

From a linguistic perspective, inflectional morphemes have three important characteristics. First, an inflectional morpheme usually has a semantic basis. The English plural marker -s expresses the meaning of more than one, for example. Thus, a grammatical morpheme is essentially a morphological device to express a grammaticalized meaning. Second, a language usually has a limited number of grammaticalized meanings and inflectional morphemes. In contrast to the numerous and ever expanding lexicalized meanings, the grammaticalized meanings are not only limited in number but also remain stable over an individual's life span. For example, English has eight inflectional morphemes, which is unlikely to change soon. Finally, languages differ in what meanings are grammaticalized and thus expressed morphologically. As a result, they differ in what inflectional morphemes are employed. For example, Korean marks honorific meaning morphologically, English marks singularity and plurality meanings, and none of these is morphologically marked in Chinese. As will become clear soon, all these three linguistic characteristics have an impact on the acquisition of inflectional morphemes in an L2.

From a psycholinguistic perspective, whether a meaning is grammaticalized has a significant impact on the routine encoding of messages in language processing. The singular and plural meanings are grammaticalized and morphologically marked in English. As a result, the singular and plural meanings form a routine part of message encoding for native speakers of English when countable nouns are involved. Reading the word *cats* in a sentence such as *I saw the cats* will not only activate the meaning of cat, but also the meaning of more than one. In contrast, for speakers of Chinese which does not mark the singular and plural meanings morphologically, reading the word *mao* (cat) in the same sentence context (*wo kanjian mao le, I saw the cat(s)*) would only activate the meaning of cat; no singular or plural meaning is activated, unless it is preceded by a singular or plural modifier (i.e., expressed lexically). Similarly, in speech production, in responding to the question of "what is under the table" when two cats are there, an English native speaker has to have two meanings activated at the message level before responding with "cats" (i.e., *cat* and *plurality*). The presence of the plural marker in the language forces a native speaker of English to encode the plural meaning. In contrast, a Chinese native speaker does not have to encode the plurality meaning in responding to the same question in Chinese because the correct response is "mao" whether there is one or multiple cats. In short, the difference in the grammaticalization of meanings leads to different pattern of semantic encoding and activation in different languages.

This impact of grammaticalization of meaning on message encoding is widely recognized in psycholinguistics. For example, while discussing what is represented in preverbal messages in speech production, Levelt (1989) explicitly stated that "languages differ in the kinds of semantic features that are grammatically acknowledged. As a consequence, the encoding of messages is not the same for speakers of different languages" (p. 106). He illustrated this point by suggesting that English speakers have to have temporal meaning such as "past" represented in the preverbal message, but Chinese speakers do not (Levelt, 1999, p. 94). A similar view is put forward in Slobin's theorizing of thinking for speaking (Slobin, 1996), who suggests that "one fits one's thoughts into available linguistic forms" (1987, p. 435, cited in Slobin, 2003).

The presence of a grammaticalized meaning at the message level is not only a direct consequence of whether a meaning is morphologically marked in a language, but also serves an important function of activating the right morpheme in speech production. Almost all language production models (e.g., Dell, 1986; Eberhard, Cutting, & Bock, 2005; Levelt, 1989, 1999), postulate that the selection or activation of a linguistic element (in this case, a lexical or morphological item such as a plural marker) is driven by the elements in the higher representations (e.g., semantic features in the preverbal message). The meanings represented at the message level determine what inflectional morphemes will be activated or selected. Thus, the right meaning should be present in the message. "Otherwise the morphology cannot come out right" (Levelt, 1989, p. 104). Furthermore, such meaning-to-morpheme activations are automatic, as envisioned in Levelt's model. No attentional resources are required in the process. In the earlier example, the plural morpheme -s in an English speaker's response "cats" is automatically activated by the plural meaning at the message level.

To sum up, when a meaning is morphologically expressed, it is routinely activated at the message level in language processing. Languages differ in what meanings are grammaticalized and morphologically marked. As a result, speakers of different languages have different patterns of semantic activations. For example, a number meaning (singular or plural) is routinely activated in connection with a countable noun in English, but not in Chinese.

If the above analysis is correct, a psycholinguistic explanation can be offered for the morphological congruency effect: L2 learners face very different tasks while learning congruent and incongruent morphemes and this difference in turn leads to differences in how the two types of morphemes are acquired, their acquirability, and the ultimate learning outcome.

To begin with, L2 learners face very different tasks while learning a congruent versus an incongruent morpheme. In the former case, because the related meaning is grammaticalized in the learner's L1 and thus is part of routine message encoding and activation, the learner's task is to link this activated meaning to the right morphological marker in L2. For a Russian ESL speaker to use the English plural morpheme correctly, for example, the plural meaning is already part of what is routinely activated at the message level as a result of learning a number-marked L1. Now, he or she has to learn to link this meaning to the right plural marker -s in English. In learning an incongruent morpheme, however, one faces two tasks: a) the activation of a grammaticalized meaning that is not routinely activated in L1 processing, and b) linking this meaning to the right L2 morpheme. For example, in order to use the same English plural marker correctly, a Chinese ESL speaker has to first learn to routinely activate and represent the plural meaning at the message level.

This difference leads to a difference in learning outcome. Establishing a link between the encoded message and the right L2 morpheme may take a considerable amount of time. Furthermore, one has to strengthen this link so that the meaning-L2 morpheme activation becomes automatic. Before this is achieved, an L2 learner may rely on explicit knowledge and may continue to demonstrate inaccuracies. However, given enough experience in the target language, building and strengthening this link is an achievable outcome. After all, individuals have to continue to learn to build new links and connections in adulthood. Thus, highly proficient L2 speakers are able to demonstrate nativelike performance in using congruent morphemes.

Incongruent morphemes represent a very different scenario. I want to suggest that the development of new grammaticalized meaning may be subject to maturational constraints in that it becomes extremely difficult after early years of life, particularly after the establishment of one's first language. It may be related to the stable nature of meaning grammaticalization, which makes it unnecessary for individuals to develop new grammaticalized meanings during one's life time after the learning of L1. In this regard, one may compare the development of new grammaticalized meanings to the development of new phonological categories for speech perception. Both grammaticalized meanings and phonological categories share two common properties: They are limited in number in a language and they remain stable in one's life time, the latter of which means that once they are developed, there is no need to learn new ones. If Kuhl (2000, 2004) is right in suggesting that the perceptual map of phonological categories is laid out very early in life and becomes very difficult to alter later, the same can be true for the grammaticalized meanings. The pattern of semantic activation involving grammaticalized meanings may be finalized in the process of learning one's L1 and becomes very difficult to change.

Consequently, even highly proficient L2 speakers are not able to automatically activate a meaning that is not grammaticalized in their L1. In productive use of L2, this means that there is no semantic representation at the message level to activate the English plural marker among Chinese ESL speakers, for example. In L2 comprehension, an incongruent morpheme does not automatically activate its related meaning in a NNS' mind, either.

Now L2 speakers are left with one more option to get the incongruent morphemes right: the use of their explicit knowledge. The usages of inflectional morphemes are usually quite straightforward, and such usages are usually part of what is emphasized in L2 instruction. Thus, L2 speakers should have explicit knowledge about them at their disposal. The successful use of explicit knowledge, however, depends on two things: one's desire for accuracy and the availability of attentional resources. When such desire and attentional resources are available, nativelike performance can be achieved. Otherwise, non-native performance results. This explains the discrepancies observed of NNS in offline and online tasks. For example, the NNS in Jiang (2004) showed a high accuracy in the GJT but non-nativelike performance in the SPRT.

Figure 7.2 illustrates the main ideas of this explanation. A crucial component of nativelike competence in inflectional morphemes such as plural and tense markers lies in the presence of a grammaticalized meaning at the message level in language processing. In L1 use, a grammaticalized meaning is a routine part of semantic activation at the message level. A link exists between a grammaticalized meaning and the related morpheme. This link allows the automatic activation from a grammaticalized meaning to the right morpheme in L1 production and the encoding of the grammaticalized meaning from input processing in comprehension (left part of the diagram). This meaning-morpheme route is referred to as Route 1 or R1. In L2, different processes are involved in the learning and use of congruent and incongruent morphemes. In the case of the former, Route 1 is available because the grammaticalized meaning related to a congruent morpheme is routinely activated as a result of learning the L1. A learner needs to learn to link the meaning to the right L2

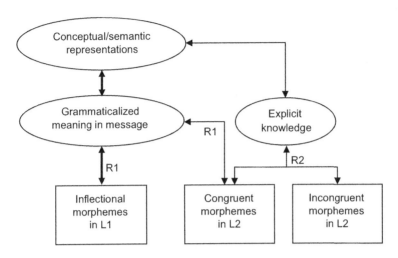

Figure 7.2 The Acquisition and Use of Congruent and Incongruent Inflectional Morphemes in L2, as Compared to L1 Morphemes

morpheme and strengthen this link such that the meaning-morpheme activation becomes automatic. Nativelike competence is achievable in this case because adults have the capacities to build new links. The automatization of this link takes a great deal of practice, and before this is achieved, one may have to rely on explicit knowledge, which is Route 2 or R2.

For incongruent morphemes, however, Route 1 is not available because of the lack of a correspondent grammaticalized meaning at the message level (as a result of L1 learning and maturational constraints). Consequently, L2 learners have to rely on Route 2 in using incongruent morphemes. By relying on Route 2, L2 learners can still develop a high level of accuracy in using incongruent morphemes under some circumstances. However, this high accuracy can be best seen as a result of increased efficiency in applying explicit knowledge. No matter how efficient this process is, as far as it requires a desire for accuracy and attentional resources, Route 2 is cognitively different from the automatic meaning-morpheme activation of Route 1 and is not optimized for real-time morphological processing. Thus, even steady-state L2 learners do not possess the same kind of linguistic competence as native speakers do in the area of incongruent morphemes.

A central component of the explanation offered above is to attribute the difference in the learning and processing of congruent and incongruent morphemes to whether a related meaning gets automatically activated and represented at the message level. A related meaning is available at the message level for a congruent morpheme and, as a result, the nativelike Route 1 can

be adopted. A meaning correspondent to an incongruent meaning is not activated at the message level, so Route 1 is not available. For this reason, it is
appropriate to refer to this framework as a meaning activation model of L2
morphological development and processing.

7.5.2 Testing the Proposal

To test this explanation, a sentence-picture matching study was conducted
(Jiang, Hu, Chrabaszcz, & Ye, 2017). In the experimental task, a picture of
three objects was first presented on a computer monitor. It was then followed
by a sentence that was presented above the picture. The participants' task
was to decide whether the sentence correctly described the physical relationship or properties among the three objects in the pictures. The critical
manipulation in the study was the two versions of a "match" item. As is illustrated in Figure 7.3, a match item was one in which the sentence described
the physical relationship of the picture correctly and thus required a Yes
response. This match item had two versions. They shared the identical sentence, e.g., *The bike is above the tall basket*, but the two versions differed in the
accompanying picture. In one version, there was only one basket, and thus
the picture matched the singular word *basket* in the sentence in number, but
in the other version, there was more than one basket, and thus the sentence
and the picture did not match in number. We refer to them as number-match
and number-mismatch conditions, respectively. Note that the task required
the participants to pay attention to the physical relationship among the three
objects, not the number of objects. Since the sentence described the relationship of both pictures correctly, the expected response was Yes to both
versions.

Several mental processes were conceivably involved in performing the
matching task. First, broadly speaking, one had to recognize the objects, note
their physical relationship or properties, and encode and store this information

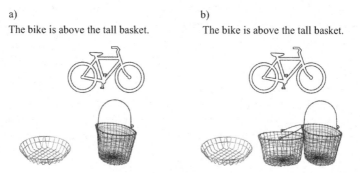

Figure 7.3 A Test Item in the Sentence-Picture Matching Task

in the mind. Then, the sentence had to be processed and its message stored. Finally, the two messages were compared to see if they matched. If they did, a positive response was in order. Otherwise, a negative response was generated.

The use of the sentence-picture matching task in combination with the number-match/mismatch manipulation in English should allow us to determine whether singular/plural meanings are automatically activated and involved in performing the task. In a language that morphologically marks number and thus the singularity/plurality meanings are routinely and automatically encoded in language processing, a singular meaning would be activated in association with the word *basket* and a singular or plural meaning would be generated in association with the picture of basket depending on whether there was one or two baskets. The test items in the number-mismatch condition entails a mismatch in number between the sentence and the picture (i.e., a singular noun *basket* and the presence of multiple baskets). If the singular meaning is automatically activated, even when participants are asked to pay attention to physical relationships among the three objects in the picture, we would expect the participants to automatically and subconsciously notice this mismatch in number in the number-mismatch condition. This information would contradict with a "match" decision based on the physical relationship, thus causing a delay in reaching a Yes response. No such delay would be expected for the number-match condition. Thus, if the number meanings are automatically activated, a number-mismatch effect would occur in that participants would take longer in responding to number-mismatch items than number-match items.

This number-mismatch effect should not occur if we translate the sentences into Chinese and ask Chinese NS to perform the same task. In this case, there is no singular or plural meaning associated with *lanzhi* (basket), as Chinese does not mark the number meanings, and thus, there should be no number-mismatch effect.

To sum up, by comparing participants' reaction times (RTs) in responding to the number-match and number-mismatch items, we could determine with reasonable certainty whether singular and plural meanings are automatically activated in language processing. The automatic activation of the number meanings would result in a number-mismatch effect, that is, a delay in responding to the number-mismatch items. If no difference is found, we can reasonably conclude that no grammaticalized singular/plural meanings are activated and involved in the process of performing the task.

Three experiments were conducted. The first one was intended to confirm the usefulness of the method by testing native speakers of English and Chinese in their respective L1s. If the method was sensitive enough to capture the activation of the singularity/plurality meanings, only native speakers of English would show a number-mismatch effect. Native speakers of Chinese were not expected to do so while performing the task in Chinese. Two versions of the stimuli were created, one in English and the other in Chinese. English and Chinese NS performed the task in their respective language. Consistent with the expectation, English NS showed a number-mismatch effect but Chinese NS did not. The second experiment was the main experiment in which a group of L2-proficiency-matched advanced Chinese and Russian ESL speakers were tested in the same task in both their L1s and L2. Three versions of the stimuli were used: the English version, the Chinese version, and the Russian version. The Russian and Chinese ESL participants represented L2 learners for whom the singular/plural distinction was a congruent and an incongruent one, respectively. If we were correct in suggesting that only meanings grammaticalized in L1 get automatically activated in L2 processing, only Russian ESL speakers would produce a number-mismatch effect. Chinese ESL speakers should show no difference. The results confirmed the predictions. Experiment 3 was done to reinforce our interpretation of the results of Experiment 2 by demonstrating that the method was powerful enough to detect the activation of lexical meanings among Chinese ESL speakers. When lexical items such as *many* and *several* were used to manipulate number matching, Chinese ESL speakers showed a number-mismatch effect. Taken together, the findings of the three experiments provided supporting evidence for the view that a meaning grammaticalized in L1 gets automatically activated in L2 processing among advanced L2 speakers, but a meaning not grammaticalized in L1 does not.

7.6 Conclusion

Whether adult NNS are able to develop nativelike competence in morphosyntax is an ongoing debate. The examination of NNS's sensitivity to morphosyntactic violations in sentence processing provided some online evidence for answering this question. This line of research has shown that morphological congruency may affect the successful acquisition and nativelike processing of L2 grammatical morphemes. A theoretical explanation is provided, along with some preliminary evidence, for explaining the morphological congruency effect. Other factors that have shown to affect L2 morphosyntactic development and processing include violation distance, phonological realization, and L2 proficiency. However, the findings are by no means consistent. Some of the inconsistency may be attributed to experimental conditions under which data were collected. For example, encouraging participants to pay attention to grammatical accuracy, e.g., as a result of requiring them to perform a GJT, is likely to increase the probability of NNS noticing errors in the stimuli, thus inflating their nativelike performance. Having entire sentences in front of the participants, as is often the case in eye tracking studies, may also increase the likelihood of grammar checking, resulting in the same inflation. Consistency in results across studies may improve if data are collected in experimental conditions where the participants pay minimum attention to grammatical accuracy and where the involvement of explicit knowledge is unlikely.

Notes

1   Other online methods that are also used in this research, but to a lesser extent, include sentence matching (e.g., Bley-Vroman & Masterson, 1989; Gass, 2001) and the congruency priming paradigm involving the shadowing and lexical decision task (Guillelmon & Grosjean, 2001; Scherag, Demuth, Rosler, Neville, & Roder, 2004).
2   Note that in a GJT, a judgment decision is made only after a participant has finished reading a sentence.
3   Included in this review are 14 ERP studies of morphosyntactic sensitivity among NNS published in journal articles. Many ERP studies (Guo, Guo, Yan, Jiang, & Peng, 2009; Hahne, 2001; Hahne & Friederici, 2001; Pakulak & Neville, 2011; Sanders & Neville, 2003) explored NNS' sensitivity to other structures, such as phrase structure violations, and are not included. See Meulman, Stowe, Sprenger, Bresser, and Schmid (2014), Morgan-Short, Sanz, Steinhauer, and Ullman (2010); Morgan-Short, Steinhauer, Sanz, and Ullman (2012); van Hell and Tokowicz (2010); and Steinhauer, White, and Drury (2009) for more ERP studies on the topic.

References

Ainsworth-Darnell, K., Shulman, H. G., & Boland, J. E. (1998). Dissociating brain responses to syntactic and semantic anomalies: Evidence from event-related potentials. *Journal of Memory and Language, 38*, 112–130.

Allen, M. D., Badecker, W., & Osterhout, L. (2003). Morphological analysis during sentence processing. *Language and Cognitive Processes, 18*, 405–430.

Bannai, M. (2011). The nature of variable sensitivity to agreement violations in L2 English. *EUROSLA Yearbook, 11*, 115–137.

Barber, H. & Carreiras, M. (2005). Grammatical gender and number agreement in Spanish: An ERP comparison. *Journal of Cognitive Neuroscience, 17*, 137–153.

Bialystok, E. (1997). The structure of age: In search of barriers to second language acquisition. *Second Language Research, 13*, 116–137.

Bialystok, E. & Miller, B. (1999). The problem of age in second-language acquisition: Influences from language, structure, and task. *Bilingualism: Language and Cognition, 2*, 127–145.

Bley-Vroman, R. (1989). What is the logical problem of foreign language learning. In S. M. Gass & J. Schachter (Eds.), *Linguistic perspectives on second language acquisition* (pp. 41–68). Cambridge: Cambridge University Press.

Bley-Vroman, R. & Masterson, D. (1989). Reaction time as a supplement to grammaticality judgements in the investigation of second language learners' competence. *University of Hawai'i Working Papers in ESL, 8*, 207–237.

Chen, L., Shu, H., Liu, Y., Zhao, J., & Li, P. (2007). ERP signatures of subject and verb agreement in L2 learning. *Bilingualism: Language and Cognition, 10*, 161–174.

Coughlin, C. E. & Tremblay, A. (2013). Proficiency and working memory based explanations for nonnative speakers' sensitivity to agreement in sentence processing. *Applied Psycholinguistics, 34*, 615–646.

DeKeyser, R. M. (2003). Implicit and explicit learning. In C. Doughty & M. H. Long (Eds.), *The handbook of second language acquisition* (pp. 313–348). Malden, MA: Blackwell.

Dell, G. S. (1986). A spreading-activation theory of retrieval in sentence production. *Psychological Review, 93,* 283–321.

Eberhard, K. M., Cutting, J. C., & Bock, K. (2005). Making syntax of sense: Number agreement in sentence production. *Psychological Review, 112,* 531–559.

Ellis, R. (2002). Does form-focused instruction affect the acquisition of implicit knowledge? *Studies in Second Language Acquisition, 24,* 223–236.

Ferreira, F. & Henderson, J. M. (1990). Use of verb information in syntactic parsing: Evidence from eye movements and word-by-word self-paced reading. *Journal of Experimental Psychology: Learning, Memory, and Cognition, 16,* 555–568.

Flege, J. E., Yeni-Komshian, G. H., & Liu, S. (1999). Age constraints on second-language acquisition. *Journal of Memory and Language, 41,* 78–104.

Flynn, S. (1989). The role of the head-initial/head-final parameter in the acquisition of English relative clauses by adult Spanish and Japanese speakers. In S. M. Gass & J. Schachter (Eds.), *Linguistic perspectives on second language acquisition* (pp. 89–108). Cambridge: Cambridge University Press.

Foote, R. (2011). Integrated knowledge of agreement in early and late English-Spanish bilinguals. *Applied Psycholinguistics, 32,* 187–220.

Foucart, A. & Frenck-Mestre, C. (2011). Grammatical gender processing in L2: Electrophysiological evidence of the effect of L1–L2 syntactic similarity. *Bilingualism: Language and Cognition, 14,* 379–399.

Foucart, A. & Frenck-Mestre, C. (2012). Can late L2 learners acquire new grammatical features? Evidence from ERPs and eye-tracking. *Journal of Memory and Language, 66,* 226–248.

Franceschina, F. (2001). Morphological or syntactic deficits in near-native speakers? An assessment of some current proposals. *Second Language Research, 17,* 213–247.

Frenck-Mestre, C. (2005). Eye-movement recording as a tool for studying syntactic processing in a second language: A review of methodologies and experimental findings. *Second Language Research, 21,* 175–198.

Frenck-Mestre, C., Osterhout, L., McLaughlin, J., & Foucart, A. (2008). The effect of phonological realization of inflectional morphology on verbal agreement in French: Evidence from ERPs. *Acta Psychologica, 128,* 528–536.

Friederici, A. (2002). Towards a neural basis of auditory sentence processing. *Trends in Cognitive Sciences, 6,* 78–84.

Garnsey, S. M., Pearlmutter, N. J., Myers, E., & Lotocky, M. A. (1997). The contributions of verb bias and plausibility to the comprehension of temporarily ambiguous sentences. *Journal of Memory and Language, 37,* 58–93.

Gass, S. M. (2001). Sentence matching: A re-examination. *Second Language Research, 17,* 421–441.

Gillon Dowens, M. G., Guo, T., Guo, J., Barber, H., & Carreiras, M. (2011). Gender and number processing in Chinese learners of Spanish: Evidence from event related potentials. *Neuropsychologia, 49,* 1651–1659.

Gillon Dowens, M. G., Vergara, M., Barber, H. A., & Carreiras, M. (2010). Morphosyntactic processing in late second-language learners. *Journal of Cognitive Neuroscience, 22,* 1870–1887.

Guillelmon, D. & Grosjean, F. (2001). The gender marking effect in spoken word recognition: The case of bilinguals. *Memory and Cognition, 29*, 503–511.

Guo, J., Guo, T., Yan, Y., Jiang, N., & Peng, D. (2009). ERP evidence for different strategies employed by native speakers and L2 learners in sentence processing. *Journal of Neurolinguistics, 22*, 123–134.

Hahne, A. (2001). What's different in second-language processing? Evidence from event-related brain potentials. *Journal of Psycholinguistic Research, 30*, 251–266.

Hahne, A. & Friederici, A. D. (1999). Electrophysiological evidence for two steps in syntactic analysis. Early automatic and late controlled processes. *Journal of Cognitive Neuroscience, 11*, 194–205.

Hahne, A. & Friederici, A. D. (2001). Processing a second language: Late learners' comprehension mechanisms as revealed by event-related brain potentials. *Bilingualism: Language and Cognition, 4*, 123–141.

Hahne, A., Mueller, J. L., & Clahsen, H. (2006). Morphological processing in a second language: Behavioral and event-related brain potential evidence for storage and decomposition. *Journal of Cognitive Neuroscience, 18*, 121–134.

Hawkins, R. & Chan, C. (1997). The partial availability of Universal Grammar in second language acquisition: The 'failed functional features hypothesis'. *Second Language Research, 13*, 187–226.

Hawkins, R. & Liszka, S. (2003). Locating the source of defective past tense marking in advanced L2 English speakers. *Language Acquisition and Language Disorders, 30*, 21–44.

Hinz, J., Krause, C., Rast, R., Shoemaker, E. M., & Watorek, M. (2013). Initial processing of morphological marking in nonnative language acquisition: Evidence from French and German learners of Polish. *EUROSLA Yearbook, 13*, 139–175.

Jia, G. (2003). The acquisition of the English plural morpheme by native Mandarin Chinese-speaking children. *Journal of Speech, Language, and Hearing Research, 46*, 1297–1311.

Jiang, N. (2004). Morphological insensitivity in second language processing. *Applied Psycholinguistics, 25*, 603–634.

Jiang, N. (2007). Selective integration of linguistic knowledge in adult second language learning. *Language Learning, 57*, 1–33.

Jiang, N. (2012). *Conducting reaction time research in second language studies*. London: Routledge.

Jiang, N., Hu, G., Chrabaszcz, A., & Ye, L. (2017). The activation of grammaticalized meaning in L2 processing: Toward an explanation of the morphological congruency effect. *International Journal of Bilingualism, 21*, 81–98.

Jiang, N., Novokshanova, E., Masuda, K., & Wang, X. (2011). Morphological congruency and the acquisition of L2 morphemes. *Language Learning, 61*, 940–967.

Johnson, J. S. & Newport, E. L. (1989). Critical period effects in second language learning: The influences of maturational state on the acquisition of English as a second language. *Cognitive Psychology, 21*, 60–99.

Keating, G. D. (2009). Sensitivity to violations of gender agreement in native and nonnative Spanish: An eye-movement investigation. *Language Learning, 59*, 503–535.

Kuhl, P. K. (2000). A new view of language acquisition. *Proceedings of the National Academy of Sciences of the United States of America, 97*, 11850–11857.

Kuhl, P. K. (2004). Early language acquisition: Cracking the speech code. *Nature Reviews Neuroscience, 5*, 831–843.

Lardiere, D. (1998). Case and tense in the 'fossilized' steady state. *Second Language Research, 14*, 1–26.

Lardiere, D. (2007). *Ultimate attainment in second language acquisition: A case study.* Mahwah, NJ: Lawrence Erlbaum.

Levelt, W. J. M. (1989). *Speaking: From intention to articulation.* Cambridge, MA: MIT Press.

Levelt, W. J. M. (1999). Producing spoken language: A blueprint of the speaker. In P. Hagoort & C. M. Brown (Eds.), *The neurocognition of language* (pp. 94–122). Oxford, UK: Oxford University Press.

Lim, J. H. & Christianson, K. (2014). Second language sensitivity to agreement errors: Evidence from eye movements during comprehension and translation. *Applied Psycholinguistics, 36*, 1–33.

Long, M. (2003). Stabilization and fossilization in interlanguage development. In C. Doughty & M. H. Long (Eds.), *The handbook of second language acquisition* (pp. 487–535). Malden, MA: Blackwell.

McDonald, J. L. (2000). Grammaticality judgments in a second language: Influences of age of acquisition and native language. *Applied Psycholinguistics, 21*, 395–423.

Meulman, N., Stowe, L. A., Sprenger, S. A., Bresser, M., & Schmid, M. S. (2014). An ERP study on L2 syntax processing: When do learners fail? *Frontiers in Psychology, 5*(1072). doi:10.3389/fpsyg.2014.01072

Molinaro, N., Barber, H. A., & Carreiras, M. (2011). Grammatical agreement processing in reading: ERP findings and future directions. *Cortex, 47*, 908–930.

Montrul, S., Foote, R., & Perpiñán, S. (2008). Gender agreement in adult second language learners and Spanish heritage speakers: The effects of age and context of acquisition. *Language Learning, 58*, 503–553.

Morgan-Short, K., Sanz, C., Steinhauer, K., & Ullman, M. T. (2010). Second language acquisition of gender agreement in explicit and implicit training conditions: An event-related potential study. *Language Learning, 60*, 154–193.

Morgan-Short, K., Steinhauer, K., Sanz, C., & Ullman, M. T. (2012). Explicit and implicit second language training differentially affect the achievement of native-like brain activation patterns. *Journal of Cognitive Neuroscience, 24*, 933–947.

Mueller, J. L., Hahne, A., Fujii, Y., & Friederici, A. D. (2005). Native and nonnative speakers' processing of a miniature version of Japanese as revealed by ERPs. *Journal of Cognitive Neuroscience, 17*, 1229–1244.

Mueller, J. L. & Jiang, N. (2013). The acquisition of the Korean honorific affix (u)si by advanced L2 learners. *Modern Language Journal, 97*, 318–339.

Ojima, S., Nakata, H., & Kakigi, R. (2005). An ERP study of second language learning after childhood: Effects of proficiency. *Journal of Cognitive Neuroscience, 17*, 1212–1228.

Osterhout, L. & Holcomb, P. J. (1992). Event-related brain potentials elicited by syntactic anomaly. *Journal of Memory and Language, 31*, 785–806.

Osterhout, L., McLaughlin, J., Pitkänen, I., Frenck-Mestre, C., & Molinaro, N. (2006). Novice learners, longitudinal designs, and event-related potentials: A means for exploring the neurocognition of second language processing. *Language Learning, 56*(s1), 199–230.

Pakulak, E. & Neville, H. J. (2011). Maturational constraints on the recruitment of early processes for syntactic processing. *Journal of Cognitive Neuroscience, 23*, 2752–2765.

Roberts, L. & Liszka, S. A. (2013). Processing tense/aspect-agreement violations on-line in the second language: A self-paced reading study with French and German L2 learners of English. *Second Language Research, 29*, 413–439.

Rossi, E., Kroll, J. F., & Dussias, P. E. (2014). Clitic pronouns reveal the time course of processing gender and number in a second language. *Neuropsychologia, 62*, 11–25.

Rossi, S., Gugler, M. F., Friederici, A. D., & Hahne, A. (2006). The impact of proficiency on syntactic second-language processing of German and Italian: Evidence from event-related potentials. *Journal of Cognitive Neuroscience, 18*, 2030–2048.

Sabourin, L. (2001). L1 effects on the processing of grammatical gender in L2. *EURO-SLA Yearbook, 1*, 159–169.

Sabourin, L. & Haverkort, M. (2003). Neural substrates of representation and processing of a second language. *Language Acquisition and Language Disorders, 30*, 175–196.

Sabourin, L. & Stowe, L. A. (2008). Second language processing: When are first and second languages processed similarly? *Second Language Research, 24*, 397–430.

Sabourin, L., Stowe, L. A., & de Haan, G. J. (2006). Transfer effects in learning a second language grammatical gender system. *Second Language Research, 22*, 1–29.

Sagarra, N. & Ellis, N. C. (2013). From seeing adverbs to seeing verbal morphology: Language experience and adult acquisition of L2 tense. *Studies in Second Language Acquisition, 35*, 261–290.

Sagarra, N. & Herschensohn, J. (2010). The role of proficiency and working memory in gender and number agreement processing in L1 and L2 Spanish. *Lingua, 120*, 2022–2039.

Sagarra, N. & Herschensohn, J. (2011). Proficiency and animacy effects on L2 gender agreement processes during comprehension. *Language Learning, 61*, 80–116.

Sanders, L. D. & Neville, H. J. (2003). An ERP study of continuous speech processing: II. Segmentation, semantics, and syntax in non-native speakers. *Cognitive Brain Research, 15*, 214–227.

Schachter, J. (1988). Second language acquisition and its relationship to universal grammar. *Applied Linguistics, 9*, 211–235.

Scherag, A., Demuth, L., Rosler, F., Neville, H. J., & Roder, B. (2004). The effects of late acquisition of L2 and the consequences of immigration on L1 for semantic and morpho-syntactic language aspects. *Cognition, 93*, B97–B108.

Schmidt, R. W. (1983). Interaction, acculturation, and the acquisition of communicative competence. In N. Wolfson & J. Manes (Eds.), *Sociolinguistics and second language acquisition* (pp. 137–174). Rowley, MA: Newbury House.

Shibuya, M. & Wakabayashi, S. (2008). Why are L2 learners not always sensitive to subject–verb agreement? *EUROSLA Yearbook, 8*, 235–258.

Slobin, D. I. (1987). Thinking for speaking. *Proceedings of the Thirteenth Annual Meeting of the Berkeley Linguistics Society, 13*, 435–445.

Slobin, D. I. (1996). From 'thought and language' to 'thinking for speaking'. In J. Gumperz & S. C. Levinson (Eds.), *Rethinking linguistic relativity* (pp. 70–96). Cambridge, UK: Cambridge University Press.

Slobin, D. I. (2003). Language and thought online: Cognitive consequences of linguistic relativity. In D. Gentner & S. Goldin-Meadow (Eds.), *Language in mind: Advances in the study of language and thought* (pp. 157–191). Cambridge, MA: MIT Press.

Steinhauer, K. (2014). Event-related potentials (ERPs) in second language research: A brief introduction to the technique, a selected review, and an invitation to reconsider critical periods in L2. *Applied Linguistics*, 1–26.

Steinhauer, K., White, E., & Drury, J. E. (2009). Temporal dynamics of late second language acquisition: Evidence from event-related brain potentials. *Second Language Research, 25,* 13–41.

Tokowicz, N. & MacWhinney, B. (2005). Implicit vs. explicit measures of sensitivity to violations in L2 grammar: An event-related potential investigation. *Studies in Second Language Acquisition, 27,* 173–204.

Tokowicz, N. & Warren, T. (2010). Beginning adult L2 learners' sensitivity to morphosyntactic violations: A self-paced reading study. *European Journal of Cognitive Psychology, 22,* 1092–1106.

Traxler, M. J., Pickering, M. J., & McElree, B. (2002). Coercion in sentence processing: Evidence from eye-movements and self-paced reading. *Journal of Memory and Language, 47,* 530–547.

van Hell, J. G. & Tokowicz, N. (2010). Event-related brain potentials and second language learning: Syntactic processing in late L2 learners at different L2 proficiency levels. *Second Language Research, 26,* 43–74.

VanPatten, B., Keating, G. D., & Leeser, M. J. (2012). Missing verbal inflections as a representational problem: Evidence from self-paced reading. *Linguistic Approaches to Bilingualism, 2,* 109–140.

White, L. (1989). *Universal grammar and second language acquisition.* Philadelphia: John Benjamins.

White, L. (2003). Fossilization in steady state L2 grammars: Persistent problems with inflectional morphology. *Bilingualism: Language and Cognition, 6,* 129–141.

Epilogue

As a person who has used a typologically different second language as the working language for the past 25 years and who did not have significant experience in the language until his 20s, I have always felt that using an L2 is very different from using an L1, even after many years of immersing in the L2. Delivering instruction in an L2 remains mentally more demanding and tiring, for example. In writing, there is often a feeling of uncertainty about whether my expression is sufficiently accurate, appropriate, or engaging. In reading, English words do not seem to invoke my memories, incite my emotions, or conjure up mental images as much as my L1 does. As Eva Hoffman put it:

> The words I learn now don't stand for things in the same unquestioned way they did in my native tongue. "River" in Polish was vital sound, energized with the essence of riverhood, of my rivers, of my being immersed in rivers. "River" in English is cold—a word without an aura. It has no accumulated associations for me, and it does not give off the radiating haze of connotations. It does not evoke.
>
> (1990, p. 106)

My experiences as an L2 speaker have convinced me that there are some fundamental differences in the representation and processing of a non-native language, as compared to that of a native language, just as my own persistent plural errors have convinced me that certain aspect of a non-native language is not acquirable for adult learners, at least for those from a typologically different language background.

A major motivation for writing this book was to give myself an opportunity to survey the field of second language processing in search of research findings to support this conviction, or to identify research topics that may lead to such findings.

While doing so, I have in my mind psycholinguistic findings as such the Stroop effect (Stroop, 1935) for showing automatic nature of lexical access and the McGurk effect (McGurk & MacDonald, 1976) for demonstrating the bimodal nature of speech perception. The first finding shows that individuals name the colors of printed words much more slowly when the color and the word meaning do not match (the word *red* printed in yellow and thus has to be named yellow). In the second finding, individuals tend to report hearing something different from the actual stimulus (the stimulus /ba/ heard as /ga/) in the presence of a visual input of someone pronouncing /da/. These findings help reveal an otherwise undiscernible cognitive process in a simple linguistic task in a highly replicable and interpretatively unmistakable way. Thus, these are extremely inspiring and powerful findings.

Supposedly, second language processing research should also produce findings that can help illuminate what is qualitatively different between L1 and L2 representation and processing in a similarly powerful way. These findings should be consistent with our intuition as second language speakers but go beyond our intuition in uncovering the underlying cognitive processes responsible for L1–L2 differences, these findings should represent relatively simple linguistic phenomena that can be observed in a linguistic task repeatedly with high consistency, and their findings can be interpreted in a straightforward and unmistakable way in relation to the cognitive processes they help reveal.

After four years of intensive looking, now I can ask where we are in search of such findings.

SLP research has undoubtedly produced many findings that demonstrate differences in L1 and L2 representation and processing. Age effects and L1 effects in L2 processing are two of them. They reflect how these two L2-specific factors can affect L2 representation, processing, and acquisition. This research has also helped discover some specific processing phenomena that are particularly interesting. For example, given the same set of stimulus words for a word association task, L2 speakers tend to produce more form-related responses than L1 speakers do, and they produce orthographic priming effect (*restaurant→rest*) where L1 speakers do not (Section 4.3.1), and given the same set of high- and low-frequency words, L2 speakers tend to produce a larger frequency effect than L1 speakers do (Section 4.5.2).

In spite of these findings, SLP research faces at least two limitations. The first one is a lack of replicability and consistency. Many L2 processing findings either have not been well replicated or do not get replicated across studies. Conflicting findings have been obtained in the study of almost all major topics such as the relationship between AOA and phonological processing (Section 3.3), the role of L1 in word recognition (Section 4.4), the use of syntactic information in L2 sentence processing (Section 6.3), the role of working memory in L2 sentence processing (Section 6.4), and nativelike sensitivity to morphosyntactic violations among NNS (Section 7.3).

A second limitation is related to the interpretation of the findings. Many L2 findings are subject to multiple interpretations and thus they do not help reveal a cognitive process in an unmistakable way. The larger frequency effect in L2 word recognition, for example, has been explained in at least three different ways, and multiple proposals have been made to account for age effects in L2 phonology. Moreover, most of these alternative explanations remain as speculations that are yet to be developed into specific and testable hypotheses for empirical scrutiny. Thus, there is a great deal of uncertainty about how we may relate these findings to the pursuit of the uniqueness in L2 representation and processing.

Due to these limitations, current L2 processing research has produced few research findings in the same caliber as the Stroop effect and the McGurk effect. There are few findings today that we can replicate or have replicated with high consistency and interpret with full confidence and in unanimity. The limited progress may reflect some inevitable complexities involved in L2 processing research. For example, L2 speakers usually represent a less homogeneous population than L1 speakers as far as both language proficiency and learning conditions and thus processes are concerned. Many learner and linguistic factors are more likely to affect L2 than L1 learning and processing. The limited progress also means that we need to search for more innovative research paradigms or more clever design ideas to isolate the right L2 processing phenomena for our purpose.

To end on a positive note, though, nearly four decades of SLP research has helped accumulate a tremendous amount of knowledge about L2 processing in terms of research techniques, theoretical frameworks, and empirical findings. Every finding in this research is important in one way or another and helps pave the way in our search of what is unique in L2 representation and processing. I am hopeful that the moment will come in the near future when we can say to people outside of our field with confidence and in unanimity: look, this is how using a non-native language is cognitively different from using a native language and that is why.

References

Hoffman, E. (1990). *Lost in translation: A life in a new language*. New York, NY: Penguin Books.

McGurk, H. & MacDonald, J. (1976). Hearing lips and seeing voices. *Nature, 264,* 746–748.

Stroop, J. R. (1935). Studies of interference in serial verbal reactions. *Journal of Experimental Psychology, 18,* 643–662.

Index

Made in United States
North Haven, CT
12 May 2022